SHAPING S-CURVES

Shaping S-Curves

Choreographic Process in Odissi

Kaustavi Sarkar

Suggested citation: Sarkar, Kaustavi. Shaping S-Curves.
doi: https://doi.org/10.5149/9781469698786_Sarkar

ISBN 978-1-4696-9877-9 (paperback: alk. paper)
ISBN 978-1-4696-9878-6 (open access EPUB)
ISBN 978-1-4696-9879-3 (open access PDF)

Published by J. Murrey Atkins Library at UNC Charlotte

Distributed by the University of North Carolina Press
www.uncpress.org

In memory of Guru Poushali Mukherjee

❦

TABLE OF CONTENTS

Introduction

Angular Oscillations

TILTING MY HEAD on the left and raising my right leg with flexed foot and bent knees without shifting the S-shape in the body that remains grounded in the left leg, I test the resilience of the curve on the left side—hips and rib cage counterbalancing one another. This is the ultimate test of Tribhangi, an S-shape, that I encounter day in and out in my long association with the dance form over three decades.

The above anecdote grounds the kinesthetic principle of opposition that presupposes a two-step procedure—first of isolation and then of integration in the dancing Odissi (an eastern Indian traditional art form from the state of Odisha) body (Banerji 2010). *Shaping S-Curves: Choreographic Process in Odissi* is also a two-staged performance of technical grounding and creative potential. This book weaves materialities and dreams in the *Tribhangi*: the quintessential S-curve in Odissi dance. Odissi is a complex art form given its inherent imbrications with both dance and music borrowing inspiration from scholar Anurima Banerji's invitation in "The Epistemic Politics of Indian Classical Dance" to "imagine Indian classical practices differently" given their inherent regional specificity and interdisciplinary content (2023, 192).[1] It is designated as a classical dance form by Sangeet Natak Akademi, India's premier art institution based in New Delhi (India's capital city) and there is an emerging parallel political, social, and cultural movement for bringing Odissi music to the national fore as a culturally unique rigorous form of music that is not captured by the existing genres of music recognized in India (Tandon 2005). Odissi vocal accompanists Nazia Alam and Rupak Kumar Parida won the Ustad Bismillah Khan Yuva Puraskar, the prestigious national award given to artists under the age of forty by Sangeet Natak Akademi, in 2009 and 2020, respectively (Barik 2022). In this genre, music and dance are inseparable in the case of Odissi as the choreographer simultaneously works with the music and rhythm composer and the dancers to create. As a professional Odissi soloist, I speak from my grounding in solo dancing and my collaborations with musicians and choreographers to show how creative processes as well as daily technique practices are grounded in particularities of Odishan cultural ethos.

The oppositional materiality of the dancing body is best captured by scholar andartist Nandini Sikand's book title, *Languid Bodies, Grounded Stances,* also intuited in my inaugural cohesion around bent knees and deflected torsos (Sikand 2016). An oppositional interface grounds my dancing body in counterpoint and tensile strength. Guru Kelucharan

Mohapatra style emphasizes upon immobility of hips. This stringency also makes visible lucid torso curvatures. Hips act as fulcrum for the torso and the legs to operate freely with the highest range of motion. Isolation and opposition remain key in physical control of grounded footwork and circular upper bodies. This tension constitutes the centrality of both physical strength and affective multiplicity in the moving body reveling in its knee-bends, ankle-flicks, toe-heel-flat footwork, rooted spins, and a deep melting into the floor. The gestural interface of subtlety, minimalism, and visibly apparent ease demands significant control in the form of hand-eye coordination where cultivation of a focused gaze determines the virtuosic ingenuity of the performer.

In this introductory chapter, I position myself as a practitioner demonstrating the meaning, purpose, and ethos of solo Odissi dancing. Although there is a growing literature exploring critical historiography, sensory-somatic-affective potential, assessment, clinical and therapeutic benefits, and democratic ethos and standardized education-assessment, there remains a lack of deep understanding of the practicing body (Kaktikar 2024). In a book-length inquiry, I engage the dancing body to explore its performative and epistemic limits (Sen-Podstawska 2019). Odissi repertoire emerges from invocatory exercises and ends with hopes of liberatory gestures. Invocation of the earth seeking permission to stomp one's foot incessantly on it then leads to a sequence of technical, musical, and textual elaborations. The last element seeks freedom from the act itself simultaneously noting the impermanence of the materiality and the epistemological significance of the dancing body as witness to the act of performance. After grounding the philosophical paradigm of the dancing body in the second chapter, I briefly sketch the oppositional grounded languidness through technique, conventional repertoire, and new choreographies. Having been trained in the Guru Kelucharan Mohapatra style of Odissi, I ground my practice in its principles of isolation, opposition, and coordination. Isolating parts of my body, maintaining an echo in my torso with every footwork ensuring immobile hips, and coordinating all of these various movement possibilities foreground the aesthetic hallmark of my training. However, I have branched out by learning repertoire in multiple other styles, namely Guru Debaprasad Das, Guru Surendranath Jena, and Guru Pankaj Charan Das through my research and grant-funded projects in order to avoid myopic and hagiographic association with one particular domain within Odissi, which has pluralistic foundations.

Finally, I have prioritized researching the creative process of making a solo dance composition because a detailed scholarly analysis of this music and dance symbiosis is missing from existing literary records. Working with music and rhythm composers, namely Shyam Kalyan, Anirban Bhattacharyya, Ramprasad Gannavarapu, M. A. Jyothi, and Agnimitra Behera among others, I have explored the symbiotic relationality across the musical and choreographic infrastructure. Book chapters explore the technical infrastructure and the creative process at large; specifically focusing on the works of two important choreographers, Rohini Dandavate and Maya Kulkarni, who I commissioned to make solo works. These works show the pluralistic and layered investments of the solo dance creators, which pushes open the field in new directions and provides deeper context for understanding the form in diasporic and global contexts. In closing, I reiterate the importance of understanding the specificity of the S-curves as numerous artists around the world dedicate their lives to its practice, philosophy, and artistry as a way of life in itself.

The practicing Odissi dancing body is at best a spectacular phenomenon and at worst an act of temporal disjuncture due to fossilization in historical time with no way of apprehending its meaning. Its possibility of meaning-making is occluded to the general public at large who is not familiar with the codes of the dancing body. In this book, it is my priority to make transparent the meaning-making procedures operational in movement. I investigate the theories undergirding the movement principles alongside the philosophical significance of the S-curve. Technical grounding of the form gives it a unique visual distinction, departure of which automatically takes the presentation outside of the parameters of its formal principles. However, experiments to expand the limits or the contours of the dance have been common creative experimentations in the field (Tandon, "Classicism on the Threshold of Modernity"). The thesis of this book is that the spiraling S-curve of the *Tribhangi* is grounded within a philosophical worldview that simultaneously prioritizes material cyclicality as well as imaginative departures.

Recuperating the Dancing Body

As one of many instructors of Charlotte Ballet's (premier ballet company in Charlotte) five-week 2024 Summer Intensive, I was asked to reconsider costuming for the final informal showing. As a female identified Indian dancer, I rarely associate bindis (adhesives or colored agents worn on the forehead in between the eyebrows) with religiosity. A bindi is worn by both male and female artists and is more of an ornamental, cultural, and aesthetic feature than a religious ideal. Bindis are not exclusively used in dance but also worn by general public as a fashion accessory. In a discursive analysis of the bindi, communication studies scholar Mary Grace Antony argues how the bindi is a complex signifier that although once considered as a quintessential symbol of Indian femininity, is also a performative identifier of resistance, activism, and political affiliation. Simplistically, it is possible that the Christian controversy around the bindi as a quintessential identifier of a Hindu woman might have a role to play in my students' parents' refusals to comply with my costuming convention (Antony 2010). Part of the problem, perhaps, lies within the interrogated conflation of Indian dance with Hindu essence since the majority of the repertoire concentrates on Hindu myths, episodes, narratives, poetry, and prose. Banerji notes that "much of the rhetoric, both in the scholarship and in communities of practice, assigns a devotional purpose to classical dance, especially by emphasizing its nexus with temple culture in the present or past; secular, educational, economic, entertainment and political values are usually relegated to the fringes (Banerji 2023, 202). But, at large, the request to reconsider costuming (in case of the bindi) even for remote religious associations also illustrates that there is a serious lack of understanding shrouded in a series of misgivings about Indian dance.

Spatial and temporal domains remain the central axes on which the dancing body operates with varying degrees of curvature and intensity. Yet, what does the Odissi dancing body accomplish? I argue that it is a process of intensification, deepening, and discovery. Its investment with the body-mind complex to accomplish epistemological processes goes through these three stages. The first stage utilizes technical infrastructure to raise the affective potential to its highest possible degree. Codified vocabulary and expressive tools of communication—physical, verbal, production-related, and emotional/ ideational—together enable the rallying up of intensity in performance. This artistic intensity then provides a subsequent stage of deepening nurturing, holistic attitudes toward the body-mind complex, nuanced ways of understanding the ecologies of practice, and complementarity across collective wisdom and individual flair. In this stage, dance becomes a way of knowing as well as a knowledge base. As both a means and an end to the epistemological process, the dancer finally is able to discover the meaning and purpose behind the act of dance. According to Africanist aesthetics scholar Omofolabo Soyinka Ajayi, dance is integral to African way of life and acts as a base for knowledge accumulation over time (Ajayi 1989). Using material limits of space, posture, appearance, gaze, space, and time, the African dancing body transcends material limits into ancestral and spiritual realms. This finality of spiritual discovery is technically encoded in the definition of the dancing Odissi body with *Moksha,* meaning freedom from the cycle of birth and death, as its final destination. This, the final stage of my analysis, is one of individual discovery beyond both the kinesthetic and the verbal. Its domain lies within and exceeds the material limits of the body and the cognizing mind. Every cellular membrane intensifies, deepens, and discovers for itself the purpose of the confluence of technical rigor, cultural accumulation, and a subjective delight, which individuals determine in multiple ways—aesthetic, spiritual, religious, and theatrical. Below, I focus on the solo dancing format to further exemplify this individualized process.

The dancer on stage takes the responsibility of the content to communicate to an audience. Communication to the viewer takes precedence in the technical infrastructure of the movement itself. The *Sachi* (looking sideways) presupposes the sides as the end of the seating in the proscenium theater. During training and rehearsals, the dancer does not look completely sideways. Rather, the gaze stops at about forty-five degrees from the front to ensure that the audience does not see too much of the sclera or the white portion of the eye. While the technique, choreography, and production maintain communication etiquette, the dance also takes ownership of the content—intellectual, literary, percussive, melodic, philosophical, and kinesthetic. *Nritta Hastas* or pure dance gestures, such as *Anjali* (hands joined at the palms), *Swastika* (hands joined at the wrists), *Kartaka* (hands interlacing fingers) etc., are examples of nonverbal usage. Although, *Anjali,* commonly used in yoga studios in the United States at the end of a session, might have a deeper meaning (ranging from paying respect to honoring one's inner strength), its usage in movement can be purely a kinesthetic abstraction without any verbal interpretation. Yet, gestures remain the semiotic conduits of the dancer as each gesture comes with an array of meanings and possibilities. This way, the viewer always has the discretion of interpreting the semiotic codes conveying ideas, emotions, or mapping the musical content. So, the frontal nature of the dance is because of the inherent responsibility of the dancer to ensure vivid and vibrant communication to the audiences who are presupposed within the technical formalities of every movement.

The communication of the content occurs in multiple stages and depends upon the type of information being conveyed. Communication of music, text, rhythm, and physical movement occurs in different modalities. Musical mapping occurs through gestural, postural, expressive, and percussive registers. Using *Nritta Hastas* to glide over the melodic notes while performing footwork that accents the percussion, the dancer primarily takes ownership of the music ensuring its visualization for the viewers. The expressive takes into account the mood of the *Raga* or the melodic mode or multiple *Ragas* that provide the compositional base for the music. It is often seen that the dancer makes it a point to show the mathematical exactitude of the complex rhythmic frameworks that constitute the Odissi music. Just as a vocalist takes joy in teaming up with a percussionist on stage, the dancer also plays a call and response strategy with the percussionist, either in person while live accompaniment or within the recorded audio track. Sometimes movement appears for movement's sake without an added burden of further meaning-making. Percussive footwork, gestural motility, or postural stasis might act as bridges between sections in a piece. For example, in *Bichitro Anondo* (*Enigmatic Bliss*), choreographer Rohini Dandavate used a rhythmic section to act as a bridge from the first thought pattern to the second.[2] In this way, the section provides a respite for the audience from constant verbal meaning-making. The section provides some percussive structure ensuring the continuation of parallel mapping of music and dance. But, the choreographic treatment of a musical section conveys the primary intent of the choreographer. For *Bichitro Anondo,* the musical variation of *Ta Jham Ta Rita Jhena*, provides some transitional respite between two sections of the song composed by Nobel laureate Rabindranath Tagore. Finally, and most importantly, the dancer takes charge of verbal meaning-making. *Abhinaya* or expressional performance requires the highest degree of virtuosic performance. In Odissi dance, the understanding and processing of expressive content is far more important than physical display of flexibility and strength. This continues to remain its primary difference from Western concert dance, where the verbal and the expressive remain secondary to the abstract materiality of the dancing body.

Text is central to Odissi dance putting to use codified vocabularies of gesture to convey content. Most commonly used languages are Oriya (the language originating from Odisha), Sanskrit, and Hindi. However, dancers from non-Oriya heritage often use their languages, such as, Bengali into dance compositions. *Bichitro Anondo* is one such choreography where a Bengali song has been repurposed into a *Sabhinaya Pallavi,* which means a combination of *Abhinaya,* meaning expression, and *Pallavi,* meaning melodic and percussive elaboration. *Bichitro Anondo* intersperses melodic and percussive registers with textual content. In such cases, the musical and the textual blend into one another in the musical composition and the choreography through a collaborative compositional process across music and dance. Poetry is also used in many pieces as the textual content is expressed as recited and not as sung lyric. Meaning of the words and sentences are usually presented with the help of the vast gestural vocabulary that codifies every part of the body from head, neck, eye, chin, cheek, rib cage, sides of the body, hands, wrists, fingers, waist, legs, knees, feet, etc. Usually a word-by-word gestural translation is followed by a more general import of a sentence structure. This literal treatment of text is then further elaborated through a series of contextual information, metaphorical interpolation, and poetic imagination. In Debasish Pattnaik's choreography *Mon Bayaro Banko Churore* (translated as my beloved's curled locks of hair), the protagonist is compared to a full moon shining its light on the city limits. Although, the hand gesture shows the moon using the *Chandrakala,* it has layered signification showing not just the real-world variant but also its analogical counterpart.

This way textual usage in movement is multilayered and its interpretation is deeply subjective given the array of possible meanings of each gestural usage. While gesture is central to expressing textual content, postural stasis and motility as well as percussive footwork are often important means of intensifying a particular motif.

Movement in Odissi dance is laden with abstract and narrative meaning as I research the locus and intent behind generation and reception of artistic material. Its affective potency is paramount given its primary function of communication to an abstract or often imagined audience encoded within the technical infrastructure. Movement engages in a literal and conversational modality although it undergoes significant aesthetic stylization. Further, movement is also imbued with rhythmic signification, gestural ornamentation, postural degrees of freedom, musical proliferation, and other nonverbal modalities of communication. Multiple constituents cocreate a piece of work—namely, poetic verses by historical or contemporary writers, scriptwriters, melody and rhythm composers, choreographers etc. It is possible that the poetic intent differs from that of the scriptwriter and the choreographer might bring in a completely different orientation. For example, in the traditional composition of Kavisurya Baladeba Ratha's composition *Lila Nidhi He* was reinterpreted by Guru Kelucharan Mohapatra's choreographic intention. In a similar way, Dr. Dandavate reinterpreted creatively Kabiguru Rabindranath Tagore's lyric in her piece *Enigmatic Bliss.* The choreographic reinterpretation does not lie within literary hermeneutics. Rather, it follows principles of dance composition while indulging in creative departures from authorial intent. So, literary content and devices, while significant in Odissi, do not have the last word. Rather, the creative output is always a push and pull between text, music, and movement. Odissi music scholar Dr. Sangita Gosain noted that Odissi music places emphasis on literature. So, musical liberty that often distorts pronunciation and lyrical integrity, is not welcome within Odissi's creative flow. This shows how meaning-making in Odissi is a balancing act across narrative, communicative, melodic, percussive, and choreographic choices that together ensure the curvilinear flow in *Madhyam Laya,* that is, in medium speed, neither slow (*Vilambit*) nor fast (*Drut*). The elaborate signification process of codified gestural vocabularies will be further explored in subsequent chapters.

The structure of communication within movement, expression, and performance relies on agential code-switching by the performer on multiple accords. Irrespective of content, the dancer as the content provider is a specialist who simultaneously performs, acts, dances, and witnesses. Embodied motility engages in physical expansion and contraction in space alongside marking percussive accents mapping the rhythmic framework. Movement in time and space leading to bodily changes remain central to the dance. But subtle changes in the dancer's thought pattern primarily affects the reception of movement. In this way, Odissi is unique given its simultaneous usage of movement and expression. Usually, in dances such as *Kuchipudi* and *Bharatnatyam,* the dancer emotes to textual content using gestural vocabulary only. However, in Odissi, the dancer simultaneously uses the entirety of the dancer's tool kit to showcase content complicating binary deployment of gesture and footwork as noticeable in other dances. Simultaneous engagement with multiplicity engages the entirety of the body-mind complex in such a way that the dancer is required to remain nimble, agile, and present to ensure code-switching.

FIG. 1: Claiming Lineage: Author with her teacher Guru Poushali Mukherjee a performance (Kolkata, December 22, 2019). Reproduced with permission from Debojyoti Dhar.

Dance then becomes a constant agility across the content, its communication, and the transition between the two. In order for the content to land in a realistic fashion, the dancer takes ownership of theatricality. Yet, the next moment might be one of check-in resulting in a zooming out of the particular character, narrative, story, situation, emotion, thought, rhythmic pattern, or melodic mode, to the larger public. The public is never in real-time and in real-scale. Rather, the viewer is an imagined entity occupying the frontal periphery of the gaze. The dancer's gaze returns to that imagined center time and again to ensure a direct checking in with the pulse of the audience, but it is never with a single person or a group of people. The audience in the proscenium remains in the dark and even if the dancer is able to see the viewers, the gaze typically goes into the infinite horizon to an imagined group or individual recipient. This checking-in also requires a physical rest, which I will later theorize as *kinesthetic pause*.

Checking-in with the audience is as important as a daily check-in as an artist invested in keeping the art alive as life-breath. As a practitioner of Guru Kelucharan Mohapatra style of Odissi (under the tutelage of Guru Poushali Mukherjee from Kolkata and Guru Ratikant Mohapatra and Guru Sujata Mohapatra from Bhubaneswar), I present my stylistic perspective although one that is deeply imbued with my investment in daily practice. This work is limited in many dimensions due to its particular focus on the solo format, but it makes legible cultural and artistic labor of the South Asian dancing body that is illegible, imperceptible, and impenetrable, leading to glaring mistranslations. In its true sense, Odissi is an interdisciplinary art form with sculpture, painting, architecture, music, and literature serving its skeletal framing. In this way, dance brings other art forms to life functioning as a metaphysical bridge to other arts serving as a repository and disseminating their collective wisdom. So, exploring epistemic limits of kinesthetic attention of the dancing body becomes significant. This is the first book-length inquiry into the South Asian solo practitioner's tool kit, which is not overdetermined by the conservatism of tradition or seduced by imported understandings of innovation. Rather, this is a manual of a creative individual who defines the relationship between technique and choreography in Odissi that is particular to the culturally situated practice of dance.

A Word on Structure and Agency

Knees bend as I pivot my right heel and switch my body-weight from the back to the front leg. The echo of this twisting motion is echoed in my rib cage as I deflect my torso to the left and rest my head on the right. Experiencing a moment of stasis with the sideways deflection of my head, I stretch out the pause infinitely through the rest of my body. This results in a sensory mode of extending attentiveness to stillness that creeps its way into the dance through movement qualities prioritizing a curvilinear arc between rest and motion. I enter the proscenium with this gait garnering presence—emotional, intellectual, experiential, and performance—to start yet another reflective process of intensification, deepening, and discovery. This is a quintessential entry into the proscenium theater repeated in conventional Odissi repertoire and practiced time and again by dancers in the studio. Practice is central to the dancing body's ability to function with exactitude, rigor, and understanding. It challenges unnecessary separation of the body and mind (Reckwitz 2002) given its simultaneous processing of context, experience, and activity (Green 2009). In the above anecdote, I share my experience of entering the concert space in Guru Durga Charan Ranabir's choreography with the familiar gait of heel-pivots. The activity of pivoting in the context of Guru Debaprasad Das style, which is different from my training within Guru Kelucharan Mohapatra style, provides me a unique yet familiar feeling in my practice and performance. These three elements of activity, context, and experience layer and unfold into one another in dynamic proportions according to practice theorist B. Green. Garnering all of my body and mind, muscles and joints, thoughts and emotions, and senses and feelings, I start yet another round of entering the stage-space, which is an arena of alchemical exchange and experiments with freedom. The freedom in the studio or on stage primarily lies in testing limits of the body and mind. The studio has a controlled ecosystem without the added pressure of the penetrating gaze of the audience. However, it is also limiting in terms of alchemical exchange of energies that enhances the generative intensity during a performance. Generation of emotions during the solo recital bear experiential, felt, sensorial, and mental dimensions. Execution of footwork primarily relies on mathematical acuity, speed, and strength. Gestural precision lies on a controlled energetic dimension that controls the contours of the fingers without making them look either limp or taut. So, attentive detailing to text, rhythm, music, and emotion is the central hallmark of the dancing body. Yet, I want to free myself of constraints in order to experience presence in the moment given that the exercise for the dancer is to experience freedom from any externally or internally imposed criteria or parameters.

In search of my agency and to make the form my own, I seek out moments of my being within the uber coded structure of technique and creative experimentations of choreographic intent. In between the technique and creative imagination, I search for my footprint. I look for the performative resonances through the materiality of my body. Materiality of the dancing body prioritizes ideation and sweat in the same vein, foregrounding the primacy of the relational nature between embodied actions, conceptual frameworks, and felt emotions. The field of Odissi experiences an authority of practice with existing codes and conventions, often limiting the scope of agential action, for the dancer. As a dancer seeped in this living tradition of orthodoxy and authoritarian practice, I have a visceral reaction against this hierarchy. Responding to this notion of emergent practice in a larger tradition, scholar Donna Mathewson Mitchell notes that the practitioner "develops a relationship to practice that engages their agency, in relation to the broader tradition" (2013, 416). Overall, the point is to transcend the experience, activity, and contexts of my movement to experience a moment of silence—one that is imbued with epistemic awareness of being, revealing, creating, performing, responding, connecting, and nurturing in dance. Structured pauses, as described in the anecdote at the beginning of this section, further that specific investigation into kinesthetic attention. Structured practice becomes the organizing principle of my body-mind complex navigating the curvilinear grounds of technique, the negotiation of flow of thought and movement in creative manifestations, the deepening of affect in imagistic dramaturgy, the interplay with regionally specific modalities of music, and basis for collaboration with dancers and choreographers.

My daily dance practice, also known as *Sadhana,* has shifted since I started Odissi at the age of ten with Guru Poushali Mukherjee. At that time, I followed instructions, focused on bodily strength and remembering content, and found freedom within my guided dance sessions. My relationship with my daily dance practice has shifted over the years. Odissi practitioner and scholar Nandini Sikand notes how Odissi dancers use their *Sadhana* (which has a wide variety of meanings and functions in dance, spirituality, and philosophy) for scholarly, creative, and traditional interpretations of their integrity with their artwork. Making content my own is a post thirty-five phenomenon where I am able to activate my embodied strength and agility with an empathic and cognitive understanding of kinesthetic, literary, musical, percussive, and philosophical content that undergird performance in this art form weaving pluralistic registers in dynamic relationalities; a phenomenon exemplified in the foregrounding of the physical (Fig. 2) and the emotive (Fig. 3). At this point, I question the centrality of the cognitive as well as the apparent neutrality of ideation as a desensitized mental exercise (Dawn 2025). Movement encompasses all of my being, activity, and experience where objectifiable cognitive thinking is complementary to emotional expressivity, sensorial awareness, affective presence, rhythmic acuity, and melodic flow. I find it hard to grasp the philosophical separation of an intellectualized being as different from the situated contexts of the body. In this vein, I echo van Manen's phenomenological view of existence as felt, sensed, and cognized since my dancing body is

FIG. 2: Guru Poushali Mukherjee in a slightly bent physical posture during a performance (Kolkata, December 22, 2019). Reproduced with permission from Debojyoti Dhar.

FIG. 3: Guru Poushali Mukherjee absorbed in an emotional moment in a slightly bent physical posture during a performance (Kolkata, December 22, 2019). Reproduced with permission from Debojyoti Dhar.

dynamically engaging in all three acts together, or separately, and in various combinations at any given moment in time both simultaneously as well as sequentially (Van Manen 2023). In the dance studio, one hones in on focus that then sharpens the ability to grasp the world in its material complexity. I have to know my spacing as well as my timing impeccably well. I stay attuned to the musical notes and textual meaning. I continue to remember to communicate while charting the multiple registers of movement. Text and music are deep investigations of their own. So, the dancer's metaphysical outreach to these forms is itself imbued with infinite philosophical depth and improvisatory potential. I will investigate music and text with greater depth in my deep dives into choreographic processes in chapters five and six. So, the dancing body's ability to remain present at every instant with sensitive and sensible awareness is unique especially given the layering of music, text, and rhythm with the additional communicative function. Moving away from assuming knowledge as cognitive, I sensitize my dancing body to explore experiential dimensions of my practice.

I organized my research process around my daily dance practice while supplementing my studio-based data collection with creative collaborations with other artists—choreographers, music composers, and dance educators. I kept a journal of my daily solo dance practice that provided detailed systematic reflection into the performance process. I reflected on anatomical, expressive, musculoskeletal, as well as affective dimensions. Apart from researching my own studio work, I applied for federal, state, local, and regional grants to interview as well as work with other artists who have been trained in styles other than Guru Kelucharan Mohapatra style. Switching styles within the form is looked down upon with extreme disdain. One can think of this as deflections by Russian artists from the Soviet Union to the United State during the Cold War era. While the latter is a political deflection, the former example of my seeking knowledge of other styles is to be inclusive of difference within the broader genre of dance. However, I have received significant backlash on social media as well as faced boycotting due to my decisions as a scholar and researcher that impinge on conventions in my life as an Odissi artist and disciple of teachers steeped within Guru Kelucharan Mohapatra.

My year-long collaborations on artistic and educational projects with Ratna Roy (trained under Guru Pankaj Charan Das) and Bani Ray (trained under Guru Durga Charan Ranbir who trained with the Guru Debaprasad Das, which is a style in Odisha) broadened technical, affective, and performative dimensions of my practice. Ohio Arts Council's Traditional Arts Apprenticeship grants allowed for a year-long working opportunity with New Jersey-based Odissi artist Bani Ray Deubler who is an exponent in Guru Debaprasad Das style of Odissi. Having worked in ensemble choreography that premiered in January 2023 with Colorado-based dancer Madhavi Rao had already deepened my understanding of Guru Debaprasad Das style given Rao's initial training in this form. A faculty research grant from the University of North Carolina at Charlotte supported my year-long collaboration. Roy has directly learned from Mahari Sashimoni Devi, who was a temple-dancer in Odisha and also an inspiration for my doctoral dissertation, "Mahari Out: Deconstructing Odissi" that was published in 2017 (Mahari means temple-dancer). Little did I envision that five years later, I will encounter Mahari Sashimoni Devi once again through her tutelage of Dr. Roy. I have also interviewed NYC-based Odissi dancer Radhika Jha (Guru Surendranath Jena style) and collaborated with Connecticut-based dancer

Urmila Mallick (Nrityagram style) to further broaden my knowledge-base in Odissi. Radhika Jha trained under Guru Surendranath Jena notes how his style relies heavily on sculptural specificities. Urmila Mallick notes the expansive and demanding repertory of Nrityagram, globally the most popular Odissi conservatory known for their professionalism and artistry. I do not claim to have a comprehensive embodied understanding of all existing styles currently in operation in the field. Rather, I show how my semantic and epistemic investments in the technique and repertoire of Guru Kelucharan Mohapatra style shift through my exposure to other stylistic characteristics.

In addition to these immersive working sessions, I organized, facilitated, and led week-long symposia in performance and scholarship that further supplemented my understanding of the grounding and creative forays in this form. The aim behind these sessions was to provide a structured platform where artists could share their views on the educational, artistic, and performative dimensions of Odissi through lectures, performance, teaching, or performance. In 2021 and 2022, two virtual conferences called *Shaping S-Curves: Choreographic Process in India* and *Pluralism in Odissi: Forms and Aesthetics* respectively focused on the creative and the technical grounds of the dance (Čurda 2024). Both these conferences were online, free, and attended by Odissi dancers, choreographers, educators, and scholars from the international community. Though these two conferences were held online due to restrictions of in person gathering during the COVID-19 pandemic, they allowed for an online gathering of Odissi enthusiasts sharing and learning from one another. The 2021 conference focused on the choreographic process that is directly tied to the theme of my book. The 2022 conference allowed me to think more broadly outside of my training and investment within Guru Kelucharan Mohapatra style of Odissi. I do not make claims to understand the other styles completely. However, the presentation of multiple stylistic and aesthetic traits broadened my horizon about the understanding of Odissi technique. In 2023, I worked in person with veteran artist, Guru Aruna Mohanty, artistic director of Odisha's premier institution, Orissa Dance Academy, at the *Sadhana: Art and Philosophy of Curvilinearity* conference. Working with Mohanty for ten days in the studio furthered my knowledge base about the contemporary practice of Odissi in Odisha. In 2024, I organized "Odissi Odyssey" where I rehearsed and performed a duet with Debasish Pattnaik from Bangalore (a southern Indian city). Mohanty is steeped in Guru Kelucharan Mohapatra style, like me, through her training with Guru Gangadhar Pradhan (a direct disciple of Guru Kelucharan Mohapatra). Performing with Pattnaik, who is trained in Debaprasad Das style, gave me direct visceral experience of stylistic difference within the execution of movements in the two styles.

I devised a nine-celled matrix to capture nuances of my practice-based methodology in my scholarship, performance, teaching, and organizational leadership in the professional domain of Odissi. It provides a relational, generative, and dynamic representation of performance, teaching, and creativity to capture the nonlinear and interdependent nature of the complexities of practice that asserts a conversational dynamic across given structure and personal agency. The horizontal axis represents the structures of music, text, and movement that impact the performative output. The vertical axis represents the stakeholders (choreographers, composers, dancers) in solo movement repertoire. It is important to note the simplistic and reductive nature of this matrix given that it obscures other players in the business of teaching and creating in

TABLE 1. Nine-Celled Matrix Exploring Structure and Agency in Odissi Dance

	Music	Text	Movement
Dancer	What are the virtuosic, performative, affective, communicative, and expressive registers that reach the audiences generating a sync across artistic production and reception in the sonic realm?	How can I weave in agential interpretation of text in my execution of verbal information primarily through semiotic codes?	What curvilinearities am I insinuating in the space-time continuum and how can these signify meaningfully to audiences from diverse backgrounds and knowledges?
Choreographer	What are the subtle intentions and physical motifs edifying a particular work in the kinesthetic framework where the audible dancing body merges with live musical accompaniment or recorded audio tracks?	What strategies and degrees of literary immersion does the choreographer need in order to create a series of gestural, postural, and percussive commentaries on existing textual authority?	What is the role of personal signature and stylistic annotation in the creative act?
Composer	What is the melodic and rhythmic infrastructure setting the primary abstract tone of ornamentation?	How can making explicit the correlation of text with music composition impact the creative process?	What is the particularized process of creating music for dance?

Odissi, such as the arts administrators, policymakers, scriptwriters, and organizers. However, I have chosen this representation in order to foreground the priorities of my practice-based methodological focus primarily on the dialectical relationship between music and dance. Each of these cells investigates a particular question in the solo-dancing repertoire largely asking: How does music, text, and movement interweave into the creative process and the execution? Across music, text, and movement, I explore the epistemologies of curvilinearity, one that is simultaneously independent and in conjunction with other markers of structure in the dance. Representing my methodology in a snapshot, this table explores the epistemic limits of the form I live, breathe, and be.

Grounded and Languid in Praxis

My grounded and languid practice of the lower and upper body, respectively, is suffused with South Asian performance theories and philosophies that *Paribartita,* make a horizontal eight-shaped curve, with my dancing body, which collects, organizes, sifts through, and collates data for this book project. This project inquires the creative process in the dancing S-curves of Odissi. Through my immersion in the dance form for the past three decades, I develop a process involving gathering data, reflecting on the content, and assimilation of repertoire

FIG. 4: Smaranika Jena of Odissi Research Centre fame in *Chauka* (square). Reproduced with permission from Jeff Cravotta.

syncing intellectual analysis as well as my experiential reality. While I start with interviewing, collaborating, organizing, and observing, I make it a point to establish embodied pathways of sedimentation of the gathered information as experiential knowledge through daily practice of footwork and expression. From this place of gathering, processing, and assimilating, I write about the dancing body where praxis becomes central to the organization of thought and flow of writing. How do I know in dance? What do I know through movement? What are the philosophies undergirding my daily praxis? I investigate the philosophical import behind the theory and execution, such as knowing the theory of *Bhramaris* (spins) and practicing them on the Marley floors of Robinson Hall for the Performing Arts at the University of North Carolina at Charlotte. I dedicate the next chapter to investigate the inflection point of the S-curve grounding the languid through stasis as well as percussive accenting by the heel, toe, and flat surfaces of the feet.

Practice presents the templates, trends, and flowcharts central to my research of agential inquiry. Where am I in the dance? Am I in the thought or footwork, gesture or expression? In the

FIG. 5: Smaranika Jena of Odissi Research Centre fame in *Tribhangi* (S-shape). Reproduced with permission from Jeff Cravotta.

dance studio, I start with a warm-up routine of Vinyasa yoga. After stretching and centering, I do the sound and soundless exercises as laid out in the *PathFinder* published by the Odissi Research Centre under the leadership of performer, educator, and scholar, Guru Kumkum Mohanty. This leads into the practice of what is conventionally known as, "Stepping" comprising of a numerically progressing footwork regimen in the postures of *Chauka* (square) and *Tribhangi* (S-Shape) (Mohanty 1985).

Ta Tathi Naka Thini/ Ta

Stepping is typically bound by the four-beat rhythm structure called the *Ekatali. Ta Tathi Naka Thini/ Ta.* This rhythmic refrain repeats in at least three speeds—*Vilambit* (slow), *Madhyam* (medium), and *Druta* (fast)—grounding the lower body in a dialectic of symmetry-asymmetry, square-S shapes, and a plethora of ways of bearing, sharing, and gesturing of body weight. For example, footwork in *Tribhangi* requires a certain melting onto the ground by the supported leg complemented by buoyant articulations by the gesturing leg. After the centering within yoga, exercise, and stepping, I engage with the conventional progression of the traditional repertoire—namely, *Mangalacharan, Batu, Pallavi, Abhinaya*, and *Moksha.* These are typically choreographed pieces that constitute the five-segment constitution of the performative arc. One starts processing new material only after grounding the body within the conventional repertoire. This ensures that the emergent languidness and nimbleness to start exploration in artistic imagination and embodiment as the body, then, is deeply entrenched within the ethos and parameters of Odissi. A typical practice session takes anywhere between two to four hours. In the second chapter, I theorize the philosophical basis of this repertoire. Below, I focus on the practical components of practicing and mining information within and through practice.

Grounded with fundamentals and convention also stretch, transform, and personalize the notion of time. The soloist requires stamina to hold audience attention for an extended period of time; anywhere between twenty minutes to two hours. Pieces tend to be fifteen minutes on average. Performing continuously for that duration requires cultivation of focus, centering, and stamina. So, the long stretched out practice, ranging from its conditioning, technique, and repertoire, is also a way to ensure growth and improvement in physical stamina and mental focus. My practice generates, processes, and analyzes the data—in the form of movement sketches, musical collaborations, costuming conventions, productions requirements etc.—illuminating epistemic and semantic possibilities of the dancing body. What differs my usual from my inquiry-based practice-based research lies in the explicit taking stock of the conditioning process, technique curriculum, and traditional repertoire to then theorize about the larger trends, trajectories, and inflection points of movement and its choreographic body. I maintain journals noting progresses, failures, and discoveries in these practice sessions.

In order to understand the choreographic process, I work with choreographers to commission solo and ensemble works. This way, I engage with the various elements in the creative process, ranging from ideation to script writing, music composition to rhythmic variations, and introducing to building upon a choreographic motif. Articulation of this creative process through embodied processing in and through my daily lived experience of the *Sadhana* places practice at the heart of my methodology. While I inform myself of theoretical definitions

FIG. 6: Author performing with Tamara Williams at UNC Charlotte Dance Faculty Concert, Charlotte, January 23, 2023. Reproduced with permission from Jeff Cravotta.

of *Sadhana* within various disciplines of Indian philosophy, religiosity, spirituality, and ritual practice, I prioritize the creative process at the heart of choreographic making. In this way, *Sadhana* is indelibly a process of inquiry and discovery. The analytical and the creative would weave into my technical encoding in dance through the cyclical working through existing material and exploring new work. I would have one-on-one work sessions with choreographers two or three times a week. In these sessions, movements would go through a research and development process. Multiple iterations of movements or facial expressions would be presented on the table. From these options, one or two would be finally make it to the work. Each piece would take about three or four months. I delve into the detailed choreographic process in Odissi in the Chapter 4. Here, it is important to mention that the infiltration of this creative input from the choreographer would feature in my daily practice. I familiarize, understand, process, and go through what I call a process of sedimentation of the newly gathered motifs.

Although this text explores the agential embodiment in solo dancing, I have also sought out peers as collaborators to complicate, challenge, expand, and nuance my creative process. In this dimension, I have focused on South-South collaborative processes foregrounding my political position of enforcing aesthetic diversity by pluralizing the center constituted mainly of Western concert dance aesthetics. South-South collaboration allows me to consider other non-Western practices—such as Yoruba-inspired movement genres as well as Afro-Brazilian modern dance technique, Silvestre—in connection to my creative and collaborative process. On March 4,

2023, I premiered *Tapa: Fervent Triggers* at CounterPulse in San Francisco (Dandavate 2023). *Tapa* means heat. This was an evening-length production featuring choreography by Dr. Rohini Dandavate, Tamara Williams, and Rosangela Silvestre (founder of the Silvestre technique) held to the fore important environmental and social justice issues such as climate change, forest fires, and mass shootings in the United States. This production orients the artistic in and through the traditional, the spiritual, and the philosophical. Creativity, in this collaborative process, lied in invoking Yoruban spirits alongside Odishan sculpturesque figurines (Reckwitz 2002). Myth, memory, and contemporary political and environmental disasters that plague our daily lived experiences find breathing space in *Tapa*. I danced solo three pieces created by Dandavate in Odissi, namely, *Fire, Trigger,* and *Enigmatic Bliss* with live singing by Hindustani classical vocalist Anirban Bhattacharyya. Interspersing my solos were solos by Tamara Williams and Rosangela Silvestre in Yoruba and Silvestre dance forms, respectively. While Rosangela danced in silence, Tamara was accompanied by a live drummer, Luciano Xavier. Williams and Silvestre's dances carried the flow of the overall program centering the devastation and havoc caused by human greed and utilitarianism. *Tapa* ended with all three of us on stage with the live musical accompaniment by Luciano Xavier's lilting percussivity and Anirban Bhattacharyya's ornamented vocalization. In a subsequent journal-length exploration, I return to the notion of aesthetic pluralism of collaborative cosmogonies while making choices around costuming, music, and choreography. However, it is beyond the scope of this text, which primarily uses the S-curves as points of departure or of landing.

During my research inquiry, I worked very closely with music to understand the relationship of the dancing Odissi body to music. During the three-year (2021–2024) period in consideration, I worked with three music composers over multiple projects and spent a year collaborating with a vocalist trained in Indian music, Anirban Bhattacharyya that resulted in the performance of *Tapa* also mentioned in the above paragraph. In traditional parlance, Odissi repertoire is performed to sung lyric, verbal syllable characterizing musical note, rhythmic beat, or other instrumental approximation, voice modulation, or nonverbal vocalizing. The lilting characteristic of movement—what Ratna Roy refers to as the oceanic ebb and flow—is derived from the music while simultaneously shaping the timbre, affect, quality, and aesthetic of the musical accompaniment. Roy's first lesson with Guru Pankaj Charan Das was at the Puri on the beach.The musicality of the waves with its incessant gathering, rising, and dissolution was crucial for Roy's affective learning of the subtle, energetic detailing that characterizies torso movement. Heightening my affective and experiential concurrence with music during my studio practice, I paid greater attention to music and the musicality. I worked with music composers in a variety of compositions ranging from traditional to contemporary takes on the tradition to departing significantly from the Odissi idiom, especially through my forays into experimental dance forms, *Yorchha* (the contemporary Indian dance technique rooted in social justice created by Ananya Chatterjea) and *Shilpanatanam* (the contemporary Indian dance technique rooted in Indian traditional storytelling idiom created by Maya Kulkarni) (Chatterjea 2013). By notating these compositions and analyzing them, I gathered how music and movement achieve Roy's oceanic lilt in Odissi. Earlier, music would provide the sonic accompaniment to my guided dance practice. Nevertheless, in this research process, I developed a conscious engagement with the guided sonic activity by paying specific attention to the representation of the music in dance, on one hand, and taking note of integral requirements of the dance by necessitating changes in the musical compositions, on the other. The back and forth between the dance studio and the composer's pre and post mastering and mixing at the music studio allowed the choreographic process to come to fruition and achieve communicative efficacy. This particular push and pull between dance and music constitutes a significant aspect of the creative process within Odissi.

Music and dance are integral to the practice of Odissi. Separation of dance and music is an alien concept for Odissi where the body itself is a rhythmic instrument with its own accord. Against this dance studies perspective of finding a separate ontological existence of dance in and through movement, I present a culturally situated understanding of Odissi's complementarity with its musical interface while noting creative and artistic choices. Odissi music has a unique regional flavor that is markedly different from Hindustani music from northern India and Carnati music from the south as noted by scholar Itishree Sahoo in her book-length investigation of Odissi music (2009). Located at the confluence of the north and south, Odissi music has developed a mellifluous tenor and structure that complements the flow of Odissi dance. Melody and rhythm together constitute the pillars of the dance choreography. During the creation process, the choreographer works with two composers representing melody and rhythm. In the conventional Odissi repertoire, music plays an important role. The five-part progression from *Mangalacharan* (Invocation), *Batu* (Fundamentals), *Pallavi* (Musical Proliferations), *Abhinaya* (Narrative Elaborations), *Moksha* (Spiritual Emancipation) has distinct characteristics in each segment. Separating music and dance is impossible in the context of Odissi. Sometimes, I have to make a case for the importance of music in Odissi, especially in my current situation in US higher education. I believe Western concert dance trends of complicating relationships to music are interesting experimentations that can inform the practice of Odissi composition only after one first attempts to understand the intricate webs in which dance and music are co-constituted in the field of Odissi. The *Invocation* has a three-fold musical structure, which starts with a rhythmic construct, enters into evocative singing, and ends on specific musical composition. *Batu* introduces choreographically and musical the various instrumentation (string, percussion, etc.) used in the music. *Pallavi* is where the musical climax is attained in terms of speed and virtuosic composition, especially of fast-paced percussion. *Abhinaya* peaks the dramatic intent of the dancer as poetic verses are repurposed into affective movement that is sensorially and emotionally charged for narrative meaning-making. Lastly, *Moksha* starts on a rhythmic note but ends on a quiet mode of centering the body-mind phenomenon through the chanting of the om syllable. Each of these segments will be elaborated in Chapter 3 focusing on both technique and repertoire.

As noted above, musicality is ingrained in the dancing S-curves of Odissi. At this point, I want to elaborate upon the quintessential curvature that has been the defining feature of my art form. *Tribhangi* is a tri-bent posture that resembles the shape of the letter S. Distinct bends at the knees, waist, ankles, hips, elbows, wrists, and neck allow for inflection points for directional changes in flow and expression. Technically speaking, a movement phrase involves a series of inflection points, points definitively marking a change in the direction of the curvature. The S-curve draws strength from the technically grounded lower body in Odissi. This requires significant training and practice of feeling, being-with, and melting into the ground. There is an entire pedagogy of grounding while introducing strong, efficient, speedy, buoyant, and percussive footwork. Slapping the foot into the earth in heel-toe-flat articulations map onto the corresponding beat-structure played on the *Mardala* (drums) by the percussionist. In comparison to the Western concert dancer, the Odissi dancer covers much less space because virtuosic movement lies in rhythmic complexity rather than spatial coverage; polyrhythmic coordination rather than physiological extension; affective juxtapositions rather than stoic presence. This teaches the body to have a center of gravity that is lower than the usual height of the dancer. Further, this equips the dancer with the ability to bear body-weight and maintain the centralized, closer-to-the-earth core in spatially wide movements. Oftentimes, there are plural embodied vectors of energetic configurations occurring in the same movement. For example, the third stepping of *Chauka* (square posture) has percussive footwork in the lower body juxtaposed with circular arm movements. The torso works as an echo deflecting sideways to the stamping of the third beat on the ground; the right foot sends the rib cage to the left and vice versa. The grounding further allows for crisp pivots along a vertical axis, always maintaining a languid circularity juxtaposed with staccato percussivity.

In my research, I focus on the various entry-points of this marking the S in the dancing body across creative and technical registers. Providing an illusion of ease and flow, the S-curve requires significant musculoskeletal strength resulting from an elaborate training regimen. I elaborate further on sculpting and mobilizing the S with directional clarity, circular juxtapositions, percussive complexity, affective flow and upper-body flexibility while discussing choreographic experimentations by scholar and artist Rohini Dandavate. Below, I share a snapshot of a small gestural phrase from Dandavate's *Bichitro Anondo* in the S-curve while maintaining a one-legged balance.

Knees bend as I lift one leg off the ground. The lifted ankle deflects to the side with an energetic extension through the toes. Finding my center of gravity in this one-legged balancing act, I push my rib cage to the right. I bring my arms above my head in a measured circularity as preparation for the next gesture. My fingers gather into codified Asamyukta-Hasta-Mudras (single-handed-gestures)—namely, Alapadma (cascading fingers) and Hamsasya (tips of index fingers and thumbs touch leaving free the remaining three). Alapadma positions itself right above my head while the Hamsasya shakes gently drawing a circular arc ranging about ninety degrees. It starts from the top where the Alapadma is stationed and ends at shoulder level. My eyes follow the Hamsasya Mudra as it travels from the top of my head to my side. It lands next to the shoulders finishing in Kapithha Mudra (tips of index and thumbs touch while the remaining fingers wrap themselves into the palm). All this while, with my eyes following the travel of the Hamsasya and its eventual realization in Kapitha, my neck moves side to side processing a different rhythm. Travel from the Alapadma to the Kapithha determines the duration of this motion. The complexity of the knees, ankles, toes, torso, hands, fingers, eyes, and neck form a loosely integrated whole with its own partial volition rather than centralized control and management by a unified self. But I feel the warmth, the brilliance, the exuberance, the nurturing, the life-inducing, as well as the scorching heat that engages, sustains, and organizes the entirety of the physical and affective complex. From start to finish, I might have completed just a second in clockwork time.

This gestural expansion of the arms with slight deflections of the neck, torso, head, eyes, etc., has a semantic function. It symbolizes the sun. The *Hamsasya* showcases the rays radiating from the sun. The landing of the movement is in stasis where the establishment of the sun becomes complete. Its depiction started with the initial preparatory moves involving knee-bends and raised hands. This is a typical cadence of an Odissi movement. It has a measured preparation. Its main activity determines the longevity of the movement. And before its dissolution, there is a static moment to register the denotation of the particular movement. This example shows the depiction of the sun through a phrase. I now turn to the epistemic processes involving this example. How do we understand that this movement depicts the sun? Audiences versed in Indian aesthetic theory recognize the *Mudras* and draw respective conclusions accordingly. Similarly, the dancer is able to complement the physical complexity of the movement through sensory, affective, and emotional registers. These registers ornament the expressivity of the dancing body. The facial emotions continue the semantic labor of signification although through an initial epistemic processing and organization by the dancer. Demonstrating a real-world object via the aesthetic visualization of a semantic conjuring of an epistemic process illustrates the sheer complexity of the dancing Odissi body (Banerji 2019).

The S curve traffics in grounded languidity where the juxtaposition of the lower body as grounded, rooted, earthy, and heavy juxtaposes with the torso's affective flow and flexibility as well as the gestural interface, particularly specifying the three pairs of neck-torso, hand-eye, and torso-wrist in coordination where the sequence varies depending on the affective valence. Returning to the previous example of the sun can further elaborate upon the gestural upper body. In sequential progression, deflections of the neck and the torso occur simultaneously as preparatory conditions for the arm movements. The gaze with the circularity of the hand, in this example showing the radiating solar power, reaches its climactic point with the completion of the phrase. In this case, *Hamsasya* converts into *Kapithha* marking the ending point. The hand-eye coordination registers a marked completion via the wrist-torso equation. The definitive placing of the wrist in *Kapithha* allows the torso to register the full arc of the phrase. This makes the way for the gaze to return to the front as the dancer never loses sight of the primary responsibility of acknowledging, communicating, conjuring, and story-boarding with the audience (live or imaginary).

The content of movement synthesizing poetic reflections, rhythmic acuity, technical grounding, and affective efficacy weaves in the performer's twisting geometries simultaneously foregrounding performative being, experience, and knowing. The dancer uses the S as an instrument to deliver content. The same S is also the grounds of being for the dancer in which experiences ebb and flow in and through the curvilinear geometries. Between two divergent thoughts, melodies, rhythmic progressions, and poetic verses, the dancer curates a definitive pause. This moment of stillness of the body and mind allows for a performative respite, which is crucial from the standpoint of artistic reception. This pause allows for the landing of a particular frequency before the next comes along. In this kinesthetic pause, experiential affective grounds merge with content deliverables within the abstract processing marking the dancing body (Ehrenberg 2015). In the Odissi body, the quintessential twist marks this kinesthetic stillness, which marks the ebb of the prior and merging within its folds the flow of the successor.

The twist allows for changing orientations. Physically speaking, this means changing the frontal scope in varying degrees, but metaphorically, it makes space for the dancer to change focus from the realistic representational to the experiential and sensory. Further dissolution of the senses into the movements of ideation foregrounds the cognitive processes in action during the flow of the movement. Reflecting on either cognitive processing of content or on experiential grounding in the senses, the dancing body is the instrument of abstraction of both external content and internal experience together resulting in the performative efficacy. The changing orientations of the twisting body become grounds for regenerating communicative efficacy across the dancer's ontological existence, felt emotions, and epistemological processing.

In addition to my solo studio praxis encompassing painstaking exactitude, infinite complexity, and indeterminable experiential cognition, I encounter the grounded and languid form in various contexts and in pluralistic capacities. My practice across my technical grounding and with peers in music, choreography, dramaturgy, and production as guided by my research questions has a community-embedded dimension. I define community as a shared collective created through the practice of dance. Since my primary location is higher education in the United States, I work with communities invested within and interested in the practice of Odissi. This also includes community-building and community-creation activities. I have developed a community research project called the *Dance and Community Research Institute* focusing on arts consulting, assessment, and outreach initiatives in the Indian diaspora.[3] Through this project, my dance practice also stretches to educational contexts. I work with K–12 populations, adult learners, as well as professional dancers, scholars, and educators.

Through my home department via continuing education efforts, I organize regular workshops, reading groups, and performance opportunities for professional development for the latter population. I teach Odissi to students ranging in age from four to fifty. I work with diverse demographic as well as with different learning styles. My research in teaching and assessing movement through grant-based projects is beyond the scope of this book project, but it is important to note that I spend over five hours per week teaching this art form in Indian diaspora community contexts, dance conservatories, and public arts schools as well as to professionals in the field of Odissi who want to further their solo performance practice. Community-engaged practice enables me perspective outside of the ivory tower of academic distance and so-called objectivity. I refuse to lose touch with my practice in order to theorize it while understanding the need for discourse around my art form for critical depth and longevity. My work in the diasporic Indian communities dealing with minors gives me spaces of introducing love for art education and showing students a pathway to a career in the arts. One of my students, Shalini Basu from Ohio, was the first recipient of a Young Arts award in Odissi dance. The community-embedded dimensions of my work provide me with a broader perspective on art-making and art-education, instilling in me the importance of creating work that is democratic in approach, culturally appropriate, and widely accessible. It is important for me to question and call out existing historical trends that continue to create hierarchies within the dance form through racial, gendered, sexual, casteist, and classist biases. I engage with my technical infrastructure in creative, nuanced, and socially just ways to inform my movement, scholarship, teaching, and outreach.

I synthesize the myriad content I gather through various dance-related activities through periodic and systematic reflections. Journaling across the sites has documented particular experiences. Periodic reflections on activities via structured feedback mechanisms further help in articulating and streamlining the creative process. I reflect on the practice-based processes of my performance as my research questions seep into my performances. Through feedback, informal discussions, and structured talk-backs, I gather information about the reception of my artistic work. Post-performance reflections make their way into my daily practice as I work on the feedback toward further improvement especially in communicative efficacy. At this point in my career, I am invested in articulating for the broader public the unique storytelling and narrative capacity of my dancing body. Criticism and critique coexist with regular practice for Odissi that constitutes my being. Odissi is imperfect, like any other cultural artifact. But, its uniqueness lies in its grounded curvilinearity and its infinite elasticity. The entire process is one of centering the acquired into the core of my dance creating embodied and neural pathways via repetition. A dialectical engagement with the body through theorization, philosophizing, and critiquing Odissi across a myriad of contextual platforms as mentioned above keeps open the intellectual ambition of change and transformation of both me and the form. I speak about this desire for seeking freedom within dance in the last chapter based on Odissi's own concluding segment called *Moksha*.

Chapter Outlines

The introduction, "Angular Oscillations," segways into Part I, which focuses on *Grounding Technique in Philosophy*. This book is structured to give an overview of certain philosophical currents operational within the contexts of dance. This necessitates some in-depth investigations of the dancing body—its technical investments, creative potential, and choreographic existence. Although readers seeking a general idea of Indian dancing might find it difficult to grapple with the large passages exploring the philosophy-theory-practice of the S-curves, they are necessary to fully cognize, analyze, and perhaps, critique, the particularized meaning-making processes in function in Odissi (Warde 2005).

In "Chapter 1: Inflection Point: Nondual Basis for Curvilinear Gestures," I explore the philosophical potential of the twist, the S, and the inherent non-graspable orientation of the spiraling dancing body. Drawing from Indian philosophical literature, I show how the spiral foregrounds an inflection point—one that is typically of a directional valence moving away from a definite direction after exhausting its scope of a sequential progression of intensity, deepening, and discovery. "Chapter 2: Curvilinear Immersion" returns to the materiality of the dancing body as woven into its technique and traditional repertoire. I discuss the strong technical grounds upon which the dance holds its own. I also show how the repertoire and the technique remain in constant dialectical engagement where the expansion of the one lead to changes in the other.

Part II, "The Creative Triad of Music, Text, and Movement," attends to the tripartite attention musicality, meaning-making, and kinesthetic communication. "Chapter 3: Kinesthetic Pause: Breaking the Fourth Wall" explores the creative process in creating new works within the Odissi genre. I show how text, music, and rhythm form a tripartite treaty for a traditional repertoire although imagined in new light and imagination.

"Chapter 4: Going Back to the S: Rohini Dandavate in Motion" and "Chapter 5: Tangential Departure from the S: Maya Kulkarni in Action" are dedicated to case studies of working with two choreographers: one within the form and the other outside the form.[4] These two chapters show how the dancing body can continue its exploratory inquiry into practice across pluralistic investments in movement. "Conclusion: A Pedagogy of the Self" argues that the solo dancing body is primarily an epistemological process where the primary motto lies in attaining freedom from its material grounds created by text, music, and movement.

"Inflection Point" provides the theoretical underpinnings of embodied curvilinearity. Curvilinear motility presupposes multiple directional vectors in the spatial organization of movement. Given the complex isolations of various parts of the body complemented by an overall coordinated embodiment remains unique to curvilinear gestural and postural dancing. Investigating the points of directional shifts, this chapter grounds the movement in theoretical explorations of inflection points within Indian philosophical traditions. What does it mean to encounter an inflection point? Finding parallels across Indian movement and philosophical traditions, especially in their individual pursuits of *Moksha* or freedom, I argue that an inflection point in Odissi movement is the point of change where the initial stage of isolation turns over to the second stage of finding coordination across the infinite and inexhaustible possibilities in the dance. I note that the inflection point is both a physical feature when the curvature flips direction as well as a philosophical grounding that ties the entirety of the curvilinear ethos. It questions the notion of 'efficiency' and 'smartness' that I feel are prejudicially prioritized as choreographic hallmarks in twenty-first century Euro-American contexts.

"Curvilinear Immersion" aspires to cover the range of skills that Odissi dancers need to navigate the grounded languidity of its formal complexity. It provides the theoretical basis of its vocabulary primer alongside the kinetic phraseology.[5] Furthermore, it shows the functional usage of its animation of the sculpturesque in the conventional repertoire. Through explorations of the canonical archive of the solo dancing body in choreographic works by Guru Kelucharan Mohapatra, Guru Debaprasad Das, and Guru Pankaj Charan Das, this chapter-length inquiry provides an account of performative mileposts that ground the curvilinear gestures. Exploring both technique and repertoire, it shows the cyclical nature between performance and training in this form.

This chapter aspires to cover the range of skills that Odissi dancers need to navigate the grounded languidity of its formal complexity. It provides the theoretical basis of its vocabulary primer alongside the kinetic phraseology. Furthermore, it shows the functional usage of its animation of the sculpturesque in the conventional repertoire. Through explorations of the canonical archive of the solo dancing body in choreographic works by Guru Kelucharan Mohapatra, Guru Debaprasad Das, and Guru Pankaj Charan Das, this chapter-length inquiry provides an account of performative mileposts that ground the curvilinear gestures. Exploring both technique and repertoire, it shows the cyclical nature between performance and training in this form.

If technique is internal organization of the body via the aesthetic, semantic, and epistemic capacities based on standardized elements of Odissi education and professional practice, choreography is expansion of scope of this body-mind mapping through external cueing across a dramatic arc in constant conversation with music. Choreography starts with an inspiration, namely, an artistic yearning, a musical mode or *Raga*, a poetic verse, a philosophical thought construct, a desire for social change, or even a desire to preserve the quintessentially traditional flow of Odissi that gets disguised with spectacular developments like speed, flexibility, and strength in recent times. Since the beginning of the 1950s, there have been significant developments in the field of Odissi choreography even though the lack of book-length inquiries to this process makes this artistic labor invisible to higher education. Scriptwriters, music composers, rhythm composers, choreographers, and dancers work collaboratively toward establishing a new work. Any piece of work draws forth a dramatic arc through interspersing rhythmic elements, narrative pieces, and inflection points marking necessary changes in the flow of the work, which also emulate the quintessential flow of the dance form. The timeline also varies depending upon the exact deliverable. Evening-length productions take much longer than a single solo work. Audio recording, sound engineering, and sound arrangement requirements add production elements that are to be considered within the timeline. In general, there is a constant back and forth between the choreography and the melody-rhythm composition. The choreography starts with a template provided by the composers, but the choreographic journey comes up with its own specific requirements in terms of adding, subtracting, manipulating, and changing the existing template. I elaborate upon this process in "Kinesthetic Pause: Breaking the Fourth Wall" through the voice of numerous choreographers, scriptwriters, music composers, and dancers presenting upon vignettes from their practice at the 2021 virtual conference *Shaping S-Curves: Choreographic Process in Odissi.* The name of this conference also inspires the title of this book. Transcribing the virtual sharing and analyzing this data provides the content for the fourth chapter that elaborates upon the creative procedures mobilized in the making of content.

In my research inquiry into freedom of expression via empowering the gaze of the solo mover, I work with Dandavate in the idiom of Odissi and with Kulkarni in her signature dance form called *Shilpanatanam*. In Chapter 5, I note that working with Dandavate has been crucial in understanding the lilting flow of Odissi's curvilinearity. Dandavate laments the loss of curvilinear engagements to spectacular jumps and spins in the contemporary Odissi performance circuits. Dandavate's training in Odissi took place in Kala Vikaash Kendra, an institution in the city of Cuttack in Odisha. Here, she received training in dance, music, and literature and toured with their professional company. Her well-rounded exposure to Odissi differs from my dance-specific focus. She is cognizant of the music and rhythm in an integral manner and uses the movement to visualize the music in its full capacity. In this way, the lilting music is complemented with the curvilinear dancing that according to her, is the primary responsibility and ethos of the Odissi dancer. Dandavate's dancing gaze is an organizing force. The gaze becomes the mode of creation and dissolution of phrases resulting in meaning-making and communication of meaning through a constant and modulated communication with the imagined audience.

While the visualization of Odissi's lost curvilinearity remains Dandavate's primary investment, Kulkarni's *Shilpanatanam* wants to elongate an experiential thought through gesture, posture, footwork, and facial expression. *Shilpanatanam* is a novel approach to Indian performing arts that I grapple with in Chapter 6. *Shilpa* in its broad meaning includes sculptures, paintings, and architecture while *Natanam* refers to movement, expression, and rhythm. *Shilpanatanam* can be described as choreographic visualization bringing static images to life with movement and narratives. The dance in this case becomes a metaphor and moves beyond the sculpturesque quality typical of the traditional idioms. Sociologist Robert Perinbanayagam characterizes Kulkarni's challenge to traditional dance formats in his book-length compilation of essays *Dialogues, Dramas, and Emotions* (2023). He notes that in Kulkarni's choreographic visualization, "characters and situations are transformed into metaphors for one human experience or another" (41). *Shilpanatanam* departs from the regimented and structured focus on the devotional and metaphysical poetics of Indian dance. Unlike Odissi's devotional cache, *Shilpanatanam* is secular in intent and cosmopolitan in approach. For instance, Kulkarni's creation, Plato's search for reason becomes the driving purpose in the *Allegory of the Cave* (2010) with visual artist and dancer Mesma Belsare; my own work, *Impossible Romance* (2022), which I elaborate upon in this chapter taps the fable construct in literature; Bharatnatyam dancer Sonali Skandan's *Adventures of a Naughty Honey Bee* (2021) is a flight of fancy. Kulkarni's vision comes through movements and expressions that draw deeply on literature, visual, and plastic arts, but the dance is front and center, it is the story and the text. This freeing of the dance form while in conversation with the allied arts is a liberating experience for my creative inquiry.

Choreographic freedom grounds within the trajectory of liberation ingrained within the repertoire itself. One can argue that Odissi's Brahmanical systems of organization and interpretation of freedom in the form of *Moksha* is fundamentally flawed given the continued casteist gatekeeping of the form and caste-based violence on a daily basis. I do not claim to undo centuries of oppression through my claims to creative freedom especially in the wake of Hindu majoritarian politics of violence, but I intend to find spaces of artistic ingenuity and sociopolitical awareness through creative choreographic gestures. This trend, I hope, will filter back into the form as it grapples with its troubled histories of marginalization and normalizing discourses that find added advantages in adhering to power structures. In my search for freedom in performance, choreography, and music, I depart from the traditional technical construct of Odissi and collaborate through an ethos of South-South collaboration (Hickling-Hudson 2004). South-South collaboration across pluralist aesthetics removes Western concert techniques as the center in my search of freedom of aesthetic diversity in contemporary contexts of higher education and concert performance in the US. I work with techniques and technicians who center an ecological embedding of the dancing body and does not abstract it away as a discrete entity (Roy 2023).[6] In my collaborative research, I find that the South Asian dancing instrument is uniquely positioned to engage potent and efficacious communication through nuanced expression. The gaze is a powerful tool that my Odissi training provides to my dancing tool kit that is simultaneously engaging and pedagogical for myself and my viewer. In closing, I write about *A Pedagogy of the Self* as an ode to my inquiry into freedom within my dance practice.

Notes

1. In "The Epistemic Politics of Indian Classical Dance," scholar Anurima Banerji, known for her astute critical historiography of Odissi dance, notes the debilitating legacy of "classical dance" in promulgating casteist and Hindu nationalist state power that was birthed within the colonial apparatus and continued by postcolonial Indian authorities maintaining an archaic and hierarchical worldview of

categorizing the folk, the tribal, and the classical, which is at the top of the pyramid. While a sociopolitical interrogation of the nationalist appropriation of Odishan art is beyond the scope of this book, I choose to focus on a keen analysis of the practice itself. This book is primarily an aesthetic analysis of the solo format of Odissi dance as it is popular to dancers worldwide.

2. In Bengali, *Bichitro* and *Anondo* mean strange and joy, respectively. This piece explores the duality of power and dissolution in daily lived experience borrowing inspiration from the COVID-19 pandemic, border politics on immigration, and environmental pollution.

3. Appendix IV: Handbook for Dance and Community Research Institute is dedicated to laying out the foundations of my community-engaged research initiative that works with scholars, artists, educators, professionals, community personnel, as well as youth through a variety of initiatives geared toward social change. Since 2019, when it started with just a membership of one hundred, it has grown through many initiatives across the United States.

4. Appendices II and III (Appendix II: Continuing Education: A Student's Praxis and Appendix III: An Undergraduate Seminar in Dramaturgical Expression) provide further resources in pedagogy focusing on the lived experience of the dance. While Appendix II is a dancer's reminiscence of continuing education in movement, Appendix III provides a template of an undergraduate seminar in creative process.

5. In Appendix I: Model Progressions, I provide a teaching toolkit for progressions along K12 as suited to National Core Arts Standards in dance education. My pedagogical philosophy lies in academic integration and building creative leadership.

6. I co-perform with Yoruba cosmogonies through my duet with Africanist scholar and practitioner Tamara Williams.

References

Ajayi, O. S. 1989. "Aesthetics of Yoruba Recreational Dances as Exemplified in the Oge Dance." *Dance Research Journal* 21 (2): 1–8.

Antony, M. G. 2010. "On the Spot: Seeking Acceptance and Expressing Resistance Through the Bindi." *Journal of International and Intercultural Communication* 3 (4): 346–68.

Banerji, A. 2010. *Odissi Dance: Paratopic Performances of Gender, State, and Nation*. New York University.

Banerji, A. 2019. *Dancing Odissi: Paratopic Performances of Gender and State*. Seagull Books.

Banerji, A. 2023. "The Epistemic Politics of Indian Classical Dance." In *Performance Cultures as Epistemic Cultures, Volume II*. Routledge.

Barik, R., et al. 2022. "Nazia Alam: Young Singer from Odisha Making a Difference." *India Art Review*.

Chatterjea, A. 2013. "On the Value of Mistranslations and Contaminations: The Category of 'Contemporary Choreography' in Asian Dance." *Dance Research Journal* 45 (1): 7–21.

Čurda, B. 2024. "Virtual and Physical Ways of Being Present in Odissi Dance Networks in Bhubaneswar in India." In *Being There, but How?: On the Transformation of Presence in (Post-)Pandemic Times*, edited by S. Dümling and Z. Wang. Verlag.

Dandavate, R., K. Sarkar, R. Silvestre, and T. Williams. 2023. *Tapa: Fervent Triggers*. Counter-Pulse.

Dawn, S. 2025. "Understanding Similarities and Exploring Possibilities of Using Somatic Dance/Movement Aspects of Odissi Dance for Social, Cognitive, and Emotional Development in Population with Autism Spectrum Disorder." *Journal of Dance & Somatic Practices* 17 (1): 9–25.

Ehrenberg, S. 2015. "A Kinesthetic Mode of Attention in Contemporary Dance Practice." *Dance Research Journal* 47 (2): 43–61.

Hickling-Hudson, A. 2004. "South–South Collaboration: Cuban Teachers in Jamaica and Namibia." *Comparative Education* 40 (2): 289–311.

Kaktikar, A. 2024. "Locating Odissi in the United States: Dancing Through Curricula, Teaching Methods, and Assessment." *Journal of Dance Education* 24 (2): 117–24.

Mathewson Mitchell, D. 2013. "Thinking Through Practice: Exploring Ways of Knowing, Understanding, and Representing the Complexity of Teaching." *Asia-Pacific Journal of Teacher Education* 41 (4): 414–25.

Mohanty, K. 1985. *The Odissi Dance Path Finder*. Vol. 1. Odissi Research Centre.

Perinbanayagam, R. 2023. *Dialogues, Dramas, and Emotions: Essays in Interactionist Sociology*. Bloomsbury.

Reckwitz, A. 2002. "Toward a Theory of Social Practices: A Development in Culturalist Theorizing." *European Journal of Social Theory* 5 (2): 243–63.

Roy, S. 2023. "Dissonant Intimacies: Coloniality and the Failures of South–South Collaboration." *The Sociological Review* 71 (6): 1237–1257.

Sahoo, I. 2009. *Odissi Music: Evolution, Revival, and Technique*. Br Rhythms.

Sen-Podstawska, S. S. 2019. "The Transient 'Ideals' of the 'Odissi Body' and the Changing Place and Role of Odissi Dancers in History." *Świat i słowo* 1 (32): 133–51.

Sikand, N. 2016. *Languid Bodies, Grounded Stances: The Curving Pathway of Neoclassical Odissi Dance*. Berghahn Books.

Tandon, R. 2005. *Classicism on the Threshold of Modernity: Expanding the Physical Parameters of Odissi Dance for Contemporary Audiences*. Trinity Laban Conservatoire of Music and Dance/City University London.

Van Manen, M. 2023. *Phenomenology of Practice: Meaning-Giving Methods in Phenomenological Research and Writing*. Routledge.

Warde, A. 2005. "Consumption and Theories of Practice." *Journal of Consumer Culture* 5 (2): 131–53.

PART I

Grounding Technique in Philosophy

CHAPTER 1

Inflection Point

Nondual Basis for Curvilinear Gestures

SIMPLY DEFINED AS THE moment where a curve changes direction, the inflection point can provide a prism for understanding the curvilinear bearings in Odissi dance. In my analysis of the S curve's inflection point, I will present a dancer's perspective on embodying the form that refracts the artist's experiencing of the world at large. The points of inflection cannot be mathematically enumerated in the dancing persona because it is not possible to configure with exactitude the vagaries of subjective thoughts, emotions, still poses, and kinetic movements. However, one can perhaps simplistically think of the three stages of development for the dancer as possible inflection points for the S. The three stages of intensification, deepening, and discovery for the dancer to reach a deeper understanding of the form, are described in the Introduction. While the first is visible in the artist's physicality and emotional sentiment, the second is perceptible in the dancer's absorption into the dance. The third is imperceptible and opens up newer epistemologies of practice, being, and experiencing in and through dance. More mature artists operate on the second and third stages while amateurs and young artists operate on the superficiality of external and perceptible intensification. In this chapter, I will show the infinite processes of isolation and integration that provide the fundamental organizing principle. This chapter is not a mathematical exposition of the inflection curve. Rather, I turn to Indian philosophical thought. Scholars have pointed out the use of *Darshana* (meaning insight or vision) or of *Aanvikshiki* (meaning rational investigation) as possible alternatives to understanding philosophical writing in India (Adamson and Ganeri 2020, 14). Investigation is considered central to all branches of study and the primary mode of entertaining epistemological processes and epistemic limits. In this vein, listing and enumerating the parts of the anatomical and musculoskeletal dimensions, the expressive registers, and the musical infrastructure becomes as important as reconnecting and integrating the infinite polarities into an abstract whole. Isolation and integration are also the hallmarks of the dancing Odissi body as it makes way into a seamlessly fluid gestural existence where the percussive accenting of time coagulates with the mellifluous infinitude of emotional depth and strength of communicative character. Broadly, inflection points can be pluralistically determined as stages of development or bidirectional shifts across isolation and integration.

Isolation of the infinitely divisible dancing body partners with the overall integration of the four expressive registers—the physical, the verbal, the ornamental, and the emotional—in order to establish the primary inflection across the grounded and the languid. The grounded requires a certain melting into the ground with temporal clarity of the percussive intonation. The languid, on the other hand, lacks a sense of temporal accent. Rather, it takes up space as the sprawling upper body expands into the crevices of the musical flow. Both the lower and the upper body are embedded in the curvilinear logic made possible by a set of inflection points—those that are physically palpable and visible. The curvilinear arc quintessential for the Odissi body has an overarching organizing principle of a defined initiation, a prolonged execution, and a definite concluding point marked by an embodied echo, which marks the transitional phase for the beginning of the next movement. Stasis and motility go hand in hand in the curvilinear gestures of the dance. So, a series of inflection points are at play in the execution of the interplay across the sculpturesque and the languid. However, the inflection points can also be more subtle and in the plane of intellectual, emotional, sensory, and aesthetic processing of material that has a direct impact on the physical domain. Circling of the wrists, for example, is an example of ornamentation that adds certain points of accented intensities in a movement arc. This circular motion adds higher density of movement to certain nodal points across the entirety of a particular phrase. Verbal meaning-making undergirds the development of phrase, especially in the expressional repertoire, where the enactment, expression, and communicative efficacy lie on multiple planes of composition and execution, only called to action at the performer's discretion. The subtle expressional ability of the body also partners with the emotional bandwidth of the dancer. This creates sinusoidal waves of enhancing and diminishing emotional intensities. Here, inflection points register moments of multiple emotional surges alongside a paucity of emotions. This further heightens the dramatic intensity of the dance.

Overall, I suggest that ultimate goal of Odissi or *Moksha,* meaning freedom is best understood in an embodied integration of mental, physical, and aesthetic registers. In *Advaita Vedanta*, non-dual philosophy, *Moksha* is defined as removal of ignorance. Equating this epistemological exercise with that of my dancing body, I argue that the primary purpose of Odissi is embedded within an epistemological investigation of freedom, but freedom is independently and subjectively defined by dancers on their own terms. I am not proposing an objective reality that each dancing body aspires to. In this way, I question the knowing-what with the knowing-how. Embodied integration of the body-mind complex questions the Cartesian split of the body-mind arguing for inflection points within the dancing body as nodal bearings of varying degrees of deepening into an inquiry-based investigation. In a three-part organization, I will discuss the metaphysical dimensions of the dancing body, its ability to inflect infinitely across its multiple dimensions (subjective and objective), and the epistemological basis of freedom.

Dancing Metaphysics

"The identification of liberation with the nature of self which is already and always attained and the emphasis on the removal of ignorance in the mind lead logically to the view that liberation is possible here and now. It is not an end that must await the death of the body since ignorance is not synonymous with the fact of the self's association with a body, but with the erroneous identification of the self and the body. It is not the absence of a constitutes liberation, but the elimination of ignorance about the nature of the self" (Rambachan 2006, 101).

A cultural and religious insider might go through the entire gamut of the repertoire through a spiritual bent (Rambachan 2014). Invoking the divine, the dancer grounds movement in basic elementals of Odissi posture and gesture. The climactic possibility of the physical is reached in the third element, negotiating speed and technical display of virtuosic control of physical dexterity, musical knowhow, and rhythmic knowledge. The fourth section allows the dancer to connect with the emotive content that touches upon a yet another dimension of individual personhood. Finally, the dancer seeks liberation from the dancing body. The entire repertoire is then organized as a ritual for the spiritual insider. However, one must note that Odissi is a highly popular concert dance practice and it is practiced by people of various nations with multiple or no religious affiliations that differ from the Indic perspectives. So, it is not uncommon to see Odissi being performed with a range of performative, cultural, and spiritual perspectives.

The first repertoire-element also known as *Mangalacharan* presents an invocation to the regional ethos of Odissi. It pays its respects to the land of Odisha by honoring its Indigenous deities and presenting rituals that are akin to the historical practice of the dance form. It emphasizes lineages of learning and transmission by prioritizing the act of surrender by playing with loosening the sense of egotistic identification of the material at hand. The second segment lays the foundational elements basic to the structure, composition, and further ornamentation of the dance form. It lays out postural foundations, gestural rubrics, and points to the musical infrastructure—use of percussive, wind, and string instruments—grounding the dance. The third element is a physical blossoming of the art form with melodious and percussive experimentation. This segment presents the highest degree of virtuosity in terms of speed and technical precision. It is here that the upward trend in physical infrastructure hits an inflection point as the fourth segment requires virtuosic emotive capacity. The physical caliber of the dancers is considered important in the form, and its scope is presented in the third section. However, the mettle of Odissi lies in quiet, centered, emotive, and sensory transcendence of the physical through the dramaturgical. *Moksha*, the fifth segment, continues the quietude established previously in the fourth section.

In the last element in the traditional repertoire, the dancer starts with a percussive segment and ends on a meditative note. *Moksha*, the culmination of the five-part repertoire, starts with an invocation marking the beginning on a note of surrender to the material being performed. The creative and performance-oriented strengths of the dancer are not glamorized in this traditional set-up where the premise lies in the ability to find freedom of the self and from the self. The dancing self makes its way into the performance with a multipronged focus where the dancer experiences, objectifies, feels, senses, thinks, emotes, and communicates. In these variegated developments, the dancer dissects the dancing self from multiple angles finding the locus of experience from within as well as in relational and objectified approaches. This bidirectionality of the self—emerging aesthetics from within as well as that which is externally induced and results in an aesthetic distance—loosens the inseparability of the self with the body-mind complex. In this way, perhaps, the dancing self is closer to the Advaitic worldview as enunciated in the above quotation. In Advaita, the dualistic association of the self with the body is considered a fallacy. Rather, the body is considered to be an appearance of the real self that is "already and always attained." I argue that the inflection point lies in the spiraling into or the pointing out of the erroneous identification of the self with the body. As in dance, the body is part of the self, but it cannot exhaust its scope as it renders itself across multiple parameters of gesture, posture, footwork and expression, the latter again differentiated by the physical, the verbal, the emotive, and the ornamental.

The dancing body traverses multiple perspectives in its organization of movement material that is expressive of literal, percussive, melodic, and kinesthetic content. The dancer checks in real-time with the viewers while reporting to, appearing to be, and being the characters, emotions, situations, and circumstances. Being-appearing and subsequent real-time nudging of content such that the viewer is being enfolded within the communicative registers of the dance makes the exercise one of constant code-switching. In the performance, the dancing body is simultaneously the visualization for the flute as well as the string instrument alongside the percussion. It is possible the footwork maps the rhythmic framework while the torso moves to the flute and the hands visualize the *Gamakas*: musical ornamentations played by the string instrumentalist. So, the being of the dancers is literally split alongside three separate coordinated registers. Isolated parts stay integrated with the logic of the music, text, or movement at various parts. But the dancing body questions a monolithic understanding of a mentally-coded being given its varying moving parts operating in stages of isolation and integration. Reality in this framework is literally the temporally congruous intermittent check-ins with the audience, where the artist ensures to generate a sense of curiosity through the constant code-switching across being and appearing.

According to religious studies scholar Anantanand Rambachan, in Advaitic ontology there is a hierarchical organization of being, appearance, and reality. In *Advaita Vedanta*, the non-dual consciousness, also known as *Brahman,* is the reality that apparently appears to be the universe as we perceive it while "nothing in the phenomenal world is ontologically necessary" (Sinari, 1972, 289). In one perspective, non-dual consciousness regards the phenomenal world as unreal. But. ultimately *Brahman* itself appears as the world at large and according to Deutsch, the knowledge of this nondifference leads to *Moksha* (Deutsch 1973, 65). So, freedom is defined as the ability to know the real nature of self as nothing but the non-dual consciousness or the *Brahman*. This appears simplistic in the case of movement where the phenomenal world is abstracted into the curvilinear folds of the body—gesture, posture, footwork, etc. Ornamentations of embodied being and appearing questions the simplistic separation of being, appearing, and the real—as the dancing body proves all of it to be varying stages of the metaphysical reality. The dancer, while code-switching, is building upon the previous kinesthetic exercise. In this way, experiential awareness in movement in building upon from one movement to another as the dancer switches across appearing, checking-in, and being. Pluralization of the self across the multiplicity of imaginative creativity alongside the empiricism of the body-mind complex questions the hierarchical model of Advaitic reality of *Brahman* that makes it unnecessary and unreal the empirical and the creative.

However, the dancing body builds upon the Advaitic framework to provide a nonhierarchical organization of being, reality, and appearance that are in constant flux in the processes of abstraction and sensate technicities. To the dancing body, the knowing of self is itself an exercise of multiplicity and freedom lies in the ability to code-switch from the phenomenological experience to mental abstraction to psychological conjuring to emotional mapping to kinesthetic sensation (Sinari 1972). For the dancer, both the real and the apparent have strong valences and one is not overpowering than the other. The dancer does not create a hierarchy of self and non-self. In many ways, the knowledge of this nondifference leads to the freedom in and through movement (Shima 1983). It is probably for this reason that tenth-century scholar of *Advaita Vedanta*, Vachaspati Mishra, foregrounds the importance of experiential meditation as an important factor in acquiring liberation (Ranganath 1999). He named his school of thought Bhamati after his wife who was a dancer (Roodurmum 2002). I strongly believe that his naming convention was not merely for appeasement but rather had a deeper insight of the dancing body's ability to emulate the experience of nondifference of being and appearing in its closest spiritual simulation and abstraction (Miśra 1880). The reason for this naming convention is beyond the scope of this essay, but I stay committed to exploring this in my subsequent scholarship (Ruzsa 2021).

Moksha as defined in Indian cosmology is bound to lack the exactitude given its apparent spiritual ontology. Language is bound to lack the specificity of this supramundane experience given its inherent translation from (Rahula 1974, 35). For our purposes, I am not invested in exploring the supramundane elements. Rather, I am curious about the promise of freedom as doled out to all Odissi artists with the conventional repertoire. In exploring its philosophical basis, I hope to cast a deeper understanding about the concept of *Moksha*. All codified terms have an array of meanings depending upon their ontological, epistemological, and functional significance. For example, the gesture *Pataka* (single-handed gesture with a firm palm and straightened fingers) has an entire array of functional usage. It is used to show actions, things, and events. It can show negation, a horse, and a cool evening breeze among many other entities. In a similar manner, the term *Moksha* can imply gaining freedom or gaining knowledge. Naming something can cursorily explain but never exhaust the entirety of that entity. So, trying to explain the liberative state in dance, perhaps, can shed some light onto the existential, experiential, and communicative dimensions of *Moksha* as seen in my Odissi dancing body. This further qualifies Rambachan's 'psychological' understanding of freedom. I critique Rambachan to argue that *Moksha* is not just a psychological understanding (Rambachan 2006). This presents an embodied dimension to freedom that enables a pluralistic, aesthetic, and creative view of the self, quite contrary to a stable identity tied to a body-mind complex.

I claim that there is infinite freedom in the dancing body despite its painstaking codifications, choreographic injunctions, musical phraseology, and textual parameters. This is primarily due to the infinite possibilities of paying attention to at any given moment. The dancer, with practice, makes the physical and kinesthetic dimensions muscle memory. Further, the expressive, felt, and emotive dimensions register as recognizable psychological states that are repeatedly practiced (in order to achieve them in shorter and shorter durations) and available in the performer's tool kit. While these states are freely available, at any given point in time, the performer can choose to deepen focus on any particular body part, thought, musical note, percussive sound, or textual meaning. So, the performer has the infinite freedom to choose from a plethora of options at any given moment in time. Such freedom allows for moment-to-moment discovery. The dancer is not dancing merely from memory. That can happen during practice sessions. But during the performance, the dance is discovered at every single instant. This makes each iteration of a piece performed by the same artist completely unique as the dance is discovered at every single moment. This way of understanding freedom lies in its creative and aesthetic capacity. Freedom to explore in real time is encoded in the entirety of the practice.

When analyzed across the performative arc of the Odissi repertoire, freedom can be defined in a slightly different manner. Here, one can think of *Moksha* as 'freedom from.' Here, freedom is more epistemological in nature. Ignorance of the dancing self as inherently and kinesthetically constructed at each iteration of the dance and the supposition of a stable identity attached to a body-mind complex are reversed with the 'freedom from' notion. Freed to see multiplicity and difference at the core of the construction of the self that then becomes a creative process, dance takes to task the simplistic Advaitic psychological system as articulated by Rambachan. In dance, the self is free to create from an array of possibilities with their infinite capacity of meaning-making resulting in a unique experiential construction. Below, I further describe the qualitative dimensions of choreographic freedom, which is particular to each performance irrespective of content and the choreographer's intentions.

In many ways, freedom in dance can incorrectly imply losing oneself in the dance. The self is not held as a unitary instrument anymore. Rather, it disintegrates with the requirements of music, text, and choreographed movement. Such a loss of individuality also lacks communicative efficacy. The communicative function of the solo dancing body is necessary to sustain durational dance recitals that traditionally can span up to over two hours. Furthermore, the traditional dancing body has a pedagogical function woven into its performative folds. The dancer is supposed to communicate and the locus of such 'taking toward' of information has a directional valence to it. This directional function emerges from an embodied being, one that is cognizant of its multiplicity and creative capacity. Nevertheless, the communicative controls do not result in the loss of the self in dance. I will explain more about the communicative deepening in the next section.

Instead of losing the sense of being, *Moksha* refers to 'freedom to' and 'freedom from': a creative and an epistemological becoming as noted earlier. This requires a combination of the epistemological, the ontological, and the phenomenological to operate simultaneously. The dancing body is invested within its empirical existence, but is also a witness of itself as it carries out its communicative function, creating an aesthetic distance between the self as known inside and outside of dance. Finally, it notes the pluralistic and changing dimensions of the self in performance. All three embodied dimensions institute a fundamental difference of the conception of the self, one that is then able to grasp the infinite breadth of freedom associated with the dancing body.

I have tried to explain the freedom imbued within the *Moksha* element of the solo Odissi repetition on its own terms without concern of whether it is a realizable state. The purpose of this section is to unpack the term in dance using its philosophical principles in *Advaita Vedanta*. *Moksha* is considered to be the highest inflection point that is the goal and purpose of the dancing body. But there are multiple stages in between to ensure intensification, deepening, and processes of discovery into the dance. In the next section, I start unpacking the changing inflections of the dancing body as necessary to attain its communicative efficacy.

Aesthetic Communication

Virtuosity of the solo artistry lies in *Abhinaya*, expressional movement (Kapur 2024). Etymologically speaking, *Abhinaya* refers to 'taking toward.' This implies both an action and a direction (Coorlawala 1996). Also implied is some content that is being taken toward a particular receiver of that material. A single expressive gesture implicates content, its carrier, the act of carrying, and the receiver. In many cases, the creator of the content namely the choreographer, music composer, script writer, musicians, and sound engineer among many others, especially in the case of traditional repertoire, is different from the dancer who is the generator and carrier of the same (Srinivas 2014). Discussing the clarity of this communication process is instrumental in analyzing the dance. In popular usage, *Abhinaya* refers to both the generic expressive movement as well as the fourth element of the Odissi repertoire. This fourth element tests the ability of the dancer to simultaneously be, experience, and emote to communicate emotional intelligence and subtlety. There is a vast technical literature of this expressional control in Indian aesthetic theory (Coomaraswamy and Gōpālakr̥ṣṇa 1917). Assimilation of such techniques by the dancer are central to be able to effectively emote in dance through hand gestures, physical postures, felt emotions, facial expressions, production elements (costuming, jewelry, etc.), and verbal meaning-making, often as sung lyric. In order to analyze this aesthetic communication, one needs to inquire into the agential subjectivity of the dancer and the ability to communicate effectively.

The communication in the dance emerges from an embodied yearning to reintegrate the isolating impulse of the technical infrastructure. The nature of this 'taking toward' has its own logic, which is quite different from linguistic transmission. Dramatic intensity is central to this passing on. In order to raise the dramatic quotient, technical density is aggravated with multitudes of footwork tied to percussive play or ideational plurality with its imprint on subtle facial changes. The first is an example of kinesthetic exercise while the second shows the equally important and choreographed cognitive dimension in Odissi. This intensification is physically and/or intellectually demanding but it is still at the individual experiential realm. In order for it to transfer to the live audience, it requires further assimilation. This is the next stage where the agency of the dancer takes over the movement material. This agential responsibility of the aesthetic motility of the body-mind complex provides the foundational grounds for the communicative dimension to flourish. The dancer has the liberty to communicate in different ways: in first person, narrating as the self in identification with the dancing body; in second person, addressing the audience directly; or in third person, narrating an existing storyline like a *Sutradhar*, the narrator connecting multiple scenes or stages in the development of the narrative. In most instances, the dancer navigates all three communicative dimensions, often being and experiencing as well as reflecting and reporting back on dramatic episodes. Thus, while communicative efficacy requires a sense of agency, the suspension of it is equally crucial such that the dancer can reflect on the multiple dimensions modulating an effective dramatic forefront. This dramatic modulation is necessary for gaining the audience's attention. So, a simultaneity of a sense of agency partners with an equal degree of agential suspension creates the dramatic intensity necessary for the dance. Reason, thought, ideas, logic, and their effective organization are as important as the movement of the head, eye, neck, hands, feet, sides of the body, and foot postures. Integration of the physical dimensions with their expressional infinitude with the cognitive and emotional counterparts, occurs on the foundation of agential suspension of the self. The impetus for the yearning to integrate comes from the dancing body's communicative function leading to efficacious transmission of information across the creation and reception of the dance work. I will now turn toward the content of this communication.

The physical body retains significant importance and promises in the aesthetic act of creating curvilinearity. The lower body utilizes the floor in creative ways to cover space and mark time. Soles of the feet act as percussive surfaces with multiple sonic reverberations accompanying the particular and technical playing of the percussion instrument, the *Mardala*. Intricacies of footwork mandate articulation in flat, heel, and toe configurations alongside the use of the sides of the feet in placement or in movements grazing the ground with momentum. Ankles gain special importance in Odissi given that this idiom does not allow the straightening of knees. So, the emphasizing of the heel on the floor requires significant deflection in the ankles. Geometric and angular foot movements complement circular grazing of the floor with the toes. Circular movement of the feet utilizing range of motion in hip sockets is another characteristic feature of Odissi technical prowess. Transposing the circularity of the hip joints onto the rib cage, the upper body provides more easily discernible cues to the curvilinear project. Circling of the torso while maintaining immobile shoulders and hips characterizes and differentiates Guru Kelucharan Mohapatra style of Odissi as researched and taught by *Srjan*, Guru Kelucharan Mohapatra's institution in Bhubaneswar, Odisha. Having trained in this style, I verify the many hours of training required to ensure such bodily control. However, the virtuosic control also comes at a cost of reducing a more fluid upper body motion, as seen in Guru Pankaj Charan Das style. I encountered Guru Pankaj Charan Das style during my year-long research with Ratna Roy, who has been trained under Guru Pankaj Charan Das in Puri, Odisha. Stylistic differences aside, the circular isolation of the rib cage continues to provide Odissi with its unique curvilinear aesthetic. Finally, whole arm movements qualified further with wrist isolations, cascading of fingers in symbolic gestures, *Mudras*, and elbow holds organized sequentially in curved pathways provide the quintessential feeling of curvature. For example, the common movement of *Abarta Puspita*, meaning the cycle of a flower from bud to bloom, encompasses a circular movement of the forearms with wrists circling from *Alapadma* (bloom) to *Katakamukha* (bud) to *Alapadma* (bloom) while the lower body creates a semi-circular arc. Spatial and rhythmic organizing of *Abarta Puspita* has a definite inflection point where the upward curvature flips to a downward progression. Use of hands with momentum and inertia always realize in a visible end-point with a feeling of energetic containment. In a way, the energy is never dissipated or thrown outward. Rather, the hands provide an excellent and visibly legible mode of energetic recycling in circular configurations. In this way, *Abarta Puspita* is a micro-example of an inflection point. Its deployment in the eighth *Chauka* having eight distinct feet movements (flat-flat-toe-flat-brush-heel-flat-flat) has a symmetrical inflection with the fifth step (brush) functioning as the point where the curvature changes direction. As visualized across a dual complementarity, every bodily part is brimming with energetic containment through technical encoding.

FIG. 7: Geometry and Poetry go hand in hand in the dancing metaphysics of Odissi: Author in a Performance in Columbus on November 18, 2018. Reproduced with permission from Kash Naraian.

Geometric complementarity of percussive-lower and circular-upper bodies partners with verbal meaning-making in the form of poetic recitations or sung lyric. Text and its literary integrity remain a crucial component. Literary works of epic status in Sanskrit and Oriya have periodically made their way into choreography. Meaning is delivered through facial expressions and gesturally by concentrating on each word or the overall sentence. Sometimes, movement and the text are complementary and the dancer communicates only the purport or the essence of the literary composition. Analogy and metaphor are often used for verbal meaning-making and its delineation through expression and movement. Alongside the energetically contained physicality, a range of activities occur in the dancing body that may or may not necessarily have a physical counterpart. Sensory projections of textual content perhaps, provide a starting clue and also are closest to physicality. This immediately results in experiential reactions, such as the parting of the lips into a smile. The process of meaning-making in dance is transparent where the mental speculations are openly shared with an imaginary audience. The dancer also engages the entire gamut of expressive possibilities—imaginative flights, somatic absorption, and emotional congruence—to further flesh out the verbal import. Such, speculative thought processes reflect on the dancers' faces as one goes through the text in real-time with the audience, unfolding the entirely in short outbursts of thought and emotion. Theatricality and linearity of progression remain key to verbal meaning-making. In order to achieve that, the soloist makes a subsequent case for the prior gestural elaboration. This case is typically made to the frontal audience who remains a fellow participant in the performative process and in meaning-making. The dancer resolves the sensory, somatic, experiential, and emotional into a communicative function requiring an intellectual resolution. Both the performative speculation and resolution are communicated in transparency toward an audience who is expected to follow along in the coproduction of meaning. A physically induced pause functions as a punctuation necessary for registering of verbal content to then move on to the next set of textual material, one that goes through another cycle of speculation and resolution. Typically, the speculation and sensory-somatic experiences culminate in an intellectual resolution, which then allows for an aesthetic distancing from the text in consideration, allowing for moving on to subsequent texts. This infinitesimal moment of physical pause and textual suspension has a purely communicative purpose. Theatrical communication and its delineative conventions are strongly interwoven into embodied meaning-making. This kinesthetic pause remains a point of inflection—one that is inaugurated and guided primarily with mental processes while retaining significant embodied resonance. For example, movement delineating 'the changing color of clouds' could possibly engage the eyes projecting upward to the sky as if seeing the colors change from blue to grey with an experience of joy and wonder about the magnanimity and grandeur of nature. Not just the eyes and the face, the dancer experiences the moist clouds viscerally and the clenching of the musculoskeletal system becomes part of the manifestation of the verbal meaning-making. Thus, sensory projections, experiential reactions, transparent speculations, intellectual determinations, imaginative flights, felt emotions, and regular audience check-ins make verbal meaning-making an engaging exercise.

Costumes stitched from the *Sambalpuri* handloom, jewelry, and *Tahia* (headdress) are significant to the reception of the traditional Odissi soloist (Das 2021). The headdress made out of wood pulp has a circular structure that sits firmly on the hair tied in a bun near the neck. In addition to the circular structure, there is a conical structure that secures itself at the top of the bun. This piece resembles and refers to the architectural edifice of Odishan temples, which feature designs blending circularity with a conical linearity. These shapes also feature within the ornaments worn on the ears, neck, arms, wrists, waist, chest, and feet. While ornaments are worn across the gender spectrum, the *Tahia* is typically worn by women presumed to have long hair and thus, tied in a bun. This stereotypical imposition on women bearing the temple structure on themselves has an additional significance. It points out the blurring of the ritual and the performance in the dancing body as the same materiality traversed across the temple and concert spaces in various historical times. The concept of preparation in order to engage with the dance is directly borrowed from ritual contexts. Odissi's elaborate facial makeup with exaggerated kohl-stained eyes and eyebrows and red lips complement the equally extensive costuming convention. The act of getting ready is a meditative act and prepares the dancer, irrespective of gender, for the recital. The act of intricate design abstracts its way from the exterior costuming, jewelry, and floral head-décor toward the interiority of movement. Efficiency is not a virtue in this art form where the circuitous longer path is chosen over the linear short-cuts. So, the element of ornamentation exists in the curvilinear folds of the body and the movement. Such ornamentations also exist in the contours of facial expressions as dancers engage in subtle head-eye-neck gestures to elaborate expressive content as if filigreed jewelry. The point of interiorization of filigree from the silver jewelry to the body-mind complex in movement and expression remains an important feature in the virtuosic execution of curvilinearity, also embodied by the borders of handloom *Saris* used to stitch the costumes.

Dual complementarity of the physical body, kinesthetic pause to register verbal meaning-making, and interiorized filigree culminate in the generation of the sentiment in an elaborate paradigm of being-doing-communicating-experiencing-performing. Anchored in a stable emotional parlance, the dancer maps out in real-time the experiential process of occupying a range of sentiments, such as love, compassion, joy, sadness, anger, fear, courage, disgust, and peacefulness. The emotional landscape is mapped in an analytical fashion with causes—one that remains the substratum and others that further trigger—and effects—immediate and involuntary experiential reactions alongside a series of transitory states echoing the primary emotional state. This emotional mapping encompassing a range of possibilities requires practice of facial expressions and their particular pairing with codified gestural vocabulary (head-neck-eye-hands-feet), using the body to convey the import of the dance to the audience. In this elaboration, the linearity of the story no longer remains primary. Rather, it is the intensification and the elaboration of a sentiment that remains key to engaging audiences who are then able to experience in their own right a personalized emotional journey depending on the dancer's ability to make transparent the emotional landscape. So, the dancer's job is to carry toward the audience the full spectrum of emotional proliferation in order for the audience to simultaneously and in real-time, be involved with the intensity. The semiotic significance is necessary but remains secondary to the elaboration of sentiment. This performative analytical depiction is far from the reductionist field of computational sentiment analysis (a natural language processing technique) that reduces each sentiment to a positive, negative, or neutral. Far from a judgmental reduction, the dancing body becomes a mosaic of complex emotional experiences that also stays away from utilitarian tendencies. This infinite elaboration of the mental, cognitive, imaginative, and emotional borrows from felt experience as well as imitation. Partly emerging from the self, partially imagined, and to an extent imitated, *Cittavritti*, the alterations of the mind, do not simply remain a mental exercise but rather involve perspiration, trembling, and becoming teary-eyed among numerous other possibilities. Making the psychological movement an embodied and communicative idiom, the dancing body broadens the description of dance as beyond musculoskeletal. The mental journeys across the emotional substratum, excitant, ensuant, and ancillary feelings do not have a one-to-one correspondence in gesture or embodied movement. Rather, the inner landscape informs the enactment as well as the embodiment of both felt and communicative realities for the dancer. In this manner, the dancing body sketches out an emotional filigree for the audience—one that the latter can only experience with a visual lag different from the ornamental filigree of costumes and physical gesture.

Central to the enunciative capacity of the dancing body is the possibility of seeing and being seen. The dancer uses the gaze to see as well as to visualize an entire gamut of imaginative concoction to an audience. Physical curvilinearity complements the curvilinear alterations of the mind and their visual assemblage on the face through a series of facial contortions. Such alterations are also somatically experienced and made apparent either through voluntary or involuntary experiential reactions. Difference between the modes and means of representation blur as the phenomenal reality (the felt emotions in tune with the literary content being expressed) loses value and significance. The content of the dancing—verbal, kinesthetic, emotional, and sentimental—does not matter at the end of this exercise as the audience is absolutely set free to latch onto their own experiential attunement. The reaching of that stage requires a real-world referent. The dancing body-mind complex has the job to attune the person dancing as well as its viewership to the phenomenal materiality via analogy, imagination, generation, manifestation, and imitation. However, the purpose is to then transcend the phenomenal reality of difference and merge with an act of witnessing created through an aesthetic distance between the subject, the content, the expression, and its reception. The reception is both by the dancer as well as the viewer. In this way, the dancer is the first recipient of the performative content and in this fashion, becomes the primary witness to the pluralistic display of sentiment. The analytical and ornamental treatment of the verbal and kinesthetic reality allow for, what I refer to as the inflection point, for the witnessing to ensue. An aesthetic distance between the content and its subjective elaboration and reception, encounter a key moment of transformation as the cognitive processing changes direction (Fort 1998). This starts with the dancer who becomes a witness to the expressivity ensured by the dancing body. The witnessing furthers to the viewership in attunement with the dancing body's phenomenal, imagined, and conjured realities. This aesthetic distance, also known as *Rasa*, is the final culminating moment in the dancing body, which results in an inflection point, freeing the form from its contents. The philosophical exposition of this inflection point forms the basis of the dancing body in the first place as its entire training paradigm then rests on the culmination of this aesthetic distancing. This results in a feeling of mutual witnessing and attunement between the dance, the dancer, and the audience, blurring distinctions of time-space embedded within the phenomenal world. There remains an experience of oneness in the dance within the material embodiment of flesh, blood, tears, joy, and curvilinear folds of grounded languidity. In the following section, I further expand upon the act of witnessing that provides an epistemological import of an aesthetic dimension.

Epistemological Gestures

What do I know about the dance? What conceptual and practical abstractions and assumptions ground my claims? As a soloist embedded within the form, I enjoy epistemic privileges. My claims about my practice inevitably have blind spots. Yet, I find the glossing over of my dancing body and its inevitable correspondence with conceptual frameworks, to be a gap in existing systems of knowledge. The dancing body has epistemic perspectives and is embedded within epistemological predilections. I make a case for an inquiry-based kinesthetic exercise where logical sequencing of expressive content occurs in simultaneity with emotive experientiality. Movement material unfolds in layers switching registers to foreground a discovery of the self as an epistemological process. The self becomes the grounds for all of being, experiencing, and inquiring. Through unknotting of content and unburdening of technique, the dancing body focuses on ways of embodied knowing as a dynamic formation of embodied resonances. This primarily draws upon the fundamental problem of the inadequacy of the erroneous notion of the self as limited by time-space. Rather, in movement and expression, the dancing body has a plethora of experiences, that can erode this erroneous clinging to. The act of taking toward the viewer a part of the self in varying proportions and possibilities has the potential of loosening the grip of one's identification with body-mind empiricism. Rather, the witnessing of the dance by the agential suspension of the dancing self, has the potential for unknotting this erroneous conflation. The process of unknotting results in the removal of ignorance, which is the false identification of the material body with concomitant series of mental speculation and sense gratification. But the latter are primary to the dancing body who uses these mental and sensory faculties to finally achieve a degree of kinesthetic stasis and mental lull. I define this momentary inactivity as the *kinesthetic pause*, where I claim the occurrence of inflection points—inflecting between different registers—to psychologically reach a sense of inactivity, that is, a state of embodied calm. In this way, I define freedom as an embodied process where one experiences this inflection point of physical and mental stasis. Such is the import of the term *Moksha* where the mind does not deflect to newer knowledge about things in the real-world. Rather, it is knowledge about changing dimensions of the psychologically aware and kinesthetically active embodied beings that can experience a new way of knowing, one that is not clogged with an abundance of quantitative data-points. This is an epistemological discovery by the dancer as the dancing body experiences a qualitative difference in its investment within and encounter with movement and its various paraphernalia.

The stylistic mode of presentation requires a certain set of movement, emotions, and expressions to showcase choreographic content. There is a range of materials that enter into constituting and subsequently, visualizing the content. The exteriority of the movement is consequential to an inwardness of emotion, aesthetic, motion, thought, concept, and action. The intensity of this inwardness then results into communicative efficacy for the performer and choreographic generation for the creator. This is the philosophical basis of the choreographic process rather than an interest in creating "new" movement material from within the basic vocabulary and stylistic considerations. Vocabulary, style, and syntax are also significant in the creative process. However, they appear as important practical investments as a consequence of the initial inwardization. In his book *Inwardness*, Jonardon Ganeri maps the geography of the mind by examining metaphors used to explain interiority. Ganeri's cosmopolitan spirit of inquiry across Buddhist, Hindu, Islamic, Chinese, and Western philosophy shows pluralistic ways of thinking about the modifications of the mind (2021). The gaze has also been an important tool to connect the exterior with the interior with subsequent physicality and thought patterns.

The gaze of the dancer is instrumental in the conjuring of meaning and aesthetic. Using eyes to communicate information remains central to tying all the different paraphernalia of movement. Dancers navigate between contemplative, communicative, narrative, emotional, sensate, and kinesthetic registers. Dr. Rohini Dandavate's recent choreography *Trigger* explains the varying shades of aesthetic within Odissi. *Trigger* is inspired by the loss of youth potency due to gun violence and indiscriminate school shootings. In this fifteen-minute solo *Abhinaya*, the dancer establishes the memories of lost lives by taking the audience on a journey through memories. Kids' aspirations of cheerleading and sports inspired abstract movements with high energy. Identification markers such as balls, pompoms, etc., were held through gestural suggestions instead of actual props. The gaze remains key as the solo dancer creates a scene of the basketball field with multiple players playing on the defensive and the offensive. The entire piece is woven by the *Sutradhar*, the third person communicator or storyteller, who takes it as his responsibility to share the entirety of the piece coherently with an audience. This communication with the audience is not literal; it is an abstract communication that is key to establishing a constant throughline between what is danced and what is received. As the *Sutradhar*, the dancer checks in with viewers from time to time to ground the narrative appeal while weaving in the contemplative, the emotional, and the sensate, modulating the varying dramatic urgencies of the piece. The gaze, then, becomes the throughline between these various possibilities of movement. However, the gaze remains misunderstood in the concert mechanics where presence is not measured by the animation of the eyes. Rather, eye movements are considered flirtatious and an easy way of grabbing audience's voyeuristic attention.

The following quote from the medieval text on *Advaita Vedanta* called *Dṛg-Dṛśya-Viveka* is an inquiry into the gaze to establish the distinction between the "seer" (*Dṛg*) and the "seen" (*Dṛśya*) (Deutsch 1980):

Rupam Drishyam Lochanam Drik
Lochanam Drishyam Manoh Drik
Manoh Drishyam Sakshi

Swami Nikhilananda translates the above as follows:

> The form is perceived and the eye is its perceiver. It (eye) is perceived and the mind is its perceiver. The mind with its modifications is perceived and the Witness (the Self) is verily the perceiver. But, It (the Witness) is not perceived (by any other).
> (Nikhilananda 1952)

The seer-seen analysis removes the ignorance of identifying the self with the body-mind complex and the world of names and forms. This is the non-dualistic Advaitic position where the world of names and forms are eventually dissolved into the witness consciousness that remains as the grounds of all reality. According to *Advaita Vedanta*, *Brahman* is the ultimate reality that simply appears as names and forms as the universe (Das 1954). This is a metaphysical methodology of inquiry into the self not identified as the body-mind complex but as *Atman* (the witness-consciousness). The foundational interpretive principle for *Dṛg-Dṛśya-Viveka* is that the seer and the seen are different (Krishnan 2023). The seer is relatively unchanging, singular, and unaffected by the manifold changes and forms of the seen. These verses navigate between the materiality of the body and the world exterior to it. It notes how the real world is perceived by the eyes first and then the mind perceives the imagistic abstraction. The mind perceives the conditions of the eyes to be that the mind is the subject and the eyes are the object. Finally, the mind becomes the object of investigation. It is proposed that the unchanging *Atman* (the self) that is the witness consciousness is the subject, which is beyond perception and is no longer an object of linguistic or epistemic investigation. Here, the form stands in for all sense perceptions, the eyes for organs of perception, and the mind consisting of the intellect, memory, and ego. Every human being can take the aid of this *Dṛg-Dṛśya-Viveka* to discern her real nature as the *Atman*. The removal of ignorance, which identifies one with the body-mind complex, is considered ultimate liberation (*Moksha*). *Moksha* has been an integral aspect of my dance career as the climactic piece in my solo Odissi repertoire that I have performed for durations ranging from thirty minutes to two hours over the past two decades as a soloist. However, I have never inquired its devotional, metaphysical, or philosophical underpinnings beyond the sweating, heaving, and ecstatic dancing body. So, in my methodological inquiry into curvilinearity and its quintessential inflection point, I seek such a non-dual emphasis on the merging of the subject and the object as the dancer becomes the dance. To my kinesthetically charged body-mind complex, I find sufficient similar charge between the *Drik Drishya Viveka*'s first few verses as noted above and the famous quote from the *Abhinaya Darpana* (Khanna 2023).

Yato Hastatato Drishtiryato Drishtistato Manah
Yato Manastato Bhavvoh Yato Bhavastato Rasaha
(Vallabh 2013, 31)

This passage is instrumental in determining the central role of the gaze in negotiating hand-eye coordination across pluralistic investments of the lower and the upper body in rhythmic cycles and a strong emphasis on textual, affective, emotional, and aesthetic pursuits—all occurring simultaneously at a singular moment in the dance. This further qualifies how the central principle of the dance lies in the distillation of personalized emotions or *Bhava* through the aesthetic distancing of *Rasa*. Aesthetic stylization and subsequent presentation of personalized movements, emotions, thoughts, states of being, and sensations is the primary purpose of the dancing body operating at the juxtaposition of expression and communication. The *Bhava-Rasa* dialectic is the theory of dance-theater on which movement is woven. It provides the affective basis for movement with or without explicit literal or verbal content. In here, the dynamic of the seer and seen takes on a different journey altogether. The visual facility is the seer while the hands are the seen. The seer changes to the mind as the seen becomes the eyes themselves. The next two stages are further categorized through *Bhava* and *Rasa* until it stops at the universalizing implications of aesthetic fervor, flavor, and distance that impersonalizes the entirety of the personal negotiation of the acting by the actor or the dancing by the dancer.

The uncanny semblance of these chosen verses from the *Dṛg-Dṛśya-Viveka* and the *Abhinaya Darpana* to me speak volumes about the Advaitic parallels of the performative enterprise. The negotiation across the interior and the exterior are made intelligible through existential and experiential sentience, rather than investments with mere and moot imitation of the material reality. While one is explicitly in the context of embodied performance that needs the emotional as well as the proprioceptive, the other is an embodied modality of discerning one's nature as the witness consciousness. The cursory resemblance between the two led me to investigate the connection across the two modalities of engaging with the body and the mind. In classical Advaitic knowhow, the choreographic process would be reduced to play of *Brahman* or the eternal existence-consciousness-bliss. However, for choreographic purposes, I find this interesting given that it reorients our thinking of materiality itself in the creative repurposing within Odissi. The negotiation of the kinesthetic intelligence and awareness are always made possible by the sentience of the dancing self. Implicating the aesthetic, the cognitive, the psychological, and the cultural, movement can result in what Anita Vallabh calls as the "ecstasy of liberation from the restless activity of the mind and the senses, which are the veils of all reality, transparent only when we are at peace with ourselves" (30). The key phrase here, is 'restless activity,' the cessation of which is necessary for the epistemological discovery (Vallabh 2013). So, the purpose of *Moksha* in Odissi is similar to Advaitic liberation, which is the removal of ignorance by a targeted quieting of the body-mind complex and curbing its constant flow toward exteriority.

Spiraling Out - Spiraling In

Odissi dance, known for its spiraling circles, draws inspiration from the oceanic waves of Bay of Bengal that brushes the shores of Puri, a beach town in Odisha. Puri is often visited by Bengalis from Kolkata via a day trip by road or an overnight by train. Puri's beaches are imprinted in my mind-body as a young Bengali learning Odissi in Kolkata. As an adult, Odisha becomes my home as I start working as a company member for *Srjan Guru Kelucharan Mohapatra Nrityabasa*. Puri hosts the magnificent Jagannath temple, home to movement as ritual practice since the twelfth century. Movement, once part of temple worship of Hindu deities, became a concertized expression with its preoccupation with terms such as technique, choreography, performance, and style. The waves of the ocean influence the circular pathways and geometry constructing movement in Odissi dance. I remember Guru Poushali Mukherjee refer to movement in Odissi as "half-circles and full-circles" throughout my tenure as a student in her dance studio in Kolkata, India. The curvilinear trajectory of Odissi has inspired many artists from around the world. In this section, I analyze the philosophy—its meaning, purpose, significance, ontology, mechanics, epistemology, value-system, ethical grounds, and aesthetic principles—undergirding Odissi's quintessential spiral. A spiral is a change of orientation along the same axis without entailing a change in space. The spiraling torso hinges at the hips in order for the spinal column to articulate a comprehensive circular pathway in the vertical direction. An example of the movement of the arms with progressive restrictions at the knuckles, wrists, elbows, and shoulder joints illustrates the spiral that can be realized both in the horizontal and vertical dimensions. Cascading one's fingers restricts movement at the knuckles whereas spiraling of the palm hinges at the wrists. Hinging at the elbow gives freedom for a forearm spiral while spiraling at the shoulder joint allows for simultaneous or sequential circular arcs at the elbow, the wrist, and the knuckles. The mechanical description of the spiral shows that it requires certain geometric and spatial limitations to realize its trajectory. An anchored hinge allows for the spiraling motion. Its mechanical trajectory is along its own axis. Once unhinged, it no longer allows for the spiraling arc to take shape. Waves remain hinged with the ocean as they arise from within the depths of the water and dissipate at the shores into foam, surf, and mist. The apparent hinging of the waves to the oceanic depths provides a working metaphor for my movement as the Odissi spiral seems to emerge from nowhere and dissolves in a similarly inconspicuous manner. Memory of Puri's sea waves trigger a return to my roots—a young Bengali Odissi dancer navigating Kolkata and Bhubaneswar while enrolled as an undergraduate student—that have hinged my own spiraling inwards toward introspection and centering in the depths of this art form.

The dancer does not resemble or imitate the real world. The connection to physical reality, as we deem it, is a process of dissolution. Dissolution of the real world occurs in a processual abstraction of four steps. First, it sets itself apart from its ecological moorings as an individual empirical entity. Second, it merges itself into its empirical settings. Third, it abstracts the real world into its gestural, postural, and sensory mediation. Finally, it maintains a sense of equanimity irrespective of the emotional content of the dance. This is the overarching philosophy of the dancing body-mind system as it connects to literary, kinesthetic, choreomusicological, and dramaturgical dimensions. I argue that curvilinearity is a gradual dissolution of gross to subtle matter. In the Indian philosophical system, the body-mind complex is a material entity. The body is considered gross matter while the mind with its thoughts, ideas, emotions, feelings, concepts, and opinions forms the subtle materiality. The process of curvilinearity is hinging the exterior universe to the interiority of the body in a three-dimensional capacity. The spiraling of the external to the internal grounds all movement and its geometric configurations. The sensory perception plays a mediating role in this gradual process of abstraction. The pivoting of the self is crucial in this metaphoric dissolution. In the following paragraphs, I describe this process of dissolution across the physical and the mental dimensions noting the process of hinging as central to the quintessential curvilinear spirals of Odissi. As a consequence, I present how the spiraling is deeply grounded in Indic philosophical systems.

The human body is considered to be constituted by earth, water, air, fire, and space—from space emerges air, from air comes fire, from fire comes water, and from water emerges earth. The process of movement is to understand and manipulate these various dimensions of the body-mind complex. The goal is to attain freedom either within dance—as performed within secular perspectives—or from dance—as practiced by religious insiders who are devotees of Lord Jagannatha. Movement can be creatively generated and deployed across a wide range of dispositions—sensory dissolution of the external world, emotive delineation of narrative content, abstract articulations of curvilinear geometry, spiritual quest for the true nature of self, and the collapse of the kinesthetic to the ethereal. As noted above, the physical world develops gradually from space to earth. So, technically, there is a way of involution possible that folds back the process of evolution all the way back from earth to water to fire to air and to space. But, according to non-dual philosophy, all matter is rolled back to the ultimate nature of the self that one can access only through ultimate liberation—also the final goal in Odissi repertoire. Advaita proposes that there is the witness-consciousness different from the body-mind complex and liberation lies in knowing the self as such. According to Advaita, the association of the individual human with the body-mind complex is illusory and erroneous (Barua 2015). This understanding of the self does not have any material dimension. This self cannot be perceived by the senses or described as a stable identity; it is completely immaterial, unattached, formless, and an apparent witness to the play of the universe. True happiness lies in realizing one's own nature as this unattached and formless association that is one all-pervading universal across the living and the nonliving entities of the universe. The point of Advaitic study is to simply point toward that reality of the self. The notion of pointing is a directional shift. It is a shift in orientation of an entity. It is not a movement in space—from earth to heaven—or in time—from birth to death—or even in form—from one body to another. Rather, it is a turning, a pivoting, a spiraling, and an orienting of the central axis of the body. I draw the philosophical potential of the Odissi dancing body from this Advaitic orientation. Identifying oneself as the body-mind, different from a physical universe, contrasts sharply with the notion of the self as the immaterial seer ever-free from the material world with its infinite mutations. Advaitic wisdom lies in this knowledge of the self that removes the ignorance of identification with the material world by noting that the universe appears superimposed on the ultimate consciousness of the self. The final wisdom is a spiraling motion, one that I see value in connecting with the primary movement motif of Odissi dance.

The primary purpose of movement, then, is material dissolution in order to attain ultimate freedom. Freedom is defined as removal of the ignorance of egoistic identification of the self with the body-mind entity moving in the universe. Rather, the self is considered as the immaterial reality—the ultimate consciousness in which the material universe including the body-mind complex arises as waves arise in the ocean. The whole premise of stillness and motion becomes a contemplative meditative exercise of mindfulness and discovery of one's true self as ever-free. *Darpana* is a dance pose found in the sculptures of Odisha. In this pose, a dancer looks at the mirror. This is physically shown by the Odissi artist in a variety of pieces composed by old and new choreographers. I learned *Basant Pallavi* choreographed by Guru Kelucharan Mohapatra when I began studying Odissi at the age of ten. The main rhythmic section in this piece uses the *Darpana* as a postural variation. I found this same posture in an item called *Lohori* choreographed by Guru Subikash Mukherjee, that I learned in January 2023 after nearly three decades of learning *Basant Pallavi*. Sculpture is a very important element in the postural determination of the dancing body. The sculpturesque creates the vehicular containment of movement across stillness and motion. In particular, the reflecting metaphor of the *Darpana* can also provide a strong link to recognizing the true nature of the self in and through the endeavor of sculptural motion. In this context, I am reminded of a particular verse from a popular ancient classical Advaitic text called the *Ashtavakra Samhita* composed by the sage Ashtavakra. According to Nityaswarupananda's translation of Ashtavakra's *Samhita*:

> The image in the mirror has no real existence. It is a mere appearance. Only the mirror exists. Similarly, only the Self exists. Body, mind, etc. have no real existence. It in only by being superimposed on the Self that they appear to exist. Just as the reflection cannot affect the mirror, so body, mind, etc. cannot affect the Self (8).

In this context, movement is one's pointing toward this ultimate knowledge to set oneself free from material bondage. This is a purely spiritual exercise attained through knowledge removing the ignorance of false identification of the self with the body-mind complex.

By and large, movement is a two-step process—one which progresses away from the center and the other that returns toward the center. The former is one of infinite isolations with codified gesture, posture, spatial, and temporal concerns. The latter is a tendency to integrate across sensory, somatic, sentimental, and creative solutions. Simultaneity of the push and pull between isolation and integration makes the experiential and visual reception of Odissi unique. The push and pull are not merely alternating one another. Rather, they exist in a myriad configurations with as many creative possibilities as the choreography demands. Depending on the number of variables in question, the center can be of two-dimensional or three-dimensional structures. Distinct changes in direction of melodic or rhythmic progression can be noticed in the *Raga* and *Tala* formats. Treatments of melodic modes or *Raga* for a certain duration add to the overall effect and intensity of the piece. Similarly, rhythmic changes function as percussive variations for the dancer. An elaborative treatment of musical intonations is beyond the scope of this text. However, it must be noted that music is key to Odissi dance. Vocal, instrumental, and percussive counterparts introduce multiple key points where the dance changes direction. Music provides a layer of commentary alongside the textual and the choreographic. Odissi artist and arts administrator Kumkum Mohanty describes beats forming the center in a rhythmic progression as inflection points in the rhythm where the rhythm changes direction to return to the center. This is yet another example of noting how time is also organized in circular configurations. Melodic modes always return to the original refrain after going through a series of variations in a traditional *Pallavi* format. Such instances are further examples of returning to the center either along the circumference of the circle or toward the radius of a two-dimensional circle or a three-dimensional sphere.

Curvilinearity of form in Odissi dance is visually apparent in its circular and semi-circular arcs embodied by various parts of the dancing body. The curvature requires a definite inflection point at which, mathematically speaking, the second derivative of the function representing the curve changes sign, switching from being concave upward to being concave downward, or vice versa. Inflection points serve as critical points of analysis in various fields, such as mathematics, physics, business etc. helping to understand and predict changes in complex systems. In this chapter, I investigate the inflection point as it relates to the curvilinear trajectory of the dancing Odissi body. For example, the eighth step in the squared posture or *Chauka* requires a circularity of the hands accentuating elbows, wrists, and gestures—*Mudras*—be paired with circular torso motions and footwork that also has a half-moon trajectory in the lower body. I describe the philosophical basis of my experiential encounters with movement. I theorize my movement in resonance with medieval Indian philosophical systems. This is because I find similar exegetical interpretations in philosophical texts, such as fifteenth-century philosopher Sadananda Yogendra Sarawati's *Vedantasara,* which reflect my embodied experience of performing the solo repertoire (Nikhilananda 1931). *Vedantasara* has a similar pathway from invocation to liberation, which is analogous to *Mangalacharan* (invocation) to *Moksha* (liberation) in the canonical solo organization of an evening-length recital. Both my embodied repertoire and the text start with an invocation, that is, bringing into one's thought, action, time, and space, to the Guru or the teacher. They both are embedded within the Hindu religious praxis with their orthodox conventions, such as accepting the divine authority of the sacred texts or the *Vedas*. While I acknowledge the Hindu worldview within which Odissi dance is embedded, here, I enter into an exegetical-philosophical-experiential analysis questioning the value of the movement experience through the convention of invocation to liberation. I expound upon my relationship with movement establishing it as a mode of knowing. Thinking, reasoning, and analyzing the experiential nature of the curvilinear inflection point through the fundamental question of how the body knows prioritizes lived experience in sync with sensory-emotional-intuitive insights. Movement becomes the grounds where knowledge occurs. In this sense, I argue that movement is an epistemological premise of seeking and discovery of existential being.

Perceptive investigation into experiential movement presents a plethora of information in gesture, posture, rhythm, expression, feeling, thought, communication, and an aesthetic connection to the real world while encoding collective embodied wisdom generationally transmitted from the teacher to the student. The detailed codification of the dancing body in technique and its artful navigation in choreographic creation allow for layers of information packed into gestural communication. Often there is a semiotic abstraction occurring in the gestural as one can see the full bloom in the *Alapadma* (a single-handed gesture where the fingers cascade resembling a flower). Such packing of information is also true for posture as the square or the *Chauka* resembles the primary male Hindu deity called *Jagannath*. Rhythmic complements to the dancer's footwork build communicative surfaces dominated by the speed, the tonality, and the numerical constructions based on the structure of the traditional *Tala*, or rhythm-cycle. Facial expression follows an analytical treatment of the subject at hand through multiple causes and pluralistic effects. The strength of the expressive results in the ability to take the audience through a series of nuanced changes to portray one stable emotion. For example, if I want to establish the emotion of wonder, I might sequentially go through a series of other emotions like inquisitiveness, disappointment, and epiphany to then finally land on surprise. I might bookend the emotional elaboration with the feeling of wonderment as a way of introducing the topic and then going through a series of argumentations through my nonverbal communication. Furthermore, costume and other production elements also hold significance and meaning in the creation of the dance. Thus, the entire body dynamically holds meaning that is beyond the verbal. Specifically, movement in my Odissi dancing body becomes an epistemological agent, which primarily relies on analogy my own inquiry into the body-mind complex being present in the space-time continuum.

In this chapter, I lay out the philosophical basis of what I theorize as the inflection point, central to moving in Odissi dance. I speak from my embodied experiences as an Odissi dancer while drawing from Indic philosophical perspectives to situate the traditional solo Odissi repertoire, from *Mangalacharan* (invocation) to *Moksha* (liberation), arguing that the inflection point is a constant reminder for the dancer to return to the dance. Movement, in this case, becomes the primal matter that constitutes the dancing body-mind complex along with the worlds of imagination the dancer conjures and sets into motion. In this way, I champion the curvilinear movement foundation in the art form that blends embodiment and stone, stasis and flow, and finally, grounding and the languid. I ground inflection points in its kinesthetic specificities. While there is a physical dimension, I question a lopsided focus on the physical dimensions through an emulation of Western concert practice. In conjunction to interrogating incongruous impositions from outside, I also critique orthodoxy crippling within the aesthetic dimensions within the form.

There is a physical dimension of the inflection point in the physical vocabulary as well as phrasing. To illustrate, I focus on *Chhapaka*, a footwork with a definite bodily accent. It allows the body to quickly change directions while being nimble and supple in its grounded materiality. *Chhapaka* remains a distinct inflection in the body as it covers space. So, the slapping of the foot on the earth is not about marking a percussive accent or about making a mark on the earth with a heavy sound. Instead, it is about covering space. It is about leaving one position to navigate to another horizontally. This can also entail a change of direction and orientation of the body. So, the movement vector of the footwork is simultaneously downward and sideward. Simultaneity of vertical and horizontal vectors of *Chhapaka* marks its distinctness from all other footwork. Furthermore, phrasing in Odissi is sinusoidal in nature bellowing outward and inward like the ocean waves with definite inflection points of changing directional drifts. There is always the inflection point that brings the expansion of movement back to the central base baseline. There are crests and troughs marking modulations in the motion. A typical phrase might consist of a preparatory motion, building up of a motif, a climactic stasis, tearing down of the departure from the center, and a static ending. The phrasing typically follows an arc with an ascending and a descending curvature. The climactic moment is also the inflection point marking an energetic containment throughout the course of movement. Movement, energy, and emotional intensity rise to a crescendo, touch a dramatic chord, and return to the oceanic stillness one finds in the middle of the sea. One can map this kinesthetically, energetically, performatively, and emotionally. It is not uncommon to see veteran artists sit in one place and perform long durations of *Abhinaya*, or expressional performance. Even in such renditions of minute gestural motion and subtle facial expressions with intentional use of eye, neck, head, and *Mudras* (hand gestures), the dancer can follow a sinusoidal graphical configuration. For example, a simple semicircular arc of the feet and the arms can start with *Chhapaka*, reach its crescendo in the grounded square or *Chauka*, and culminate is its nascent culmination in the quintessential S-curve or *Tribhanga*. This presents a simple example of the cycle of the sun with the rising and the setting demonstrated with gestural comportment: *Mukula* (fingers closed as a bud) to *Alapadma* (cascading fingers as a full bloom) to *Pataka* (fingers held together with straight palms). The beginning and the ending emulate sculpturesque postures as found in the temple-sculptures. Choreographic motifs, in that case, is the resultant navigation between one point of stasis to another. This is a simplistic depiction of movement that can be far more complex based on abstract, textual, and musical parameters. The graphical configuration of a typical movement phrase follows a sinusoidal curve. However, dancers today are experimenting with thematic variations as well as movement choices, patterns, and constantly manipulating the standard in interesting ways.

This book addresses a lacuna in dance scholarship about Odissi dance. Odissi has its regional specificities and conventional practices that need to be cognized, critiqued, and grappled with on their own terms. Let us take the example of the warm-up process. One can imagine the framing of the dancer right from the preparatory process before the performance. The solo Odissi artist does not warm-up with weights and extensions before a performance. Rather, warm-up takes the form of centering and meditative contemplation. I am not arguing for sloppy technique and lack of proper warm-up. It is definitely important to cultivate an explicit regimen of stretching and body-conditioning before dancing. Odissi dancer and scholar Bijayini Satpathy trains herself and her students with an elaborate warm-up routine in order to prepare the body for movement. She is known for her training of her lower body using weights. Yet, my point is, Odissi is not just about the body, and the warm-up regimen needs to reflect complementarity of body-mind through a constant conversation between the physical, mental, kinesthetic, emotional, and communicative faculties. In order to achieve this at a high degree, contemplative centering of the mind is equally important as the stretching and extension of limbs. Furthermore, the field itself wrangles with orthodoxy and inertia about certain conventions and norms. For example, while the expressive aspect of movement is dealt with in painstaking detail in the field, I believe that the communicative dimension lacks sincere engagement by Odissi choreography. The communication requires paying attention to the audience's needs, desires, makeup, and demographic composition. But traditional Odissi pieces are performed with a degree of propriety and orthodoxy. The repertoire is as if set in stone and needs to be unchanged despite the changing reality of the concert-stage and other performing mediums. I focus on addressing this lacuna in the sixth chapter while describing my work with choreographer Maya Kulkarni in her signature-technique called *Shilpanatanam*.

References

Adamson, P., and J. Ganeri. 2020. *Classical Indian Philosophy: A History of Philosophy Without Any Gaps, Volume 5*. Oxford University Press.

Barua, A. 2015. "Ideas of Liberation in Medieval Advaita Vedānta." *Religion Compass* 9 (8): 262–71.

Coomaraswamy, A. K., and D. Gōpālakṛṣṇa. 1917. *The Mirror of Gesture: Being the Abhinaya Darpana of Nandikeśvara*. Harvard University Press.

Coorlawala, U. A. 1996. "Darshan and *Abhinaya*: An Alternative to the Male Gaze." *Dance Research Journal* 28 (1): 19–27.

Das, A. 1954. "Advaita Vedānta and Liberation in Bodily Existence." *Philosophy East and West*: 113–23.

Das, T. K. 2021. "Sambalpuri Handloom Weavers' Livelihood: An Analysis of Western Odisha Clusters, India." *The International Journal of Community and Social Development* 3 (3): 215–35.

Deutsch, E. 1980. *Advaita Vedānta: A Philosophical Reconstruction*. University of Hawaiʻi Press.

Fort, A. O. 1998. *Jivanmukti in Transformation: Embodied Liberation in Advaita and Neo-Vedanta*. State University of New York Press.

Ganeri, J. 2021. *Inwardness: An Outsider's Guide*. Columbia University Press.

Kapur, A. 2024. "Abhinaya." In *The Routledge Companion to Performance-Related Concepts in Non-European Languages*, edited by E. Fischer-Lichte, T. Jost, and A. Schenka. Routledge.

Khanna, V. 2023. "Can You See the Seer? Approaching Consciousness from an Advaita Vedānta Perspective." *Diversifying Philosophy of Religion*: 279.

Krishnan, P. 2023. "Using Transition Systems to Formalize Ideas from Vedānta." *Studia Humana* 12 (3).

Miśra, V. 1880. *Bhámatí: A Gloss on Sankara Acharya's Commentary on the Brahma Sutras*. Channulal.

Nikhilananda, S. 1931. *Vedanta-Sara of Sadananda*. Advaita Ashrama.

Nikhilananda, S. 1952. "The Three States (Avasthātraya)." *Philosophy East and West*: 66–75.

Rambachan, A. 2006. *The Advaita Worldview: God, World, and Humanity*. State University of New York Press.

Rambachan, A. 2014. *A Hindu Theology of Liberation: Not-Two Is Not One*. State University of New York Press.

Ranganath, S. 1999. *Contribution of Vacaspati Misra to Indian Philosophy*. Pratibha Prakashan.

Roodurmum, P. S. 2002. *Bhāmatī and Vivaraṇa Schools of Advaita Vedānta: A Critical Approach*. Motilal Banarsidass Publishing.

Ruzsa, F. 2021. "Vācaspati Miśra." *The Encyclopedia of Philosophy of Religion*: 1–4.

Shima, I. 1983. "On Avidya and Adhyasa in Bhamati." *Journal of Indian and Buddhist Studies (Indogaku Bukkyogaku Kenkyu)* 31 (2): 923–27.

Sinari, R. 1972. "The Phenomenological Attitude in the Samkara Vedanta." *Philosophy East and West* 22 (3): 281–90.

Srinivas, C. S. 2014. "Significance of Rasa and Abhinaya Techniques in Bharata's *Natyasastra*." *IOSR Journal of Humanities and Social Science* 19: 25–29.

Vallabh, A. 2013. *Abhinaya Darpanam: An Illustrated Translation*. B. R. Rhythms.

CHAPTER 2

Curvilinear Immersion

In this chapter, I visualize the technical foundations as well as its expressive departures in multiple stylistic associations. The S-shape brings its plumbline of symmetrical harmonization of body weight (Hon and Goldstein 2005). Deflections from the central axis remain alive so as to keep the richness of the curvilinear aesthetic as the primary neutral. The neutral position, in this case, is based in curvilinearity of the spine with its concomitant hip-torso deflections that balance out the S-shape. The dancing body categorically maintains a constant connection with the speculative and cognitive dimensions of the mind. Every posture, gesture, footwork, and expression is loaded with the possibility of being, doing, communicating, sensing, feeling, thinking, acting, imitating, characterizing, personifying, and abstracting. This manifold potential gives the dancing body-mind an infinite array of possibilities to choose from. The goal remains efficacious communication to the viewer through an integral being in the dance. The curvilinearity of the S-shape is complemented by the constant inflection points of the dancing mind to ensure efficacious communication.

Trained in Guru Kelucharan Mohapatra style, I am limited to my conservatory education. I do not claim proficiency in styles other than Guru Kelucharan Mohapatra's Odissi lineage. However, I broaden my curvilinear horizons by working extensively with artists outside of my immediate lineage. I explore the solo body holding in its folds the possibility of inflection points. Mining my own daily studio practice of material that was learned two decades ago with that absorbed during research within pluralism in the form, I question the curvilinear neutrality of my body. What is its efficacy and toward what end does the form engage with my lived experience? I argue that Odissi technique's embodiment of curvilinearity serves as a template for its theatrical potential constituting the wide range of investments across experiential, artistic, apprentice-learning, religious, cultural, spiritual, philosophical, and performative areas.

Intentional navigation of space and time provides the impetus within the form to simultaneously isolate and integrate manifold investments as well as body-parts. Bends remain central to defining the folding and unfolding of movement—one that does not necessarily need to cover large swathes of space. Rather, these folds determine the extent of kinespheric extensions (Ylla Boix and Panhofer 2025). More importantly, the dance foregrounds connection across the multiple constituents of a single movement through physical deflections alongside thought patterns. The gradual transition from *Sithilapataka* (hand gesture with slight cascading of fingers) to *Pallava* (hand gesture with slightly greater cascading of fingers than *Sithilapataka*) with the wrist slightly bending to mark the changing degrees of deflection connects to what I refer to as the gazem acting as the central organizing principle in the earlier chapter (Janaki 1992). It is possible that the gaze is not necessarily following a parallel relationship with the wrist deflections and the cascading fingers but its lived experience of visualizing movement remains central to the curvilinear folds of both the *Sithilapataka* and *Pallava* and also the transition from the former to the latter. Thus, the folding and unfolding constitute the primary mechanics of curvilinearity in the dancing body. The body is as important as the visualizing potential of the dance. This is sometimes done explicitly with hand-eye coordination. Sometimes, it is more implicit acting as an organizing mechanism without a visibly palpable parallel link between the visualization, on one end, and the sculpturesque stasis and curvilinear motility, on the other.

I organize the chapter by first looking into the curvilinear basis of the dancing body across stylistic pursuits. After establishing the technical grounds, I show its expressive luminosity in conventional works that are deemed canonical. I conclude the chapter by noting how curvilinear gestures are always a work in progress as the embodiment and expressivity emboldens and empowers with curvilinear deepening into the traditional construct or finding migrant and itinerant values that add on to the soloist's tool kit over the progression of a career spanning over a life-time in many cases (Jackson 1996).

Sculpting the S

Technique is a complex category that provides a methodological pathway to a desired outcome with a requisite amount of attentive repetition (Inderbitzin and Levy 1998). The practice of moving the body in S-shaped curves while attending to its emotional, sensory, psychological, and physiological constructs remains the hallmark of Odissi technique. Circularity and curvature remain the physical grounding for curvilinear expression. It is not the mere revealing of the mind through the body. Rather, it is a holistic construction of thought patterns and geometric arcs—together revealing the potential of dance. In this way, technique is not a reductionist stepping stone to choreography or making dances; it is instructive of the infinitude that is dance, bringing up a multitude of themes. Noted by dance-scholar Irene Velton Rothmund, technique implies "not to have reached a goal, not having to strive for perfection, [but] the feeling of freedom, of being in the moment, and of dwelling in dance" (Rothmund 2015, 20). Aspiring to cover the range of skills that dancers need to navigate the grounded languidity, this chapter unpacks the formal complexity through anatomical deflections, kinesthetic properties, and deepening the understanding of embodied stasis and motility. While the physical control remains paramount, the technique as it is taught today, lacks providing the immense conceptual understanding that is equally important in order to justify the luminous revealing. The conceptual clarity is equally significant and its expressive modalities through the body, language as in sung lyric, costuming, and felt articulations in the mind and intellect. In this chapter, I provide a holistic view of dance technique grounded within the animation of the sculpturesque while constantly finding holistic intent behind these negotiations with motility. In this rearticulation of traditional techniques of movement, I stand in solidarity with contemporary Odissi practitioners with a similar critical dance studies approach to their legacies of traditional dance forms (Kaktikar 2024).

Having trained with and worked for companies affiliated with and founded by the Mohapatra himself, my practice is embedded within Guru Kelucharan Mohapatra style. Although, my analysis is limited to my embodied understanding through one specific lineage, it delineates the languid and the grounded that defines Odissi as a globally popular concert practice. Having trained on the technical precepts of the *Odissi Dance Pathfinder* as published by the Odissi Research Centre under the leadership of scholar and artist Kumkum Mohanty, I claim that the abstract arcs created by movement across space and time follow curvilinear drawings of multiple planes. Subtle change in levels via knee bends in standing postures complementing circular arcs of the arms alongside neck and head isolations portray one of many examples of the complex processes of isolation, opposition, and coordination present in the dancing body's curvilinear geometry in one spot. The curvilinearity also shows up across space especially in gaits, spins, and jumps.

In order to reveal the curvilinear geometry, I start with noting its postural, gestural, and affective dimensions constituted by the head, neck, eyes, torso, waist, sides, hands, fingers, wrists, thighs, knees, calves, ankles, feet, legs, hips, mind, intellect, ego, and memory among other constitutive parts of the human condition. Embodied connection of expressive registers requires a deeply felt access to one's emotions, feelings, senses, and memories to be capable of recognizing this state of the mind while familiarizing oneself with the angular deflections of the wrists. This practice of agential embodiment of the physical materiality and the mental articulation filtered through the performative ego is a technical injunction. This requires serious investment in the body and its constant connection to mental speculations, intellectual determinations, inquiries, imaginations, and memory-based articulations of the dancing body. Although, I conjecture the solo dancing body's technical investments, it needs to be noted that this moving system is a communicative mechanism. It presupposes the presence of an audience—one that is always impersonal without any necessary materialistic contact. The communicative function automatically makes this moving entity a relational construct. This remains in addition to the relational investments that the dancing body co-constructs according to the demands of the narrative given that Odissi is primarily a storytelling medium using metaphor as the primary mode of communication. Thus, technical geometries do not merely instruct and reform the physical body. Rather, they organize being, experiencing, knowing, and connecting the multiplicity that is the individual dancing body as well as its embeddedness in a larger ecosystem of other spatial, temporal, and objective dimensions. The latest research in dance technique pedagogy espouses collective and explorative learning for elucidating inquiry-based and relational possibilities (Dryburgh 2021).

The primary postures of the dancing body determine the subtleties of weight shifts and angular deflections from the central axis. Departing from the linear spinal column reflect emerging degrees of difference in postural stasis. The same footwork—for example, a simple triplet of heel, flat, flat—looks absolutely different in multiple postural possibilities that undergird all movements in which the hips can be turned in or turned out, deflected sideways or held firm, while providing the central balancing mechanism in the dancing body. Subtleties of posture also provide the dynamic perception and possibilities. The postural stance is mapped according to minute degree changes of sidewise deflections from the central axis in varying axes of symmetry.

Bhanga is the generic term for posture. *Sama Bhanga*, *Ardha Bhanga*, *Chauka*, and *Tri Bhanga* provide increasing degrees of dynamism in the standing body with deflections of the torso and the hips alongside knee-bends with hips moving from a turned in position to a complete turn-out. The *Chauka* is a symmetrical stance with turned out hips, bent knees, and hands raised to the shoulder height with elbows creating ninety-degree angles. *Tri Bhangi*, on the other hand, is an asymmetrical stance where the body creates an S-shaped curve with highly deflected torsos and hips. The entire weight of the body is usually held on the back leg with the front free to move as a gesturing maneuver. While *Chauka* and *Tri Bhangi* are postures with hips turned-out, *Sama* and *Ardha* are, more or less, stances with hips turned in although the degree of symmetry varies. The *Sama* is a completely erect posture with weight equally shared between the two legs while the *Ardha* is the same as *Sama*, except that it drops all its weight onto one leg or the other. Consequently, the hip deflects toward the weight bearing side with a slight bend in the opposite knee. In all four of these *Bhangas*, the upper body is held erect with a straight spine. There are four more body positions—*Sama*, *Abhugna*, *Aabhugna*, and *Prabhugna*—that increasingly tilt the spinal column toward the sides or the front or the back. The torso deflections—side-to-side, front-and-back, and circular—stretch the malleability of the spine while holding the end-points at the neck and the tailbone in place. So, varying degrees of bending of bodily joints enables postural complexity that characterizes the movement and acts as a vehicular conduit for the gestural, affective, and percussive dimensions of bodily extremities.

This postural basis is primary in the construction of the culturally situated dancing body, but it also retains conflicting positionalities on the construction of these given postures as named above. For example, Guru Debaprasad Das style does not deposit the entirety of the body-weight on the back leg in the S-shape. Here, the two legs bear equally the weight of the body, and both legs becomes weight-bearing and gesturing simultaneously. Getting into the detailed training methodologies of each style is beyond the scope of this text, which is a broad outline of the form based primarily on my stylistic association.[1] However, I want to flag the limitations of my analysis and the subtle shifts and changes between styles and teaching methods. This makes standardization of the form an impossibility. I believe this retains the relational and individual imprinting of the self in the technique itself and not just in the choreographic pursuit. Technique, here, is not a fossilized entity. Each generation takes it up for debate and interpretation based on understanding and embodied capacity. The folding and unfolding results only from significant investment into the technical paraphernalia that starts right from understanding and experiencing postural subtleties. The dancer listens to the body in the unfolding of technique. Dancer and artist Rebecca Enghauser refers to this phenomenon as developing *listening bodies* as infinite interpretive possibilities emerge with such acutely keen attention (2007). This is what I meant by attentive repetition written at the beginning of this section. Attentive repetition is crucial to the grounding of technique in one's own perceptual body and not just as an external set of standards and limitations.

Dance technique sculpts the S-curve, catalyzing the head, the waist, and the knees in continuous and constant conversation. Even though the body is not consciously drawing curvilinear geometries that have a visual identifier, curvilinearity and its tripartite modular formulation of embodiment denote the foundational basis of attention required by the mover. For example, the same movement can be performed by attending to the tripartite model in multiple postural configurations. *Sama* refers to the straight body marking equipoise. *Abhanga* has slight hip deflection to one side or the other adding degrees of freedom to *Sama's* equilibrium. *Chauka* and *Tribhangi* have turned out hips while in *Sama* and *Abhanga* hips are turned in. *Chauka* is a square stance emulating *Jagannath*—hands suspended shoulder-height make ninety degrees at the elbows and bent knees extend toward the tall toe. *Tribhangi* creates an S-shape with three distinct bends at the head, waist, and knees. As vehicles for all motion or stasis, *Bhangas* in their exemplary templates look like temple sculptures in Odishan temples, namely, Rajarani, Brahmeswar, Jagannath, Konark, Lingaraja, Parashurameshwara, and Mukteshwara (Sahoo 2012). However, their role lies construing a moving meditation given the constant and alternating pull and push between the three nodes of its curvilinear configuration. The postural return of every movement makes the dancer navigate between degrees of deflection, groundedness, and nimbleness. The footwork and the hand gestures have the ability to make the body depart from the postural gravitas. Yet, the dance happens in the balancing act across postural stasis and gestural mobility. I end my collaborative ensemble piece *Sama: Equanimity/ Equity* (2022) with a meditation on the four *Bhangis* as the dancers—Urmila Mallick, Deepa Mahadevan, and myself—minimally move one leg without losing ground-contact to sequentially travel across *Sama*, *Abhanga*, *Tribhangi*, and *Chauka* while returning in the reverse order back to *Sama*, noting the sculptural degrees of angular deflection in these postures while simultaneously paying attention to activating the tripartite nodal structure (Sarkar 2024).

Tribhangi is a quintessential characteristic providing a modular template for the tripartite attentive simultaneity. The S-curvature can be multiply identified in the body. It can arise from three distinct bends at the shoulder, elbow, and wrist; ankle, knee, and hips; or hips, waist, and neck. Stasis and dynamism are subtly manifest. It is not a simplistic dichotomy between standing in one spot and moving in space. Even while standing, the body can have degrees of dynamism depending on the deflection from the central axis of various parts, such as the head, eyes, neck, torso, hand, waist, hips, knee, and feet. The posture in stasis has a preponderance of *Shirobheda*, the deflected head position while in dynamism, and it uses *Gribabheda*, or neck deflections. Dynamism in *Tribhangi* can be articulated without changing the weight-bearing leg (Kothari 1980). This is articulated by movements of the gesturing leg complemented with the knee-bends of the weight-bearing leg. The *Tribhangi* posture is also effective in spatial coverage. This is made possible by actively switching weight across the two feet. This complicates the one-to-one correspondence to direction, symmetry, and asymmetry that is accomplished in stasis. For example, according to Guru Kelucharan Mohapatra style, in the right *Tribhangi*, the weight of the body is borne by the left leg while the right leg is free to articulate balancing (such as foot positions *Lalita*, *Uttalita*, *Ullalita*, etc.) and sonic gesturing (such as foot positions *Bilagna*, *Parsni*, *Utparsi*, *Kunchita*, etc.). The same *Tribhangi* on the right can no longer sustain exclusive weight-bearing by the left leg in motion although asymmetry is not completely lost—one leg can continue to bear more weight than the other since the basic premise of asymmetry needs continuous attention. This differential weight-bearing continues to articulate the S-shapes in the body. Below, I describe the S-curve in stasis and in motion respectively where the latter is defined as a necessary switching of the weight-bearing leg.

The body becomes a kaleidoscope of pluralistic tendencies while carefully examining the relationship of the torso, the footwork, and the knees. Differing experiences can be registered while discussing direct cause and effect relationships between the placement of the toe, the heel, or hitting the ankles together. This plethora of activity is particular to the S-shape of the *Tribhangi* because the weight-bearing leg at the back controls the vertical motion. The gesturing leg controls the torso motion—*Dakshachala* (right torso), *Bamachala* (left torso), *Prushthachala* (front torso), *Agrachala* (front torso), and *Prachala* (circular torso) (Sarkar 2013). Let us examine two movements to examine this coordination across the upper and the lower bodies. In the first example, the dancer sits in *Tribhangi*, hitting the floor with the gesturing leg with the flat surface, the heel, and the toe. Here, there are two competing tendencies. On one end, there is a side-to-side torso movement. On the other, the knee ever-so-slightly contracts and releases for an up-and-down movement. Sometimes the one-to-one correspondence with footwork and torso is completely broken apart like in the second example. In this step, the dancer presses the balls of the gesturing leg behind the weight bearing leg in *Tribhangi*. The movement constitutes of a toe, flat, and ankle hit. The footwork echoes in the torso in the form of lingering circularity. The knees move independently, coordinating multiple directional tendencies in the dancing body. Both the toe placement and the ankle hits trigger a circular movement of the torso while the knee continues its role in adding and taking away vertical extension for the dancer.

While a static movement requires the weight bearing leg to hold most of the dancer in order for the gesturing leg to articulate isolations of the heel, toe, ankle, etc., the mechanism is different for movements covering space. Footwork in Odissi navigates a dancer from one point to another. This covering of space requires the Odissi body to maintain vehicular conduits within the four postures, such as the *Tribhangi*. In movement across space within *Tribhangi*, the dancing body does not maintain the strict dichotomy of weight-bearing and gesturing legs. Rather, both legs do both activities while maintaining the S-shape using the spine, hips, waist, neck, knees, and feet. A particular moment in Guru Kelucharan Mohapatra's *Mohona Pallavi* illustrates this possibility. In the *Antara* section, the dancer tilts the upper body toward the gesturing leg as if the torso is pulled by an invisible string from the ceiling. Maintaining the tilt in the upper body, footwork carries the dancer across the space. By alternately contracting and releasing, the knees interrupt the horizontal linearity. In addition to horizontal spatial coverage, the dancer maintains a vertical movement while contrasting the grounded lower body with a significant tilt in the upper body. The surfaces of the feet slap into the floor with flat, heel, and toe articulations. The torso responds to the triggers made by the footwork where both feet navigate weight of the body as the dancer traverses space blurring the dichotomy of the weight-bearing-leg and the gesturing-leg in static *Tribhangi*.

Sculpting the S-curve is different for three-dimensional rendering than in two dimensions. The side-to-side dynamism as described in the above paragraph is a two-dimensional movement. Turns and nonlinear movement across space makes three-dimensional movement possible. Here, it is possible that the weight-bearing leg remains the same such as in the *Biparita Bhramari* or the spin in *Tribhangi*. The weight-bearing leg shifts in active navigation of the stage space such as in *Caris* (postural conduits) or *Paada Sancharas* (footwork). Let us take the example of the *Lalita Parsni Pada Sanchara*, which requires soft toe and heel manipulations on the floor maintaining a lilting curvilinear aesthetic. This movement is like a fish-like gait requiring continuous adjustment of toe-heel in the lower body and torso-neck in the upper body maintaining immobile hips. Grazing the floor and tracing the weight-bearing leg, the toe journeys toward the heel, which then twists from the hips to switch from the gesturing to the weight-bearing leg. The journey of the other toe begins in a twisting and curvilinear motion in space. *Bhramaris*, turns, further add to the three-dimensionality of the S-curve. *Biparita Bhramari* is a one-legged spin in *Tribhangi*—right *Tribhangi* spins from the direction of the right shoulder and vice versa. This movement gathers momentum for the gesturing leg that hits the floor and creates a circular arc in space followed with the spin. Sometimes the weight-bearing leg hits the floor vertically to generate the torque-like motion for the body. In these ways, the S-curve accomplishes various degrees and kinds of curvilinear movement in a pluralistic relationship with space.

Sculpture as historical archiving of the movement provides a sensate palette to technical embodiment of the tripartite S. An understanding of Odissi's heightened aesthetics is remiss without a discussion of sculpture. Abundance of temple sculpture as evidence of Odissi's curvilinearity in stasis has been noted by scholars. In her discussion of the laws of movement in the form, Odissi scholar Anurima Banerji argues that textual lineages gain precedence over lived experiences of historical practitioners where the sculptural serves the role of citing cultural and historical continuity through its power of symbolic language and aesthetic parameters engaging with the viewer's senses and emotions to provide a state of heightened experience (2021). Emotional fervor is also the goal of Odissi's mobile maneuvering of Odisha's static sculptural program. In *Indian Temple Sculpture*, architect John Guy notes similarities between sculpture and dance in Indian temple sculpture (2007). Like in dance, "dramatic tools of stagecraft—gesture, expression, passion, and color" were deployed by the Odishan sculptors (Guy 2007, 123). Emotional tenor in dance corresponds to the sensate palette weaved by the sculptor. The expressivity weaves through the contours of the whole body and not just the face. Degrees of dynamism of the body map through deflection from the central axes and degrees of joint flexion. Intricate hand gestures articulate the energetic detailing of the sculptural extremities. Odishan sculpture realizes a heightened level of expressivity distilling and freezing in time a dramatic action—one that the contemporary artist decodes through embodied channeling of sculptural stasis.

One cannot understand the affective resonance of the dancing Odissi body without a discussion on *Rasa*, which means sensual flavor or fervor (Pollock 2016). *Rasa* explains how art creates feelings in the audience. The performer uses gestures, expressions, movements, and voice to "cook" these emotions, just like ingredients in a recipe, so that the audience can experience, connect, reflect, and enjoy a deeper sense of beauty and meaning. The role of *Rasa* in Indian aesthetic theory across performing, visual, and literary arts is paramount. Sifting through the vastness of its literature is beyond the scope for this embodied curvilinear construction. Here, I primarily focus on the practicing body and its technical paraphernalia that are central to the compounding of *Rasa* through elements of performative control, display, and expression. *Rasa* is the complex theory of affective performativity allowing the viewer to experience the performer's expressivity through an aesthetic distance. It is the primary purpose of the dancing body whose virtuosity is not measured through technical precision or expressive acumen. Rather, the ability of the dancer to generate *Rasa* separates an involved artist from others. The degree of involvement increases with age, maturity, and experience.

Rasa pervades all aspects of this dance providing a rich theoretical basis to emotional expressivity. Deeply influenced through Abhinavagupta, in my practice, I am focused on deliberate dissolution of the patriarchal through the aesthetic and the philosophical, one that emboldens the narrative musculature of the dancing body (Rastogi 2013). Abhinavagupta's commentary on *Rasa* has elaborated upon the density of stylized aesthetic expression through action and actualization. Andrew Ollett shows strong parallels between literary connotations and action-oriented precepts in Abhinavagupta's aesthetics (2016). While attentive repetition is crucial to actualizing the geometric harmony of embodied materiality, attentive to narrative expression refers to a careful analysis of embodied meaning—both point to the integrity of the holistic body-mind complex questioning all semblances of dual configurations of the body and the mind.

Embodied resonance is vital to meaning-making by the mover. Often, meaning is restricted to subjective abstractions of the physical world. Other times, it can refer to abstract movement without any representative impulse internally or externally generated. A large portion of the training consists of codified gestures—a flick of the head or the neck or the eye, a configuration of fingers either as single-hand or double where the two hands join at wrists, sides, palms, fingers, and a plethora of other possibilities. The gestural landscape is an infinite array of meaning-making as each one is comprised of a series of meanings. Gestural imprinting often goes beyond the mere one-to-one verbal semiotic signification to larger ritual, cultural, and spiritual ethos as seen in the use of minimalism in gestural usage by dancer and scholar Rekha Tandon's theorization of the dancing Odissi body from a practitioner's perspective (2023) as well as by scholar and practitioner Sabina Sen-Podstawska's sensory-somatic configuration (2019). The contextual use determines its final symbolism.

In particular, the gestural interface of the dancing Odissi body is detailed with an array of codifications of *Mudras*, hand gestures, allowing for a nuanced reading of movement as stylized semiotics. *Asamyukta* or its single-handed complement *Samyukta* or double-handed connotations. The *Odissi Dance Path Finder* classifies the *Mudras* according to two sources. One is the lineage from Bharata's *Natyasastra* while the other draws from oral histories and textual representations in Odisha's regional representation (Muni and Ghosh 1956). The connection of *Mudras* to text and literal meaning is central to the communicative potential of the moving body as well as its organizational impulse. *Path Finder*'s categorizing of the *Mudras* as single-handed, double-handed, and pure-dance hand gestures shows the complex and arrayed possibilities of gestural communication (Chatterjea 2007). The pure-dance *Mudras* are defined as "hand gestures used in non-expressional dance conveying aesthetic beauty of form without connotation" (Mohanty 1985, 41). Some pure-dance gestures are also used for their connotative implications.

Where does gestural signification end to instill felt markers of a holistic embodied potential? Verbal communication through gestural interfacing is not the only modality of expression. Rather, the stylization lies in abstract portrayal of aesthetic and formal nuance. In addition to the pan-Indian *Natyasastric* lineage, there is the regional influence from Odisha. In my two decades of Odissi dancing, I have used single hand gestures namely *Bastra* (clothes), *Tambula* (beetel leaf), *Puspa* (flower), *Bana* (bow), and *Sukhachanchu* (coy) and double hand gestures, namely, *Padma* (full bloom), *Gabakshya* (window grills), *Mayur* (peacock), *Ubhayakartari* (making love), and *Pradeepa* (oil-wick lamp) in various pieces. For example, *Bastra* (clothes) features in the second big category of the Odissi repertoire called *Sthyayee* that shows the foundational elements of the dance form. These gestures with regional specificity really cater to the dancing ethos of Odissi that abstracts Odisha's cultural mapping into its curvilinear motions. I continue to deploy regional gestures, such as *Padma* (lotus) in my last public performance of *Bichitro Anondo,* a choreography combining elements of musical as well as poetic elaboration. While I learned *Sthyayee* as a beginner in 1991, I commissioned a solo choreography *Bichitro Anondo* by Rohini Dandavate in 2021, pointing toward the imprint of Odisha's regional ethos in my persona, psyche, and performativity through gestural imprinting over two decades. Subtle, nuanced, linear, and nonlinear configurations oversee the gestural imprint in the dance where meaning-making is simultaneously poetic, reflective, metaphorical, communicative, performative, stylized, somatic, sensory, intellectual, emotional, and cultural. The mover traverses multiple domains of imagination and realism. Choreographic imagination travels in imagistic elaboration of a textual verse in ways that enrich the gestural tapestry. But the curvilinear dancing body remains as an ephemeral construct beyond its mere meaning-making possibility. It layers signification with realization where a methodical unfolding of material—felt resonances of somatic, sensory, physical, and mental elements, etc.—goes into subtle layering of imaginative content with curvilinear formality.

The gestural overlay of postural grounding, perhaps foregrounds the verbal and the communicative over the abstract formality of technical embodiment. Embodying the square and the S-shapes require inner-thigh strength that does not get communicated across to the lay viewer although the seasoned dance practitioner can appreciate the technicity over and above the representational impulses. Gesture continues to have its apparent emphasis on the verbal and the communicative. The subtlety of the dancing body comes into play through revealing and obscuring the multiple layers of being, communicating, describing, and showing. As a solo practitioner, my technical grounding in gesture also seeks a methodological intervention into the epistemological possibilities of the moving body. Gesture comes closest to verbal meaning-making in the dancing body in a semiotic signification, one that we attribute to linguistic communication. My practice-based methodology continues to investigate the technical embodiment of gesture into the epistemological significance asking the processes of knowing revealed within the dance artist. There exists a vast literature on gesture and its possibilities of denoting meaning. This canonical body of knowledge remains a significant training element infusing signification and meaning-making as an integral component of technical embodiment. But these stays restricted to the learning community, which makes it totally opaque to the lay audience. Gestural obscuring is an important reason for the opacity of the traditional dancing body and its loss of relevance to contemporary audiences. Part of this can be overcome by the emotional and the affective as noted below.

Facial expression in the moving Odissi body is a combination of the sensory, the felt, the physiological, the cognitive, and the aesthetic. Sensory inputs from the real world reciprocate the inner processing, filtering, and communicating of the same through the same senses. This act becomes essential in the simple act of seeing. Eyes as sensory apparatus simultaneously sees and shows as noted by Kazuyuki Funatsu from the traditional Indian theories of expression (2001). Funatsu compares the traditional Indian affective histrionics with American psychologist Paul Ekman's Facial Action Coding System (Ekman and Friesen 1978, 155). On one hand, through a series of passionate, frightened, humorous, tearful, charming, ferocious, inflamed, serious, distressed, and disgusted glances they show the felt emotions of the dancer. On the other hand, these same glances visualize into fruition worlds of action units of the joyful, terrible, funny, fearful, heroic, and amazing with their multitude of entities—characters, situations, personality traits, and communicative registers. Stylized sentiments simultaneously bring to bear the felt, the described, the sensed, and the communicated. Integrating a multitude of isolations, the face is the vehicular conduit for affective display with its codifications across eyes, separating eyeballs, eyelids, and eyebrows, nose, lips, cheeks, chin, etc. This integration and isolation take years of practice and a serious understanding of the movement material. Understanding the material becomes crucial to the success of its execution in a form where the physical virtuosity of curvilinearity remains subservient to the curvilinear ethics of communication and expression.

However, the regional currency further nuances this body of work as the dancing Odissi body communicates in a different measure than the southern Indian dances, such as Bharatnatyam. A starkly regional flavor of subtlety overlays affective nuance where precision and exactitude also gain a curvilinear dimension. Instead of linearity and directness in communication, facial expression combines a subtle, long-winded, and stylized affective appeal. Deflections and tilts of the head and the neck pair up with almost every precise postural stance or expansive gestural flair always noting the necessity of nonlinear modules. Communication of verbal content, which is often integral to the facial scope, also occupies this curvilinear space. I will return to the use of text while discussing the choreographic process in the next chapter. Virtuosic currency needs a constant tuning of the body-mind complex feeling, sensing, and communicating in layers and waves both abstract and narrative motion. Head, eyes, and neck add flavor to every languid and grounded movement. For example, the mechanical repetition of circling the head in *Alolita* has multiple purposes. First, it loosens the musculature allowing for smooth head tilts. Second, it adds the expressive tenor of movements. In *Bichitro Anondo*, I use the *Alolita* while moving around the stage in a circle to express my bodily joy in the activity. Third, it adds weight to the gesturing upper body that otherwise lacks the grounded weightiness of the lower body. This weight, on one hand, adds to the aesthetic deepening of an abstract movement. On the other, it communicates inviting the viewer in the abstract depiction of metaphorical, narrative, or intensely emotional content. With the intensity of eye expression characterized with the respective expansion and contraction of eye muscles in conjunction with the necessary emotional tenor, pairing of musculature and expressivity occurs in, what I call, narrative musculature. This concept pairing the gesturing face with the body toward emotional, aesthetic, or rhythmic expressivity finds greater resonance in Chapter 6 where I discuss the stretching of Odissi's curvilinearity in contemporary choreography.

Affective display and phenomenology remain a scalar modulation of this narrative capacity—one that is simultaneously powerful and subtle. Narrative musculature is not in the strength of directness of communicative methods or linearity of subject matter. Rather, it lies in a currency of obscuring and revealing measured resonances for poignant expression retaining the regionally informed cultural ethos. Ritual efficacy has been instrumental in the historical formulation of Odissi that played on secrecy, a religious studies discussion that is beyond the scope of this book. Premised on *Mahari* (temple-dancer) ritual dancing, Odissi borrows specific ritual elements. The morning ritual called *Sakhala Dhupa* used to be accompanied with *Batu*, the second major category of the Odissi repertoire (Bharne 2022). The bedtime ritual called the *Pahuda Alati* used to be accompanied with the singing of poet Jayadev's *Gitagovinda* (Marglin 2019). *Gitagovinda* is a significant text in Odissi *Abhinaya* (expressional movement). It is considered to embody the highest expressive ethos for its nuanced deliberation on the acting potential of the dancing body.

Obtaining sensory inputs and indirect precepts about the world at large, and mental perceptions bereft of immediate signification to the external reality, movement allows the experiential to thrive. Such access to the sensory, indirect, and direct states at the performer's beck and call requires training and practice. More than practice, it requires bridging of being and knowing. Content is not just to be practiced. It is to be primarily understood and eventually actualized in every cellular membrane of the moving phenomenon. Verbal meaning connected to language merge with the phenomenological and the experiential in order to provide actualization of the performative content. This actualization of performance abstracts away from the layer of signification and representation, retaining itself as the witness to such meaning-making and pointing to the integrity of the embodied materiality. For the dancer, this means incessant physical practice alongside perfect intellectual understanding to then transcend the body-mind dichotomy and experience the holistic nature of embodiment. Being in the performance in separate faculties of intellectualizing and experiencing remain mere transactional and linguistic means to explain the phenomenon and procedures of knowing that is instilled within the folds of dance technique. In this capacity of actualizing across being, experiencing, and knowing, I note how the musculature itself becomes a literary imagination of sorts, a narrative development of one's own journey to knowing oneself. To my understanding, movement technique purposefully can critically construct the self as a holistic being embedded in an ecosystem of reciprocity through felt sensory markers.

Historically speaking, ritual action and literary discourse have shaped the contemporary avatar of the dance form in discussion, but I find a promise of its critical reconstruction enfolded within its very folds of curvilinearity. This text is not about reiterating the mechanical dimensions of Odissi technique. Rather, it is a nonprescriptive and experimental tryst with technique as crucial to revealing possibilities within the dancing body transcending externally mandated material distinctions and barriers. This philosophical freedom remains within Odissi's primary purpose (alongside its concluding repertoire element) of *Moksha*. This technique is instructive of linking meaning not just as a property of a text but also linking meaning to action. In this light, the ritual actions of historical temple-dancers (*Maharis*) become imbued with meaning not just for their ritual symbolism but also as their humanistic potential as operational in the real world. In a similar manner, dance technique itself links the text to the action, the being to the experiencing, the performing to the knowing. It must be noted that grounded square stances retain their ritual symbolism to *Jagannath*, and the geometric abstraction of that shape into the experiential knowing as inhabiting and dwelling within that embodiment in space and time. In this dimension, the actualization in dance occurs beyond the immediate meaning making possibilities of the movement symbolic or experiential aspects.

Momentary and endured experiences shape the process of actualization of movement visualization. Visualizing abstract curvilinear geometries differs from narrative visualization. In movement, the technique invests in creating an entire spectrum of tenacity and capacity for narrative visualization. This happens through codified gestural nuance where invoking a certain head flick or wrist deflection evokes an array of narrative connections already delineated in textual domains and often reinforced in studio pedagogy. More importantly, the visualization comes into life through the training of the mental, psychological, emotional, and intellectual domains and their concomitant but nonlinear connections with the musculature. As I critically reconstruct the technique, I refer to this practice-based visualization procedure as narrative musculature. Divvying up the various faculties of the mind—speculative, determinative, appropriative, and temporal—the dancer can change the tenor of expression, presentation, and communication. One must note that this internal dialogue is a cyclical and nonlinear process. It does not necessarily follow any strict linearity. The dancing body speculates, determines, imagines, dreams, resolves, and appropriates all these functions in its communicative dimension only to repeat the cycle in no particular order. But this internal dialogues is not an easy function. Its kinesthetic possibilities are profound as the artist makes possible a plethora of activities to come to fruition to its audiences and in turn able to isolate and integrate, deepen and intensify, and reflect and introspect into the ability to bring to bear the process of actualization in the choreographic visualization.

One possible pathway for the art making is perhaps to start with the mental dialoguing. Speculative dimensions make transparent the real-time unraveling in the dancer—one that makes solo dancing a process of discovery and come alive. In real-time, the dancer unravels an existential condition through deepening into a felt emotion or a sensory input. This speculative dimension is usually followed by the determinative function where a particular choice is made. In this choice-making, the dancer lands on a particular actualization trajectory. The path has been chosen for the visualization to then occur. Further along, the dancer goes back and forward on the temporal spectrum to dream, imagine, and remember various dimensions that further characterize a situation or an experience. All of these then result in the dancer's individual self, appropriating the multifarious mental dimensions as a single storytelling exercise. Here, the solo dancer is the *Sutradhar*, translated by theater scholar E. T. Kirby as "the holder of the thread," responsible for narrative continuity (1974). In this way, dance technique teaches the artist to simultaneously *to be* and *to show* (56). This continuous and consistent mind-body chiasmus makes it impossible to note when the dancer is using one or the other. In this way, the solo dancing body also knows the integrity of its holistic identity embedded in a relational ecosystem constituting of people, ideas, feelings, and sensory inputs. Visualization of movement in this case becomes actualization of the holistic system where curvilinear geometries merge in and out of curvilinear thought patterns. Thus, momentary speculation and endured determinations create a plethora of emotions and feelings to further enhance the particular emotional tenor that the *Sutradhar* holds as a continuous thread clewing the entirety of the piece (Kariya 2023).

The experiential dimension remains paramount in channeling the performative efficacy. Geometries are a close limiting adjunct to this expressive tenor that primarily characterizes

Odissi dance. This is very different from linear storytelling in the theatrical domain. Dance allows for the density of the existential moments—the fleeting as well as the endured—to deepen and surface in the moving body where actualization occurs simultaneously independent of and in conjunction with the narrative content. The continuous switching between the attentive repetition between perhaps, inner thigh strength for *Uttalita*, a perfect S-shaped one-legged balance, and again, the agential ego as the *Sutradhar*, but one with convincing communicative efficacy, marks virtuosity. The mere ability to hold a balance or to communicate would not make the mark. Rather, the ability to transition with kinesthetic pauses and efficacious affect requires technical training into not just physical but emotional mapping. Experiences partner with knowing and feeling in this complex activity. In this way, procedural actualization holds greater value and importance than the final product. Independent of the content, the dancing body becomes an experiential vehicular conduit for a curvilinear trajectory, where the point across is the curvilinearity of the procedural. The point is not the linearity of storytelling. Content, in this case, remains the prompt for embodied mapping of suggestions, actualizations, and visualizations—all of which then point to the viewers' own predilections with form and content in their daily existences. Movement, then, helps in the evoking of a certain continuity across the spectator and the performer, devoid of the narrative or kinesthetic content. The unraveling and the procedural reveal the daily grind and make transparent techniques of aesthetic embodiment of that conflicting positionality constituting the human condition. Being and knowing become significant places of departure in techniques of the dancing body as they bring to light the ontological and epistemological dimensions of existence and consciousness.

Mobilized in space and time, attentive repetition and narrative musculature critically construct the dancing body in motion. Focusing on motility in two and three dimensions, movement, emotions, sensations, feelings, and imaginations constitute the progression in spatial and temporal domains. Procedural knowing through action results from sculpting degrees of freedom within the spine without necessary displacement in space. Spatial stasis can complement temporal motility bearing marks of degrees of curvilinearity. This is perhaps the beginning grounds of motion in the technical constitution, since the training starts with postural navigation with the hips, knees, and waist. The next stage comes with preferably minimal coverage of space but a plethora of rhythmic acuity through footwork. Such mobilization of rhythm is a direct attack on the percussion-making movement as a commentary on the temporal progression, organization, and deflections. Gestural motility has more verbal connotations as noted above although footwork, gesture, and posture can have multiple axes and interpretations across abstract and representationally expressive registers. Taking toward the audience, Odissi technique marks minimal spatial usage to ensure deterring from its communicative potential. Grasping the audience's attention remains paramount and primary through internal and external marking of space and time through attentive repetition and narrative musculature, as noted above.

Space is geometrically marked through internal and external maneuvering of the dancing body. Dancing activities do not necessarily result in the movement from one spot to another. It is possible that the dancer focuses on footwork with turned in or turned out hips in the exact same place with heel-toe-flat articulations of the feet, turns and jumps with landing occurring underneath the dancer, and gesturing by the upper body continuing the act of communication through motion. The movements, here, result primarily, in alterations within internal spacing of the body—curving of the spine, folding of the sternum, deflections of the neck, head, eye, and torso, and angular changes of joints such as knees, elbows, and hips. Spatial coverage of the dancing body occurs in specific curvilinear geometries actualized by circular arcs created by the various parts of the body in isolation, opposition, or coordination—principles that I discuss later in this section. The curvilinear arcs are best demonstrated by circular leg movements in varying degrees of hip turn-out accompanied by the articulation of foot positions both in one spot as well as across space. Studying the foot movements is necessary because movement originates in the lower body while the upper body responds sequentially echoing the melting of the foot on the ground. *Paada Sancharas* create serpentine, circular, cyclical, spiraling, and curving pathways in space negotiating body-weight between the feet with hips that can be either turned in or turned out. The movements make way for travel with varying degrees of contact between toes and heels on the floor or the front of the foot along the ankles, calves, and back of the knees. In *Sthitabarta*, the dancer grazes the floor with the big toe in a counterclockwise direction, eventually pivoting on the heel to rest the body-weight on the other leg to let the toe-grazing to start on the other side (Mohanty 1985, 54). This sort of frontal movement is also repeated in the *Susama Paada Sanchara* allowing for soft footfall toward any direction with one foot initiating the move toward displacement and the other joining the first in the new position. This exact same movement with an added jump introduced during the landing at the new spot dons a different name *Ashwa Utplabana* (54). It is important to remember that the dancing Odissi body is erect and frontal—shoulders remain in the same vertical plane as the hips—with a high degree of spinal spiraling and facial expression directed toward a viewership. So, even though movements can cover three hundred and sixty degrees in space, they return to the front and center in order to maintain uninterrupted communication. The spiraling and curvilinear pathways created by the feet eventually make their way into the gesturing arms, undulating spines, and the oscillating torsos.

The entirety of movement in Odissi is bound in *Tala*, a rhythmic cycle with a designated set of beats, and the movement always ends on the first beat or *Sama*. The dancer learns the rhythmic structure alongside learning the movement. Verbal illustration of an entire piece through the *Ukuta*, mnemonic syllables played on the *Mardala* (two-headed drum), with appropriate representation of *Tali* (claps), *Khali* (indicator of a directional change in the *Tala*), *Laya* (movement of the units in the *Tala*), and *Bhaga* (compartmentalization of the units in the *Tala*) is part of the dancer's training. Hence, Odissi movement is temporally woven in cyclical renditions, although the number of beats of the *Tala*, its tempo, and speed determine the pace of the cycle. The percussive density of the dance depends on the layering of rhythm, text, and melody, each of which leads into the other with short, crisp *Manas* or *Tihais* (fixed syllables that repeat three times in the same pace and end on *Sama*). This occurs in varying degrees of spatial coverage.

In concluding sketches to critically embodied reconstruction of the technique, I vouch for the transferable skills and movement principles of the dancing Odissi body. The principles of isolation, opposition, and coordination string the curvilinear geometric arcs characteristic of the dancing Odissi body. Isolation of the head, neck, eye, arm, hand, wrist, elbow, torso, hips, knees, ankles, toes, heels, and flat surfaces of the foot allows for the sequencing of gestural and postural movements to achieve specific geometric frames. Opposition is key in terms of coordinating the movement of two isolating body parts. In the Guru Kelucharan Mohapatra style of Odissi, footwork is accompanied by a corresponding shift in the torso (space between the shoulders and the waist) in the opposite direction while maintaining static hips.[3] This oppositional principle takes the form of an echoing movement, especially because of the foot stamp leading to the torso deflection. But, rarely in a particular movement does one have only the involvement of the feet and the torso. The dancer quite always coordinates all parts of the body in isolation while some parts remain in opposition. The wrists and the neck often have a binary relationship, especially in *Tribhangi* footwork. While the torso and the neck remain in opposition, the wrist moves in the same direction as *Gribabheda* (neck movements). The circular arcs of the arms and the feet gain their curvilinear color through the corresponding minute adjustments in the head and neck movements. Linear movement is quite rare in this body of dance. Even where it emerges, such as in the *Utsyandita Paada Sanchara* where the toe grazes a linear distance in front of and crossing the supporting leg, the preparatory move of reaching to the toe from the balls of the foot and the concluding gesture of the stamping of the flat surface of the foot after the toe graze adds curvature to the move. The microcosmic look at the technical details leads to perceiving the curvilinear arc of the dancing body.

A Quick Survey

A quick survey of the dancing body from head to toe notes the particularities as well as peculiarities of meaning-making through embodiment and verbal gesticulation. I start with the gaze, showing its instrumental organizing role following its philosophical exposition in the above section. Then, I bring a discussion on gestural articulation delineating its importance in constructing meaning through precision as well as pluralistic interpretive possibilities. Moving on to the lower body, I note the particular deployment of the knees and feet. I string it all together through a discussion of how a choreographic motif takes shape from stasis and concludes in a static configuration.

The gaze is primary in situating the dance although the viewers are intrigued to connect the onstage viewing experience to the real world. Accessibility is always a partial exercise. The choreographic intention is partially translated. Yet, the dancing body has a representational modality connecting the abstract rendition to the real world. Here, I am reminded of prominent dance studies scholar Susan Leigh Foster's four delineations of modes of representation, namely resemblance, imitation, replication, and reflection (1986). According to Foster, resemblance presents a real-world event through its physical attributes, imitation leaves little doubt among the audience, replication presents systemic coherence, and reflection tangentially alludes with a lot of artistic liberty. While imitation and reflection remain on the opposite sides of the spectrum, resemblance and replication are present along the two extreme positions in terms of establishing representational valence. Foster notes that "imitation depends on a spatial and temporal conformity between represented entity and danced step" (65). One could see a high degree of realism bordering on Foster's definition of imitation in Odissi movement.

However, gestural abstraction nuances this possibility to a great extent. Codified gestures can make the dancing body appear as a palimpsest of verbal information. Say, the dancer shows the sun. His rendition of the sun through the *Alapadma* (full bloom gesture) may communicate the sun but might also be confused with another meaning given that the *Alapadma* has an array of meanings and usages. So, contextual usage of gesture configures meaning-making in the dancing body that needs further elaboration than Foster's simplistic modes of representation might allow.

Gesture can constitute an entire array of communicative potential in dance. It is a richly codified system that can literally stand alone as sign-language. Audiences well-versed in gestural codification can literally translate the dance in verbal terms. This is especially true for *Abhinaya* that typically is based on poetic verses, sung lyric, or prose. Signification in choreographic form through gesture presupposes a working knowledge of *Mudras* and their *Viniyogas* (intended usage). It is up to the choreographer as to how realistic the dance wants to be. Is it important for the dance to abstract certain attributes from the real world or present a one-to-one correspondence with reality. Movement is valued on precise apprehension of a realistic portrayal bordering on Foster's imitation. Yet, the gestural translation of dramatic characterization, narrative storytelling, and real-world phenomena is abstract at best. This is because every *Mudra* does not have a singular attribution in terms of meaning-making. There is an array of meanings associated with each *Mudra*. This way there is the possibility of gestural slippage as in, there is always the possibility of slipping into another meaning attributed to the same *Mudra* in the *Abhinaya Darpana*. This, I argue, complicates the complete imitative possibility of gestural movement. Further, metaphoric elaboration of a certain attribute or character through an array of possibilities, also known as *Sanchari*, remains the pinnacle of virtuosic movement in Odissi dance. So, depth and maturity are prized over extensions and line in the form. This shows how important it is to center the mind such that perfect hand-eye coordination is accompanied with emotive, sensory, and perceptive registers setting the stage for virtuosic movement. In this way, though Odissi dancer Pranati Mohanty's *Abhinaya* moves audiences to tears, in terms of concert aesthetics in the West her dancing will not be considered virtuosic to begin with. Rather, Bijayini Satpathy's movement is legible as virtuosic because her movement, with strong emphasis on physical conditioning, translates to the trained eye in Western concert practices. Gestural, communicative nuance with seamless dramaturgical connections to the kinesthetic, the sensory, and the emotive constitute meaning-making in Odissi dance complicates simplistic, realistic connotation with perceptual being and sensate characterizations of meaning, characters, stories, and abstract rhythmic patterns.

In this section, by isolating parts of the physical dancing body, I hope to share the particularities of motion within the dance form and its connection to meaning-making. The semantics of technique were explained in the introductory chapter through its pedagogical implications. I focused on the grounded languidness noting the melting of the lower body into the earth and a distinct circularity of the upper body mapping its oceanic scope. In this section, I talk about the gaze and the gesture from the upper body. Gestural articulation and connecting the dance by the dancer's gaze are not particular to Odissi. Other Indian dances such as Bharatnatyam, Kathak, Manipuri, and Mohiniattam also use the gaze and gesture in poignant ways. However, there are particular ways in which gestural gaze and gazing gestures in Odissi are imbued with a regional ethos. They emerge from the land of Odisha and pedestrian communication has crept into art through choreographic abstraction, stylization, and ornamentation. Below, I continue to focus on knee movements resulting in level changes and *Chhapaka*, a footwork used for quick directional switches and reorienting the physical body that is particular to Odissi.

Squared-posture *Chauka* and the S-shaped *Tribhangi* requires markedly different manipulations of the knees. In *Chauka*, the knees remain bent at approximately ninety degrees, deflecting as the hips turn out. Ideally, the form requires complete turn out. However, like in ballet, it is an anatomical impossibility for many. Training in the form can be injury prone given forced turn out from the knees and the ankles to supplement the incomplete turn out of the hips. I make it a point to honor different body types and abilities and work with the facilities available, rather than forcing an anatomical impossibility that will surely lead to short-term and long-term physiological damage. In any case, the bent knees of the *Chauka* more or less maintain the same degree of angular deflection despite the changing nature of footwork—the articulation of the heel, toe, and the slapping of the surface of the feet on the earth. Weight is equally distributed between the two legs and the hips remain square. This provides a grounded aesthetic that then contrasts sharply with the lyrical upper body. The torso floats in circular or angular deflections countering corresponding footwork above immobile hips establishing Sikand's grounded lower body and a languid upper body. *Tribhangi*, on the other hand, also carries forth a similar dichotomy of lower and upper halves even though the mechanics are quite different. Here, the hips do not remain square. The body is asymmetrical, skewed to one side with the torso and the hips deflecting at opposite sides of the central vertical axis. The feet do not equally share the weight-bearing burden. Instead, *Tribhangi* has a weight-bearing leg and a gesturing leg. The former manipulates knee movements vertically, controlling level changes of the dancing body. The latter controls horizontal expansion and contraction of the leg by controlling the angular deflection of the knees. In *Tribhangi*, the knees determine kinespheric extension and contraction where the kinesphere is defined as the largest spherical container the dancing body might extend during the course of the dance. Unlike in ballet and modern and contemporary dance, the expansive capacity of Odissi is limited to anatomically bent configurations as the wrists, elbows, knees, hips, shoulders, neck, and waist remain flexed marking an energetically contained aesthetic rather than dissipation or display of energy and line respectively. Thus, the knees are instrumental in deciding the levels of the dancing Odissi body. They either maintain a singular level, as in *Chauka*, or create level changes vertically, as in *Tribhangi*. Overall, the deflected knees are instrumental in grounding the dancing body, melting and molding the dance onto the earth as its sculptural counterpart found on temple-walls of Odisha.

Mobilizing the S

Repertoire in dance blurs formal (rhythmic, curvilinearity, etc.) precepts with ideational (narrative, philosophical, social justice, etc.) inspirations. Current generations of artists repurpose the form or brings to bear socio-politically relevant content to the artistic process. Scholars and practitioners use their creative-making as a continuum of their traditional learning either in foraying into other linguistic domains (outside the conventional usage of Sanskrit and Oriya in the canonical repertoire) or other musical inspirations (outside of the traditional Odissi music that forms the basis of its rich repertoire). However, this can be contested as Odissi scholar, practitioner, and educator Aadya Kaktikar notes how artists, namely Ramli Ibrahim and Ananya Chatterjea have changed the landscape of the dance form (2024, 120). Before proceeding with this section on Odissi canonical repertoire, I want to reiterate that having been trained in Guru Kelucharan Mohapatra style, my writing on choreographic process comes from working with dancers and choreographers invested primarily in this stylistic domain. While Kaktikar's conjecture might also be contested depending upon individualized and ethnocentric perceptions about who has the right to change the form, it must be noted that Chatterjea is trained under Mohapatra style and Ibrahim's pedagogy lies within Guru Debaprasad Das style. Further, my entry into the history of Odissi through erasure was through a temple-dancer's (also known as *Mahari*) dancing body, that of Sashimoni Devi *Mahari*, who I encountered in *Given to Dance*, a documentary created primarily to showcase Mohapatra's senior student, Madhavi Mudgal. Sashimoni Devi *Mahari* represents another style of dance although patriarchal predilections continue to erase her voice even in her miniscule presence within Guru Pankaj Charan Das style. I want to ensure that my writing does not reinforce existing hierarchies and practices of erasure. In order to mitigate this, I have conducted practice-based research into other styles of Odissi. I work with Seattle-based Ratna Roy, student of Guru Pankaj Charan Das. Roy reminisces how Sashimoni Devi *Mahari*, who she lovingly called Dungri Apa, would teach her the affective quotient. Also, I train with New Jersey-based Bani Ray, California-based Bidisha Mohanty, and India-based Debasish Pattnaik who are direct disciples of Guru Durga Charan Ranbir, a direct disciple of Guru Debaprasad Das. I briefly interview and work with New York-based dancer Radhika Jha who has trained in Guru Surendranath Jena style of Odissi. I must caveat this subsequent writing work by declaring that my training is lopsided toward one style and my research non-equitably supportive of all existing styles and lineages. It must be remembered that all these lineages conjectured have a male progenitor, noting the patriarchy inherent in the formulation, as well as self-proclaimed and perpetuated through authoritative control of dissemination and discourse.

This section discusses the arc of the Odissi repertoire as practiced in the solo format. One can unnecessarily construct a binary between objectification and agentic display in the currency of the solo dancing body. Questioning such a dichotomous impulse, I draw evidence from over twenty years of professional practice in solo performance. I speak from my inquiry-based approach to performance where every studio practice or concert event becomes an opportunity for me to investigate into my performative progression as an epistemological construct. I have elaborated upon the epistemological inflection point of the dancing body earlier. In this section, I show how the repertoire creates a kinesthetic and energetic cadence for structural inflection points to occur where text, movement, and music blur in the knowing-doing of the self, in turn, spiraling to the pluralistic construction of the body-mind complex, always already in construction and only known in contextual conditions. I also juxtapose my voice with that of many other solo Odissi practitioners. For some of us, the practice is primarily aesthetic. Others have a devotional relationship with the form, recognizing themselves as adhering to organized religion or as spiritual beings. Some maintain a physical-somatic relationship with a deeply felt phenomenological connection. The Hindu religious connection is at the forefront and remains a continuous tension in the form as it travels outside the borders of the Indian nation-state and negotiates in high art concert spaces.

The repertoire, in its formative years, was modelled on Bharatnatyam, the first dance to be recognized by the Indian nation-state. Although I am an Odissi artist, I have over fifteen years of training in Bharatnatyam under Guru Moushumi Bhor Bhattacharyya and Guru Priyanka Sarkar Niyogi (also my elder sister). Here, I categorically argue that the trajectory of the Odissi repertoire is unique and differs from that of Bharatnatyam on which it was loosely structured. The first piece in the repertoire, also called *Mangalacharan*, is an invocatory piece with multiple segments. They are, *Mancha Pravesh* (entry into the stage), *Puspanjali Pradan* (offering flowers), *Bhumi Pranam* (salutation of the earth), *Dev-Stuti* (prayer to the deity), *Sabha Pranam* (acknowledging audience), and *Trikhandi Pranam* (salutation to deity, guru, and musicians). This invocation is followed by *Batu*, which shares the fundamentals of the dance, such as posture, costumes, ornamentation, and musical instrumentation depicting the *Veena* (string instrument), *Bashi* (flute), *Manjira* (metal cymbals tinkling), and *Mardala* (double-headed drum). The percussive peak of the repertoire is executed in the rhythmic as well as melodious elaborations of the next category called *Pallavi*. However, the affective quotient, or the *Rasa*, reaches its apotheosis in *Abhinaya* or expressional performance that comes after *Pallavi*. The typical repertoire consists of five segments—*Mangalacharan*, *Batu*, *Pallavi*, *Abhinaya*, and *Moksha*. *Moksha* shows the dancer's desirous surrender to the spiraling nature of movement on a solemn note of one-pointed centering and focusing. In this capacity, the trajectory of the Odissi repertoire is very different from that of the Bharatnatyam, which ends in a rhythmic crescendo with the *Thillana* marked by high-speed jubilation. *Moksha*, on the other hand, is a meditative rendering toward a centered resolution.

The Odissi repertoire used to be much shorter and unsegmented. Often termed as *Margam*, meaning pathway, it is premised on the solo dancing format of the *Mahari* ritual specialist. Odissi scholar Nandini Sikand (2016) acknowledge the role of restructuring the Odissi *Margam* on the *Mahari* repertoire although the founding gurus were mainly *Gotipuas* in their childhood. However, the traditional repertoire is constantly updated with artistic and choreographic intervention, a creative labor that remains illegible and unacknowledged to dance critics and lay audiences, as noted by artist and academic Ananya Chatterjea while discussing the critical reception of the Odissi dance company *Nrityagram*'s performance of *Vibhakta* in New York (2007). This obscuring occurs in emphasizing cultural and historical continuity over disruption and innovation. However, this artificial binary of the old and the new again falls apart in the solo dancing body that has to make its own every single choreography, however, old or new, in order to energetically and aesthetically connect to the source material and communicate with the larger audience.

The beginning of the repertoire is marked by a ritual paradigm borrowing from *Jagannath* culture (Mali 2024). The dancer enters the stage to ritualize through certain action-steps that have direct bearing with the temple-ritual paradigm. Central to this inaugural entry remains a certain relational acknowledgment of the time-space to be subsequently inhabited. It is assumed that the dancer is only the visible manifestation of the pedagogical system and the ritual ancestral lineage marking the dance's footprint into historical antiquity. By offering flowers and verbal injunctions, the mover acknowledges the dancing self in material continuity with the ritual programs, the teaching and learning methods, the musicians' repertoire, and the audience. This ritualized beginning of the evening-length program situates the perceptually sacred dimensions of the form within the perceived secular contexts of the concert environment. The ritualized foundation provides the primary framing of the dance on top of which the technical—focusing on structural foundations, musical proliferations, and textual elaborations—rest in chronological progression.

The dancer enters the stage in serpentine footwork and torso spirals. The orientation of the movements provides the audience access to the ritualized organization of space. The dancer brings flowers in *Puspaputa* (cupped hands) and offers them at the front-center usually few paces ahead of the primary center stage. This undoubtedly marks the arguably religious and ritualized beginning of the piece while also ensuring that the rest of the dance happens behind the flower offering. It would be inauspicious to step on the flowers and also inconvenient and dangerous for the artist to actualize turns and jumps on its slippery surfaces. In any case, the *Puspanjali Pradan* (offering flowers) sets the tone for the rest of the evening. A deification of the religious and spiritual dimensions occurs in rhythmic as well as gestural expression. For example, at the beginning, the percussive *Bols* (mnemonic syllables) *Tat Ta Ta ke Ta*, the *Puspaputa* hands invoke *Jagannath, Subhadra, and Balaram*—the three deities installed in the *Jagannath* temple of Puri. It is to be noted that the dance also takes place without the flower offering or *Puspanjali Pradan*. It is possible that there are multiple events lined up and no time to clear the flowers for the next piece where dancers might trip on them. In any case, the variant of *Tat Ta Ta ke Ta* is performed in *Anjali* (hands joined in prayer). While the *Puspaputa* version uses *Shirobheda* (sideways head tilts), the *Anjali* format deploys *Gribabheda* (neck movements). Both versions mark the presence of the divine trio—*Jagannath, Subhadra*, and *Balaram*—although the slight gestural shifts of the head and neck and the double-handed gestures document the choreographic imprint on the traditional repertoire. I learned this material from my first teacher, Guru Poushali Mukherjee, who was trained under Guru Kelucharan Mohapatra, also the choreographer for this invocatory expression. I am not sure if Mukherjee's pedagogical infusion or Mohapatra's choreographic imagination led to these slight changes in the invocatory ritual premise. However, a promise of nuance and subtle curvilinear gestures is laid out in clear expansive sketches. These foreground the curvilinear canvas of the entirety of the Odissi repertoire. Such subtle nuances make their way for the subsequent technical expansion of the dance.

After introducing the ritual backdrop, the solo dancer moves along in the repertoire to then present the technical infrastructure. This is accomplished in *Batu* where the primary purport remains to showcase the physical embodiment of the formal. Cursorily, expressive registers—both sonic and visual—that create the foundational basis for the formal find their seeds implanted. Music constitutes an important pillar for the dance, but its proliferation comes only in the third element or the *Pallavi*. *Batu* provides a voice to the orchestral instrumentation that function in kinesthetic collectivity with the soloist. Furthermore, sculptural stasis and ornamental aesthetics are brought to the fore in this. Overall, *Batu* points to select foundational parameters that undergird the technical precepts. Setting the strong foundations—corporeal, gestural, musical, and sartorial—allows for the repertoire to then pursue specific tenets of the dance. Establishing the *Chauka* and the *Tri Bhanga* at the outset provides a postural weightiness to the form strongly demarcating a heavy lower body with energetic containment of the upper body. Negotiations of bodily weight through pelvic positioning determine the receptivity of the footwork. For example, the same *heel, flat, flat* looks very different in the S-curve than in the square stance. Further, the movement looks even more different once it is used to move in space rather than hit on-stop. The upper body is especially communicative through gesture—gesturing musical instrumentation or bodily ornamentation. Positioning of the arms and the holding of specific *Mudras* coupled with sidewise spinal deflections during the *Veena* (string instrument) and the *Banshi* (wind instrument), determine the corporeal depiction of Odissi's musical infrastructure. Costuming is an important component of the dancing body's expressivity. Showing the wrapping around of a *Sari*, creating and wearing a flower garland around the hair tied in a bun, portraying the swinging of ear-rings, and putting on a bindi while looking at a mirror are examples of alluding to the aesthetics of the ornamented dancing body. While some movements have historical continuity, the choreographic labor in creating this genre holds strong as it displays in every aspect and category of Odissi dance. The embodied symbolism of the structural foundations achieves a choreographic complexity and performative flair with each individual representation.

Structural edifices created by the second element makes way for delving deeper into the specificities of each in subsequent progression. Music becomes the first to be expanded upon followed suit by text. Verbal and musical registers find their creative expansion in *Abhinaya* and *Pallavi*, respectively. One note of clarification about musical construction and conventional usage is important to be delineated about the term *Pallavi*. According to the Harvard dictionary of music, *Pallavi* refers to a refrain in Carnatic compositions from southern India, which is often also an elaborately improvised type of metered music. Given its intricate weaving of music and rhythm, mathematical precision remains key in choregraphed gestures as the dancer and the musician departs from, plays around, and finally arrives at *Sama*, the first beat in the cyclical rhythmic signature. *Batu*'s structural interweaving of the sonic with the visual provides a segway into visualizing the sonic. The structural setting creates a strong base for musical proliferation in the form of gestural complexity and intricate footwork. Musical experimentation with tonal notes and percussive beats reaches an apotheosis in *Pallavi*. The musical intensity rises to a crescendo as the dance usually starts slow and increases its speed along the progression of the song. It refers to the metaphor of blossoming with the climax portraying the manifestation of a rich tapestry of intricate gestural, postural, and percussive complexity as articulated by the expressive surfaces of the feet. The *Pallavi* usually has a musical signature that characterizes the dance. The dance returns again and again to the musical refrain as a haunting reminder of the cohesive organization, an example of which is *Ta Jham Ta Rita Jham* from Odissi scholar Rohini Dandavate's choreography *Bichitro Anondo* (2021). Usually, the slow start to a *Pallavi* is accompanied by torso movements paired with eye, neck, and head motions. As the music gains momentum, the movement represents the variations of the *Mardala* as well as the multiplicity of vocal, wind, and string instrumentation. Musical notes as well as rhythmic beats alternate to create a sense of rolling progression across musical variety. *Pallavi* is divided into the *Sthyayee* and the *Antara* with the former establishing a melodic mode, also known as *Raga*, and the latter offering a distinctive variation in that same mode. For example, *Bichitro Anondo* deploys Raga Mishra Sarang, combining a number of *Ragas* belonging to the same family. In the dance, we see three distinct variations in the melodic treatment using the same words as before, such as *Ta Jham Ta Rita Jham*. *Pallavi* ends on a faster tempo, the feet usually articulating more beats per the standard rhythmic cycle. The dance is tightly wound to the rhythmic cycle, which starts in a slower tempo at the beginning only to increasingly gain momentum along the progression, ending on a climactic high. This high can be compared to that after the last element of the Bharatnatyam repertoire, namely the *Thillanna*. This climactic high of physical exuberance achieved only to visualize the musical proliferation of a certain melodic mode undergoes a definite inflection point as it curves toward the most substantial category of the repertoire, *Abhinaya*.

Apparently, text is held in high esteem in the traditional construction of curvilinear containment. The inflection beyond the kinesthetic proliferation categorically moves to more solemn containment of energy and exuberance through verbal expressive gymnastics—one that is less about the visual and more about emotive and narrative capacity. This return from the musically exuberant to the textually composed retains the angular inflection as far as the entirety of the Odissi repertoire is concerned. This is strikingly different from the linear progressive rising trend in the Bharatnatyam repertoire, which ends with the *Thillanna*. This has been noted earlier, but there is another subtle point about the role of text in Odissi. While music and text are held in paramount importance in the conventional and canonical repertoire in the Odissi genre, I want to point out that it is not about the text as such, but the code-switching of the dancing body that is actualized by the usage of text, which marks the potential of world-making in *Abhinaya*. On the surface, the body is a semiotic carrier of meaning and messaging often reflecting, reiterating, refracting, and debunking conventional norms (Anoop 2012; Coorlawala 2004). But, in my embodied practice-based research into the category of *Abhinaya*, I claim that its primary resonance lies in simultaneously showing and effacing the verbal content. Usage of gesture, both codified and pedestrian, points to its semiotic capacity and also features another array of meaning-making possibilities since gesture and meaning do not have a linear one-to-one correspondence. So, the gestural infrastructure, while referring to the textual, has the possibilities of meaning-making beyond the one-to-one translation of words or sentences in significatory codes. As a dancer, I feel the promise of *Abhinaya* lies in this multi-arrayed potential of improvising—being and showing—multiplicity and always maintaining the possibility of a cognitive surplus. This surplus is beyond the access of communication while simultaneously enriching the act of taking toward meaning from the dancing body to that of the viewer, but the technical paraphernalia of this expressive capacity itself is intricate and vast. Using an elaborate tool kit, the dancer presents literary expression from a chosen text interspersed with choreographic intensification in the form of *Sanchari*, meaning elaboration. *Sanchari* is an expressive tool used by the choreographer to deepen a particular moment, concept, relationship, character, and persona. This tool is at the heart of *Abhinaya*. The dancer uses the *Sanchari* to nuance, tailor, and personalize the expressive quotient of the piece. The expressive intensity rises with the dancer's affective contouring of the text using choreographic detailing—gestural nuance, postural complexity, bodily carriage, facial manipulation, and subtle footwork—to forward the narrative arc of the dance. The narrative is usually nonlinear and metaphorical, posturing of a variety of topics ranging from the philosophical to the prosaic and the political to the environmental.[2] Serious interpretation of text or of non-textual elaboration of dramaturgical intensity carries the signature markers of *Abhinaya*. This is the most emotionally intense portion with elements of both *Natya* (expressive gesturing) and *Nritta* (formal movement not necessarily tied to verbal meaning). While percussive intensity is at the highest in the performativity of the *Pallavi*, I experientially claim that the expressive quotient reaches its peak during the *Abhinaya*. The curvilinear arc follows as one crescendo is followed by another creating a complex mesh of juxtaposed curving pathways for the Odissi *Margam*. The goal of this pathway is to evoke *Rasa*, which is invoked the most in the *Abhinaya*'s expressive quotient.

The *Margam*, or pathway, presents a dramaturgical arc weaving musical, textual, and choreographic elements in a serpentine bond. The invocatory ethos sets the tone of the journey of the dance by the dancer. The dancer never loses sight of the viewer maintaining a personal yet impersonal tone of affective and stylized communication throughout. The tenor of this communication differs across the *Margam*, ranging between technical, musical, and textual communication. The choreographic manipulation of the form reaches its apotheosis through the musical and textual influences afforded within the *Pallavi* and the *Abhinaya* formats, respectively. This choreographic complexity is juxtaposed with performative intensity in the centering observed in *Moksha*. Thus, the pathway demonstrates multiple aspects of the form in its technical virtuosity, affective quotient, and musical complexity. At various junctures, the performative adorns different valences—its intensity lies in geometric execution of the square *Chauka* or in precise counting of rhythmic beats through intricate footwork or in soulful characterization of a literary phrase depicted poetically in *Abhinaya*. The embodied exposition of percussive intensity in the *Pallavi* differs from the affective deepening that takes place in the *Abhinaya*. The emotional modulation through facial expression and kinesthetic details allow variations throughout the repertoire feeding into the arc of the pathway. The dancer's ability to perform complex routines in high tempo in *Pallavi* juxtaposes with the meditative calmness of *Moksha* alongside the ethereal and ever-elusive intersection of the philosophical, narrative, and textual elements of *Abhinaya*. There is no virtuosity meter in this form since its dimensions are infinite with the sole purpose of generating *Rasa*. I believe choreography intervenes to transform mere technique or skill to *Rasa*. The choreographic pathway, thus, has the purpose of evoking *Rasa* in the process of the performance. The traditional *Margam* creates this through a deliberation on embodied processing of form, music, and text.

Choreographic experimentation in Odissi complicates the traditional *Margam* through structural as well as deconstructive interventions. It is rare today that the Odissi artist gets to perform a traditional repertoire because of time constraints or other curatorial adjustments, such as thematic considerations, costume changes, cultural representation in international contexts, etc. The choreographer takes the considerations of framing a piece into the creative process. Sometimes external trappings of framing inspire a new work, while other times one sees creative desires emerge from within. *Bichitro Anondo* is one such choreography that intersects musical and poetic elaborations by Nobel laureate Rabindranath Tagore combining elements from the categories of both *Pallavi* and *Abhinaya*, hence the name *Sabhinaya Pallavi*. In this piece, choreographic imagination adds a separate dimension to the musical and the poetic as the choreographer Rohini Dandavate connects Tagore's lyrics with contemporary crises of the pandemic and refugeeism. Another category that does not fit neatly in the five-part *Margam* belongs to pieces that superimpose percussive and verbal experimentation. The masterpiece by Guru Kelucharan Mohapatra, *Ardhanariswara* (meaning half-man-half-woman) depicting eighth-century philosopher Adi Shankaracharya's verses, juxtaposes lyrical expression with percussive developments. The latter emerges from both drums as well as string instrumentation. Rhythms emerging from the *Mardala* as well as the sitar are explored in footwork and gestural traces continuing the narrative development, merging, and malleability of gender across the primary characters, the male *Shiva* and the female *Parvati*. By superimposing existing categories, the choreographer tries to structurally complicate the *Margam*. On another note, the creative process starts from a deconstructive oeuvre where the artist starts with the elements of the form and goes ground up to create a piece that might work across existing category markers. While *Bichitro Anondo* is a structural experiment, *Ardhanariswara* is a deconstructive maneuver.

Linear or nonlinear and conventional or experimental pathways culminate into the meditative centering. Beyond the verbal exposition, where the story dissolves in the dance, there is silence—the silence of a focused and centered body. In this body movement reduces and eventually stills. This is no longer sculptural stasis because sculpture has its own degrees of dynamism. This is silencing the body-mind complex to intensify the dance of centering. This dance is about reducing dynamism while simultaneously intensifying focus and meditative absorption. The expressive intensity of the Odissi repertoire culminates in the meditative calmness of *Moksha*. *Moksha* begins with a rhythmic component moving on to a verbal section that emphasizes the cyclical nature of *Srishthi*, *Sthithi*, and *Pralaya* (meaning creation, preservation, and destruction). The dancer performs single-legged balances, *Virabhadrasanas*, in three directions before descending to the floor through the gradual portrayal of the journey to the self. The body is at the center of movement, and the entirety of the repertoire is a spiraling act of returning to the self. The borrowing of the *Yogic* posture in this section marks the aspirational and performative that is left to each dancer to interpret. This entity is entirely dependent upon the dancer's positionality and access to the form. Odissi dancer and scholar Scheherazaad Cooper argues that "not every Odissi dancer is necessarily Hindu, or even 'spiritual', for that matter" (2013, 342). The performative vision of Odissi is an embodied lived experience that varies according to the individual embodiment by the dancer and the respective interpretation. Thus, the dancer's interpretation of the emancipated self is deeply connected to technical ability, rehearsed practice, expressive ethos, and dominant philosophical principles. In any case, the curvilinear arc of the repertoire manifests itself through the culmination of the *Moksha*, marking an end to the progressive development of invocatory elements of *Mangalacharan*, structural foundations of *Batu*, musical proliferations of *Pallavi*, and textual elaborations of *Abhinaya*.

FIG. 8: Prepping Students: Author with 2025 Ohio Arts Council Traditional Arts Apprentice Tanisha Mukherjee during her Graduation Recital Prep on September 27, 2020. Reproduced with permission from Arup Atarthi.

FIG. 9: Prepping Students: Author with mentee Anushka Maharana during her Graduation Recital Prep on July 3, 2021. Reproduced with permission from Surit Maharana.

Curvilinear Returns

Dance, with its technical infrastructure and repertoire-led inflection points, makes arbitrary the bearing of music, text, and ornamentation on its registers. The dance becomes one with the self—the embodied complex executing the kinesthetic gesture. This spiraling back into the embodied after a ritualized pathway across multiple elements frees the dancer in the dance. The dancer is not tied to the visual or the sonic, the verbal or the percussive. The dancer finds freedom in the movement beyond its exploratory potential to visualize, describe, and communicate. The return is a spiraling aesthetic foregrounding the curvilinearity of the form, the content, and the expression. Beyond these three, the curvilinear aesthetic nuances the entirety of the philosophical grounding foundational to the premise of *Moksha*, the proposed possibility of finding freedom in the dance. Technical embodiment of the curvilinear undergirds the philosophical spiraling after multiple trysts with the invocatory, the fundamental, the proliferative, the elaborative, and the emancipatory. The solo dancer becomes a methodological embodiment of an epistemological inquiry about the body-mind complex. But this inquiry is embedded in the imaginative, in the musically inspiring, in the metaphorical, in the ancestral, and in the materiality of the dancing body

The repertoire from *Mangalacharan* to *Moksha* can be grounded in ancient and medieval South Asian philosophical traditions as noted earlier. An introductory engagement with South Asian philosophy and Odissi has been accomplished in delineating the theoretical purport behind the curvilinear aesthetic. As bookends to a methodological pathway, *Mangalacharan* and *Moksha* as invocation and culmination, respectively, grounds an experiential dwelling in the body. This kinesthetic dwelling is simultaneously aesthetic and epistemological. The curvilinear spiraling is a dance of passionate engagement and its momentary dissolution pointing to the philosophical removal of ignorance about the self as an interplay, a performance of sorts in a state of constant intertextuality. Concepts and narrative, musicality, and kinesthetic maneuvering influence the manifestation of the creative vision. Sometimes people, places, stories, emotions, and circumstances create the ideational fabric. Other times, abstract musicality—either through melodic or percussive elaboration—determines movement generation. Emotional connectivity remains constant with a fundamental and constant acknowledgment of an audience. The nuanced expressivity that comes only after years of embodied repetition with conceptual clarity is quite hard to achieve. Rarely, when a dancer accomplishes such an achievement, the audience is transported, realizing the promise of introspective contemplation as the primary significance and everlasting potential of Odissi repertoire. Corporeal engagement of the body has a methodological grounding across conceptual, emotional, and sensory registers to produce such exuberance—one that charges the self as well as its audiences in transformational valencies.

In closing, I return to a solo practitioner's individualized practice-based research perspective. The execution of repertoire requires an awareness that is different from display of technical rigor. There are multiple approaches to the manifestation of Odissi's nuanced aesthetic depending on the philosophical outlook of the practitioner. Odissi's promise of transcending the exterior and entering an inner landscape overlaps movement, meditation, and contemplation. Unlike Western concert practices, Odissi loses its layered meaning-making with a mere analytical outlook, such as mapping Odissi's use of the body, energy, time, and space. Stepping back into the internal awareness and perceiving the body as a toolbox allows for a corporeal cooking from which Rasa is tasted. A conscious engagement of the body, breath, energy, mental faculties, and emotions can happen with the spinal cord as the starting point of movement according to the Bihar School of Yoga. Quieting the mind to enter into an internal landscape acknowledges internal points of reference through which it is much easier to let go of habitual stiffness and identify areas in the body in need of release.

Dancer and scholar Rekha Tandon engages such a corporeal performative approach deeply influenced through her investment in Tantric philosophy that grounds the awareness deep within the corporeal experientiality (Tomlinson 2018). Odisha is the land of Tantra. Tantric philosophy and praxis have deep-seated implications within the form and its creative manifestation. Tandon's corporeal mapping across genres takes deep inspiration from eminent South Asian dance studies scholar Kapila Vatsyayan's work in interdisciplinary understanding of Indian dance. Curvilinear symmetry creates a space that is deeply charged with philosophical intonation deploying the body for ritual purposes while explicit ritualized outlets for the dance no longer exist. Tandon makes movement choices after sieving through her philosophical lens in a laboratory experimentation of trial and error. The process of choosing travels across genres, styles, and mediums as philosophical rigor complements choreographic skill in creating materials ranging from solo works for intimate audiences to large multimedia productions involving multiple dancers and media projections. Kinesthetic conjuring emanates energetic detailing of the dancing body taking the audience into an inquiry into the self. The form itself uses movement and breath to facilitate mental and emotional faculties in order to create a play of energy. A lay audience sees the rounded movements of the Odissi body and, perhaps, connects through emotional registers. Experienced connoisseurs of art sieve the energetic details through the kinesthetic enterprise and experience the beauty of the embodied through the transcendental. Stepping back into the internal awareness, the dancer conjures the body as an energetic mapping of what Tandon theorizes as the *Yantra*, which is a geometrical diagram. The physical body is not negated. Rather, it is central to the conjuring of energy that touches both dancers and audiences.

Odissi is a popular global art form that has stylized representation in music and dance. Its choreographic, performative, practical, and pedagogical elements need to be engaged with on its own terms in scholarship, which is currently lacking. In addition, the choreographic process particular to the form given its particular, culturally situated and specific investments with text, music, and literature need unpacking and not assumed away or denounced by postmodern trends of *movement for movement's sake* in Western concert dance. The dancer experiences the changes in directions physically through quintessential *Chhapakas*, emotionally through the multiple *Cittavrittis,* sensorially through the visualizing capacity of the gaze, as well as in a culminating capacity in the final act of becoming the witness to one's own dancing. Such is the basis of the curvilinearity of the Odissi dancing body encompassing multiple dimensions of being, experiencing, and feeling.

Notes

1. In Appendix I, I provide Model Progressions of teaching and learning based on anchor standards. This is a teaching toolkit primarily created as resource for educators.

2. I had toured with a production by Orissa Dance Academy in Cleveland where a social menace of rape, connecting to 2015 high-profile gang-rape of Nirbhaya was depicted in choreographic subtlety and aesthetic nuance.

3. In Appendix I, I present a case study of the presentation of traditional repertoire in pre-professional dance training. In this appendix, I create a teaching aid where I talk about 'Mancha-Pravesh,' meaning first entry into the stage. This terms marks a debut solo recital of an aspiring soloist. In this teaching aid, I present a case-study of a student recital along with the varying aspects necessary for actualizing this vision.

References

Anoop, M. 2012. "Nāṭya, rasa, and abhinaya as semiotic principles in Classical Indian dance." *Semiotica* 2012 (190): 111–131.

Banerji, A. 2021. "The Laws of Movement: The *Natyashastra* as Archive for Indian Classical Dance." *Contemporary Theatre Review* 31 (1–2): 132–52.

Bharne, V. 2022. "The Ritual Landscapes of Hindu Temples." In *The Routledge Handbook of Cultural Landscape Heritage in The Asia-Pacific*, edited by K. D. Silva, K. Taylor, and D. S. Jones. Routledge.

Chatterjea, A. 2007. "Contestations: Constructing a Historical Narrative for Odissi." *Nordic Theatre Studies* 19.

Cooper, S. 2013. "The Alchemy of Rasa in the Performer–Spectator Interaction." *New Theatre Quarterly* 29 (4): 336–48.

Coorlawala, U.A. 2004. "The Sanskritized Body." *Dance Research Journal* 36 (2): 50–63.

Dryburgh, J. 2021. *Re-Envisioning Dance Technique Pedagogy*. Middlesex University.

Ekman, P., and W. V. Friesen. 1978. "Facial Action Coding System." *Environmental Psychology & Nonverbal Behavior.*

Enghauser, R. 2007. "Developing Listening Bodies in the Dance Technique Class." *Journal of Physical Education, Recreation & Dance* 78 (6): 33–38.

Foster, S. L. 1986. *Reading Dancing: Bodies and Subjects in Contemporary American Dance.* University of California Press.

Funatsu, K. 2001. *Kinesics in Natyasastra Tradition*. Shinshu University Library.

Guy, J. 2007. *Indian Temple Sculpture.* V & A Publications.

Hon, G., and B. R. Goldstein. 2005. "From Proportion to Balance: The Background to Symmetry in Science." *Studies in History and Philosophy of Science Part A* 36 (1): 1–21.

Inderbitzin, L. B., and S. T. Levy. 1998. "Repetition Compulsion Revisited: Implications for Technique." *The Psychoanalytic Quarterly* 67 (1): 32–53.

Jackson, C. 1996. "Managing and Developing a Boundaryless Career: Lessons from Dance and Drama." *European Journal of Work and Organizational Psychology* 5 (4): 617–28.

Janaki, S. 1992. "The Hand-Gesture Pataka in Natya." In *The Traditional Indian Theory and Practice of Music and Dance*. Brill.

Kaktikar, A. 2024. "Locating Odissi in the United States: Dancing Through Curricula, Teaching Methods, and Assessment." *Journal of Dance Education* 24 (2): 117–24.

Kariya, D. P. 2023. "Rasa Analysis of Girish Karnad's *Hayavadana*." *Vidhyayana* 9 (1): 17–27.

Kirby, E. T. 1974. "The Shamanistic Origins of Popular Entertainments." *The Drama Review* 18 (1): 5–15.

Kothari, S. 1980. "The Use of Masks in Indian Dances and Dance-Dramas." *The World of Music* 22 (1): 89–106.

Mali, D. K. 2024. "Exploring Jagannath Culture: The Intersection of Devotion, Rituals, and Literary Traditions." *Integral Research* 1 (4): 1–9.

Marglin, F. A. 2019. "Two Rituals of the Devadasis in Jagannath's Temple: (Followed by Conclusions in a Confessional Mode)." *Journal of Vaishnava Studies Online (Beta)* 27 (2).

Muni, B., and M. Ghosh (1956). *Natyasastra*. Manisha Granthalaya.

Ollett, A. 2016. "Ritual Texts and Literary Texts in Abhinavagupta's Aesthetics: Notes on the Beginning of the 'Critical Reconstruction'." *Journal of Indian Philosophy* 44 (3): 581–95.

Pollock, S. 2016. *A Rasa Reader: Classical Indian Aesthetics*. Columbia University Press.

Rastogi, N. 2013. "Quintessentiality of Camatkāra in Rasa-Experience: Revisiting Abhinavagupta." In *Abhinavā: Perspectives on Abhinavagupta: Studies in Memory of K. C. Pandey on His Centenary*, edited by N. Rastogi and M. Rastogi. Munshiram Manoharlal Publishers.

Rothmund, I. V. 2015. "Dance Technique-Meanings and Applications." *Nordic Journal of Dance–Practice, Education and Research* 6 (2): 13–23.

Sahoo, D. 2012. "SIT: A New Dimension for Promoting a Destination: A Case Study on Religious Tourism in Odisha." *JOHAR* 7 (1): 41.

Sarkar, K. 2013. "The Frigid Description of the Dancing Body." *Performance Research* 18 (6): 38–45.

Sarkar, K. 2024. *Dance, Technology, and Social Justice: Individual and Collective Emancipation Through Embodied Techniques*. McFarland.

Sen-Podstawska, S. S. 2019. "The Transient 'Ideals' of the 'Odissi Body' and the Changing Place and Role of Odissi Dancers in History." *Świat i słowo* 1 (32): 133–51.

Sikand, N. 2016. *Languid Bodies, Grounded Stances: The Curving Pathway of Neoclassical Odissi Dance*. Berghahn Books.

Tandon, R. "Practice-Research in Odissi Dance: The 3 Bindu Approach to Embodying Sacred Geometry." *International Journal of Arts Architecture and Design* 1 (1): 22–30.

Tomlinson, D. K. 2018. "The Tantric Context of Ratnākaraśānti's Philosophy of Mind." *Journal of Indian Philosophy* 46 (2): 355–72.

Ylla Boix, R., and H. Panhofer. 2025. "The Kinesphere: A Systematised Literature Review." *Body, Movement and Dance in Psychotherapy* 20 (1): 4–21.

PART II

The Creative Triad of Music, Text, and Movement

CHAPTER 3

Kinesthetic Pause

Breaking the Fourth Wall

Introduction[1]

CHOREOGRAPHY FOR THE CURVILINEAR dancing body goes beyond an investment in technique prioritizing conceptual organizing of music and text. Musical and textual dimensions lead the choreographic oeuvre in traditional repertoire. *Pallavi* or musical proliferation weaves melodic and rhythmic dimensions into posture, gesture, and mapping footwork (Banerji 2010). *Abhinaya*, or expressive repertoire, grounds the movement into the verbal domain, such as the philosophical, textual, and literary (Kothari 2022). In her doctoral dissertation *Analyzing Music and Dance: Balanchine's Choreography to Tchaikovsky and the Choreomusical Score*, Kara Yoo Leaman notes how while ballet master George Balanchine's choreography focused only on the skill of providing "a visual complement to music," Odissi choreographers require musical as well as poetic literacy and artistry (2016, 5). Visualization of a particular story, a melodic mode, or a philosophical precept charts a pathway toward affective efficacy. In this chapter, I explore how the landing of the performative content remains woven into the choreographic dimensions.

In this case, the creative process is a dialogical process across scriptwriting, music composition, and choreography, where the code-switching occurs during the communicative impulse. I define this moment of choreographic congealing as the *kinesthetic pause*, a moment of stillness, aesthetically drawing from an array of influences across sculptural curvature, melodic progression, verbal meaning-making, that retains an empathetic bringing forth of a creative impulse toward an imagined viewer. In this process, choreography retains a pedagogical influence of pointing to the viewer the dynamic difference across form and content. Content loses its primacy. What remains is formal complexity stilled toward the *Sthayibhava* in the viewer, the basic emotional state aestheticized through creative discourse. The Brechtian fourth wall created to prevent passive consumption could be an interesting parallel to artistic creation and reception in Indian dance that blurs the boundary between performer and spectator (Pillai 2023). For example, *Abhinaya*, or expressive storytelling and framing, situates the audience as participants rather than observers, inviting reflection rather than illusion. The audience is encouraged to remain fully conscious of both the artistry and its import onto the viewer's embodiment and psyche.

Solo dancing in the Indian arts context remains illegible to artistic reception. Sheer lack of scholarship creates a false perception that they lack artistic dimensionality and depth. The mover as well as the movement are perceived as lacking creative capacity and intellectual rigor. I derive inspiration from artist and scholar Karen Nicole Barbour who uses solo dancing as a methodological engagement toward advocacy of solo performance as research (Barbour 2012). Distinct bodies of knowledge inform the creative unpacking of form and content across historical archives as well as contemporary thematic structures. Embodied methods unique to the formal specificities such as the echoing of the torso with corresponding footwork, center the process of creation and dissemination. Interdisciplinary influences across Indigenous literary and visual arts offer an embodied modality of knowing and being—one in which the performer and the viewer remain in creative suspension during the performance. Embodied knowledge and imagination remain at the forefront of solo performance, making it primarily an iteratively creative act in every manifestation (Barbour 2011).

Theorizing the creative process behind solo dance, this book project is a theoretical intervention, addressing these discursive lacunae. Some of the questions addressed in this chapter are: How does the creative process begin? What is the purpose of creative interplay across dance, music, and text? What is the role of the solo dancing body in this germination of ideation and formal particulars? What is the relationship between the choreographer and the dancer? What are the defined roles of scriptwriting and music composition? Which kind of relation does one have with the music? What comes first: music or movement? How much of the choreography is the choreographer's solipsistic visualization and how much is composed through dialogical engagement with the dancer? At the outset, I lay out the distinct dimensions of allied arts in the creative process. Establishing the choreographic arc through the triad of text, movement, and music, segways into the development of the original theoretical concept of the *kinesthetic pause*. I end with grounding the creative ethos in the philosophical and regional dimensions of the land of Odisha (Majhi et al. 2024).

The Triad

Inspiration can be multifaceted in varying degrees of combination of the textual, the musical, the imagistic, the emotional, and the contextual as the poetic arc builds through increasing intensities. Poetic certitude provides primacy of metaphor in the serpentine organization of the dancing body. Alongside metaphoric appeal, inspiration comes from a rich linguistic tradition of literary texts as well as those focusing on performance theory. Movement is drawn from the numerous Sanskrit (*Natyasastra*, *Abhinaya Darpana*, *Sangeet Ratnakara*, *Gitagovinda*) and Oriya (*Sangita Muktavali*, *Natya Manorama*, *Sangita Narayana*, *Abhinaya Chandrika*) language treatises that have been available to the canonical composition of movement. The sung lyric is as important as melodic and percussive markers. Musical centering occurs through melodic and percussive influences in many cases, especially in traditional repertoire demonstrating technical acumen. Sculpture and palm-leaf painting weave into numerous choreographic processes either as entire movement motifs or as punctuating transitions. The emotional takes precedence in expressive repertoire as the dramatic arc materializes through narrative

FIG. 10: Pathos Series 1: Author Painting Increasing Degrees of Emotional Intensity at a performance in Durham Arts Council on June 25, 2025. Reproduced with permission from Arun Kumar.

and metaphorical progression. Contextual events draw inspiration from the everyday, special events, historical stories, social justice, environmental justice, etc. The traditional canon is lacking in politically conscious engagements with the world. In many ways, the canon functions in a performative vacuum, indulging heavily with religious, spiritual, philosophical, and ephemeral precepts. My first teacher of Odissi dance, Guru Poushali Mukherjee, told me in my very first class with her that Odissi dance consists of half-circles and full-circles, a motto that has stuck with me over the last forty years of my engagement with the curvilinear aesthetics. One sees the curvilinear neutral throughout the movement variations across bent knees, deflected necks, circular torsos, adjusted hips, and restrained expressions.

FIG. 11: Pathos Series 2: Author Painting Increasing Degrees of Emotional Intensity at a performance in Durham Arts Council on June 25, 2025. Reproduced with permission from Arun Kumar.

Beyond the square postures and S-shapes, there is an infinite variety of physical templates from which artists draw inspiration from and carve their dynamism. Postural stasis and dynamism as demonstrated with their degrees of departure from spinal linearity is at the fulcrum. They act as vehicular conduits onto which further etching of gesture, footwork, expression, and rhythmic exuberance occur. Constant and conscious weight shifts from one leg to the other, connect the dancer with the earth in an indelible manner. Repercussions from the feet flow through a sequential adjustment of hips, torso, and the neck. This is the most defining element of the movement as it lends a curvilinear flow through constant weight-shifting, grounding the

FIG. 12: Pathos Series 3: Author Painting Increasing Degrees of Emotional Intensity at a performance in Durham Arts Council on June 25, 2025. Reproduced with permission from Arun Kumar.

dancing body within every transition. Dance scholar Sunil Kothari noted how the S-shape was achieved through the manipulation of the torso to avoid "exaggerated hip movements" (2022, 60). Dynamizing sculpture has been an integral part of choreographic inspiration although over the years, various artists have chosen to disagree with one another about the nature and extent of that dynamism. For example, Guru Surendranath Jena's student, dancer and author Radhika Jha, notes how her teacher spent years with Odishan sculpture to find meaning, purpose, and permission to make the stone move (2024). His choreography looks significantly different from that of Guru Kelucharan Mohapatra, Guru Pankaj Charan Das, and Guru Debaprasad Das. It must be noted that there are varying degrees of sculptural dynamism in every style of Odissi although it might not be the sole differentiating factor of the choreography.

FIG. 13: Pathos Series 4: Author Painting Increasing Degrees of Emotional Intensity at a performance in Durham Arts Council on June 25, 2025. Reproduced with permission from Arun Kumar.

Whether in amplifying metric perturbations or in aligning string to percussive instrumentation, dance and music share a parallel relationship where the visual and the kinesthetic often bear a synced affinity. In traditional pieces, such affinity can often be predictable as musical influences continue to infuse emotional valence and rhythmic flair into the dance. In experimental choreography, this symbiotic relationship is sometimes questioned. Diving into experimental dimensions of avant garde work that stretches the formal dimensions of the continuity across dance and music is beyond the scope of this chapter, which focuses primarily on repertoire, although it is explored in Chapter 6's discussion of the choreographic work of Maya Kulkarni. The relationship of music with movement can be both didactic and interpretative

FIG. 14: Pathos Series 5: Author Painting Increasing Degrees of Emotional Intensity at a performance in Durham Arts Council on June 25, 2025. Reproduced with permission from Arun Kumar.

depending on the usage. The choreography is mathematically precise owing to the rhythmic accompaniment, often bringing a positivist approach. Systematic examination of musical structures, forms, and notational details across harmonic resonance and dialogical conversations establish a framework interacting in a graphical intersection of the melodic mode and rhythmic mesh (Vatsyayan 1963). For instance, the vocalist may expand upon the main melody while sustaining a parallel connection with the dancer's gestural vocabulary. Accompanying string and wind instruments presents simultaneous variations. These add on to the density of dynamism in the work. Finally, percussion converses rhythmically with the melodic infrastructure. The dancer's footwork maintains a symbiotic anointing with the percussionist.

FIG. 15: Pathos Series 6: Author Painting Increasing Degrees of Emotional Intensity at performance in Durham Arts Council on June 25, 2025. Reproduced with permission from Arun Kumar.

Music can also yield interpretative liberty due to its expressive nuance where the dancer internalizes and glides over the tones and lyrics through gestural improvisation. Vocalist, lyricist, and arts administrator, Dr. Sangita Gosain, who sang for Odissi for the first time in 1987, notes that Odissi music is the support that makes choreography possible. In an online music workshop organized by Odissi Alliance of North America, Gosain notes how lyrical meaning-making is central to the art of Odissi music. She goes on to note how collaboration is the central crux of this process between music composer, subject matter experts, the choreographer or the guru, rhythm composer, and the performer. Typically, choreography happens in a hierarchical domain of a guru working with the student on new pieces. Gosain notes how Guru Raghunath Dutta worked with music composer Rakhal Mohanty to create music for expressing dramatic mapping of a complex psychological mindset for a theatrical presentation adopted from an Oriya text called *Sita Banabasa* (the forest exile of protagonist Sita) (Panda 2017). Percussive composition is inspired from the mindset of the central character. This shows how an emotional inspiration underlies the artistic process in a layered and step-wise progression of the choreographic tiers. Noting how choreography does not distort literary, musical, and percussive enunciation, Gosain says that "we do not have any right to add our engineering into canonical pieces of choreography" (Oana 2023).

The aesthetic and artistic must align across the board to bring the choreographic creation to fruition. The seed thought of the choreographer goes through a process of expansion and growth through research, consultation, and collaboration. The process of choreographic abstraction allows for selective prominence to certain elements of the imagination in order to marry effective storytelling with efficacious visual imagery. The choreographer needs a working knowledge of music—both melodic modes and lyrical phrasing—especially to address musical notes corresponding to emotional mapping. The drafting of an initial sketch of the music following the emergence of a script is then tried out in the dance studio as the choreographer sculpts the dancing body or bodies in accordance with the music. Music creates an appropriate emotional tenor as the *Saptak* (seven notes) allow for infinite creative potentiality. With just the change of *Ga* (short for *Gandhār*, *Ga* is the third note in the basic scale), from the *Shudh* (natural) to the *Komal* (flat), evocation of *Veera* (boldness) switches to *Karuna* (pathos). The musical tradition needs to be maintained especially the alignment of the music with the orally received lyric. The bright, open, and stable sound converts to a softer, more plaintive emotional melancholy.

Musicologist Itishree Sahoo notes that Odissi is a triad of song, music, and dance called *Samprada* in ancient Odisha (Sahoo 2025). *Maharis* or the temple-dancers were appointed as *Samprada Nijoga* for their daily ritual offering as well as specialized performativity during festivities. This triad is quite similar to the conceptualization of *Sangeet* by aesthetician Sarangadeva (Trivedi 2019). Sahoo laments the disciplinary split imposed on Odissi whereby the dance is separated from the music that is integral to the form since it bears the regional ethos of Odisha, which attributes the present formal musical structure of Odissi to the performance repertoire of the *Maharis* in the Jagannath temple at Puri while going through a meticulous chronology for the *Mahari* repertoire. In a detailed analysis regarding the naming of Odissi music, ethnomusicologist David Dennen presents diverse sources to note the complexities of naming and the ontological nature of music from the state of Odisha (2013). Dennen contends with the celebrated cultural activist Kalicharan Pattnaik's (1966) claim to Odissi music's individuality through a discussion around its pan-Indian situatedness (Dennen 2013, 74). A detailed discussion around the autonomy of Odissi music is beyond the scope of this project. However, it is impossible to disengage the music from the dance and vice versa as Odissi refers to the simultaneous curvilinearity in lyric and motility.

The solo dancing body cultivates focus distilling individuated influences from text, music, and movement into a distilled pattern of garnering attention and communicating to an audience. Choreographic impetus lies in garnering that focus across multiple music and movement patterns and dramatic arcs either supported with a textual appendage or emotionally generated without the use of any explicit text. Scholar Rosella Simonari notes how literature was used to develop poetics as well as personality in American modern dance (2019). Text is integral to the creative process as the choreographer often derives inspiration from the literary and the literal word for movement innovation as well as creating dramatic arcs in the piece. Odissi is textually guided in terms of its technical nuances as laid out in ancient and medieval texts or in using a vast plethora of literary works in its choreographic renditions. Oriya and Sanskrit are most commonly used languages although Hindi, Bengali, English, Marathi, and other regional Indian languages have also been used. Dance and literature[2] are intimately connected in the curvilinear kinesthetic folds as symbolic imagery simultaneously invokes the cognitive and the evocative. Musicologist Itishree Sahoo questions a simplistic adaptation of Odissi dance to music outside the *Samprada*, that is music that does not maintain cultural integrity across the triad of song, music, and dance. She notes how songs in regional languages *Mythili* and *Brjbhasa* can claim allegiance to medieval Oriya lyric, noting that she is not proposing unnecessary conservativism and rigidity. She urges for thoughtful experimentations instead of violently imposing music from other genres onto the dance.

Text is often a semiotic device in the composition as the symbolic is codified in hand gestures, a prior knowledge of which enables a smoother viewing experience. Julia Ayau, who navigated both Western concert as well as Odissi dance training during her undergraduate thesis project, predicts that "in presenting Odissi dance to non-Indians, the archetypal emotions and universal themes may be readable, but the precise symbolism will be lost on those not familiar with Indian culture" (2017, 5). In the concluding essay of the anthology *Migrations of Gesture*, editors Carried Noland and Sally Ann Ness note how in the conditioning of linguistic symbolism, which builds as a skill after sustained training and engagement, "gesture itself is not under attack" in the context of democratizing communication (2008, 275). An array of meanings accompanies any single gesture with context-specific usage alongside the dancer's emotional residues, colors the particular context of presentation. South Asian performance studies scholar Ketu Katrak writes how gestural usage goes beyond the literally signified since it borders on the metaphorical, the evocative, and the inspiring. Katrak notes how codified gestures function as precision as well as evocative tools in representing and depicting cultural contexts (2001). Beyond the semiotic and the symbolic, gestural signification also borders upon the creative. This has been noted especially in the choreographic repurposing of gesture by Astad Deboo as a sinewy intervention of its own and not as a tool of substitution (Katrak 2024).

The role of text in evoking emotion has been explored within the choreographic ethos of the artist. The meaning communicated through gestural symbolism when imbued with the emotional resonance continues to invoke and inspire. Universality of emotion needs to be the sounding base on which the literary can be built through gestural signification. Signification achieves its efficacy once the distinctive embodiment of the dancer has contemplated upon, processed through, and distilled via expressive modalities. Actions, moods, emotions, events, ideas, personifications, and characterizations parallel the literal overtones through the choreographic process as oriented in space and time. The poetic rhythm of the text ruffles with the vibrations of the air disturbing the dancer's space-time continuum in order to achieve choreographic efficacy (Meglin and Brooks 2016). Different choreographers place text in differing valence—invoking emotion, infusing psychological monologuing, or inviting cognitive analysis—although scriptwriting has become an important artistic endeavor in Odisha. Odissi dancer and writer Ranjana Dave notes how choreography operates within a particular stylistic ethos for individual choreographers (2016). In Dave's words, "the ethos of a form, however, is a highly individualistic concept, which wildly varies in scope and meaning for each artiste attempting to capture it" (99).

The iconic *Ashtapadis* (eight-versed songs) from the Sanskrit text *Gitagovinda* are a musical inspiration for many choreographers (Miller 1984). This text is held at great reverence in the canon given its cultural importance as ritual accompaniment in the Jagannath temple in Puri (Kothari 1981). Evocative imagery, intricate rhythms, and devotional intensity lend to a rich repertoire for the embodiment of subtle emotions of love, separation, longing, and union (Citaristi 2022). The text is simultaneously a literary-religious touchstone but also a living performative text shaping the emotional core of movement. The literary compositional technique of *Champu* (combination of prose and poetry) as penned by Oriya poets Baladeba Ratha, Banamali Dasa, and Dinakrushna Das are also literary adaptations in Odissi. Eighteenth-century composition *Kishorachandrananda Champu* by poet Baladeba Ratha narrates a love story in thirty-four songs, one for each consonant (Dennen 2014). Sculptural precision merges with evocative expression across musical and literary influences. Geometric clarity grounds the form in ritual resonance while being a vehicular containment of mining infinite emotional depth. Visual harmony amplifies emotive intensity transcending the binary of form and feeling, presenting a dance language where technical rigor and emotional resonance exist in perfect reciprocity.

Solo choreography can be understood as a dynamic dialogue between the choreographer and the dancer, where artistic vision meets interpretive embodiment. Choreographic structure, motif, rhythm, and thematic intention are negotiated with physical vocabulary, emotional depth, and lived experience. The solo form heightens this dialogue, as the dancer becomes both interpreter and cocreator, making choices about phrasing, emphasis, and nuance. Choreography becomes a dialogical process across lineage and individuality as inherited structures open space for personal voice—both transmission and presence deepen the choreographic framework. In traditions like Odissi and other classical forms, this dialogue honors both lineage and individuality, showing how solo choreography can simultaneously preserve inherited structures and open space for personal voice.

Yet, subtle infiltration of meaning along multiple registers becomes the unifying ethos in solo dancing. The representation of content is stylized via formal acuity, which draws forth the primary intent of blurring binary distinctions. However, the content that is traditionally drawn from relies on a heteronormative and conservative schematic that, by definition, retains a jarring, casteist, and exclusionary gate-keeping for the gender and sexually nonconforming. As a critical dance studies scholar, this text does a disservice given its inability to address caste. However, that is a distinct book project of its that discusses caste questions through a detailed investigation across specific historical episodic formation alongside the contemporary practices that continue to propagate the curvilinearity on a global scale. In a sequel to this title, *Shaping S-Curves: Choreographic Process in Odissi*, I will focus on the presence of dance in the incipient stages of the formation of an Oriya ethos and consciousness. Coauthoring with poet, journalist, and scriptwriter Kedar Mishra, I will focus on *Utkal Sammelani*. It is an organization founded in Cuttack in 1882 by social reformer Madhusudan Das to fortify Odishan cultural heritage alongside its economic development. In a book-length inquiry, Mishra and I will look at the contextual folds subsumed within the historical formation of the curvilinearity of the form as we know. The promise of freedom from its own created shackles continues to elude formal strictures and creative departures in Odissi. As a scholar, I infuse the promise of freedom afforded to itself by the last canonical repertoire, which is *Moksha*.

Kinesthetic Pause

Sculptural, musical, and verbal meaning-making gain synergy in the act of choreographic meaning-making. Typically moving between moments of physical stillness, the sculpture retains its individuality. Phrasing, structures, and motifs ebb and flow with musicality and lyrical cadence. The sonorous adopts the cognitive and emotional in its sung lyric. The textual realm also provides the grounds of shaping meaning. However, the overall synergy is provided by the adoption of the imagined audience in the flow of the composition.

A combination of being, doing, and communicating, the work of the choreographer lies in effective communication of the intent and the purpose of the piece at hand. The choreographer operates within a field of posture and gesture. With appropriate physical movement and codified gesture, the communication that is usually achieved requires a certain familiarity with the codes and conventions of the technique. The choreographer's efficacy depends upon how well the dancer is able to use the variety of modalities to communicate. The kinesthetic presence of the dancer complements the visual signification and the didactic checking-in such that the audience has a variety of material and modalities to latch on to throughout the performance. The dancer simultaneously has the burden of describing a scene, personifying and enacting dialogical communication between the characters, and being in the dance across sensory, mental, contemplative, visual, and kinesthetic registers. Communicative efficacy relies on the use of a riveting gaze in order to check-in with as well as direct the audience toward aesthetic objectives or a narrative phenomenon. This prior admission of an audience's presence is then enfolded into the choreographic folds of the dancing body. In order for the artist to switch registers, the exteriorization of the performance functions independently, sequentially, and simultaneously with the interiorization of the movement material. This implies that the artist has to employ the sensory and mental faculties, focus, and visual abd kinesthetic registers in order to be, to perform, and to communicate.

The code-switching between the exterior and the interior, requires the dancer to engage the sensory facilities. In her chapter-length inquiry, "Considering a Sensory Paradigm for Odissi Dance," artist-scholar Sabina Sweta Sen-Postawska notes how the sensory inputs processed by the dancer in real-time determine the communicative potential of the choreographer (2016). Listening in movement has also been investigated in research positionality by ethnographer Sally Gardner (2012). Listening in dance and listening with dance are important activities for both the choreographer and the dancer as the role of the audience reception is presupposed in the folds of the art. Choreography does not happen in a communicative vacuum. Rather the role of reception is integrally folded within the curvilinear arcs of gesture and meaning-making. For example, in Guru Aruna Mohanty's *Abhinaya* composition *Madhave Ma Kuru Manini Mana Maye* there is a moment when the solo dancer personifies a particular entity, dialogues with another character, enacts the self's engagement with a dramatic thought, and finally, communicates with the audience self-doubt and certainty at the same time.[3] This demonstrates the layered nature of communication that also implies signification and abstraction in the same vein. It depends upon the dancer's ability to focus, which translates into the audience's ability to do the same. The choreographic genius lies within this layered nature of communication where text, music, and movement all function toward a contemplative focal point.

The crux of the choreographic process lies within the diffusion of the discrete elements that constitute a particular work. Text, music, and movement combine during the compositional process to portray the performative emergence of a new work. The text might emerge from an established canon or from the choreographer's personal explorations of the world. Similarly, the music and the movement also have their bearing in traditional fields of Odissi music and dance technique, respectively, with occasional artistic departures from the Odishan topographical and cultural landscape (Gochhayat 2016). These discrete elements interweave to activate the imagination of the choreographer. The interweaving occurs in a way where the individual elements—text, music, and movement—lose their identifiable characteristics. Musicality, embodied flow, and linguistic meaning-making enmeshe completely to bring to focus the communicative quality of the dance. The information—textual, musical, or movement-based—as processed by the dancing body communicates choreographic quirks. The discreteness of the various elements due to their embodied processing brings to attention a distillation of sorts. This distillation across multiple constituents make room for a complete surrender to the act of choreography. The solo dancer realizes this choreography through such a surrendered control, presence, focus, and communicative efficacy. The processing is one of being-doing where the combination is the basis of the communication to the audience. The control of movement and thought remains as important as the stamina to remain in a bent-knee posture, demanded by the square and S-shaped postures. Interiorization by the dancing body of the discrete elements then lead to a distilled focus by the artist. This is the end goal of the choreography as the subjectivities of the choreographer and the dancer blur along with the blurring of the text, music, and movement. I argue that the conviction reached by the dance-artist after processing of musculature, sensory inputs, mental focus, and the exteriorized performance navigates toward a communication of the choreography that then becomes a merger of interiorized intensities of text, music, and movement. What we see on stage is this conviction of the artist bringing into presence a distillation of multiple elements through a combination of being-doing-communicating. Reflexivity by the dancer and the audience together constitute the communicative efficacy of the choreography. The following few paragraphs are dedicated to investigating this reflexivity that requires a certain physical pause, but this moment is far from stillness. Rather, it is an active processual function of resolving across textual, rhythmic, and sculptural meaning-making and transitioning.

The self-reflexive addresses the exteriorization and the interiorization of content where the dance offers a unique medium of lived and creative embodiment garnering material from both in the act of weaving multiplicity (Kieft 2014). Music, text, thematic content, and postural coding provide the multiple elements that are blurred within a self-reflexive churning. The pause, in this case, if specially focused on an embodied mapping: a mind-body integration cultivating a sense of presence. One can possibly argue that cultivating presence is impossible given the multiple layering that functions in the moving body. In any given instant, one has to remember the previous phrase or remind oneself about the one to come. While this is true, the pause originates the space-time. In this way, the dancing body creates its own schemata of temporal and spatial progression. The dancer's ever-present openness to feelings, images, emotions, and a holistic being allow for the pause to function as a presentist act of wholeness (Margolin 2014). Inspired to weave *yoga*, a self-reflexive somatic idiom, into the communicative idiom of Odissi, dancer Reela Hota's *Atmamukti* (1996) choregraphed by Guru Kelucharan Mohapatra and composed by Rajan Sajan Mishra, maps the journey of the self toward ultimate freedom (Sharda 2007). Combining the self as perceived, sensed, enacted, felt, experienced, and projected, this work is one example where blurring takes precedence as the creative embodiment stands as a metaphor for the deeper philosophical insight (Ghosh 2024). Blurring programs to a greater degree, mindfulness presence than aesthetic nuancing characteristic of other kinds of pausing as shown below (Kumar 2013).

Choreographic ethos lies within sensitivity to detail where the nuances of meaning—implied in the poems or movement phrasing and shaping—result from an embodied ability to manifest the immediate, the felt, the sensate, and the energetic. Shapes and texts are only points of entry for the choreographer, whose primary strength lies within their stylistic distillation to carve out a dramatic arc. It is often said how prominent solo artists, Balaswaraswati and Kelucharan Mohapatra among many others, would revel in repetition of a particular content-theme in innumerable imaginative variants (Coorlawala 1996). These artists deal with choreography as structured improvisation as the musical variation inspires multiple interpretations. According to artist and scholar Uttara Asha Coorlawala, "repetition of the same line does not move the action further into the plot as in Western drama, each repetition clarifies and intensifies a prescribed emotional environment, that of the dominant mood" (1996, 153). Between units that are repeated, there remains a moment of respite; a pause where the distillation of each repetition is allowed to congeal. It is an infinitesimal moment, but its gravitas is communicated in choreographic intent and performative clarity. In *Choreographic Empathy: Kinesthesia in Performance*, dance studies theorist Susan Leigh Foster questions the immediate connectivity across the body of the dancer and the observer noting its mediation via sociocultural mores (2010). Studying choreography, sensation, and empathic connections from the 1700s to the contemporary era, Foster notes the changing valence of dance and corporeality. While Foster's provocation problematizes my choreographic supposition of a monolithic artistic reception, I noted above how the creative ethos in the case of Odissi solo compositions internalizes sensation and empathy into its choreographic folds to perhaps, diminish the otherwise material and abstract distance between the dance and the audience. The creativity lies in such an ability to spin, distill, stylize, and dream where the evaluative criteria lie in receptive deepening of intensity, focus, and presence. The content blurs out in the performative manifestation of the choreographic through the communicative.

Even though communication is a presupposed breaking down of the fourth wall for the dancer, the content of communication is secondary to the formal embodiment (Turner 1963). Kinesthetic embodiment of the material does not communicate the literary or the musical content (Schnepel 2012). Rather, the sensate, the dramatic, the distilled, and the blurred emerge from the performer to touch the viewer in evocative ways. According to veteran artist Madhavi Mudgal, it is necessary to inculcate the evocative through music, text, as well as production elements. Mudgal holds onto her training in the S-curve that keeps the central median alive from the top of the head to the middle of the feet. As an early generation artist, she laments the exaggerated shifts of the torso in contemporary works. She focuses on the languid S-shapes fueling transitions between phrases and sections. *Tapoi* adapts a famous poem in Oriya homes to music by Maheshwar Raut. It is a *Navakshari* poem where nine letters are grouped together. Expressive movement is woven in ensemble work where multiple clusters engage in dialogue with one another or with the audience. Mudgal likes to focus on the abstract fluidity that choreography makes possible. She does not create dance-dramas with specified characters setting in motion a fluidity across persona and subjectivity even in narrative content such as *Tapoi*. The gaze is important in this regard where the act of communication is actively woven into the kinesthetic organization. *Drishti* or the focused gaze primarily for maintaining focus and balance partners with *Darshan* that means a relational viewing or visualization. The entire choreographic act is a balancing act from one to the other. Depending upon the internalized or the externalized valence of the choreography, the work balances *Drishti-Darshan* in a dialogical back and forth.

Both sculpture as noun and sculpting as verb, share an intimate connectivity with Odissi dance that is known for its lived connections with Odissi. Artist and scholar Rekha Tandon analyzes geometric alignment across sculpture and the dancing body, noting the seminal importance of the central axis and its afforded degrees of freedom in motion (2023). Independent scholar studies the growth of secular female sculpture called *Alasa Kanyas* (languid females) in Odisha discussed in the Orissan text on temple architecture, Shilpa Prakasha of Ramachandra Mahapatra Kaula Bhattaraka (Sharman 2020). The corner niches of the temples had the *Alasa Kanyas* almost as a decorative program. Profusion of such imagery is attributed to the Shakta cult in Orissa (Dora 2002). The Shilpa Prakasha illustrates sixteen types of maidens, listed below, the study of which has informed my choreographic pursuit with undergraduate student populations in the United States (Sarkar 2019).

1. *Torana* (one forming an arch)
2. *Mugdha* (the innocent)
3. *Manini* (the offended)
4. *Dalamalika* (holding a branch like a garland)
5. *Padmagandha* (smelling the lotus)
6. *Darpana* (holding a mirror)
7. *Vinyasa* (the well-groomed)
8. *Ketakibharana* (one wearing ketaki blossom)
9. *Matrmurti* (the mother)
10. *Chamara* (one holding a fly whisk)
11. *Gunthana* (the one who hides herself)
12. *Nartaki* (dancer)
13. *Shukasarika* (One playing with a parrot)
14. *Nupurpadika* (one wearing anklets)
15. *Mardala* (drummer)
16. *Alasa Kanya* (indolent maiden)

Sculpture brings in physical stasis as a direct materiality of embodied stillness in movement (Berkson 2000). Odishan sculpture has been studied by several theorists although a detailed exposition of sculpture and Odissi is yet to be studied in a systematic way (Donaldson 2023).

Embodiment of flexibility, flow, and arches make the movement particularly interdisciplinary. Interdisciplinarity is also demonstrated in parity across psychological complexities as behavioral and personality driven mannerisms find their dynamism in motion. Movement is drawn from a variety of vegetal and floral references (such as holding a branch, or smelling or wearing a flower) as well as establishing relationship with animals (i.e., playing with a parrot) (Phyu 2004). Ornamentation as well as instrumentation remain powerful metaphors as images of anklets, drums, mirrors, and fly whisks find their way into movement motifs. Explicit mention of a dancer, *Narthaki* foregrounds the interdisciplinarity across the embodied and the stone sculpture even further.

Rhythm in dance is particular to intentional choreographic embodiment that brings to bear the minded activity of the dancing body, patterns of beats in music, and alignment of the spinal articulation (Bresnahan 2019). The name for rhythm, *Tala* also refers to a measure in sculpture noting how the same definition encompasses quantitative organizing of time and space. Physical pauses in movement often are used for spinal realignment as well as musical resolution like a *Tihai*, which is a repetition of a rhythmic phrase three times. Rhythmic resolutions in the form of *Tihai* adopt a pause in the movement that remains parallel to the choreography. However, as shown here, pauses are also adopted with choreographic liberty where dynamism in embodied movement creates intentional silencing that are often occurring with musical accompaniment. Silence in movement and that in music is a traditional construct that is still adopted by many.

Mudgal prefers pure dance (*Nritta*) through its technical and choreographic interplay with musical innovation. Her *Vistaar* (2023) uses the technical progression of the music to suture movement. Mudgal's choreography manifests patiently like the unfolding of a *Raga*, uncluttered of verbal meaning-making, while being infused with rich musical symbolism. Mudgal prefers the formal resolution with musicality across melody and rhythm as a traditional engagement with *Nritta* (Ibrahim 2024). Through gradual unfolding where movement often partners with stillness and qualitative efficacy. Four is stalky while seven has more fluidity in Mudgal's imagination as it applies to body proportions. Enlivening the negative space within the *Tala*, that is, the fractional moment of silence, perhaps, emanates from a subconscious with prior training in architecture. Rhythmic cycles inspire onstage geometric structures as she uses four dancers along a square shape to present a percussive segment in *Ekatali*'s four-beat structure (Brown 1985). Rhythm's place continues to remain integral to the music composition, choreography, and performance as each instills newer degrees of freedom and poise that weave into the dynamic adaptation.

As a corollary, melody introduces another layer of processing as a slow, unmetered introduction starts exploring from lower to upper musical registers with or without percussive pulse. Choreography adds its own intentional choice whether to glide over or accent time using gestural flow or percussive footwork, respectively. Pauses of the melodic impulse might not be as imperceptible as the rhythmically accented ends. Movement builds momentum of its own stylizing in preferred modes with repeated drone-like strokes of the *Jhala* (fast-paced rhythmic section) or the pulsating unmetered *Jhor* (a developmental musical mode between the free-flowing introduction and the highly rhythmic *Jhala*). Momentum, intensity, and high-energy climactic resolutions are restructured in choreographic scaffolding (Alfonso et al. 2022). Musical modes and proliferations find their nuanced detailing in a moving commentary as kinesthetic pauses take on the role of registering the melodic being into the folds and patterns of dance. The entire gamut of melody—from the invocatory melodic improvisation to the climactic fast-paced conclusions—is woven into embodied complexities as footwork and gestural embodiment establish signatory amulets of choreographic aura (Ram 2011).

The choreographic pause as channeled kinesthetically by the dancer is as much an exercise in mindful being as it is in physical materiality. Movement for movement's sake is beyond the scope of traditional solo dancing where the tradition of music, text, and dance technique resolve to a climactic tension. However, resolution of each individually or the three tied together occurs in not just physical resettling and reorienting, but also mental processing. Use of punctuations and conjunctions in grammatical sentence construction could be a close second to this organization of thoughtful content. Movement is simultaneously changing registers—from the verbal to the melodic, from the abstract to textual. In these cases, cognitive unloading of existing thoughts in order to reengage with subsequent performative processes become a central mechanism of creative resolution across pluralistic influences (Deshmukh 2013). Such a mental reorganizing helps in retargeting of attention of both the dancer and the viewer as presupposed within the choreographic process. This spiraling back of focusing power presupposes a proposed diminution of mental noise where signals relating to gesture, posture, and footwork, can activate sequential choreographic structures. Creative interweaving of an aesthetic of meditative reflexivity allows for the dance to remain present (Litfin 2020). Thus, the kinesthetic pause presupposes a mental poise—one that does not always result in physical stasis.

In a way, solo choreography presupposes the kinetic, aesthetic, cognitive, and physical dimensions of movement where changes in thought patterns are of equal importance to changes in musculature. Affective influences of ritual service complement literary analyses of medieval texts for choreographer and soloist Rahul Acharya. Ethnographic research inside the Jagannath Temple, where the ritual singing of Jayadeva's *Gitagovinda* occurs as a daily ritual, becomes a crucial element in his choreographic creation of the *Ashtapadis*. Acharya partners his affective ritualization with a literary analysis of multiple commentaries by Sridhara, Raghava Bhatta, Kumbha Rana, Jagannatha Pramoda, Vishvanatha, Narayana Tirtha, Krishnadeva Yati, Gopalakavi, Caitanyadasa, and Sankara Misra on the *Gitagovinda* across literary, devotional, philosophical, and theological interpretations. Both the literary interpretation and the affective ritualization of the text inform Acharya's choreographic oeuvre. Acharya's foray into saint poetess Mirabai's songs takes him to western Indian state of Rajasthan. Acharya's penchant for the affective takes his research into the museums and temples of the western Indian state of Rajasthan, especially in the Govindji Temple where an interaction with the head priest becomes a key determining factor in the choreographic process. To imbibe the life of Mirabai, he engages with the Manganiyar sect who are Muslim bards rendering Mirabai's songs (Carr-Richardson 2002). Acharya's immersion within content is an act of distillation from a place of phenomenological, cognitive, affective, emotional, and intellectual churning (Martin 2010). Overall, the kinesthetic pause infiltrates the multitude through code-switching, blurring, distilling, sieving, unloading, and decluttering in the choreographic canon of solo movement.

Unpacking of choreographic intent, formalist practices, and meaning reveals the communicative catalyst behind the organization of movement content. Movement is infused with communicative intent as a marker of acknowledging the presence of the viewer. Centering of focus through the gaze brings back the choreographic arc to a mode of exchange. This does not entail linearity of content or mere storytelling. The dance, quite contrarily, creates intensities and dramatic arcs. These remain the crux of impressionable content that the vehicular embodiment of the dancer imprints upon through a real-time communicative inspiration. Even if the dance is performed in vacuum, actions emerge around a range emotional surges to ensure that a dramatic arc registers through effective nonverbal communication. Gesture is paramount in this mode of being, doing, and communicating. Gestural codification is a rich tapestry of semiotic information encoded in three folds of the major limbs (head, hands, chest, sides, waist, feet), the subsidiary limbs (shoulders, arms, back, belly, thighs, shanks), and the minor parts (primarily face and extremities: eyes, eyebrows, cheeks, nose, lips, tongue, jaw, chin, as well as fingernails, ankles, and toes). Hand gestures with elaborate unfolding of the palms, fingers, wrists, forearms, and upper arms remain central to the symbolic and the codified condensation of verbal information.

Yet, the sensory impulses of the choreographer as well as the dancer infuse the movement with vitality, leaving traces not just in the bodies implicated by the artistic creation but also its reception. The audience's embodiment is encoded within the social communication that gesture entails right from the moment of its inception. Kinesthetic pause, in this case, refers to the moment of imprinting—one that leaves a trace in the body that registers in memory of the dance and by interpolation in the choreographer, the dancer, and the audience. The triad remains true throughout the creative process even though the audience is not present in the room during the creation of a piece. I am reminded of dance ethnologist Deidre Sklar's theorizing of the term *kinetic vitality* where she examines the gesture for its sensory, social, and cultural dimensions as it leaves a mnemonic trace in the body (2008).

Kinetic vitality of each verbal injunction partners with a simultaneity of being-doing and communicating. The gaze riveted at the center, where departures from it mandate an equal and opposite oscillating return, is the fulcrum of the situated viewer, one that is disembodied, abstracted, and absorbed into the performativity of the dancer. The mental chatter is visible on the facial expression as dialogical communication with the characters in the dance interspersed with the centered gaze for regular check-ins with the unknown, yet ever-present object of communication. The dance is an oscillating dialogue with the recipients although this communication has its own rhythm. This oscillating return introduces slight pauses in between thought experiments and embodied shapes as the text, poetic departure, and meaning-making take precedence above all else.

Virtuosic potential measured through the ability of emotive exuberance driving home a *kinetic vitality* differentiates an amateur from a seasoned artist. There is a combination of figurative abstraction and nonfigurative somatic awareness that is crucial for the *Abhinaya* portion of the repertoire. The move away from the established semiotic and the signified to the abstracted somatic and embodied is the moment of release. This release aids the process of communication and universalization of the particular emotional arc to the abstracted dramatic intensity. The felt somatic moment is the kinesthetic trace that simultaneously touches both the dancer and the viewer. Viewership as premeditated into the folds of the dance opens up the notion of a release from the figurative to the nonfigurative. Shapes, steps, patterns, texts, and words etch themselves onto the kinetic sensations of the dancer. While the ocular objectification of the art by the artist—for example, glancing sideways to communicate shyness or constricting the eye muscles to portray eerie ominousness—is the first step. It leads to the concomitant release from the visual to the kinesthetic through proprioceptive awareness—embodied awareness of the body in space-time continuum (Barlow 2018). The text is as important as the feeling, which is generated as much from muscle memory as from being-doing in the present. For example, the act of smelling a flower is partnered with the actual sensory exercise of inhalation. Bringing together imagining a floral smell with visualizing the garden in which the smell emerges, presents the virtual, the phenomenological, and the semiotic in the same vein. Sklar notes the importance of acknowledging and theorizing the somatic memory: "just as the sensations that arise for dancers during performance are virtual, in the sense of being both spontaneous—as immediate affects—and also resulting from a temporal displacement, so too is bodily memory virtual, occurring, intentionally or not, as both immediate sensation and, as a migration of somatic memory over time" (2008, 89). The universal achieved through the release of the *kinetic vitality* from the amplification of the contextualized is simultaneously embodied mnemonic traces as well as culturally and socio-politically structured and mediated. I do not assume a singular landing of meaning-making onto either the artist or the audience. However, it must be noted how the proprioceptive release of the figurative into the nonfigurative remains at the thrust of the somatic trace releasing the artist from the particular contents of the artwork at display through embodied signification and tracing (Çelik et al. 2022). In a way, the content is immaterial. What remains, is the kinesthetic imprint through the space-time motility in choreographic thought and action.

Built on a triad of emergence, stabilizing, and destruction, a cyclicality of life is proposed with the contemplative centering of the body-mind complex, which is the primary focus of the choreographic meaning-making. Dance becomes one with the dancer. Silence folds into stillness and a lack of physical movement transposes onto reducing mental activity. The face calms down; the gaze is toward the ground beneath reducing the infinitude of the ecological embedding of the dancer into the unidirectional capacity of the riveted gaze. As I close this section, I wish to reiterate that the scope of the dancing body can be summarized as a practice of focus. Stillness of the body-mind complex seems to be a necessary ingredient for such a contemplative state. The last element of the repertoire prioritizes this contemplative focus as the mental weaving and the physicality of patterned embodiment engage in a duet of reflexivity. Limitations of the embodied engage with the mentally imagined, dreamed, and gathered as the dance becomes an experiential outpouring of the residue. The physical maps onto the thought-out and vice versa. The audience experiences the aftermath of that incessantly cyclical encounter. This last element of the Odissi canon calls for a cessation of the cyclical and we see the paralleling of the body and the mind. The three postures of the yogic pose *Virabhadrasana* (also known as a warrior pose) at the concluding end of *Moksha* light up the possibility of freedom, where freedom is not defined as an escape *from*; it is defined as an escape *in*. The body and the mind parallel one another as the dancer becomes one with the dance. The phenomenological, the sensory, the proprioceptive, the cognitive, the emotional, and the physical merge within the riveting of the gaze as the repertoire ensures a promise of liberation across the socially mandated or the culturally prescribed or even the transnationally presupposed. The choreographic ethos of the dancing body is a journey into experiential awareness of the self. The transmission of this awareness to a larger public engenders a curvilinear mapping of the space-time continuum. This larger weaving reaches the final goal of a parallel dance between silencing the still, on the one hand, and stilling the silence, on the other as I refer to the silencing and stilling to both the body and mind at various moments in the temporal teleological progression.

The dance, in this regard, cannot be thought of in isolation of the dancing body, justifying my prerogative of investigating the solo performance. In this case, the term choreography functions metonymically for the etching of the originary creator. But the loss of translation is apparent. The person on whom the choreography has been commissioned at a particular historical encounter or on whom the choreographer has worked for a long duration to sequentially bring in changes into the work, has the most access to what Sklar would call the *kinetic vitality* of the piece. Durational engagement with a solo work and its eventual processing through constant practice and analytical tools bring forth the efficacy. In that state, one can see the freedom within the dance (Smith 2008).

Arc-ing Up Before Quieting Down

The canonical repertoire maintains a bell-shaped arc in affective intensity rising to a crescendo during the third traditional element which is the *Pallavi* (musical proliferations). The arc goes upward from *Mangalacharan* (invocation) to *Batu* (foundation) to eventually reach its climactic association in *Pallavi.* The affective arc comes down through *Abhinaya* (expressional movement) and meets its contemplative stasis in *Moksha* (liberation). The reaching of a crescendo and its eventual dissolution draws from the philosophical basis of freedom in and even from dance, making the form simply an exploration of degrees of physical, emotive, psychological, and performance openness. As noted earlier, participatory attention of the audience remains woven within these folds of movement and performance. Body, breathwork, and imagination create the foundational impetus for empathy and resilience as emotional congealing bring together the performative and the receptive dimensions. Precision and interpretation are not just the only modes of communicative engagement as the dance also weaves in an entire world of affective imagery. Melodic modes, or the *Ragas*, bring a certain underlying mood to the piece bringing the dance work with its multiple precise (rhythm-related) and interpretative (text-related) liberties into an organic whole (Holland 2013). The percussionist's rhythmic tally on the *Mardala* (the two-headed drum used to accompany Odissi dance), matches the footwork as complex mathematical structures are brought to bear through the feet. A strong communicative and collaborative impulse is there from the beginning of the compositional process and until the end of the performance with a live audience. For these reasons, the compositional process requires both the rhythm and the melody composer from the very outset (Mason 2012). For example, choreographer and percussionist Guru Kelucharan Mohapatra and composer and violinist Bhubaneswar Mishra have produced a plethora of compositions that form the basis of the Odissi canon. With the compositional dialogue, the choreographer etches thought, inspiration, and motivation onto a soloist. Movement for movement's sake is absent in the traditional repertoire as the collaborative and the communicative injunctions marry melody, rhythm, choreography, and dancing (Minton 2017). They journey through a period of constant back and forth in order to realize a final composition.

Kinesthetic structures are built on such an exchange of music and dance where the regional remain integral to the larger performance. Regional sonorous flavor of Odisha color the lilting aural scape of Odissi as music traditions of *Champu* and Jayadev's *Gitagovinda* shape compositional choices in dance (Pradhan 2017). Rekha Tandon notes the primal importance of sound emphasizing that the split of dance and music as separate disciplines in Western academia is often unhelpful in the rendering of Odissi (Stepputat and Djebbari 2020). Musical instrumentation—sitar, violin, flute, drums, metal cymbals—accompany parallel to the dancing body in conventional performance as the dancer's footwork often articulates the same rhythmic stresses that the percussion provides. While playing a significant role in the creative process, music requires a dialogical and relational back and forth between choreographers and composers.[4] Melodic contours of the melodic modes translate into expressive gestures. Torso movements, eye work, and hand gestures parallel the rise and fall of melodic lines. Choreographers expand upon a basic motif in dance—mirroring the improvisatory nature of music. Rhythmic energy, melodic mood, and expressive gesture coalesce into a single performative whole as artists resort to analyses, transcriptions, and notations by different partners: music composers, scriptwriters, choreographers, and dancers (Kar 2013).

The sung lyric holds importance; the poetic journey intersperses with the choreographer's intent as if the latter was a commentary on the former. Immersing in the context, connotation, history, and historical period of the poetic text renders the choreographic process an experiential traversing of time and space. In order to satisfy the creative urge in the dance field, artists make significant lifestyle choices, which points to the immersive nature of such an experiential aesthetics. US-born artist Sharon Lowen has lived over fifty years in India as a celebrated Odissi dancer under the tutelage of Guru Kelucharan Mohapatra. With a background and terminal degree in modern dance, she chose to live in India for her creative urge and ease of access to music. "I like to keep things within their own tradition," says Lowen, as she avoids bringing her two core disciplines, modern dance and Odissi, together (Mohanty 2023). Culturally specific instrumentation with a realistic flair of linguistic diction is important to supplement this dialogical back and forth across dance and music. Indigenous lilting musicality brings in alignment between the emotion and the melodic mode bound by a set of rules on progression and improvisation. Alignment allows for the merging of the dancing form with the performed content.

In addition to alignment, abstraction and intensification further diversify the choreographic process in relationship with literal meaning-making apprehending the rich literary tradition of Odisha (Samantaray and Nayak 2015). Just as the S-curve has definite points of inflexion, the narrative and the choreographic arc dissect and intersect with one another for effective storytelling. Choreographers Aruna Mohanty and Ileana Citaristi have a philosophical ethos guiding the choreographic oeuvre. While Citaristi's foray in choreography is through philosophical abstraction, Mohanty works through intensification of ideation. Emotional self-reflexivity guides Mohanty's creative process from start to finish as Citaristi's haunting imagistic inspiration makes way into a narrative visualization in dance. Elaborating upon the overall choreographic ethos as well as specific productions, the section below shows how Mohanty and Citaristi forge a philosophical agenda in dance through creative adaptation of scripting in dance. Kedar Mishra and Devdas Chhotray have been celebrated for their scriptwriting for Aruna Mohanty, and Ileana Citaristi, respectively.

Text is often indicative of larger philosophical and ideological underpinnings as Mishra's democratic politics is reflected in his scriptwriting. Mishra's scriptwriting emerges from a philosophical impulse of transforming the linear narrative depiction within Odissi. Thematic exploration of ideational multitude from text, experience, sociopolitical or personal crisis results in explication through embodied codes and symbolism that transcends time and linguistic boundaries. In his work *Eko Prosna* (2020) with Aruna Mohanty, Mishra deals with existential problems (Mohanty 2023). Fighting for gender equality, Mishra envisions women from across historical and mythical time walking together in their respective existential struggle. Mishra's liberal democratic ideology informs his work as he notes the democratic ethos of scriptwriting since choreographic imagination, rhythmic progression, and musicality engage with creative writing. Thus, scriptwriting remains a cooperative, communal, and collaborative affair through dialogue with the music composer, choreographer, and dancers. Inspired from Kumudini Lakhia and Chandralekha's multilayered, multidimensional, and multi-textual storytelling, Mishra wants to push Odissi's technical boundaries with new ideas and themes such that the deeply local Odissi dancing body can speak to global human crises. Mishra navigates the democratic alchemical possibilities of script and choreography across choreographic retention of Odissi's sensitivity and sensibility.

Poet Devdas Chhotray, in his scripting for Ileana Citaristi, notes that choreography lies in resolving and blending the technical precepts and the literary-ideational-narrative arc. Devdas Chhotray is a well-known lyricist in the Odisha movie industry. He writes scripts for Ileana Citaristi having begun with *Mahanadi* (2008) and over the years worked on *Karuna* (2010), *Kala* (2012), *Siddhartha* (2014), *Akshara* (2016), and *Refugee* (2018). These are ensemble evening-length group productions using scenic sets, props, lighting, and media projections in the backdrop. *Siddhartha* (2014) is inspired by Herman Hesse's book of the same name. Citaristi used an English translation of the original work in German for her research. Using Citaristi's artistic vision, choreographic outline, and inputs on the various acts, Chhotray transformed the book in prose to poetry that was then adopted in dance. The choreographer imagines the sketch of the production and shares it with Chhotray who creates poetry in Oriya that is then musically composed for choreography. While the choreographer holds the strings of the overall narrative arc, the poet has to fill in verses in the various sections. The narrative arc for *Siddhartha* is nonlinear traversing the river of time with a goal of self-realization across familial, ascetic, and sensual dimensions of life. Using the analogy of the river, this production drives home the importance of the present. The river has no past nor future and is present only in the now. The river goes toward the vastness of the ocean pregnant with history but with one purpose. *Siddhartha* ends on a spiritual note superimposing the transformation of Siddhartha to Gautama Buddha to the secret of the river. Choreographic choices depicting the inside turmoil of Siddhartha as he goes through different phases of life, indulging in Vedic chanting, complete asceticism, and sensual indulgence (including that of self-realization) are visualized through the contortions of a male dancer around a pole (Citaristi 2021). Ensemble choreography depicts

Siddhartha's being in pleasure as Chhotray's poetics display in musical—percussive, lyrical, and melodious—elaborations. The narrative of *Siddhartha* is built choreographically across musical transitions and poetic phrases centering the bending of the S. Chhotray is principally responsible for the narration as well. Narration has gaps, and just as in film, the choreographer has the prerogative of advancing the arc through the building of the S, that is, the filling up of the narrative arc by choreography.

Both Mohanty and Citaristi acknowledge how their autobiographical inspiration, intellectual discomfort, and mental disquietude germinate their choreography. The time spent with the thinkers is as critical as that with the musicians. The story-boarding session with the musicians communicates the way the choreographer visualizes the progression. The choreographer presents focal points to the scriptwriter who generates inputs based on the outline. After this initial grounding of the conceptual itinerary, dance and music composition go hand in hand in the compositional process that ensues. The perspective of the choreographic presentation is sometimes decided by the scriptwriter, while at other times it is the choreographer's own reflexivity.

Mohanty's coinage of the term *Samrachana* means cocreation of music composition, dance choreography, and script writing (Mohanty 2023). *Samrachana* starts with contemplation on a seed thought or *Bindu* that expands and becomes the entire world in Mohanty's inner landscape. The *Bindu* branches out as Mohanty goes into a deep meditative state from where comes the script. Herein, comes the role of a think tank, a group of intellectuals who help Mohanty elaborate upon the seed of germination. Eventually, music session, costume design, dance-composition, and rehearsals follow suit.

Concluding Proliferations

Practice is woven through a distinctive ritualized pathway, not only along the arc of the entirety of the canon, but also in the progression of each individual segment. The goal of this practice remains individually determined. For me, it is a process of inquiry into the self while exploring its possibilities of transformation. The transformational impulse is primarily epistemological. I ask: What knowledge is imbued in these practicing pathways of curvilinear spiraling? I am inspired by Jacqui M. Alexander's chapter-length work, *Pedagogies of the Sacred*, where the author traces "the ways in which knowledge comes to be embodied and made manifest" (2006, 15). Tracing Alexander's pedagogical crossings in my own pathway and weaving the five distinct steps, I find my own set of discoveries of the self through movement metaphors. The methodology inspired by practice-based research through innumerable practice sessions in the studio across the curvilinear pathway. The physical practice of a plethora of pieces corresponds to the multiplicity of pathways. The choice remains in how one chooses the path through the selection of music and text. Dance is the manifestation of multiplicity. From this multiplicity emerges the quieting, an eventual centering of the body-mind complex. In the following, I present the physicality of the curvilinear potential while interspersing the physical sketches with my self-referential and self-transformational inquiry into the dancing entity. Multiple strategies weave movement, text, and music to create a mosaic of seamless artistry. Seamlessness achieved through attention to symmetry, transitional smoothness, curvilinear mapping of musical progression, and psychological conditioning of an emotional architecture produces a dramatic intent. Every composition bears its own nuance. Thus, comprehending a comprehensive list of procedures is futile. Yet, in closing, I focus on the pacing up of the canon identified by Invocation, Foundation, and Proliferation.

Weaving serpentine spirals on the floor, I enter. I cascade into concavity with changing levels only to then expand in breath and spirit. Touch and contact maintain my alignment and balance. Bringing my palms together in various directions and positions helps in my torso deflections. Brushing the floor with my palms and my heels grounds my being into the earthy texture of the dance. Texts emerge only to subside to the ebbs and flows of spiraling motions. Description and elaboration of the text maintain a simple and literal relationship in the very first segment of the canon. The body finally arrives to the audience, or the Sabha, at the end of this Invocation after it has gone through its physical and mental centering. From this point on, spontaneity is possible. This spontaneity undergoes a distinct set of contemplative gestures in order to set the course straight for the rest of the canonical unfolding.

The physical metaphor of centering requires a certain degree of alienation from the mundane to the ritualized. The dancer has the responsibility for audience engagement. However, the externality comes at a later stage after it has turned inward. The discussion on inflection point comes in handy in this case where the outward expression is first completely halted through contemplative inwarding. While this inwardness takes many dimensions in world religious and spiritual traditions, I remain invested in exploring its physical dimension and meaning. The spiral churning and the concavity experienced in the dancing body at the initial stages create channels for the regurgitation of existing baggage. One has to go through this process first in order to then seek new inspiration—perhaps from a deity or in one's own heart—to eventually bear the responsibility of presentation. But, right from the beginning, the presentation does not take a one-dimensional monologue. It remains a humble conversation of sorts where the interaction remains at the center. In this way, the centering is never in favor of a dictatorial self. Rather, it is a pluralistic endeavor with multiple dimensions of the physical, the mental, the emotional, and the contemplative where each remains in conversation with the other and with the externality in the form of an imaginary, yet already assumed, audience. Thoughts and movements surge in the self at all times. The dancing self channelizes such waves in physically determined pathways that help in centering—the hallmark of *Invocation*.

I gesture to stringing the instrument before tugging on the strings in my S-shape. My foot steps, brushes, heels, toes, and toe-grazes pivot around the weight-bearing leg that intermittently steps to hold both time and weight. Strung by melodic registers of the string instrument is complementary to the work on the flute. As a flautist, I construct and play the flute in various poses. My vigor increases as I become the percussionist dancing with the drums playing on as well as off-beat notes. Finally, the metal cymbals add a textural difference to the percussionist's grounded tones. It is not surprising that I segue into the squared postures right after the high-pitch metal cymbals marking the essence of foundational praxis. I continue wielding the ornamental basis of my movement after laying its musical infrastructure. Instrumentation and ornamentation both provide the complex aesthetic. I end on a note of concavity, depleting my chest of any remaining air for a Prushthachala, retreating the chest to the back.

Post withdrawal and centering, the canon sets to harnessing its focus through a degree of directness as musical instruments are strung at, blown into, slapped on, and hit with. The instrumentation provides the foundational basis for the ornamentation to occur. The square posture and its afforded groundedness remain at the forefront in order to hold the tapering ornamentation. There is a direct correlation between the musical infrastructure as the base and ornamental monument installed over and above the squared mesh. Visualization of the second segment, *Foundations*, offers strength and resilience that is achieved through direct physicality. Such a claim does not necessarily imply linearity of structure and motion. The movement is still curvilinear and the aesthetic retains nonlinearity as its ornamental possession. Yet, the owning of the movement occurs in this section where a direct association of the body-mind complex to ornamental and instrumental features prioritize a degree of directness. Here, we can see the congealing of a coherent self that gathers momentum and force to share its felt expression and experience. The sense of the solo self gathers around the body-mind complex with direct associations with music and costuming. The centripetal gathering toward the self becomes self-referential as limbs and sensory organs gesture to various modalities of either aesthetic ornamentation or musical orchestration. This sense of initial pedantic awareness is slowly dissipated in a feeling of abundance and depth noting further musical and textual complexities in the subsequent canonical progressions.

> *Opening and closing the felt expression in a sinusoidal arc of crests and troughs and navigating wrists, elbows, shoulders, hips, knees, and ankles tuned with the melodic mode leaves an indelible trace. Tracing with neck deflections partnered with direct and indirect gazing reflects the heel, toe, brush, and flat footwork. The echo is controlled due to the rhythmic complexity where section breaks provide a respite between progressively difficult patterns. Creating a tapestry of rhythm and melody requires a simultaneity of building blocks and their coordinated coexistence in an organized whole. Building and dissolving abstract patterns in numerically challenging constructions and melodic variations becomes the hallmark for the Proliferations segment of the canonical solo repertoire.*

The indivisibility of abstract build-up and its organic dissolution present an exploration of the knotting of music and dance in an indelible manner where the aesthetic experience relies on the interpretation of the music. Movement knots the cognizability and appeal of the music through musculature and expression. Knotting the elements in *Proliferations* takes a winding turn to firmly establish the canonical arc of the repertoire. Artistic expression goes beyond the corporeal as the emotional intensity builds up with the energetic arcs and lines conjointly for the artist building an experience of increasing complexity and resolution. Knotting the abstract with the intense builds an epiphanic trajectory glimpsing a deeper appreciation of the art form, which eventually leads to increasing energetic waves and joyful exuberance on the visual aesthetics of the dancer. One can compare this epiphany with that of a realization of a deeper dimension of the self as demonstrated through a discussion in Indian philosophy by Ross Keating in the field of arts appreciation. In a discussion around the philosophical investigation of the human condition, ecologist Baird Callicott defines the self as a "knot, nexus, or node in a skein of social and environmental relationships" (Callicott 2017, 235). In this definitive capacity, the artist situates publicly a manifestation of the multiplicity of the situatedness. Music—rhythm and melody—becomes a metaphor for the infinite knotting that the self is constituted within. Callicott's ecologically resonant self rings well for the solo dancing body, one that is in the midst of proliferating and deconstructing multiple knots in rhythm and melody. The social and the environmental play out in the movement as the dancer continues the communicative quotient as well as quilting numerous rhythmic and melodic progressions.

Notes

1. This chapter is written after analyzing the conference presentations of attendees at the 2021 online conference *Shaping S Curves* that was the first time in history focusing on choreographic discourse in Odissi dance. The title of this book comes from the name of the conference. Hosted by the University of North Carolina at Charlotte, *Shaping S-Curves*, was a week-long online conference (June 14–19, 2021) concentrating on the choreographic footprint of the eastern Indian dance form. Over 229 people registered at the conference site and actively participated in the sessions either on the Zoom videoconferencing or on social media live telecast via questions in real-time. Choreographers, performers, scriptwriters, music composers, dance-scholars, and student-researchers participated in the conference speaking from their vantage points of theory and practice. Over the course of six days, thirty-five presenters wove the verbal, the lyrical, the poetic, the percussive, the sculptural, the philosophical, and the musical within the choreographic. Presenters shared their choreographies for concert spaces as well as dance-films, questioned casteist gatekeeping within the form, explored technological adaptations of the dance, discussed the transference between the choreographer and the dancer, delineated thematic organizing of existing choreographic works, and elucidated reconstructions and readaptations of canonical works. The traditional choreographic process wove within the dancing body literary text, percussive syllables, and musical notes. This process required a dialogical interaction between music and rhythm composition, dance-making, scriptwriting, lighting designers, scenographers, and dancers.

2. Classical Odia literature, deeply rooted in ancient oral traditions, evolved into a distinct literary tradition by the fourteenth century, marked by the development of its own script. The Charyapadas, Buddhist mystical verses, are considered its earliest poetic form. The literary landscape flourished during the Panchasakha Age (fifteenth–sixteenth centuries) with five prominent poets—Balarama Dasa, Jagannath Das, Achyutananda Das, Ananta Dasa, and Jasobanta Dasa—who contributed significantly to devotional and philosophical literature. A defining milestone was Sarala Das's *Odia Mahabharata*, a seminal work that reflected the region's linguistic and cultural maturity. Later, the Bhanja Age (eighteenth century onward) introduced a more intricate poetic style, epitomized by Kabi Samrat Upendra Bhanja.

3. I learned this piece from Guru Aruna Mohanty when she was the invited guest for the 2023 *Odissi Odyssey* conference in August 2023. Mohanty taught this piece over a week-long dance intensive.

4. The understanding and perception of musical notes are necessary for the choreographic process. Cuttack-based Odissi performer and choreographer Meera Das focuses on *lalitya*, or softness, that brings Odissi its uniqueness in the panoply of dance forms from India. The choreographic process in Odissi invests in the technicalities while ensuring that the visual result of the end product transcends the mechanical. Meera Das demonstrates her process in *Nruthya*, which emerges from Guru Kelucharan Mohapatra's *Batu*, a pure dance connoting the foundational elements of Odissi. Das starts her choreographic career with *Nruthya* by adopting similar elements—*Veena*, *Benu*, *Mardala*—from the original dance *Batu*. Creating a different set of mnemonic syllables, or *Bol-Banis*, Das's reimagining of Guruji's

Batu brings the instruments more alive with longer percussive compositions allowing more time for bodily variations. Another choreography by Das, *Moods of Rhythm* uses different body language for different percussion instruments, namely the *Mardala*, *Khola*, *Manjira*, *Ghanta*, and *Khanjani*.

References

Alexander, M. J. 2006. *Pedagogies of Crossing: Meditations on Feminism, Sexual Politics, Memory, and the Sacred*. Duke University Press.

Alfonso, S., et al. 2022. "Eliciting Awe in the Spectator: The Case of a Dhrupad-Based Dance Performance." *International Journal of Transpersonal Studies* 41 (2). https://doi.org/10.24972/ijts.2022.41.2.48.

Ayau, J. 2017. *Creating Multivalent Danced Narratives in Odissi and Contemporary Dance*. The Ohio State University.

Banerji, A. 2010. *Odissi Dance: Paratopic Performances of Gender, State, and Nation*. Seagull Books.

Barbour, K. 2011. *Dancing Across the Page: Narrative and Embodied Ways of Knowing*. Intellect.

Barbour, K. N. 2012. "Standing Center: Autoethnographic Writing and Solo Dance Performance." *Cultural Studies? Critical Methodologies* 12 (1): 67–71.

Barlow, R. 2018. "Proprioception in Dance: A Comparative Review of Understandings and Approaches to Research." *Research in Dance Education* 19 (1): 39–56.

Berkson, C. 2000. *The Life of Form in Indian Sculpture*. Abhinav Publications.

Bresnahan, A. 2019. *Dance Rhythm*. Oxford University Press.

Brown, R. E. 1985. "New Perspectives on the History of Tala." *Journal of the Indian Musicological Society* 16 (2): 13.

Callicott, J. B. 2017. "Notes on 'Self-Realization: An Ecological Approach to Being in the World'." *Worldviews: Global Religions, Culture, and Ecology* 21 (3): 235–50.

Carr-Richardson, A. 2002. *Feminist and Non-Western Perspectives in the Music Theory Classroom: A Study of John Harbison's "Mirabai Songs."* College Music Symposium, JSTOR.

Çelik, M. S., et al. 2022. "Effectiveness of Proprioceptive Neuromuscular Facilitation and Myofascial Release Techniques in Patients with Subacromial Impingement Syndrome." *Somatosensory & Motor Research* 39 (2–4): 97–105.

Citaristi, I. 2021. Personal Interview.

Citaristi, I. 2022. *Odissi and the Geeta Govinda*. Routledge.

Coorlawala, U. A. 1996. "Darshan and Abhinaya: An Alternative to the Male Gaze." *Dance Research Journal* 28 (1): 19–27.

Dave, R. 2016. "Liminal Spaces: Odissi as a Continually Evolving Form." In *Tilt Pause Shift: Dance Ecologies in India*, edited by A. E. Churian. Columbia University Press.

Dennen, D. 2013. "The naming of 'Odissi': Changing Conceptions of Music in Odisha." *Ravenshaw Journal of Literary and Cultural Studies* 3: 58–82.

Dennen, D. 2014. *Words into Music: A Study and Translation of Kabisuryya Baladeba Ratha's* Kisoracandrananda Campa. University of California, Davis.

Deshmukh, V. D. 2013. "Cognitive Pause-and-Unload Hypothesis of Meditation and Creativity." *Journal of Alternative Medicine Research* 5 (3): 217.

Donaldson, T. E. 2023. *Hindu Temple Art of Orissa, Volume Three*. Brill.

Dora, J. 2002. "Iconography: With Special Reference to the Iconography Of 'Shakta' Deities of 'Vaital' Temple, Bhubaneswar." *Proceedings of the Indian History Congress* 63: 1224–1232.

Foster, S. 2010. *Choreographing Empathy: Kinesthesia in Performance*. Routledge.

Gardner, S. 2012. "Dancing and Listening: Odissi Across Cultures." *Journal of Intercultural Studies* 33 (4): 411–25.

Ghosh, P. 2024. "Therapeutic Mindfulness Through Rasa." ಅಕ್ಷರಸೂರ್ಯ (AKSHARASURYA) 4 (1): 141–50.

Gochhayat, A. 2016. "Odisha as a Multicultural State: From Multiculturalism to Politics of Sub-Regionalism." *Afro Asian Journal of Social Sciences* 7 (2): 28.

Holland, N. N. 2013. *Music Fundamentals for Dance.* Human Kinetics.

Ibrahim, R. 2024. "Weaving Odissi Feminine: A Malaysian Perspective." *South Asian Dance Intersections* 3 (1).

Jha, R. 2024. Personal Communication.

Kar, P. 2013. "The Debaprasad Das Tradition: Reconsidering the Narrative of Classical Indian Odissi Dance History." PhD diss., York University.

Katrak, K. H. 2001. "Body Boundarylands: Locating South Asian Ethnicity in Performance and in Daily Life." *Amerasia Journal* 27 (1): 1–33.

Katrak, K. H. 2024. *Astad Deboo: An Icon of Contemporary Indian Dance.* Seagull Books.

Kieft, E. 2014. "Dance as a Moving Spirituality: A Case Study of Movement Medicine." *Dance, Movement & Spiritualities* 1 (1): 21–41.

Kothari, S. 1981. "Enactment of Gita Govinda in Neo-Classical Dance Forms." *Journal of the Indian Musicological Society* **12** (3): 53.

Kothari, S. 2022. "Odissi: From Devasabha to Janasabha." *Marg, A Magazine of the Arts* 74 (1): 54–60.

Kumar, A. 2013. "Constructing and Performing the Odissi Body: Ideologies, Influences, and Interjections." *Journal of Emerging Dance Scholarship* 1.

Leaman, K. Y. 2016. "Analyzing Music and Dance: Balanchine's Choreography to Tchaikovsky and the Choreomusical Score." PhD diss., Yale University.

Litfin, K. T. 2020. "The Contemplative Pause: Insights for Teaching Politics in Turbulent Times." *Journal of Political Science Education* 16 (1): 57–66.

Majhi, L., et al. 2024. "The Intellectual Contributions of Odisha to the Indian Knowledge System: A Historical and Cultural Analysis." *Partners Universal Innovative Research Publication* 2 (5): 51–69.

Margolin, I. 2014. "Bodyself: Linking Dance and Spirituality." *Dance, Movement & Spiritualities* 1 (1): 143–62.

Martin, N. M. 2010. "Mirabai Comes to America: The Translation and Transformation of a Saint." *The Journal of Hindu Studies* 3 (1): 12–35.

Mason, P. H. 2012. "Music, Dance, and the Total Art Work: Choreomusicology in Theory and Practice." *Research in Dance Education* 13 (1): 5–24.

Meglin, J. A., and L. M. Brooks. 2016. "Embodied Texts, Textual Choreographies." *Dance Chronicle* 39 (1).

Miller, B. S. 1984. *Gitagovinda of Jayadeva: Love Song of the Dark Lord.* Motilal Banarsidass Publishers.

Minton, S. C. 2017. *Choreography: A Basic Approach Using Improvisation.* Human Kinetics.

Mohanty, A. 2023. Personal Interview.

Noland, C., and S. A. Ness, eds. 2008. *Migrations of Gesture: Dance, Film, Writing.* University of Minnesota Press.

Oana, O. 2023. "Intro to Odissi Music by Dr. Sangita Gosain." *OANA Blog.* OANA website, Odissi Alliance of North America.

Panda, A. K. 2017. "Translation in Odia: A Historical Survey." *Translation Today*: 202.

Pattnaik, K. K. 1966. *Raga-Citra.* Odisi Kala Prakash.

Phyu, U. 2004. "Depiction of Nature in the Sculptural Art of Early Deccan (Up to 10th-Century AD)." PhD diss., University of Hyderabad.

Pillai, A. 2023. "Breaking the Fourth Wall Festival: Rediscovering Brecht's Timeless Relevance Kolkata Centre for Creativity (KCC)." *Communications from the International Brecht Society* (2).

Pradhan, M. 2017. "The Contribution of Odissi to Jagannath Cult." *International Education and Research Journal* 3(7): 99–100.

Ram, K. 2011. "Being 'Rasikas': The Affective Pleasures of Music and Dance Spectatorship and Nationhood in Indian Middle-Class Modernity." *Journal of the Royal Anthropological Institute* 17: S159–S175.

Sahoo, I. 2025. "Performing Arts: A Holistic Perspective." *Sangeet Galaxy* 14 (1).

Samantaray, N., and J. K. Nayak. 2015. "History of the Progressive Literary Movement in Odisha." *Indian Literature* 59 (3 (287): 166–76.

Sarkar, K. 2019. "De-Centring the Choreographer: Historically Inspired Interruptions/Disruptions in an Exploration Between Sculpture and Movement." *Choreographic Practices* 10 (2): 269–91.

Schnepel, C. 2012. "Bodies Filled with Divine Energy: The Indian Dance Odissi." In *Images of the Body in India: South Asian and European Perspectives on Rituals and Performativity*, edited by A. Michaels and C. Wulf. Routledge India.

Sen, S. S. 2016. "When Our Senses Dance: Sensory-Somatic Awareness in Contemporary Approaches to Odissi Dance in India." Master's thesis, University of Exeter.

Sharda, S. 2007. "Every Indian Dance Form Has a Spiritual Basis." *The Times of India.*

Sharman, S. 2020. "Secular Female Imagery in Orissan Temple Architecture: The Case of Alasa Kanyas." *Chitrolekha Journal on Art & Design* 4 (2).

Simonari, R. 2019. "Martha Graham's Letter to the World: A Dance Adaptation of Emily Dickinson." *Journal of Adaptation in Film & Performance* 12 (1–2): 33–48.

Sklar, D. 2008. "Remembering Kinesthesia: An Inquiry Into Embodied Cultural Knowledge." In *Migrations of Gesture: Dance, Film, Writing*, edited by C. Noland and S. A. Ness. University of Minnesota Press.

Smith, L. 2008. "'In-Between Spaces': An Investigation Into the Embodiment of Culture in Contemporary Dance." *Research in Dance Education* 9 (1): 79–86.

Stepputat, K., and E. Djebbari. 2020. "The Separation of Music and Dance in Translocal Contexts." *The World of Music* 9 (2): 5–30.

Tandon, R. 2023. "Practice-Research in Odissi Dance: The 3 Bindu Approach to Embodying Sacred Geometry." *International Journal of Arts Architecture and Design* 1 (1): 22–30.

Trivedi, S. 2019. "The Case of Sarangadeva." In *The Oxford Handbook of Sound and Imagination*, Vol. 1, edited by M. Grimshaw-Aagaard, M. Walther-Hansen, and M. Knakkergaard.

Turner, M. J. 1963. "A Study of Modern Dance in Relation to Communication, Choreographic Structure, and Elements of Composition." *Research Quarterly. American Association for Health, Physical Education and Recreation* 34 (2): 219–27.

Vatsyayan, K. 1963. "Notes on the Relationship of Music and Dance in India." *Ethnomusicology* 7 (1): 33–38.

CHAPTER 4

Going Back to the S

Rohini Dandavate in Motion

REGIONAL PARITY OF THE dancing Odissi body with sculpture and temple architecture in the state of Odisha grounds scholar/ choreographer Rohini Dandavate's contemporary creative ethos within curvilinearity (Dandavate 2006). Her work lies within the curvilinear idiom, one that ties her to other disciplinary mediums of Odisha. A deep dive into the architectural, the sculptural, and the embodied principles of the sinusoidal wave is a book-length inquiry of its own (Sarkar 2019). In this chapter, I merely become the canvas for Dandavate to draw forth her vision in using the regional and traditional form of Odissi to bring alive stories of contemporary relevance related to diaspora and migration. Thus, an interaction between a dancer and a choreographer tied together by their shared love for Odissi dance and desire to raise its visibility, profile, and legibility in choreography studies ensues (Gardner 2008).

Since 2020, Dandavate has created new and reimaginations of existing solo works on me that emphasize upon *Abhinaya* or expressive movement. *Abhinaya* literally means to carry forward. *Abhinaya*, or dramatic dancing, carries forward a pluralistic impulse congruent with the poetic imagination, the composer's musicality, the choreographer's expansion of the text and music through movement and expression, and finally, the dancer's embodiment and creative realization of this alchemy. The dancer's responsibility remains in being a vehicular conduit for prior existing and thematic content.

Dandavate's focus on curvilinearity remains at the center of her choreographic oeuvre. According to her, the focus on speed and athleticism has eroded the regional ethos of curvilinear deepening that marks her training and investment in Guru Kelucharan Mohapatra style. Having learned from Guru Kelucharan Mohapatra herself in the Kala Vikash Kendra in Cuttack, she is privy to the history of Odissi's incipient stages when Mohapatra was in the process of codifying his stylistic particulars. I argue that the study of relational encounters across movement, music, and text in solo works by Dandavate unfurls a dynamic kaleidoscope of multifaceted investments across an inquiry-based exploration of contemporary issues and deepening of technical precepts.

In the remaining chapter, I lay out the curvilinear implications of dramatic enactment, particular to Dandavate's choreographic complexity: paying synergistic attention to text, musicality, and movement. I show the mechanics of her choreographic process with a collaborative relationship with the melodic and the percussion composition. After laying out the verbal and musical premise of the compositional format, I analyze particular solo works attending to formal as well as conceptual paraphernalia. In closing, I identify and elaborate upon characteristics unique to Dandavate's creative making.

An Unruly Dancer

The mentor-mentee relationship is held sacrosanct in traditional contexts. Teachers get upset if students defect from one institution or educator to another. This is grounded in Indian philosophical contexts where the teaching and learning is not about content but about a relationship. The role of the teacher is to remove ignorance in the student. Dancers work with their teachers and what emerges in the process is an artistic corollary. The practice of choreographers working with professionals to make a new piece is absent at best and frowned upon at worst. Fear of ostracization and hearsay makes dancers stay within the hierarchical boundaries of singularity—the singular axis between the particular mentor with the apparently chosen mentee or vice versa. Continuation of this practice of territoriality causes significant stress and psychological repression that, I believe, is antithetical to creative flourishing. In any case, I enter this research in creative process from a desire to be chiseled upon; to experience a willing suspension of agency; to make a case for dramatic enactment; and to have a continually transformative relationality with my technical grounds. My unusual decision of working with Dandavate faced significant backlash in the community. I will not deliberate upon the value judgments, either for or against, behind my creative liberty and caveat this writing by noting its research inquiry-based prerogatives.

I borrow from dance scholar Priya Srinivasan's theorization of the *unruly spectator* who refuses to pay attention to the traditional conduits and channels of embodied display (Srinivasan 2009). My unruliness is not necessarily flamboyant or unproductive but only irrupts into practice if there is breach of equity during choreographic or compositional exchange in terms of configuring class, caste, nonbinary gender and sexuality, and other identarian markers of difference. This is never targeted at a person or an institution but rather goes toward transforming the traditional cultures of hierarchies and exclusionary practices toward more equitable grounds and futures. While I engage with the technical rigor and philosophical subtlety of the *Natyasastra* as it relates to *Abhinaya*, I stay abreast of its casteist and sexist implications (Munsi and Burridge 2012).

My first collaboration with Dandavate produced a ten-minute solo, *Nachi Meera* (2020), choreographed to a song written by the medieval female mystic Mirabai. This led to two twenty-minute productions called *Enigmatic Bliss* (2021) and *Trigger* (2023). These were close encounters with percussionist Ramprasad Gannavarapu and ethnomusicologists Anirban Bhattacharyya and M. A. Jyothi. Percussion for *Nachi Meera* (2020) was created by Guru Poushali Mukherjee, my first Odissi teacher, while that of *Enigmatic Bliss* (2021) and *Trigger* (2023) was developed by Ramprasad Gannavarapu. *Enigmatic Bliss* was based upon a song written by Nobel laureate Rabindranath Tagore. It enquires about the inherent and inevitable dualities in nature—such as light and dark, joy and sorrow—as the sung lyric was connected to disease and death during the COVID-19 pandemic. With *Nachi Meera* and *Enigmatic Bliss* focusing on social freedom and philosophical deliberation on the nature of life respectively, *Trigger* speaks to the issue of gun violence in the United States. Focusing on the voice of youth, this piece reflects on a social problem from the loss of youth potency. While working with new pieces that were made on my body, I also worked on Dandavate's reimagination of *Agni* (1998) as *Fire* (2023) based on fire. Dandavate had premiered this sixteen-minute solo work choreographed by Guru Kelucharan Mohapatra in Ohio in 1998. She performed visualizing the Indic ritual contexts of the mythical origination stories about fire and also worked with a group of modern dancers to explore an intercultural expression of fire as both life-enhancing and destructive. Dandavate's reimagining of her own dancing on my body was an interesting process on reflecting on our shared style across generational and ideational variations.

With the desire of making explicit the implicit rigor of the dancing body, I write about my encounters of performing Dandavate's choreography, reflecting on her creative and intellectual investments. Interestingly, although belonging to the same lineage, Dandavate finds my training quite different from hers and this revelation sparked my research interest in the questions: How does movement shift across generations even in the same stylistic convention? How does individual expression weave into the technical parameters? Where lies the form-content differentiation and is it a helpful analytic in the study of choreography in Odissi? And, how—and to what extent—does an inquiry-mindset activate choreographic spurts? Centering my practice from the art-making to the premier of solo works, I reflect upon the qualitative contribution to the choreographic product by the dancing body. My research into Dandavate's choreography, suggest a curvilinearity in technique as well as expression, as reimagination of existing traditional precepts. Dandavate is invested in the contemporary world with its social, environmental, and political issues, combining reason and freedom in her creative expression, while resonating with Odissi's primary purpose of *Moksha* (meaning freedom and/or transformation). She continues to explore this practice-based experiential freedom in her most recent work, another twenty-minute piece called *Azad Pankh* (2025), which is based on a poem called the "The Unstuck Feather" by poet Uday Dandavate.

Sthayi: Centering Musical and Dramatic Enactments

Sthayi functions as a stabilizing element that sustains artistic expression in Indian music as well as dramatic performance. It refers to the opening and principal section of a composition where the melodic theme is established and repeatedly returned to, creating a foundation for improvisation and development. In drama, it embodies permanence, acting as the anchor against which variations unfold. *Sthayibhavas* are the enduring emotional states that, when intensified through aesthetic stimulation and combined with transitory emotions, blossom into a fully realized aesthetic experience. Thus, in both frameworks, it signifies continuity and permanence: in music, it stabilizes the melodic journey and in aesthetics, it grounds the emotional experience, allowing art to move fluidly while always returning to a central essence.

Dandavate locates the virtuosic in the ability to evoke a subtle, restrained, focused, and calming projection through embodiment and visualization. The dancer's ability to hold a stable expression, or the *Sthaibhava*, throughout a piece with the aid of the dramatic elements while moving in the curvilinear pathways and gestures, is a significant aspect of Dandavate's choreographic priorities. Traditional Indian aesthetic theory presents the performing arts with a culinary analogy where the process leading to the arousal of *Rasa* (flavor, sentiment) is ontologically different from the elements leading up to it, such as *Bhavas* (emotions), *Vibhavas* (causal factors), *Anubhavas* (consequential experiences), and *Vyabicharibhavas* (transitory states). In this complex milieu of expression and meaning-making, the locus of *Rasa* anticipates the structural creativity and the technical dramatic enactment. Locating Dandavate's creative process at the juxtaposition of the formal constitution and aesthetic reception makes sense given her dual focus on both the structural parameters of curvilinearity and its virtuosic intent of stable focus. The constitutive and the aesthetic, both undergird Dandavate's choreographic development of a melodic mode, poetic verse, sung lyric, or abstract gestural expansion. Both structural and affective, the *Sthayi* becomes the stabilizing factor across embodied reaching of emotional and musical peaks and troughs only to return to the enduring stable grounds (Rani 2021).

Sthayi integrates the musical, the dramatic, and the kinesthetic in its curvilinear folds in the second element in the traditional repertoire. Primarily a *Nritta* (abstract movement) piece with an infusion of a dramatic enactment on textual verses, it functions as the point of stability around which the variations unfold. Recurrence stabilizes artistic variation helping audiences to establish a sense of continuity as well as transformation. Sculptural poses, intricate footwork, and rhythmic flair build up on a musical refrain that repeats a percussive phrase in complementary musical notes: *Ta Ke Dha Dha Karataka Ta Ham Jham Tari, Ta Ke Dha Dha Karataka Ta Ham Jham Tari.* Recurring movement motifs complement rhythmic and melodic anchors. This cyclical return to foundational movement sequences mirrors the principle of recurrence central to Indian aesthetics. This is an example of kinetic stability despite rapidly changing rhythmic structures. Virtuosity is defined as the ability to focus, hold on to, and build upon a kinesthetic, musical, and dramatic integration over a durational performance. While Dandavate uses the technical construct of the *Sthayi* in *Azad-Pankh*, she is interested in this cyclical return both in visual parlance as well as in sonic registers. At the center of both music and movement is the ability to cultivate a mood, not with just a discrete set of emotions. Rather, the sculptural stillness is brought to bear in the imagination of the dynamic communicator charged with carrying a message from the performance to the audience. Rhythmic, melodic, kinetic, and philosophical continuity forms the central pillar of Dandavate's choreographic oeuvre as pinned on the *Sthayi*. It functions as a stabilizing anchor, balancing freedom and order in musical creativity. According to Dandavate, the *Sthayi* allows for coherence in the unfolding of a performance.

Slow unfolding of a stable reservoir of affective resonance starts with various stimuli, which activates perceptible involuntary and voluntary reactions using gesture, posture, footwork, and facial expression. An emotional stimulus can be provided by a multiplicity of factors, namely, environmental, sensory, sensuous, musical, and relational. Involuntary reactions constitute essential features of stereotypical emotional expression; for example, sadness is often connected to lack of physical strength. Dandavate takes liberty in visualizing dramatic intent through her creative incorporation of voluntary reactions. This provides the basis for her movement generation. Dandavate prioritizes building up of the *Sthayibhava* using extensive workshopping of ideation and writing. Writing of emotional nuances to ensure subtle progression of a narrative expression or a poetic construct, unfurl the *Sthayibhava*.

During Dandavate's creative process, I have spent days in emotional mapping and writing in simple linguistic progression. I write down the step-by-step actions in order to create a particular mood. This aids in congealing the otherwise granular process of differentiation of the various constitutive forces behind the confluence of the stable. My participatory sense-making of Dandavate's vision borders on my experiential, sensory, sensuous, and felt expressions. Such a coordinated and reciprocal interaction between myself and Dandavate leads to an empathic unfoldment of the *Abhinaya* where the four differentiating traits are gestural restraint, parallel attention to movement and musicality, elaboration of expressive registers, and a calm stasis with focused communication of performative aesthetics toward the audience. I start with addressing Dandavate's unique elaboration of expressive conduits, arguing that it creates a humane and empathic register between the performance, the performer, and the theatrical enactment. Below, I show how this grounds itself as the differentiating feature of Dandavate's creativity.

The production, communication, and reception of emotion enjoy paramount importance in Indian performing arts traditions. So, rarified gestural emotive quotient has greater virtuosic merit than physical capacity to bear or extend or contort. The representation of emotion undergoes scalable proportions onstage from their existential and phenomenological counterpart. Also, the performative reproducibility of the emotional register also requires significant practice such that the duration of the performance can maintain a similar degree of emotional endurance. Practice creates body-mind connections that the performer can create and have access to whenever needed in order to present a similar work. Thus, the beginning lies in the ability to produce the dramatic enactment within the *Abhinaya*. Dandavate's elaboration of expressive registers has a literary impetus. She asks me to write my feelings and reflections about the performance. She requires me to add adjectives and adverbs, making a qualitative difference in my movement quality and simultaneously requiring me to connect my embodiment to thoughts, feelings, sensations, and emotions. The short section below describes the dynamic and curvilinear quality of both the movement and the felt emotion.

> *Gathering the sandalwood paste in her palms, she brings them to her face. The aroma lifts her spirits reminding her of the excitement (Umad-Ghumad, a rolling feeling) and her turbulent heart while noticing the dark cumulonimbus clouds around her.*

I wrote this during the making of *Nachi Meera*. There are environmental triggers, such as clouds and sandalwood pastes, and emotional intensifiers, such as an excited and turbulent heart, together building the required emotional density. The performance builds upon the *Rasic* framework of causes with their triggers and intensifiers alongside immediate and ancillary effects to produce the requisite stable emotional tenor, one that is built throughout the making of the solo work. Such elaboration of expressive registers require maturity in movement and expression and the ability to articulate in language the felt emotional landscape that Dandavate elicits from the dancer.

This short segment is a testimony to the nuanced and complex polysemic matrix that Dandavate's choreography brings to the fore through her literary configurations. The *Sanskrit* term for emotion is *Bhava*, which comes from the verbal root *bhu*, meaning to come to existence. The emotion pervades the entirety of the movement just as the aromatic sandalwood paste infuses the air around and the being within for *Meera*. The stable emotion is the underlying existential state that can be reached at through experiential production and communication of immediate reactions. The existential dimension of the stable emotion (in *Nachi Meera*, it is devotional love) is colored by the transitory emotions, such as excitement and turbulence bordering on fear. Being and performing remain coterminous although it is the production of the emotion through deliberate attentiveness and practice that gains precedence rather than the actual feeling of fear, excitement, etc. In his essay "Emotion in Motion: The Natyasastra, Darwin, and Affect Theory," South Asian studies expert Vinay Dharwadkar presents a comparative literary exercise of emotion as dealt by Bharata in performance (2015). Dharwadkar argues that Bharata's "starting point is that our emotions phenomenologically compose an enumerable and classifiable plurality: some are well-defined while others are transitory, some always accompany others while some come and go independently" (1383). Dharwadkar's description shows how duration, quality, meaning, and purpose of the various emotional registers in combinatorial creativity remain instrumental in developing the *Sthai*. Dandavate's aesthetic production integrates the verbal, the linguistic, the semiotic, and the semantic. Sometimes signification is through semiotic dissection of each word in the sung lyric while at other times, a cluster of words alludes metaphorically to a certain situation, character, and place. In *Enigmatic Bliss*, Rabindranath Tagore's composition in Bengali is translated both as *Padartha* (word-by-word) and *Vakyartha* (as a sentence). A combination of translational, metaphorical, metonymical, and suggestive meaning-making processes is at work.

Curvilinearity is ingrained within Odisha's regional ethos infusing its musical and embodied dimensions. Gestural expansion and contraction occur in parallel to musical ebb and flow—one that the psychological landscape of the dancer emulates in rising and receding performative intensities. Given the oceanic continuity of movement, Dandavate's choreography never reaches a complete halt. Sculptures stasis assumes dynamism in degrees of tilt. Imbued with the musical resonances, the stasis continues, deepening the postural conduits while movements across space expand and contract gesturally. Footwork plays a significant role in marking the percussive and grounded lower body that remains attuned to the percussionist while the upper body follows the melody. This curvilinear ethos of the grounded and the languid shows up in the musical build up and cool down of dramatic intent.

While expressive registering and musical curvilinearity ensure the production of the dramatic intent, gesture and focus carry it forward to the audience using the large corpus of the textual tradition of codified aesthetics. I identify restraint in gesture and a focused communicative intent as Dandavate's remaining choreographic quirks, which are particular to the aesthetic representation and figuration of a mimetic state. Between the domains of reality and mimesis, Dandavate conjures a world of savoring that is beyond emotional identification, cognitive reasoning, and physiological experiencing. This experience of relishing the artwork, notes philosopher Abhinavagupta, is concomitant with the act of embedding it (Gnoli 1968; Masson and Patwardhan 1974; Pollock 2016). It is not something that can be cognized or felt at a later time or in another space. The space-time-object blurring that occurs in the moment of savoring between the individuated experience of the dancer and that of the viewer remains key in this aesthetic communication.

Gestural meaning-making can be inferential, contextual, and nonverbal aesthetic production. Embodying the felt emotion is key to realizing Dandavate's choreographic vision. She really despises the flaying of arms and feet without layering intent across verbal and musical registers. In this way, it seems, she might be averse to mere abstract dynamism. Focusing on layering polysemic registers in every gesture, her work is then packed with density of information. The simple movement—a hand-eye coordinated semicircular arc starting with *Pataka* (fingers joint and held in extension of the forearm) and ending with *Suchi* (exaggerating the index finger)—can represent or visualize the environment while following the musical expansion and ebbing parallel to the arc; the words sung as lyric could continue to inform the changing facial expression along the creation of the semicircle; and the temporality, endurance, and appearance of the gesture continue to gain multiple resonances in each iteration. Thus, a plethora of meaning-making occurs at any given instant of gestural expansion. Even if Dandavate uses a paucity of gesture, there is a significant packing of intent and meaning within that simplicity. The way one interprets the presence of fire from the visible smoke, gestural communication can be a similar semiotic marker. Unlike a choreographic motif, there is a stable emotional conduit that populates the entirety of the piece, marking its cohesion across the range of emotions, musical variations, and theatrical representations. The final import is the aesthetic reception or the savoring of *Rasa* by the audience which is triggered, intensified, articulated, actualized, and finally stabilized using a range of auxiliary emotions by the performer. Dandavate works on the premise that *Rasa* is the concentration and scaling of an existential and phenomenological temporality in the confines of theatrical production. Gestural restraint and emotional immersion lead to the stabilized focus on and with the audience by the performer in order to reach the intended claim of generating an aesthetic import of the content as well as form. The topics represented, in this instance, remain valid during the validity and duration of the performance. The performative focus that enables the viewers to connect with their own inner stasis and calm, endures.

Ultimately, Dandavate's choreography in Odissi is a process of aesthetic meditation, one that relies on the immovability of the viewer's stable emotional state. Through choreographing focus and stability, she influences the viewer to cultivate a certain degree of stability in their emotional psyche. By choreographing a panoply of emotional registers to weave in the extent of the *Sthayibhava*, the viewers in turn are able to connect with their underlying experiential state irrespective of the content of the choreography (Dharwadker 2015). As Vinay Dharwadker points out, "The Nātyashāstra's boldest implication is that the sthāyi bhāvas comprise an individual subject's fundamental mode of existence in the world—that a self exists only in one or another of these long-lasting states at any given time, persists over time in a succession of such states, and has no other mode of existence "(2015, 1384). The choreographic skill enables such prioritization of focus and eventual relationality with the viewer with their own fundamental mode of existence. Focusing on the human condition and its ontological intent of a stable emotional register makes art relevant. Relevance is derived through the landscape of feelings alongside a geometric attunement to a specific cultural and regional ethos. The performance becomes a conduit for the creation and appearance of the human condition both to the performer and the viewer. Theatrical enactment starts gathering a life of its own, which resonates with the multiple entities entwined in its creation, production, and dissemination. The human registers of the *Sthyai* empathically draw the audience into its curvilinear folds. While this has spiritual resonance across religious registers in the Hindu pantheon in which Odissi transacts, operates, and functions, I believe the philosophical takeaway of conceptually, experientially, and relationally connecting to oneself through aesthetic reception of art to be the most significant.

Shaping Ss

Working across music, text, and movement, in a collaborative capacity, Dandavate works with a democratic ethos, soliciting ideas from her scriptwriters, music composers, and percussionists. Formal vicissitudes of dance and music propel her toward imaginative curiosity within a contemporary ecosystem. She uses her choreography to satisfy her inquiries into social issues. She celebrates and critiques lived experience through her art-making. It is a formal inquiry of the contemporary moment that reactivates and wrestles with the past. Formal depths seem foundational to her. Her pedagogical investments alongside her familial ties with the cultural heritage of Odisha keep her ingrained within the formal ethos (Dave 2016). However, she finds it limiting to stick to the usual theological and mythological components that constitute the bulk of traditional repertoire. Her inquiry takes into account the sociocultural reality of her contemporary existence as she subjects her artistic practice to humanistic questioning. Representation and continuity of the human condition across lived experience and aspirational futurity remain a functioning thread weaving her multiple choreographic projects together. She brings to bear a temporal weaving of the past into her present while grounding her work within a progressive journey of growth and improvement.

Spirituality, which remains the core of the traditional Odissi body, forms an underlying tonality in her composition. She borders on a calm stasis deploying the mobile only to formally satisfy her artistic vision. Satiety of the human condition through a focused, centered, and yet deeply communicative exterior creates a degree of efficacy in the carrying forward of both information and intent toward an audience. Dandavate finds points of enquiry for her artistic journey in her lived experience raised in a conservatory setting where worshiping the Guru as well as the content learned remain customary. Movement, then grounds as a pseudo-religious and pseudo-spiritual regimen. Love for the divine is not actively practiced even though it is a given and considered a basic requirement for an integral dance career. Progression in movement then becomes an activity in deepening one's *Bhakti*, or devotional quotient. Love for the divine element has been central to Indian dance forms. Rarely has inquiry been considered a valid point of departure for thematic or structural composition. Dandavate uses inquiry as a launching pad into formal and conceptual parameters. However, the inquiry that Dandavate espouses is not philosophical speculation. Rather, it brings to bear lived experience and a sense of the collective. It uses the individual dancing body toward a connected worldview, one where the individual is ecologically embedded in a divergent array of multiplicity and plurality.

Without assuming a devotional quotient as the underlying condition for success, for Dandavate, the curvilinear subtlety in kinesthesia and emotion remains the hallmark while an inquiry into the human condition drives her artistic impulse. While not critical of the formal value judgments of Odissi, Dandavate's choreographic ethos borrows from the vicissitudes of a progressive mindset to simultaneously question some of the rigidity she perceives as gripping the field and refuses to let go of her curvilinear investments. Interplay of musical tonality, grounded languidity, and textual interpretation stretch in Dandavate's imagination to constitute the curvilinear pathway in choreographic visualization. The ontological nature of reality as represented through thematic foci itself takes on a curvilinear impulse, one that is changing continuously with rising and receding waves starting from and merging back into sculptural stasis or meditative focus. Distillation of the embedded moments through lived experience distills the represented toward poetic rarefication—one that is deflected with an inquiry into the ontological nature of Odissi. Dandavate's quest into Odissi's ontological status still remains an open question. But, for our purposes here, her inquisitive building up and tearing down of intensity serves as a hermeneutic strategy, potentially interpreting the thematic content through an experiential conduit that is central to an efficacious *Abhinaya*.

Through an experiential questioning, she registers an artist statement that is deeply phenomenological and interpretative but rests within a systemic structure. The curvilinear scaffolding of her Odissi body holds its own cultural ethos and thematic valence. Holding that regional weight, she does not intend to break free from the confines but rather wishes to transcend these chains only through her inquisitive deepening into the nature of reality. As shown in the above section, her questioning rests in the ontological nature of this world. She configures her training, experience, and creativity to delve into some distressing moments of disequilibrium—forest fires, school shootings, and the COVID-19 pandemic. Returning to the equilibrium, which is not in stasis, continues to remain the hallmark of her choreographic signature. It is the premonition of an impending change and a move away from the current status quo as she leaves the possibility of such a sequel through a continuous and enigmatic questioning. Whether she subscribes to an uncreated ontological ethos or that of eternity, her inquisitive mindset drives her artistic desire primarily through the act of knowledge. Choreography has lent itself to critical inquiry and vice versa in multiple scholarly studies restricted to Euro American concert forms (Welch 2022). Dandavate's work extends this body to South Asian dance studies helping to frame how dance and choreography can be generative modes of inquiry (Carter 2020).

Knowledge of the form as well as the content in a reflective manner allows for a detached gliding over the two where the primary component is to generate a certain degree of intellectual and experiential qualities in the spectator. Reflecting on the formal complexities of the curvilinear Odissi body is at the core of this exercise. Gestural fluidity where the fingers are held with detailing and precision without any musculoskeletal strength continues to differentiate the eastern Indian dancing body with that of southern Indian dance styles. Often, I have been reprimanded by southern Indian dance Gurus for not holding my *Mudras* (hand gestures) 'properly.' Perhaps, part of it can be attributed to my artistic lacunae but the majority of this is due to what I call gestural fluidity as opposed to gestural placement. Formal strength lies in the action-oriented nature of the gesture instead of involving stasis within the gestural framework. There is energetic congruence across gesture in tune with music and text with a percussive lower body. Footwork functions as percussive interruptions to the gestural fluidity of the upper body.

The bent knees place the dancing body low to the ground while the upper body is free to conduct the spiraling, flowing, and gestural detailing marking the grounded and the languid texture of formal curvilinearity. Dandavate's absolute insistence on this energetic detailing makes her work unique in the field. Often, we see the lower body at a high degree of production or the upper body exuberant in fluid detailing. The combination that requires a tempered gathering of two distinct energetic intensities continues to remain a rarity in the field.

Knowledge of the thematic content is another reflective medium of meditative contemplation for Dandavate. The content drives the formality of the codified techniques from which a choreography is drawn. The traditional repertoire has been dealt with in the introductory sections of this book where I show how the dancing body navigates its attitudinal, musical, and textual paradigms. The canon's grounding of the body in invocatory gestures with progressive strengthening and manifesting of the musical framework that then reaches an emotional peak borrowed from literary texture, anticlimactic to a final letting go of all formal and content-driven motility, creates a curvilinear arc. Ritualistic centering of the body-mind complex at the very beginning and returning to it at the very end after having reached musical and emotional proliferations, respectively, textured through melodic/percussive and textual determinations continues to ground Dandavate's choreographic arc. Culturally situated within the ethos of Odishan culture, Dandavate is then free to explore the form-content dyad in a nonbinary format as shown below.

Through formal and contextual curvilinearity, Dandavate connects to her reality shaped by immigration, higher education, and her intercultural experiences. Climate change and forest fires are a reality to her as she experiences it first hand by being a California resident. Having raised a child in this country, she is cognizant of the imminent threat of school shootings and chooses to explore her visceral emotionality through choreography. The COVID-19 pandemic-induced uncertainty also makes way into her art-making. Thematic intrusions of her contemporary reality into the curvilinear domains of her artistic practice have a tenor of intellectual and experiential grappling. She does not seem to have a prescriptive panacea for these larger social, political, and environmental problems. Rather, she enters her practice with an inquisitive bent and hopes to maneuver her audiences into introspective questioning. The reception of her work borders on the interrogative and the experiential as she ends her work by asking her audiences to think with her. The emotional and the visceral performance intricately weaves a call to action in her work. This is not an explicit call but one that creates an experiential resonance in the interior that then can perhaps, and hopefully, lead to greater change in the society. Dandavate relies on the depth of the liberatory and transformative potential of the dancing body only when it deals with technical and performative complexities in an apt manner. Her call to action remains a meditative contemplation on the matters in hand. She needs her audience to return to their core, a centered equilibrium, which is integral for transformative action. Dandavate does not pose to have answers to these larger problems she is grappling with. Rather, she makes her artistic grappling transparent. She makes public the curvilinear channels of introspective reflection through her art.

Emotional mapping frames the carriage of each movement across points of stasis. The sculptural is channelized through a concurrence of visceral emotionality, a parallel musicality of the body, and a gestural connection to the sung lyric. This reflection is an intellectual distancing, one that is informed by cognitive processing and involves reasoning with text, music, and movement at every instance. The cognitive questioning moves the art from the emotional and the visceral toward the communicative domain. This cognitive questioning also infuses a durational depth of *staying with the question*. Surrendering to the inquiry is not the traditional surrender to the divine as we see in the traditional moving body. Dandavate's humanistic appeal to choreography introduces humility into the human condition that simultaneously critiques and resists, in the process of deepening the inquiry through repeated questioning (Ghosh 2020). The performative domain becomes an active experiential arbitrator with the viewing audience through collective questioning, and one can inger a synergistic reflection upon possible solutions. The choreography becomes an experience of collectivity building a community across difference ingrained in the cultural-situatedness of a people. This modality of repeated questioning through a persistent perceptual dialogic pays cognizance to change and contemporaneity. I have argued earlier how the sculptural stasis is programmed into the dancing Odissi body as *kinesthetic pause* in which moving from a posture to another, transitions with a pause, one where the communicative impulse is infused into the dancing body breaking its fourth wall as an independent entity. In that moment, it becomes a part of the larger whole involving the performance as well as the reception.

This moment aligns the dancer's body-mind continuum with its choreographic reality—in imagination, visualization, and description—while simultaneously connecting it to the audience. These *kinesthetic pauses* have resonance in Dandavate's inquisitive experientiality especially via hand-eye coordination. For her, the focus of the gaze is crucial to being and communication. The use of the eyes as a constant negotiator of being, seeing, and visualizing is paramount as the viewer is able to gauge the dancer's actions and create an aesthetic tapestry of the emotional centering joined with inquisitive experientiality. A constant reflecting on, and distancing and detaching from the form-content binary, through a tenor of the intellectual and the experiential creates an inquiry-based art-making. This process simultaneously questions the current status quo and suspends the egotistic ambition of finding an immediate solution. Solution is not the end goal for this artistic exercise. Rather, the call to action is meditative introspection where the dancing body can be the most effective in its traditional adherence to formal complexities. Below, I elaborate upon Dandavate's inquiry into curvilinear gesture as an epistemological premise in her solo choreography by delving into the process of inquiry where the content is communicated through reflection, distancing, and subsequent detachment, emulating the liberatory gestures of the last segment in the Odissi repertoire.

Introducing the Inquiry: *Enigmatic Bliss*

Dandavate asks a philosophical question about the problem of suffering despite the presence of joy. Her object of knowledge is not a definite answer given the deep philosophical investments into this subject matter across literature and religion. She turns to a philosophical literary composition while her mode of argumentation remains the formal infrastructure of curvilinear gestures and postures of *Sabhinaya Pallavi* (musical proliferation with verbal deliberation). The dance is organized along three binary configurations, namely, *Anondo-Koruna* (joy-compassion), *Timiro-Jyoti* (darkness-light), and *Milono-Bichhedo* (union-separation), weaving the traditional melodic elaboration of *Pallavi* with the verses in Bengali. The choreographic process honors the dichotomous depiction of bliss and sorrow, light and dark, and union and separation while alternately weaving the expressive and the percussive. Dandavate refutes any authoritative or prescriptive attempts at finding her way into this existential question and focuses on the choreography as am embodied instrument of knowing. In philosophical parlance, she focuses on *Pramana Grantha*, an intense deliberation on the methodology of argumentation (Sivananda 1960).

Enigmatic Bliss draws from Nobel laureate poet Rabindranath Tagore's song "Joyo Tobo Bichitro Anondo" in Bengali (translated by me as "Praising Your Strange Joy"). The term *Bichitro Anondo* becomes the tagline for the compositional process with a back and forth between music and dance. *Bichitro* means strange; *Anondo* means joy. This phrase from the sung lyric established embodied exploration of duality in our existential condition—across sadness and joy, light and dark, and union and separation. Art historian David Gall notes that Tagore believes in a comprehensive humanism, recognizing the need to globalize humility, compassion, and selflessness quite contrary to postcolonial imitation of Western modernity designed to foster discrimination and inequality and perpetuate social conflict (Gall 2019). Tagore strives toward freedom and fulfillment of the self through complete integration with the world. Artistic integration of the self through constructed dualities of sadness-joy, dark-light, and separation-union gives a glimpse into Tagore's world-making. In this work, I show how Dandavate's dancing body and her choreographic intent infuse the process of epistemological knowing into the artistic process. I elaborate upon the creation of this work and supplement the creative process with a choreographic analysis of the final piece grounding Dandavate's choreography as a formalized philosophical inquiry. This section establishes Dandavate's choreographic ethos as an inquiry-based reflection on the devotional surrender characteristic and quintessential of the Odissi dancing body.

Suggested by ethnomusicologist Anirban Bhattacharyya, Tagore's song "Joyo Tobo Bichitro Anondo" captures the uncertainty of the COVID-19 pandemic. Although written in 1909, this song encapsulates the moment we found ourselves with choreographer Dandavate in San Francisco, Bhattarcharyya in New Delhi, and percussionist and rhythm composer Ramprasad Gannavarapu in Mumbai. I was stuck inside the four walls of my residence in Charlotte, North Carolina. Tagore's composition brings the four of us together through the squared abstractions of the gallery feature in the video conferencing portal—Zoom. The song acts as a congealing factor bringing the various elements of the work together in an online work setting. Although this modality of online collaboration was unprecedented prior to the pandemic, it has since become commonplace for most of us who continue to be involved in the creation and production of artistic content. Alongside providing artistic inspiration and respite from the pandemic induced alienation, on a more concrete level, the song provides the linear flow of the piece as musical and percussive refrains interspersed Tagore's lyrics. Gannavarapu translates Tagore's song in *Teora Taal* (seven beats rhythmic cycle in Hindustani classical music) to Odissi's *Tripata*

Taal (seven beats rhythmic cycle in traditional Odissi music) and variations in it, both having the same rhythmic structure and emphasis (3+2+2; *Dha Dhi Na Dhi Na Dhi Na*).

> This world, which takes its form in the mold of man's perception, still remains as a partial world of the senses and the mind. It is like a guest and not like a kinsman. It becomes completely our own when it comes within the range of our emotions. Without love and hatred, pleasure and pain, fear and wonder, continually working upon it, this world becomes part of our personality. (Tagore 2007, 83)

The above quote situates emotion at the center of world-making especially in the way the individual gets to make meaning of their existence. In this capacity, the song centers the range of our emotions toward a collected notion of meaning-making with a difference—one that is simultaneously situated in cultural and regional codes while finding its resonance across pluralistic encounters. Odissi is both nationalist and majoritarian by construction. Its historical construction coincides with the larger cultural heritage project of nation-building, and it depends on Hindu cultural codes and conceptual basis for its construction and dissemination. Yet, it is reflective of the regional ethos. Further, there is linguistic tension between Bengal and Odisha. Use of Tagore's lyric has been questioned before by the Odishan community with allegations of appropriation and inauthenticity. For example, in my transliterations, I have used the particular Bengali accent that I am acculturated within. Cultural and regional tensions aside, as a Bengali seeped in Tagore as well as Odissi dance since my childhood, this was my first Odissi composition involving Tagore's song, well into the third decade of my professional career. Dandavate's translation of Tagore's, "Joyo Tobo Bichitro Anondo," is provided below (Dandavate 2021).

Long live each joyous song.
Poet, long live your compassion.
Long live formidable
all demolition of wrong.
Long live elixir
Death, suffering,
long live your solace.
Long live your luminosity,
appalling gloomy night.
Long live your love, unity.
Long live your heartbreak.

Literal interpretation of the words through codified gestures situates authorial intent as a primary voice. Word-for-word translation through gestural interface is imbued with expressive intent of the choreographer as executed by the dancer. The first sentence: *Joyo Tobo Bichitro Anondo He Kobi Joyo Tomaro Karuna* ("I praise strange multivalent juxtapositions of joy and sorrow") is established at the beginning of the dance and returns throughout the piece. Here, *Tobo* and *Tomaro* refer to an invisible entity in second person, further established by the elevation of the gaze. Eye-level communication represents communication with the viewing audience.

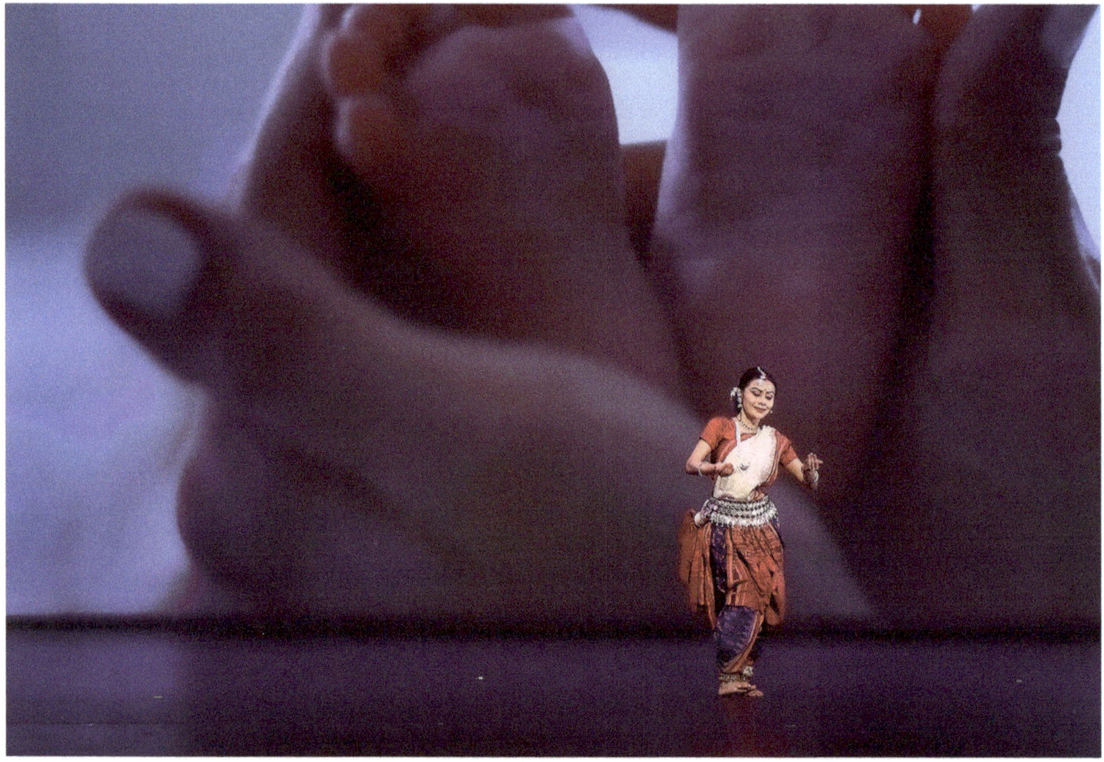

FIG. 16: Author Performing Karuna as Labor of Love at UNC Charlotte Dance Faculty Concert, Charlotte, January 23, 2023. Reproduced with permission from Jeff Cravotta.

This becomes clear with the movement description of the first sentence of the *Sabhinaya Pallavi.* The *Abhinaya* portion begins with Tagore's first line: *Joyo Tobo Bichitro Anondo He Kobi Joyo Tomaro Karuna* addressing someone as the poet and the world around as a strange place with opposite tendencies. With the gradual opening of my eyes, first looking at my right hand and then to the audience, I establish Tagore's *Joyo*, which means to praise and elevate. Then, I address Tagore's *Taba*, meaning yours, with my left hand in *Chatura Mudra* (hand gesture with thumb placed at the base of the ring finger as the little finger separates from the remaining three fingers imitating a table top). I bring my hands near my chin to project *Bichitro*, which means strange. Then, I stretch out both my hands toward the audience portraying *Anondo*, intense joy or bliss. While every word of the segment *Joyo Tobo Bichitro Anondo* accompanies a gesture in its very first iteration, such is not the case for the remainder of this first line. For the entirety of *Joyo Tomaro Karuna*, I use *Katamukha* (hand gesture where the tips of the index finger, the tall finger, and thumb touch and all the fingers stretch to their maximum capacity) to portray a compassionate heart and then I revert back to *Chatura* to consolidate acts of empathy. This analysis of the first line of the song shows the variation of fusing authorial intent with choreographic direction and finally performative execution. The words are important for the piece and

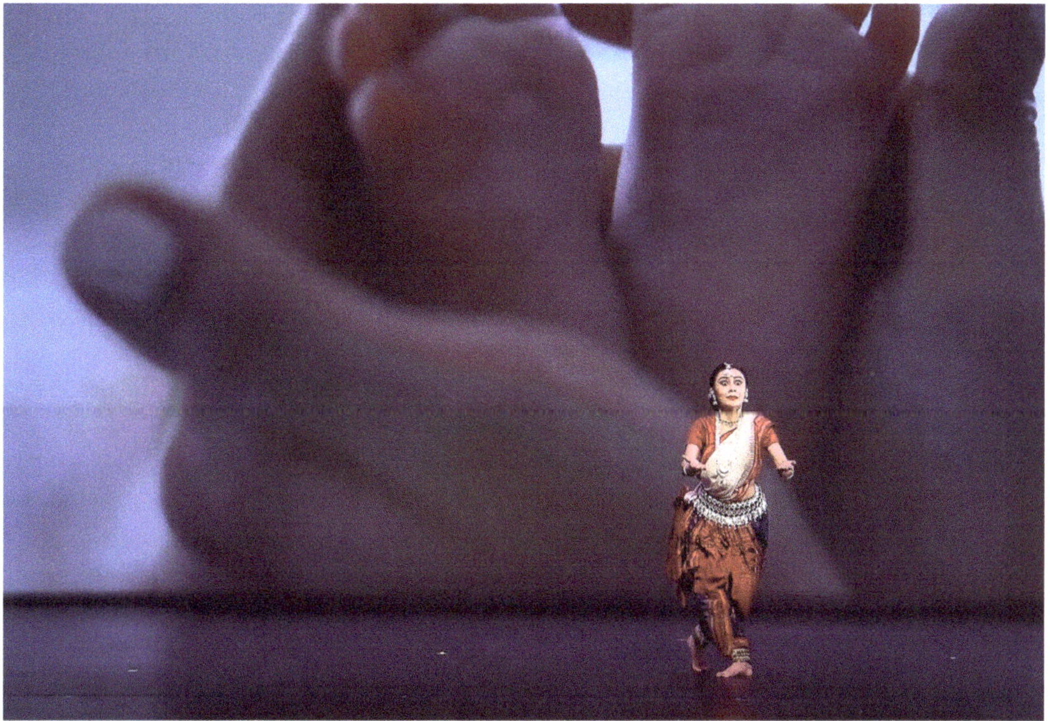

FIG. 17: Author Performing Karuna as Loss of Love at UNC Charlotte Dance Faculty Concert, Charlotte, January 23, 2023. Reproduced with permission from Jeff Cravotta.

literal translation represents Tagore's vision. Furthermore, the choreographic intention comes through with specific additions of expressive accents using the gaze to direct attention and establish strength, focus, and intensity of the narrative. The gaze when elevated, refers to the poet in question. When the gaze remains at eye-level, it performs the descriptive, representative, and visualizing functions delivered to the audience.

Sanchari, or expressive elaboration of sung lyric, draws from contemporary issues plaguing the lived realities of our daily lives. Similar to Tagore's juxtaposition of *Anondo* (joy) with *Karuna* (sadness), the dance notes the mirth of the natural environment as human mobility comes to a standstill juxtaposed with the loss of lives configured as floating corpses and mass burials. Similar juxtapositions are developed through *Timiro-Jyoti* (darkness-light) and *Milono-Bichhedo* (union-separation). While the former duo brings out the light and dark within each of us as we regenerate our daily cycle through waking, dreaming, and deep sleep, the latter is stretched toward the discourse of border politics and humanity's hierarchical organization by non-empathic othering (Nikhilananda 1952). So, authorial intention is expanded through the tool of *Sanchari* toward directions inspired from the choreographer's notebook.

Each performance is an act of assimilation, processing, and choice-making. The performer brings in an expressive capacity that differs from day to day and from every iteration of the performance and its array of rehearsals. Yet, the practice of nuanced expressivity to hold and direct the gaze is necessary to then sustain that facial subtlety in the glaring lights of the performance. The dancer needs a well-lit face in order for the expression to register. This implies that front-lights hit the dancer's eyes. Multiple iterations of repeating this same sentence through coordinated gestural, postural, and emotive registers allow for a smooth execution during the actual performance. Authorial intent is opened up through choreographic imagination and performative efficacy.

There is an array of performative registers to draw from, which include emotional, affective, abstract, rhythmic, intellectual, conversational, discursive, sociopolitical, activist, and— most importantly— the curvilinear technical injunctions. At any point, the dancer draws from one, a combination, or even all of these registers in order to get a point across to the audience. In fact, the dancer can improvise on stage and determine the perfect combination of elements depending on the performative nature and preparation for that day and iteration of the dance work. *Bichitro Anondo* broadly presents musicality of the *Raga* (melodic mode), percussive accentuation by the *Mardala* (two-headed drum), and the narrative content of the lyric extended further through choreographic imagination. Certain sections of the dance emphasize one or the other. For example, we hear only Gannavarapu's voice during the beginning rhythmic entry and the *Arasa* (rhythmic interlude) in the middle of the dance bridging the *Sthayi* (opening and principal section of a musical composition) and the *Antara* (musical variation building upon the *Sthayi*). In the bridging *Arasa*, I use multiple narrative elements, sun, sky, bird, flower, etc., to depict an environment free of human intervention, manipulation, and pollution.

Throughout the work, the choreographer wants an inner dialogue, a constant thinking through accompanying choreographic visualization. Dandavate asked me to write words accompanying my gestures. She encourages the use of adjectives and adverbs that would enhance the expressive quotient of my dance. These words are an important part throughout the piece and often stand in conjunction with Tagore's lyric, Bhattacharyya's voice, and Gannavarapu's percussion. This intellectual real-time processing kept every performance an act of choice-making and improvisation. I subdivided the piece in ten segments as pearls strung together in a thread anchored in my torso movement.

1. Entry: I enter the stage accompanied by vocal modulations and percussive notations.
2. *Sthayi*: I establish the primary musical refrain through curvilinear pathways.
3. *Anondo-Karuna*: I elucidate the first (sadness-joy) of three scenarios of duality through expansive body movement and focused gaze.
4. *Arasa Setu*: Setu means bridge. I call this *Arasa Setu* because it acts as a main anchor of change in the narrative flow of the piece. The bridging rhythmic component helps to transition from *Sthayi* to *Antara* maintaining the traditional format of the *Pallavi*.
5. *Antara*: The musical variation of the Antara is introduced, maintaining the components of the traditional *Pallavi*.
6. *Timiro-Jyoti*: The second duality (light-dark) is introduced here through gestural and expressive nuance.
7. *Antara* Returns: The Antara music returns briefly marking a narrative change.

8. *Arasa Sakhya*: Sakhya means friendship. This rhythmic section that I named *Arasa Sakhya*, depicts a friendly encounter via rhythmic elaboration. It provides a rhythmic introduction to the next section that focuses on the coming together and separation of people.
9. *Milono-Bichhedo*: In this duality depicting union-separation, I encounter US policy of separating children from their migrant parents at the borders. In the dance, I enliven this narrative through emotive registers enacting the militarized borders and their implications for the lives of both adults and children.
10. *Sthayi* Returns: The concluding section brings forth the *Sthayi* refrain in greater speed like in a traditional composition. One can hear Bhattacharyya's voice alongside Gannavarapu's percussion ending in a climactic apex matched by the dancer's seeking of an answer to riddles of union-separation, light-dark, and sadness-joy.

I enter with the lilting gait of the *Lalita Parsni Paada Sanchara* (a serpentine heel-led forward gait) mapping the vocal articulations by Anirban Bhattacharyya in the melodic mode of *Raga Shudhha Saarang* (an afternoon melodic mode). Using a circular gesture punctuated by alternating *Mudras—Alapadma* (full-bloom) and *Katakamukha* (bud)—I establish an environmental scape encompassing the various cues of the flora. My right hand rises, noticing the infinite shades of blue in the sky. When it reaches directly above me, I mark a decisive change of color owing to, perhaps, the monsoons. At the tail end of the semicircular gaze, I notice a dancing peacock at a distance. The audience experiences the dancing peacock first through my expressions—subtle eye, neck, and head movements—and subsequently in the rhythmic footwork mainly using the heel as I spin along my central axis with bent knees. This marks the entry.

Jhimi Kita Jhimi
Jham Karataka Jhenu Jhena

From the very onset, the percussive accompaniment establishes a soft aesthetic that Dandavate refers to as *Jhunk*, translated as a particular downward lilting accent specific to Oriya culture and Odissi's curvilinearity. My dancing peacock sequence qualifies the *Jhunk* by level changes and the turning in and out of the hips. Syllables on the third (*Jhimi*) and seventh beats (*Jhena*) on the *Mardala* playing the seven-beat rhythmic cycle called *Tripata*, I bend my knees to lower my level. My hips turn out, distinguishing this sudden and subtle collapse to the side from the previous movements that focus more on footwork—heel-toe articulations of the feet—and accompanying neck and torso movements. While interspersing the *Jhunk* across rhythmic accents, my upper body engages in side-to-side torso movements while the spinal column reaches back and front playfully to enact the dancing motion of the bird. The *Jhunk* continues throughout the piece, establishing itself firmly in the rest of the entry sequence through neck, torso, feet, and spine with spiraling, expanding, and circular movements before the first utterance of the primary *Sthayi*: *Ta Jham Ta Rita Jham Jhenu Ta Rita Jhena*.

Deflecting my neck in *Tirascinna* (a diagonal chin-raise) and *Prakampita* (forward and backward neck motion), extending, circling and spiraling my spine, as well as using differential movement qualities, level of hand movements, and gestural variation, I establish the *Jhunk*. The peacock dances amidst the flora, fauna, the rising and setting sun, the soft breeze, and the rippling waves of the river water. Using *Bhasa* (full-bodied gesture) depicting the flow of water, I end the prelude to the beginning of the main structure of the *Pallavi*, that is the *Sthayi*—a musical as well as dramatic concept that unifies and stabilizes the piece.

The tone of the piece oscillates between binary formulations through nuances of expressive subtlety and border-crossings, juxtaposing a differential at the central core. The rhythmic and the melodic create the aesthetic bulwark of the piece on which the narrative and the metaphorical rest. I practiced these sections separately and in small chunks before stringing the entire necklace with all ten beads. Practice allows for the dance to become muscle memory in ways that then by-pass active memorization during the performance. Although, I am not interested in analyzing the exact scientific mechanics of my performativity, I find it useful to note the processes involved in setting a piece of this length to memory and ensuring its emotive, affective, and expressive enlivening at every iteration, whether during rehearsal or in performance. The musicality and percussive inform my movement as much as the narrative appeal of text and imagination. Throughout the work, the torso remains the principal actor and the primary signifier given its incessant and continuous flow across technical, narrative, and musical imperatives.

Dandavate's choreographic oeuvre lies in enhancing Odissi's geometric arcs. She misses this arcing of the torso in contemporary works that focus on precision, spectacle, and fast-paced footwork. To address this discomfort, she experiments with *Bichitro Anondo* as a realization of the full potential of the curvilinear torso. The torso is highly pliable in this dance. It physically creates arcs through isolation of the rib cage. Furthermore, it uses the back muscles and the core muscles to enhance its movement, often in connection with the musicality. It also conjures narrative intensity through an emotional activation of the torso. Finally, it maintains a call-and-response relationship with footwork. It is commonly known that stamping the right foot leads to an echo of the torso toward the left. This is customary of Guru Kelucharan Mohapatra style of Odissi and not necessarily practiced in other styles. Given, Dandavate and my training within Guru Kelucharan Mohapatra style, this technical injunction continues to remain ingrained in my body. The oppositional basis connecting the rib cage with footwork can be described as the most transactional of torso movements given the one-to-one connections. In any case, the torso is the most expressive element in this piece of choreography given its embedding within every movement imparting curvilinearity in stillness and in motion. The torso assimilates the music, text, and rhythm of the *Sabhinaya Pallavi* as the expressive facial tremors are felt in the subtle shifts of the chest, the sides, or the back. Dandavate is successful in reorienting audience's attention to the torso through her curvilinear choreography.

Flight remains a strong metaphor as animal and human migration are juxtaposed across dimensions of border-crossing, connectivity, and transformation. Establishing the curvilinear aesthetic from the point of entry until the last *Chhapaka* (sling-shot movement), *Bichitro Anondo* weaves critical questioning through Tagore's poetry. Movement is no longer performed toward or away from the transcendental as the yardstick. The structure of the piece incorporates an alternation of musical, percussive, and textual variations with each complementing the other in order to support the dramaturgical arc. The piece starts with a feeling of wonderment, juxtaposing opposite emotions, traits, and possibilities while intermittently interjecting the question of irreconcilability. *Bichitro Anondo* ends on a questioning note where the dancer grapples with the irreconcilable differences of beauty within the form and in nature and the environmental, political, and humanitarian disasters inflicted by humans on each other. Toward the end, the climactic questioning is provided by the repetition of the first line of Tagore's song: *Joyo Tobo Bichitro Anondo,* translated by the choreographer as *Long live each joyous song.* The multiple iterations of this sentence functions as an organizing tool relaying internal bliss, external description, and a provocation. It becomes a provocative flight of imagination exploring regionally specific formal and conceptual limits. Dandavate does not need to go beyond the formal investments in order to inspire change.

The musical and percussive tenets of the piece are deeply colored by the emotional arc. Through facial expressions, gestural complexity, and embodied emotions, the dancer impresses upon the audience poignant moments, intensities, and imagery using an array of first, second, and third person voices. Use of eye, eyebrow, lips, neck, and head movements demonstrates choreographic subtleties that add meaning to the existing text. *Mudras*, or hand gestures, provide a consistent degree of stylized semiotics since gestural communicative potential supplements the textual as well as the percussive. The rhythmic accompaniment encourages more of *Nritta* (pure dance) although the choreographer weaves in embodied expressivity by coloring bodily carriage with that of a dancing peacock or encoding gestural meaning in an *Arasa* (a rhythmic section) between the melodious mapping. The primary melodic refrain *Ta Jham Ta Rita Jham* is introduced in the beginning and musical variations interject the dance at various points in the dance, setting the tone in grounded languidness. At the beginning, musical variations in multiple speeds and changing modes of delivery establish the mellifluous structure of *Raga Mishra Sarang* in the curvilinear aesthetic. Although the words of the refrain, *Ta Jham Ta Rita Jham*, remain the same, the tune changes throughout the piece bringing in subtle changes in notes evoking the feeling of curiosity. However, the primary refrain and its associated gestural and postural traces return after every musical variation in order to ensure choreographic continuity throughout the dance. While the musical section is elaborate at the beginning, the percussive takes precedence as a bridging maneuver carrying over the narrative arc of Tagore's lyrics.

In this mathematical bridge, a singular rhythmic refrain—*Dhei Ta Thin Da Dhei Ta Thin Da*—repeats in multiple variant iterations showing the sun, flowers, peacock, and birds. The *Tihai* (ending) of this *Arasa* ends with the flight of birds, a notion further elaborated upon later in the dance across the imagery of light and dark as the dancer shows the birds flying away in the day and returning to the trees at night. Gestural simulation of the world around us weaves Tagore's poetics, Ramprasad Gannavarapu's percussive compositions, and Anirban

Bhattacharyya's melody lines throughout *Bichitro Anondo* that ends on an investigation of this strange bliss.

The narrative arc of this piece starts with a sense of wonderment to reach a climactic sense of curiosity. It starts with describing the wonders of nature such as the dancing peacock, the flying eagle, the prancing deer, and the buzzing bee seeking nectar. The dance contrasts the beautiful with the grotesque in its portrayal of death, funeral pyres, and the floating dead bodies in the river Ganges during the second wave of the COVID-19 pandemic (Khakhar 2021). Portraying global trends of fear and isolation alongside the ecological balance of the nature poses contradiction as the central feature of daily life. This loss of human potency juxtaposes with the reduced pollution levels and the brief respite for the natural world—the flora and the fauna (Kinver 2021). Contradicting experiences of rejuvenation and depletion through the *Anondo-Koruna* and *Timiro-Jyoti* dichotomies are expressed in gestural semiotics, postural stability, and percussive experimentation. The dance connects the pandemic of disease to the pandemic of hatred that leads to building walls of separation between individuals as well as countries. *Milono-Bichhedo* (union-separation binary) develops through depicting love and loss induced by political tinkering and policy manipulation by nation-states. The political issue of the wall on the southern border of the US features alongside separation of migrant parents from their children. Using vivid imagery of loss, separation, and anxiety as circulating online in news and media outlets, *Bichito Anondo* is a choreographic provocation of the bewildering state of humanity that is capable of enigmatic bliss through spiritual registers, on one hand, while, on the other, can stoop down to an abyss of inflicting pain to the self and the world at large. Rhythmic interludes carry forth the narrative arc complementing the literal translation and the layering of contemporary globally transpiring experiences. The narrative arc of Tagore's song further interspersed with critical choreographic thoughts, weaves a critical consciousness within *Bichitro Anondo*.

While the symbolism of gestural signification curates the peripheral dancing body, postural nuance signifies the core through *Chauka* (symmetrical square shape), *Tri Bhangi* (asymmetrical S-shape), and *Abhanga* (asymmetrical with a slight hip deflection). The centering and subsequent decentering of the pelvic floor nuances the dancing body with varying degrees of expressivity. The grounded-centered pelvis signifies differently from the grounded-deflected one. Further, the degree of curvature differs between the *Abhanga* and the *Tri Bhangi*—the hip deflection in the former is lesser than that of the latter. Deflection from the central vertical axis adds additional degrees of dynamism to the dancing body that ensures a symmetrically balanced approach to showing expressivity and equanimity. This measured dynamism is also a common feature across dance and sculpture that, as a discipline, remains in sync historically, culturally, and contextually (Venkataraman 2003).

In addition to the vertical, the horizontal axis divides the dancing body in two halves: the upper body and the lower body. This is a significant separation in Odissi that I have described in the introductory chapter. The lower body is further nuanced by the changing levels of knee-bends. The angular bending knee is similar to the soft folds of a *Sari*. Yet, the bends firmly dynamizes the legs in *Abhanga*, *Tri Bhangi*, and *Chauka*. Odissi's characteristic curvilinearity lies in the ever-present curvature in the limbs. So, the knees never lock outward, and the legs do not hyper extend. The complete fold of the knee can be located in yoga-esque movements used in choreographic composition—say in single-legged balances such as the *Vrikshasana* (tree-pose) and depiction of the deer in *Bandhani* (a posture in which the front of one foot wraps around the back of the standing/supporting leg and the wrapped leg has a deeply bent knee).

Bichitro Anondo's unique treatment of mobilizing *Abhanga* via footwork is the central distinguishing feature. Odissi technique involves mobilization of the legs and feet via percussive footwork that are mainly practiced in the 'steppings' of the *Chauka* and the *Tri Bhangi*. Hips are turned out in both these postures. The remaining two *Bhangas*, or postures, namely *Sama Bhanga* (standing in complete attention with turned in hips and feet together) and *Abhanga* do not accompany any footwork. Yet, choreographic expansion of the form in *Bichitro Anondo* points to the degrees of dynamism located within the erect dancing body with slight deflection and turned in hips.

Intricate percussive experimentation across tonal complexity further accents the vehicular containment of footwork in postural nuance marking a presence of speed and quantitative complexity. In the preceding paragraph, I have mentioned how the reception of the footwork depends on the containing posture. The same movement—heel, flat, flat—looks very different in *Abhanga*, *Tri Bhangi*, and *Chauka*. *Bichitro Anondo* further colors the footwork according to tonal variations brought about by the percussionist's specific ways of hitting hands against the *Mardala* (two-headed drum). Soft tonal variations accompany *Bichitro Anondo*'s percussivity upon Dandavate's insistence to bring into fruition her choreographic vision. This form of percussivity further enhances the *Jhunk* defined earlier, providing a soft-lilting-curvilinear aesthetic throughout *Bichitro Anondo*. The first rhythmic construct or *Arasa* structurally marks the bridging from the *Sthayi* to the *Antara*. The second *Arasa* transitions imagistically from the construct of the light and the dark to the union and separation. This *Arasa* depicts *Sakhya* (friendship in playful commingling of bodies in space and time). The *Jhunk* is used in expressing slight appreciation and cajoling that characterizes the negotiations between friends. The mundane play of a friendship established percussively is then contrasted with the separation of states and humans inspired from contemporary immigration issues in the United States, through *Abhinaya*, or expressive subtlety. The expressive quotient remains constant in *Bichitro Anondo* across rhythmic and expressive registers.

Movement in *Bichitro Anondo* is as much about curvilinearity, interdependence of dance, music, and text as it is about positioning the dancing body in the world order inquiring, reflecting, refracting, and critiquing existing trends and the status-quo. Branching off from multiple strands of creation and performativity as enumerated below, this choreography demonstrates the multiple layers of aesthetic and political labor implicating the dancing body.

a. Tagore's investment in Asian philosophy;
b. Guru Kelucharan Mohapatra's stylistic traits of curvilinearity;
c. Dandavate's textual emphasis on movement generation and honing performative focus;
d. Bhattacharyya's acute ability to meditate on Tagore's music, lyric, and translate it to the Odissi genre;

e. Gannavarapu's dexterity in responding to Dandavate's request of generating a particular percussive soundscape that is not overbearing but mellifluous and maintains the flow;
f. My embodiment, processing, meditations, and constant improvisations of multiple registers during practice and performance.[1]

To further the experiential inquiry, I briefly explore three other works choreographed on me by Dandavate: *Trigger, Nachi Meera,* and *Azad Pankh.*

Experiential Questioning of the Grotesque: *Trigger*

The act of questioning takes a different valence in *Trigger*, a meditation on school shootings in the US. The dance is a solo work with percussive syllables and nonverbal vocal singing creating the bulk of the piece. The shooting at Robb Elementary School in Uvalde, Texas, on May 24, 2022, lead to the death of nineteen children and two adults (Hong et al. 2024). This was the launching point of *Trigger*. The dance starts with the projection of statistics on school shooting in the United States on the cyclorama (Fisher 2024). The projected images keep changing alongside the narrative progression of the dance. The dance ends on a positive note toward self-composure, prayer, and healing. After the initial offering, it renders the site of tragedy and also reminisces on the lost lives of children through their aspirations. Dandavate's rendition of the incident emerges from a place of *Karuna* (sadness), acknowledging and processing grief toward communal healing. Its linear teleological intent lies in the culmination of peace. The ending draws from a Sanskrit peace-chant drawn from the *Bridaranyanaka Upanishad*, praying for well-being, peace, and fulfilment for all (Madhavananda 1975): *Om Sarveshaam Svastir-Bhavatu, Om Sarveshaam Shantir-Bhavatu, Om Sarveshaam Purnam-Bhavatu, Om Sarveshaam Mangalam-Bhavatu, Om Shantih Shantih Shantih.*

Ending with a peace chant, this piece is composed with a faith in the possibility of communal healing, recovery, and resilience in trying times. Its utopian voice is perhaps in sync with the harmonious and symmetrical worldview of Odissi where the end is always one where the individual and the collective freedom remain overprioritized. However, the topic choice is far from the traditional realm of Odissi choreography that stays limited to mythic-spiritual-religious dimensions of the Indian cosmology. Healing feels unreal in this issue of relentless loss of youth potency. Generally, with grief there is a back and forth between a feeling of being broken as well as one of something in us that has been broken open. *Trigger* takes a stand at this back and forth across the feelings of loss and resilience, of trauma and hope. Ending on the note of peace and fulfilment, it hopes to emphasize that neither has finality in scope and existence. The ideas of both being broken and being broken open play off of one another.

It is then this play, in the form of the children's unrealized dreams, that takes precedence in the piece. Remembering the children's aspirations of becoming a basketball player, a visual artist, a snorkeler, and a cheerleader drives home the central point of play. The play of life, perhaps, can drive us forward to a point of communal healing where the point is to realize the transient nature of our existence in the larger scheme of reality. However, this view continues to find resistance from a social justice argument where the thought of leaving the lost lives to destiny's play seems like an outrageous proposition given the durational lack of state-intent to improve gun control in the United States. Furthermore, this healing activity seems unsustainable given the lack of a crisis management and follow-up plan through only periodic meetings with the impacted communities. In that case, *Trigger* falls flat. Even as I dance this work, I find myself questioning my 'spiritual escapism' and perhaps, in my performance, I am inundated with questions of purpose, significance, and relevance of such a work. I continue to grapple with an unresolved tension about my desire to inquire into this issue of losing youth to gun violencewhile noting vividly the inevitable failure of such an activity. I learn to accept that failure, as the one and only teleology for a certain choreographic situation (Bozic 2018).

Establishing Experiential Suspension: *Nachi Meera*

Nachi Meera (the dancing Mirabai) is my first experiment with Dandavate. In *Nachi Meera*, I elaborate upon Dandavate's treatment of the devotional through the poetic construction of medieval female Indian poet-mystic Mirabai (Sangari 1990). Multiple influences blend into the creative process of reimagining Mirabai. *Nachi Meera* is a pan-Indian project where an Odissi dance choreographer works on a Rajasthani (northern Indian state) historical figure with a southern Indian composer. Dandavate choreographed this in the ethos of *Baul* culture (mystic minstrels dressed in saffron who sing songs with devotional content as well as sociocultural critique). *Baul* is a heterogeneous sect of mystics in eastern India and Bangladesh who combined multiple religious and musical traditions, and since 2005, has been included in the list of Masterpieces of the Oral and Intangible Heritage of Humanity by UNESCO. Dressed in saffron, they carry their string instrument and sing devotional songs with a high degree of social, cultural, and political critique. With their distinctive clothes and musical instruments, the *Baul* culture is known for its contemporary edge to devotional content and ethos (Ganguli et al. 2019).

The dance starts and ends with the imagery of the *Baul* traversing the countryside with the *Iktara*, a one-stringed instrument. While the beginning is mellow, the end is imbued with devotional fervor, one that is characteristic of the song progression in the *Baul* genre. The song takes the form of an *Abhinaya* with text and music together weaving a series of active images—rolling clouds, weaving garlands, smelling sandalwood paste, and sweeping breeze—in the curvilinear folds of dance. The poetics, musicality, and rhythmic interludes build the dramatic intent through movement.

The layering of the *Abhinaya* is an intense culmination of multiple hues from poetic, lyrical, percussive, emotive, and devotional aesthetics. The central guiding principle remains within the *Sthayi Bhava* (the dominant expression). The *Sthyayee Bhava* is a combination of devotion (*Bhakti*) and love (*Sringara*). Mirabai's intense longing for her beloved is affirmed through her lyrical expressions (Martin 2023). Expressions of life-affirming love are abundant in Mirabai's songs where love has been equated with salvation. Mira's identity as a woman, argues John Stratton Hawley, makes her "words have an authenticity that no male poet can match" (2008, 122). Famed saint poets such as Kabir, Surdas, and Tulsidas among others had to go through all the work of "becoming" women to experience God as husband and lover (120). Although, I do not comply with Hawley's essentializing of Mirabai's gendered attributes, I acknowledge her special status as a pan-Indian figure with an unparalleled devotional fervor.

Throughout the dance, I establish Mirabai's *Bhakti-Sringara* either in lyrical translation or metaphorical exposition. Searching for *Krishna* in the environment, external and internal, *Meera* centers the devotional yearning of the *Bhakta* (the devotee). The fervor is grounded in the materiality of her beloved as the choreography culminates with Mirabai's yearning as a complete surrendering of her soul at the feet of the devoted. Poetics remain the hallmark of *Abhinaya* pieces because it provides the foundation for the subsequent elaboration in gesture and expression.

The song is a composition by Mirabai, and the dance envisions a performance as the saint poetess. This is a departure from my usual performative avatar where I maintain a fluid role of the principal storyteller and the characters portrayed by the lyrics. Here, donning the persona of Mirabai requires a sense of gravity in mood and expression. This means the constant infusion of *Bhakti* (devotion) as the *Sthayi Bhava* (dominant mood) while the description of the environment, the flora, the fauna, the clouds, and the rains continue to deepen the primary devotional enterprise. She sees him in the changing colors of the skies or in the leaps of the frogs. She experiences him in the rolling of the dark thunderous cumulonimbus clouds and makes flower garlands for his idol in the temple. The *Sanchari Bhava*, or the elaborations beyond the literal translation of the sung poem, further deepen her *Bhakti Sringara* (Sharma 2024).

While the traditional *Abhinaya* is mostly a weaving of the *Sthayi* and the *Sanchari Bhavas*, this piece incorporates another important choreographic modality, which I theorize as dialogical progression. In this piece, Dandavate asked me to verbally describe my movement and include vivid imagery through adjectives and adverbs. I found it unique to engage in the process through both moving and writing. Dandavate would ask me to compose in words felt expressions such that I draw out adverbs and adjectives. So, her devotional rendering of Mirabai's poetry was an intellectually busy exercise for me where I am in real-time consciously connecting the literary words with felt expression. The writing informed my movement as a whole, and the literary workshopping of words led to depth of expression and intent in my gestural expositions. Furthermore, it was a procedural intrusion of me as the dancer, and perhaps, of Dandavate as the creator of the movement through a dialogical progression taking the narrative forward as the *Sutradhar* (storyteller) to an audience.

The figure below is from a working session where Dandavate modified my language in order to find appropriate words for the *Abhinaya*. My words that were let go are in red. For example, words such as hastily, frantically, apprehensively, immediately, and earnestly were replaced by devotionally, spiritually, satisfactorily, experientially, and carefully, respectively. This wordsmithing entailed finding the right descriptor in the dancer's psyche that translated in facial expressions. The lyrics were interspersed with such dialogical progressions while the *Sanchari* elaborates the primary mood of *Bhakti Sringara* that is the *Sthyayi Bhava*. The embellishing of text in the form of sung lyrics, internal dialogue of the dancer, and the foundation within *Bhakti Sringara* through *Sthayi* and *Sanchari* shows the rich layering of multiple verbal codes embellishing this choreographic process and execution.

> Meera (hastily) (Bhavapurna : lot of devotion) looks hither thither following the (quaint) (divine call) trail of the flute that brings her at an immense peace and a quiet joy. Eventually, she (frantically) arrives (spiritually to a fulfifilment) at the (auspicious) doorstep of the temple. Fully satisfied and with eagernessapprehensively, she opens the door and her heart (immediately) feels a sense of relief (Santushti) (Thank God, I found you at last) springs with joy as she calmly (sufi) twirls around a few times. She realizes that it is time to make a lovely garland by showing the action of plucking flowers. She (earnestly) tells the viewers that she is going to pluck flowers, make a garland, and return back in just a second.
> She (carefully) holds out her anchal and ventures out into the forest to gather prized pieces to make the garland for her treasured one. She collects all her flowers on the ground and starts making the garland. Just to be (more) safe, Out of love and devotion, she creates one more garland to decorate her beloved with lovely fragrant flowers. Then, she takes the water jar and (softly) pours it over a sandalwood grinder. Gathering the sandalwood paste in her palms, she brings them to her face. The aroma lifts her spirits reminding her of the (excitement Umad-Ghumad Rolling of the feeling) turbulent heart within while noticing the dark turbulent clouds around.

Musicality remains a striking requirement for an *Abhinaya* as the lilting flow of the instrumentation lands, reflects, and refracts from the dancing body in nuanced ways. *Nachi Meera* is especially potent with musical imagery with the entry and exit sequences representationally showcasing the *Khanjani* (metal plates strung on wood) and *Iktara* (one-stringed instrument), respectively. Both are traditional Indian instruments that we see with Mirabai in popular iconography. *Bansuri*, the flute, maintains a strong influence as a metonymical presence of Hindu male deity *Krishna*, well-known for wielding the flute to enamor his devotees and also the sole purpose of Mirabai's devotional fervor. Finally, the percussion instrument, the *Mardala*, adds further possibilities of staccato gesturing and posturing. While the string and wind musical instruments create a qualitative holistic feel, the percussion adds a quantitative and mathematical approach to the piece. Together the *Khanjani*, *Iktara*, *Bansuri*, and *Mardala* generate a musical semiosis as the lilting cadence or the staccato tautness that the various instruments signify on their own. This metonymy connecting *Krishna* and the *Bansuri* and Mirabai with the *Khanjani* and the *Iktara* generates what I call a musical semiosis. The piece starts with the *Khanjani*, lines with a percussive *Bol* (mnemonic syllables accompanying percussion) on the *Mardala*, and moves on to vocals. Throughout the duration of the work, various strands of musicality alternate to create musical semiosis alongside the verbal and the percussive.

Percussive interruptions showcase the Odissi style of movement by expanding upon the text portrayed either before or after the *Bol*. It expands upon the *Bhava* (theme). For example, a rhythmic interlude between the repetitions of the sung line, *Umada Ghumada Kis Disi Se Aya* (where did it come from circling here and there), expands upon the lyrics with percussive ornamentation to show the density of the rolling clouds, and the intensity of thunder and lightning. The first *Tihai*—the thrice repeated percussive section that marks a distinct change in the music, paving the way for the new—focuses on the gait of the peacock and the koel. Percussion is also used to intensify the devotional elements as seen in the last rhythmscape. Here, swaying from side to side in trance, the dance visualizes Krishna everywhere, finally surrendering in *Bhakti-Sringara*.

The *kinesthetic pauses* create the necessary communicative potential for the choreography. Moving from one *Bhangi* (postural stasis in Odissi) to the other with the *Sthayi Bhava* (dominant expression of *Bhakti Sringara*) requires a moment of physical silencing. This moment aligns the dancer's body-mind continuum to her choreographic reality—in imagination, visualization, or description—while simultaneously connecting it with the audience. The use of the eyes as a constant negotiator of being, seeing, and visualizing *Krishna* is paramount as the viewer is able to gauge Mirabai's actions and create an aesthetic tapestry of the *Sthayi Bhava*. Dandavate's positioning of conjunctions as useful tools in *Abhinaya* becomes another unique choreographic strategy since the conjunctive nuances translate to *kinesthetic pauses* for effective storytelling.

Devotional surrender as imagined by Mirabai and acculturated within the *Baul* tradition lands as a literary exercise where the dancer has to constantly switch between multiple linguistic translations and performative modalities across melody, rhythm, and text. The choreographic process becomes an intellectual exercise where the notion of devotion is explored from many different angles: of gratitude, desire for freedom, offering of oneself, yearning for the Lord in case of a cultural insider, and egotistic suspension through the act of complete surrender of the body-mind complex.

Freeing the Quad: *Azad Pankh*

Poet Uday Dandavate's Hindi poem "Ek Azad Pankh" [The Unstuck Feather], translated by the author into English, inspires Dandavate's *Azad Pankh*. Dandavate connects to these poetic verses through what she calls "movement sequences" as "emotional illustrations." Cyclical deepening and intensification alongside the general ebb and flow of curvilinear tides take hold of the thematic content. In the poem, a feather becomes a metaphor for deeper thought into the meaning of life across personality transitions, curious beginnings and tragic endings of events and emotions, and phenomenological engagement with the vagaries of existence. There is a layered meaning-making across text, music, and rhythm throughout the narrative arc of the piece from epiphany to liberation to abundance and affirmation. After forty-years of marriage, Rohini Dandavate found professional inspiration in her partner Uday Dandavate's poetic imagination. She says that the first-hand view of Uday's reflective and transformative engagement with this poem "triggered in me an impulse to choreograph a dance piece to interpret and express the spirit of the poem" (Dandavate 2025).

A formal structure for the choreography was necessary to conceptualize and visualize the poetic spirit of the four paragraphs borrowed from "The Unstuck Feather." There is symbolic significance to the numerical four in Odissi with grounding in the squared posture (*Chauka*) and the quintessential repetitions in *Ekatali* with four beats. Exploring the quad continues to inspire Dandavate with the musical structure of *Chaturang* (a choreographic and compositional format having four distinct musical sections). The four sections comprise of musical composition using *Sargam* (melodious arcs), *Vadya* (percussive sections), *Pada* (sung lyric with narrative meaning), and *Tarana* (nonverbal sonic structures in a fast pace), respectively. The four-fold structural format house four selected paragraphs from the Uday's poem through an emotional mapping journeying from the limited to the limitless. Here, Dandavate ends with abundance and exuberance where the felt liberation has a phenomenological experientiality of the infinite with an expression of abundant affirmation into one's quest for meaning. Reflecting on her experiences of migrating countries, her immigrant identity presents a limited access to extended support systems and also exposes her to a global community of meaning-making and interpretations. So, the feather takes on an autobiographical resonance as she thinks of freedom within the curvilinear dimensions of the chosen idiom alongside the philosophical import of freedom axiologically grounding the dancing body. One's quest for meaning into oneself then becomes one's journey to freedom incarnate—all of which is located within. The journey referred to here is nevertheless a journey in privilege—one where immigration is self-imposed exile in search for meaning and purpose. Thus, freedom in these conduits almost always presupposes conditions conducive to being livable from which one then grounds into spiritual reflection. While this also connects with the bootstrap ethos of neoliberal thought (Stoesz 2000), it is also a spiritual training where one dives within to find liberatory impulse against societal and personal odds (Pendenza and Lamattina 2019). While this chapter does not have the scope for critique of Dandavate's particular (Motahhari 2023) or the field of Odissi's general search for freedom (Ayau 2017), it must be noted how this form operates in a nexus of privilege across class, caste, gender and sexuality, and religion as noted briefly in the introductory pages (Banerji 2010).

While the piece is created in four sections with the primacy of verbal meaning, rhythmic expositions, melodic intonations, and fast-paced melodic proliferations in each segment, the dance often blends its elements together. Often, the four elements are present in each of the four sections although one element usually takes precedence over the rest. The narrative arc of the work prioritizes the primary ethos of freedom as symbolized by the semiotic signifier of the feather. Swirling, floating, swaying, and scuddling in the air, the feather is lost and found at the same instant. To the choreographer, it finds a metaphoric appeal where it stands as the ability to rise above the daily grind through forbearance, assertion, and measured reaction for achieving one's final goal of freedom. Spotting the feather, early on in the dance, then becomes a moment of epiphany—one where the realization of ultimate freedom as the finality dawns upon the dancer representative of the human condition. In this situation, the dancer takes on the being of every individual with the innate desire and right to freedom. Moving beyond the material boundaries into a liberatory ethos, the dance ends on a note of abundance and affirmation. Dandavate finds Odissi's unique lyrical flow in her choreographic renditions while drawing inspiration from the four elements of the quad.

The primary melodic mode is *Raga Hameer* where the main melodic note is *Dhaivat* (sixth note in the octave). Dandavate asks Gannavarapu, the rhythm composer, to focus on the "Dha" note on the *Mardala*. In this way, there is a harmony and parity across the musicality and the percussion strung with the melodic tonality. The complex sonic structures across literal and nonliteral meaning-making with the overlay of the poem creates this piece a truly layered work with an exploratory nature. Dramatic element by showing the overcoming of obstacles or boundaries in the quest for freedom, allows the piece to gather its own repertoire-like arc with invocatory preludes, dense music and percussion sections, and a textual epiphany only to then dissolve in limitless abundance in the form of musical proliferation.

Closing Remarks

A simultaneous impulse of cyclical reinvigoration and restoration to complete freedom from existing boundaries animates Dandavate's curiosity. Is she ready to let go of the formal boundaries of the dancing Odissi body? Perhaps, the answer to that question will need the reader's experiential suspension while keeping the inquiry alive similar to Dandavate's choreographic ethos. Dandavate stays true to the curvilinear ethos, one that she claims to miss in the existing productions of *Srjan Guru Kelucharan Mohapatra Nrityabasa*, where both she and I have received our respective bearings in the form. While I do not find the implicit value judgment useful, it is necessary to note the erosion of the curvilinear arc over time even in one institution of Odissi dance. This is significant because Guru Kelucharan Mohapatra has trained over four thousand dancers who continue his style through global performance and teaching. Dandavate's romantic adherence to a nostalgic past of curvilinearity contrasts with that of some of her contemporaries including Guru Ratikant Mohapatra, the son of Guru Kelucharan Mohapatra. She explores the curvilinear ethos across environmental pollution, forest fires, climate change, gun violence, and the COVID-19 pandemic. Her movement develops from and mergers back into sculptural stasis as she holds on to the musical arc of the vocalist. The questioning and the dialogical grounds her emotional hues. The emotional precedes the critical inquiry that embeds choreography as primarily a task of a series of vibrations from ignorance to knowledge. *Moksha* in the philosophical treatises of *Advaita Vedanta* (non-dual textual exegesis in Indic traditions) has been referred to as the journey from not knowing to knowing (Tatu 2008). *Moksha* is defined as freedom as defined as liberation from ignorance. I show that Dandavate's choreography is not just an epistemological journey that focuses on the transformative valence. It does not make claims of liberation or of knowledge acquisition. Rather, it stays with the question.

Note

1. See Appendix II: A Dancer's Praxis where Monali Nandy-Mazumdar, a professional Odissi soloist in the US gives her theoretical, musicological, and poetic takeaways of performing this work. Dandavate's democratic and scholarly ethos infiltrates into not only her choreography but also into the preparation and execution of the work by multiple dancers.

References

Ayau, J. 2017. *Creating Multivalent Danced Narratives in Odissi and Contemporary Dance*. The Ohio State University Press.

Banerji, A. 2010. *Odissi Dance: Paratopic Performances of Gender, State, and Nation*. New York University Press.

Bozic, N. 2018. “Is This Choreography?: Choreographing Conditions for Innovative Practice in Everyday Work.” *Organisational Aesthetics* 7 (1): 24–45.

Carter, C. 2020. *Dance and Choreography as a Method of Inquiry*. Forum Qualitative Sozialforschung/Forum: Qualitative Social Research.

Dandavate, R. 2006. *Building Cultural Understanding Through Cultural Exchange*. The Ohio State University Press.

Dandavate, R. 2021. *Enigmatic Bliss*.

Dandavate, R. 2025. “Exploring Dance and Design Through Poetry.” *Medium*. https://medium.com/@rohinidandavate/exploring-dance-and-design-through-poetry-813778o1d576.

Dave, R. 2016. “Liminal Spaces: Odissi as a Continually Evolving Form.” In *Tilt Pause Shift: Dance Ecologies in India*, edited by Anita E. Cherian. Columbia University Press.

Dharwadker, V. 2015. “Emotion in Motion: The *Nāṭyashāstra*, Darwin, and Affect Theory.” *PMLA* 130 (5): 1381–1404.

Fisher, J. 2024. “Lessons Learned from the Robb Elementary School, Uvalde, Texas, School Shooting.” *Open Journal of Social Sciences* 12 (4): 78–96.

Gall, D. 2019. “Ethnocentrism and Higher Art Education: Lingering Legacies, Imperative Nondualities.” *International Journal of Art & Design Education 38* (4): 840–52.

Ganguli, M. K., L. Rafianti, and S. K. Chaudhuri. 2019. “Policy Frameworks for the Protection of Cross Border Traditional Song-Baul: A Case Study.” *Social Sciences & Humanities* 27 (4).

Gardner, S. 2008. “Notes on Choreography.” *Performance Research* 13 (1): 55–60.

Ghosh, R. 2020. “The Advaita Concept of Learning: A Pedagogic Approach.” *Philosophy and the Life-world* 22: 25–34.

Gnoli, Raniero. 1968. *The Aesthetic Experience According to Abhinavagupta*. 2nd ed. Vol. LXII of the Chowkhamba Sanskrit Series. Chowkhamba Sanskrit Series Office.

Hawley, J. S. 2008. “Mirabai in Manuscript.” In *Literature Criticism from 1400 to 1800*, Vol. 143. Gale.

Hong, J. S., A. Valido, and L. E. Robinson. 2024. “Understanding the Antecedents of School Shootings: The Case of the Robb Elementary School.” In the *Impact of Gun Violence in School Systems*, edited by J. Herron and S. R. Sartin, pp. 1–26. IGI Global.

Khakhar, P. 2021. “Shav-vahini Ganga | Ganga, the Carrier of Corpses | શબવાહિની ગંગા |.” https://agitatejournal.org/shav-vahini-ganga-ganga-the-carrier-of-corpses-શબવાહિની-ગંગા-शव-व/.

Kinver, M. 2021. “Then and Now: Pandemic Clears the Air.” *BBC News*. https://www.bbc.com/news/science-environment-57149747.

Madhavananda. 1975. *The Bṛhadāraṇyaka Upaniṣad : With the Commentary of Śaṅkaracārya*. Mayavati, Almora, Advaita Ashrama.

Martin, N. M. 2023. *Mirabai: The Making of a Saint*. Oxford University Press.

Masson, J. L., and M. V. Patwardhan. 1974. “Dhvanigāthāpañjikā.” *Annals of the Bhandarkar Oriental Research Institute* 55 (1/4): 219–25.

Motahhari, M. 2023. *Spiritual Freedom*. 88th ed. Sadra Publications.

Munsi, U. S., and S. Burridge. 2012. *Traversing Tradition: Celebrating Dance in India*. Routledge.

Nikhilananda, S. 1952. “The Three States (Avasthātraya).” *Philosophy East and West*: 66–75.

Pendenza, M., and V. Lamattina. 2019. “Rethinking Self-Responsibility: An Alternative Vision to the Neoliberal Concept of Freedom.” *American Behavioral Scientist* 63 (1): 100–15.

Rani, K. S. 2021. Katyayani Vidmahe: Rasa and Women’s Experience. In *Critical Discourse in Telugu*, 184–90. Routledge India.

Sangari, K. 1990. “Mirabai and the Spiritual Economy of Bhakti.” *Economic and Political Weekly*: 1537–1552.

Sarkar, K. 2019. "De-Centring the Choreographer: Historically Inspired Interruptions/Disruptions in an Exploration Between Sculpture and Movement." *Choreographic Practices* 10 (2): 269–91.
Sharma, B. 2024. "The Aesthetics of Opposition." *Indian Literature* 68 (4 (342)): 173–84.
Sivananda, S. 1960. *Vedanta for Beginners*. Sivananda Literature Research Institute.
Srinivasan, P. 2009. "A 'Material'-ist Reading of the Bharata Natyam Dancing Body: The Possibility of the 'Unruly Spectator'" In *Worlding Dance*, edited by S. L. Foster, 53–75. Springer.
Stoesz, D. 2000. *A Poverty of Imagination: Bootstrap Capitalism, Sequel to Welfare Reform*. University of Wisconsin Press.
Tagore, R. 2007. *Lectures, Addresses*. Atlantic Publishers & Dist.
Tatu, R. 2008. "Knowledge and Ignorance in Indian Thought." *Anuarul Institutului de Istorie» George Baritiu «din Cluj-Napoca-Seria HUMANISTICA* 6 (6): 415–21.
Venkataraman, K. 2003. "Rasa in Indian Aesthetics: Interface of Literature and Sculpture." PhD diss., University of Illinois at Urbana-Champaign.
Welch, S. 2022. *Choreography as Embodied Critical Inquiry*. Springer.

CHAPTER 5

Tangential Departure from the S

Maya Kulkarni in Action

I ENTER THE STAGE WITH *the parrot hovering around my body flying haphazardly. I gaze at it with admiration and love. "Such a warm and fuzzy bird," I skip a heart-beat as I hold him in my hand trying to attract his attention. He perches on my shoulder, walks on my arms, sits on my knees, pulls my hair, and imitates my mannerisms. I teach him to sing. At first, he fails at hitting the musical notes correctly. Eventually, he gets it and tries to one-up me. He plays hard to get flying away from my grasp and teasing me with his surreptitious appearances. Showing his antics, like going in circles on the tree-branch, he makes me laugh. I ask him to visit my lover and bring me back news about the whereabouts of my beloved. After returning, my parrot seems really aloof. I try to lure him with food and engage him in a chasing game. Finally, he discloses that he wants to explore the horizons of the sky. But he does not know that my life nests within him. If he leaves me, I die too. Alas, the choice is his to make...*

The above dramatic hook is an overview of the piece called *Woman with a Parrot* (2021) that was choreographed by Maya Kulkarni in *Shilpanatanam* (a creative movement process centering visual imagery). It was the first of a series of my experiments with Kulkarni bridging across the differences in our respective investments in different formal parameters. Kulkarni is a veteran *Bharatnatyam* (a southern Indian classical dance form with greater degrees of linearity than Odissi) artist with a long performance career in the arts spanning over six decades.[1] Despite the differences in formal particulars, Kulkarni and I have been able to work together since 2021 to create several solo works. Our binding agent remains the dramatic arc that she builds using my dancing body. Grazing the margins of curvilinear aesthetics, this series of solos does not intentionally ground the S-shape, although the serpentine continues its durational engagement and presence via the sentiment.

Shilpa means visual art and *Natanam* means dance. *Shilpanatanam* refers to moving imagery where movement animates static images—painting, sculpture, and palm-leaf sketches—through gesture, posture, rhythm, and dramatic intent. My exchange with Kulkarni is across geometry, concepts, feelings, and experiences without set assumptions and boundaries. This is a strikingly different experience from that of working with Dandavate about which I have elaborated in the earlier chapter. Dandavate and I are both students of Guru Kelucharan Mohapatra style. We speak the same language in postural, gestural, and other formal investments in movement as our mode of communication remains highly specialized. In contrast, Kulkarni and

I engage in more pedestrian terminology outside the formal limitations of any one technique as such. Kulkarni holds the story, the narrative, the dramatic, and the expressive as the center of her choreographic vision. I am surprised to read grandiose claims about originations of experiments across dance and dramaturgy in Europe in the eighties by prominent dance studies scholars. "The relationship between dance and dramaturgy originated by most accounts in the well-known collaboration in the early to mid 1980s between choreographer Pina Bausch and dramaturge Raimund Hoghe" (DeLahunta 2000, 20). This shows lack of interest and an insularity in the field of Euro-American movement practitioners.

Indian dance forms tend to exist in silos since versatility is not necessarily perceived as a requisite for professionalism in dance. Body-to-body hierarchical transmission from the teacher to the taught, often prevents intermingling across the various cultural codes as well as technical nuances embedded within each form of dance. My work starts from this curiosity of questioning and exploring intracultural difference between my embodied vocabulary and that of my choreographer. This work pushes me to think of difference as innately subtle. Kulkarni's notion of movement is similar but slightly different from mine given both Odissi and Bharatnatyam claim their lineage to ancient Sanskrit aesthetics as delineated in the *Natyasastra* and the plethora of texts following it. My technical footprint is vastly different from that of Kulkarni's, which makes the process of choreographic creation a collaborative exchange across difference, attesting to how "choreography as a practice requires opening to the embodied experience of others" (Burridge and Roche 2022, 114). I note how this practice-based research confronts my theoretical understanding, emotional investment, and practical manifestation of movement. Consequently, *Shilpanatanam* pushes me to center the dramatic intensity as foundational to performance rather than technical paraphernalia, such as posture—*Chauka* (square), *Tribhangi* (S-shape), *Abhanga* (slightly bent), and *Sama* (straight). The vehicular containment of movement through postural specificity gives Odissi its unique flavor alongside its lyricism, curvilinearity, and culturally embedded notions of Oriyaness. However, *Shilpanatanam* requires me to embody other modalities of expressivity, such as the unique use of *Shikhara* (thumbs-up gesture) as indicating a question in the Bharatnatyam vocabulary, opening up my expressive tool kit beyond enculturated confines. Thus, *Shilpanatanam* through Kulkarni's embodied investments, cultivates difference and expands my practice, one that I refer to as *performative variance*.

Shilpanatanam has been around for a decade and has been presented in all major festivals and venues in India and the diaspora. Based in the United States, Kulkarni has received multiple federal, state, and local grants. Her existing body of work ranges across emotional characterization as seen in a choreographic explorations of obsession (*A Woman with a Parrot,* 2021), desire (*An Impossible Romance*, 2022), and grief (*Rati Vilap,* 2023). The architectural and the energetic has inspired *Yakshini* (2023) situated in Odisha's Chausathi Yogini temple in Hirapur. A methodological and theoretical grounding focus on the notion of technical differences in the wake of a creative exchange across two different styles leading to subtle kinesthetic shifts. In this chapter, I focus on excavating the curvilinear sketches of my dancing body that molds to Kulkarni's dramaturgical shaping of *Abhinaya* (expressive movement). *Abhinaya* is a generic term originating in the text called the *Natyasastra* (ancient Indian treatise on performing arts) where an elaborate theory of dramaturgy is laid out in the sixth and seventh chapters (Kapur

2024). It refers to expressive movement across multiple dance forms, giving both Kulkarni and me a plethora of gestural, emotional, embodied, psychological, and theatrical techniques to draw from (Ghosh 1951). *Abhinaya* requires mastery over technical parameters restricting it to advanced learners and professionals. Works developed with Kulkarni fall into the category of *Abhinaya*, which is also the fourth element in the traditional Odissi repertoire. Odissi's curvilinearity exists in my body as it interacts with and attunes to Kulkarni's dramaturgical sketching. I argue that geometric framing through conceptual precepts finds subtle openings otherwise occluded from and restricted to the sinusoidal trajectory of the traditional postural parameters. I start my exposition by curating the methodology of working with Kulkarni. Dramatic reversal of the formal dilutes the curvilinear investments although my performative liberty is retained at the conjuring of the choreographic at a critical distance—a dancer trained in Odissi working with a choreographer attuned to Bharatnatyam.

Curvilinear Enactments: A Word on Methodology

Having trained in Bharatnatyam over eight years under Guru Moushumi Bhor Bhattacharya and Guru Priyanka Sarkar Niyogi, I have an embodied experience with the form. I believe this helped me in understanding the verbal instructions. For example, in one portion of the dance, the woman asks the parrot to spy on her lover because she wants to know his whereabouts. This is an iconic expression in Bharatanatyam that uses the gesture *Shikhara* (a single-handed *Mudra* where the thumb sticks out while the other fingers fold well into the palm), soft side-to-side neck movements, and a facial expression of curiosity effectuated with slight modulation of the opening of eyes. Having prior knowledge of this motif frames my approach into the narrative arc as I build my understanding of the moment in movement. This is important since I refrain from the easily accessible imitative potential of replicating Kulkarni's articulate facial expressivity accompanying her verbal instructions. My access to Kulkarni's form scaffolds and directs the choreographic instructions through a series of interventions. First, I decode the creative algorithms from a structural standpoint through my embodied memory of Bharatnatyam. Second, I actively intervene in the creative process through reframing ideas into my Odissi body. Third, I engage in an infinite process of deepening the movement through self-reflexivity as well as clarifying thoughts and questions with the choreographer. Thus, this process is scaffolded in difference through a dialogical encounter across embodiment, memory, and technique.

Usually, the choreographer creates and demonstrates the movement with a certain degree of clarity in terms of its arc and intensity. It is possible that the landing of the movement on the dancer does not match the choreographic vision. A process of trial and error ensues until the performative creates an impact on the choreographer. Working with Kulkarni did involve these fundamental steps, but with a few distinct characteristics. First, the work lies between two forms, limiting Kulkarni's degree of clarity regarding the choreographic landing. Second, the work erupts at the interstices of difference as the verbal or gestural inspiration is followed by my framing of the instructions according to its structural possibilities through my embodied memory of Bharatnatyam. Third, the framed material results in my trying out through its Odissi-esque translation. However, it is necessary to acknowledge that the locus of the translation from

Bharatnatyam to Odissi refrains from being a prerogative over the course of the choreography. Rather, it becomes a question of latent and prominent embodiment of aesthetics. As an Odissi soloist for the past twenty years, I am programmed to carve curvilinear arcs in space. This is quite different from the linear and sharp geometries created by the Bharatnatyam idiom. My body automatically translates Kulkarni's instructions in its most practiced aesthetic although it is able to algorithmically recognize and decode its Bharatnatyam elementals. Embodied decoding of choreographic instructions sieved through technical markers of difference engage multiple layers of processing enhancing the layered dimensionality of the final material. The layering process involves conscious intervention to mark-up the curvilinear subtleties of Odissi as well as engaging with the idiom to find new openings.

While the process of decoding is embodied with trial and error in donning on the movement material for the first time, I consider the second stage of intervention as the heart of the choreographic process with centering difference. In this process, I actively shape the contours of the motion and figure out it emotional and sensory trajectory. Although Odissi and Bharatnatyam seem to follow the same pan-Indian text, the *Natyasastra*, regional variations result in two quite different forms with varying aesthetics and intensities. However, the textual union results in somewhat of a shared vocabulary that allows common grounds of differential interpretation. The intervention is strongest with the Odissi-esque contouring of emotional, conceptual, physical, and aesthetic notions. This conscious intervention results in lilting, languid, and curvilinear geometries of the piece. Yet, I argue that this creative process at the center of difference creates an opening that otherwise would not have been available. The conscious processing of movement material through varying degrees of embodied understanding and sieved through a dominant aesthetic ends up creating fissures within the aesthetic itself. In my execution of new movement material via my dancing Odissi body engaged in a conscious process of sifting through prior versatile training and intervening in an articulation of grounded languidness, I experience an innovative throughline.

Therein lies the agency of the dancer in the choreographic articulation, reflecting the processual resolution of the determinants, a process that takes the shape of iterative trial and error until the desired goal is achieved. The shape of the kinesthetic trajectories as well as the intensity of the dramatic arc need to align in order for such a resolution to occur. It is easier to align the curvilinear aesthetic of the Odissi dancing body with the subtle expressivity of its affective intensity. What happens when the linear geometries of Bharatnatyam with its direct, sharp, and loud (to my perception) expressive aesthetics intervene? The linearity and the sharpness percolate through the dancing body as it goes through a process of finding resolution. Until the resolution is reached, the churning continues. The churning goes on until the linear, sharp, and directness of the choreographers' verbal instructions are completely resolved within the curvilinear geometric arcs of the Odissi body. A slight yet direct sideways glance or a subtle interjection of a southern Indian hand-to-chin gesture or a straightened elbow are few instances of openings that I create within the Odissi dancing body to enhance dramatic intensity as a result of a conscious deliberation on resolution across difference.

Odissi and Bharatnatyam have two very different registers of expression. The former has a subtle tone and more rounded glances while the latter is comparatively more direct and louder.

Although both follow the same theories of *Natya* (acting) as delineated in the *Natyasastra*, regional variations show in the delivery and execution of an expressive ethos. Kulkarni's expressive gesticulation in Bharatnatyam collides with my toned-down imitation of the same to eventually create the experience of what I call an *expressive fissure* in my emotionality. I diffuse certain gestures, facial connotations, and eyebrow raises, among other elements characteristic of Bharatnatyam in my repertoire through an expressive fissure, that is, a simultaneous toning down as well as coloring up of gestural and emotional intensity. I Oddisi-ize these elements through more rounded curvilinear execution as well as softened expressivity. However, to an Odissi crowd, my expression reads louder than the usual emotional tonality. After seeing the piece, Odissi scholar Rohini Dandavate told me that she could see Kulkarni in the work. This moment of perceiving the choreographer through the dancer's bodily contours or expressive fissure, leads to a certain degree of choreographic deepening, one where the technical difference provides a critical *performative variance*. This variance may be considered an innovative intervention. Without the use of verbal expression, using the moving body in stylized negotiations across styles, centering creative communication across technical conduits to present a choreographic vision mapped by a thematic arc. The aesthetic mapping of angularity, stasis, and affective intensity is a result of the process of choreographic deepening across the technical parameters of two styles. Bharatnatyam's angularity and emotional range infused my movements and expressions, respectively. A movement executed in the Odissi technique has its layers of information encoded in the body. However, when there is a juxtaposition of styles across choreographic vision and performative presence, the layering of difference is far more intense. This intensity leads to a deepening of the movement in terms of its processual translation and embodied realization. Stasis, which is Odissi's characteristic, features in this piece in order to draw parallels of the sculptural inspiration of the piece. The curvilinear arc is also toyed with and stretched significantly, as I negotiate angularity and stasis across Bharatnatyam and Odissi, respectively.

Starting with orientation on a topic, storyline, character, narrative, metaphor, or an idea, begins a series of processes from kinesthetic sketching to final production. Oscillating between music and dance and between choreographer, music composer, and the dancer, the piece organically evolves across ideation, musical visualization, and choreographic development. Significant to each piece remains a dramatic twist around which the solo evolves with a clear beginning and ending. At some time toward the end of the creative process, production elements, such as costuming, hair, and scenic design are brought into conversation with the choreography. Overall, each solo has taken over a year of development with three distinct phases: (1) Kinesthetic Sketching; (2) Music and Dance Oscillations; and (3) Dramatic Architecture. The first phase, *Kinesthetic Sketching*, refers to the preparatory research involving familiarity with the narrative and visual inspirations. This phase leads to generation of a choreographic motif that is always a combination of the embodied, the conceptual, and the emotive. The second phase, *Music and Dance Oscillations*, refers to the interaction between music and dance as a significant step of the creative process. Movement sketches provide inspiration as well as structure for the composer to develop the necessary musical arcs. This is a period of intense interaction between the composer and the choreographer as each builds upon the other's ideas. Finalization of the movement and the music occurs simultaneously as the solo enters into the last phase, *Dramatic Architecture*, where the dramatic plots and twists are deepened in both movement and production elements. Eventually, scenography design, costuming and ornamentation, and sound engineering help the solo add dramatic elements toward its premiere.

Phase I: Kinesthetic Sketching

A basic movement sketch follows a verbal mapping of the entire piece. It can perhaps be thoughts of as what dance scholar André Lepecki calls *metaphorical explosion* in an interview on dance dramaturgy by Scott DeLahunta (2000). Characterization of a piece starts with an inspiration. For example, *Woman with a Parrot* derives inspiration from a sculpture from a temple in Hampi, which is recognized as a UNESCO world heritage site for its historical significance. But the inspiration comes to Kulkarni from across a range of sites and sounds.

Inspirations come from museums and music, temples and texts, but the primary ethos lies within effective communication of the narrative footprint, which is co-constructed through the verbal, the percussive, the emotional, and the experiential. *Shilpanatanam* prioritizes the build-up of the narrative through effective organizing and channelizing of aesthetic elements that conjure a dramatic appeal. I arrive at the process of sketching a movement network where characters build and dissolve alongside sequences of pure movement as well as dramatic situations. Kinesthetic sketching allows for an initial embodiment of the kernel of an idea. This goes through a series of intense preparatory work for the dancer to hone in on the dramaturgical focus. Holding an attentive focused gaze, especially while building up and dissolving a narrative arc, requires hours of practice in focus. One of the many exercises Kulkarni has developed over the years requires the dancer to sit still and look side to side and up and down in a slow and deliberate manner while visualizing, imagining, seeing, and measuring a large mountain. Such is the power of *Abhinaya* where visualization, imagination, the act of qualitative seeing, and quantitative measuring occur simultaneously. Kulkarni's exercises remind me of singers using body-mapping to awaken their bodies and elevate their performance to greater degrees of freedom with heightened degrees of awareness (Allen 2012). The kinesthetic needs the body in conjunction with the face to communicate meaning and bring to fruition its overall structuring of space and time in motion. *Kinesthetic sketching*, therefore, holds the focused gaze in its overall mapping of a narrative arc alongside movement motifs. At this point, a conglomeration of embodied motifs present a suggestive structure. The structural mapping with primary episodic transitions helps to transition to the second phase of musical elaboration. Music is integral to the compositional process as the dance entangles in a duet with the melodic as well as the percussive.

Phase II: Music and Dance Oscillations

Music and dance are an integrated phenomenon in the world of classical Indian arts. The *Natyasastra* combines a host of performing arts in its exposition of the dramatic. Kulkarni's desire to return to the ancient text to realize her dramatic vision uses music and dance in a layered, complex, and interrelated manner. Integration of music and dance has been studied extensively in African performance although its study in the South Asian arts is inadequate

(Nannyonga-Tamusuza 2015). The *Kinesthetic Sketching* of the first phase gives rise to openly sourced music. This initial musical mapping for the first meeting eventually leads to a series of discussions between Kulkarni and the music composers. There is a constant back and forth between the choreographic and compositional minds as the dancer keeps modifying the dance to align the movement with the music created for it. Sometimes choreography yields to compositional changes. At other times, music composition gives in to changes made within the embodied dimensions.

Melody and rhythm provide the sonorous texture, influencing the communicability of the dramatic act. Both have expressive features that have mood-enhancing functions. The sonorous imbues the structuring of the kinesthetic motifs with sequential intent in an episodic progression of dance and music, together building a successful dramatic arc. Sensitive attunement between the two leads to an ideal composition in *Shilpanatanam* as Kulkarni refrains from settling for works that do not give her a sense of completion. The role of the dancer is like that of the oscillating pendulum trying to adjust to the sketching of the choreographer and the composer only to go through a series of revisions. I can vouch for this process as one producing a high degree of creative tension. The tense attunement between dance and music finally produces the end product. Finalizing the music results in setting the final choreography.

Typically sung lyric poem, melodic notes, percussive cadences, and dramatic expression characterize the model composition in *Shilpanatanam*. The logical sequencing that the dancer uses, the percussionist recites, and the vocalist maintains are all different although each has an intimate connection with the other and the parts gather to become a complete whole in an interactive and collaborative manner to bring Kulkarni's vision to fruition. One can argue that this oscillation between music and dance in *Shilpanatanam* seems similar to traditional compositions in classical Indian dance. This does not necessarily add a unique dimension to musicality. However, there are marked departures from the traditional strictures as maintained in the long lineage of practitioners. Kulkarni does not want formal limitations to dictate her choreographic vision. Eminent dance scholar Kapila Vatsyayan notes the formal parameters of classical musical compositions, "which the dancer interprets through movement by a most precise and highly complex technique of synchronization and co-ordination of the word and the gesture, the note and the movement" (1963, 37). In such cases, the degrees of oscillation from dance to music are limited. The choreography is often dictated by the musical strictures and strict formal parameters of alternating lyric and rhythm sequences, such as in *Varnam* (traditional musical compositions in southern Indian dance). While *Shilpanatanam* accesses the complexity of the traditional architectonic musical structures, it adds contemporaneity and provides a democratic voice to movement. Movement no longer remains subservient to music. Rather, it emerges as an equal player, sometimes dictating the progression of the work.

Phase III: Dramatic Architecture

Crafting intentionality into the work requires a balancing act between motion and stillness. Introducing moments of stillness ensure careful translation of the choreographic intent. Each piece is carefully filigreed in order to ensure dramatic ornamentation where movement and the narrative arc coincide to conjure the highest degree of dramatic intent. There is a predominant sentiment characterizing the solo work ensuring a continuity of meaning-making for the discerning audience. In this capacity, *Shilpanatanam* stays true to classical theories of drama as laid out in the *Natyasastra* (Varma 1960). Such a dramatic conjuring often takes the help of pictorial projections, text, dramatic overlays, elaborate costuming, and props cuing the audience at each stage of the dramatic developments. Finally, the dramatic appeal of the conventional repertoire draws from a presupposed intensity of devotional fervor within the cultural insider of Hinduism. This is not a given for Kulkarni who builds the dramatic solely on the merit of the narrative without presuppositions or prior associations. Its subject matter could be either sacred or secular. In any case, it is not assumed to provide any additional procedural orientation to the work in hand.

At the physical level, my infrastructural investments in curvilinearity configure to Kulkarni's *Shilpanatanam*, which seeks expansion from the historical mushrooming of various classical dance styles over the past century. The expansive ethos lies primarily in Lepecki's metaphorical allusions where connections, cohesions, and patterns emerge from the inherent dramaturgical arc and not from a superimposed structure. While my geometric framing does not loosen its curvilinear subtlety, there are moments of dissolution and rebuilding made possible by the narrative arc. Such dissolution of a dominant aesthetic results in moments of identitarian crises and avoided by most choreographers working strictly within the dictums of technique. Kulkarni, on the other hand, is not governed by technique. For her, the intensity of the dramaturgy is the determinant, and the technically trained body needs to carry forth the task of creating the dramatic arc. Geometric dissolution in the face of dramatic intensity creates a disjuncture within my movement, one that I have not experienced in conventional choreographic projects within Odissi. Engaging with the aforementioned processes of embodied decoding and conscious intervention, results in an altogether revised orientation.

The conscious engagement with difference in the creative process generates moments of creative spark that are not accessible when the choreographer and the dancer communicate in the exact same idiom. As I see it, there are two distinct modalities of identifying the innovative orientation. I call the first modality geometric framing since the body aims at achieving a curvilinear subtlety. The second brings up the question of managing the flow, precision, and energy in the movement that follows Odissi's quintessential curvilinear arc (as theorized in the Chapter 1) across technique and repertoire. The dramatic through multiplicity and episodic stillness, acculturates the viewer into its codes as each piece emerges as a unique embellishment in the repertoire of *Shilpanatanam*. No two pieces look alike as the form is inherently imbued with the creative process centered around the propensities of the dancing body. Sanskritist Mandakranta Bose notes how medieval texts like *Sangita Ratnakara* emphasize expressive embodied acts and flexible movement structures granting greater agency to the performer's creativity (1991). It must be acknowledged that *Shilpanatanam* provides a significant degree of freedom of movement that is the primary harbinger of the dramatic arc with the aid of music and text.

Choreo-Emotive Visualizations

Shilpanatanam grounds itself in the concept of aesthetic appreciation and savoring of content. Tenth-century philosopher and aesthetician Abhinavagupta's important commentary on

Natyasastra's theorization of *Rasa*, the *Abhinavabharathi*, provides the foundations for *Shilpanatanam's* storytelling via choreographic visualization (Ghosh 2006). *Shilpanatanam* is an intuitive creative process in poetics, aesthetics, philosophy, choreography, and music that refers to the intentional use of word, gesture, movement, costume, melody, and rhythm. It juxtaposes literary, visual, and performing arts where the narrative remains at the center. It is primarily an aesthetic-poetic construction of dance dramaturgy or dramatic dance that is narrative-driven and emotionally charged.

A word on conventional *Abhinaya* marks the points of departure of expressive faculties in *Shilpanatanam*. In Odissi repertoire, *Abhinaya* usually takes the format of the repetition of *Sahitya* (verses) and metaphoric elaboration of the literal meaning using gesture, rhythm, and metaphoric possibilities. The deepening through varied hues of expression enables a manifestation of a certain idea or emotion through simultaneous apprehension and suggestion. The mode of expression is a slow unfolding of meaning. This slow revelation is true for meaning-making in the creative process of *Shilpanatanam*. However, the choreographic format differs from the conventional format of alternating text, rhythm or melody. Since there is no particular format, each creation looks different. The narrative plot determines the direction of the storytelling maneuver. The dance progresses through slow revelation through enactment of the dramaturgical acts. Each act builds upon another resulting in the manifestation of the experiential emotions or the emotional experiences. The dance, then, becomes a light to the shadow of the suggested meaning (implied by the emotional, the cultural, the contextual, etc.) that emanates and grows slowly to be received by the audience. Apprehension of meaning through sensory perception is followed by the suggestion of further deepening that adds another degree of metaphorical appeal through actively negotiating with and navigating the experiential. It takes a marked departure from the existing body of classical Indian dance although it requires dancers well-versed in the *Sastric* (Sanskritized literary, philosophical, and theoretical texts) canon to execute its creative manifestations. At the heart of it remains the savoring of *Rasa* (translated as the mood, sentiment, or emotional tone relished in the process of artistic meaning-making) found in all traditional forms of theater, literature, visual and performing arts in India. *Rasa* remains foundational in *Shilpanatanam*'s dramaturgy.

In my theoretical interpretation of *Shilpanatanam*, I show how this Kulkarni's of work juxtaposes with Abhinavagupta's exposition on *Rasa* (Cuneo 2015). According to Abhinavagupta, the objective of theatrical performance is the evoking of *Rasa*, which lies primarily within the spectator. *Shilpanatanam*, quite similarly, places viewership at the center in its portrayal of a representative framework. A confluence of visual and performing arts, *Shilpanatanam* stands on creative adaptation and reinterpretation of culturally situated aesthetics steeped within artistic flavor, performative fervor, and aesthetic bliss, especially as articulated by Abhinavagupta. Language, literature, and poetry are metaphorically woven in the dance, which is again resisting the conventional trend of gestural translation of words in conventional choreography in the classical Indian dance forms. Movement holds precedence in this act of metaphorical weaving as the extant role of kinesthesia is mapped out toward *Rasic* generation.

Shilpanatanam can be literally translated as moving imagery where the visuality of the images transact with the kinesthetic act of dance. Movement remains key in representing a series of images that depict a narrative thread in choreographic organization. The narrative is usually nonlinear to ensure its dramatic appeal and to make the most sense in a performative progression. Dance studies scholar Susan Leigh Foster analyzes representation in *Reading Dancing: Bodies and Subjects in Contemporary American Dance* (1986). Foster describes four representative modes, namely, resemblance, imitation, replication, and reflection. According to Foster, the choreography can *resemble* the real-world phenomenon if it focuses on certain quality or attribute; *imitate* if it presents a literal presentation leaving little to no-doubt in the viewing experience; *replicate* if it presents a phenomenon, thing, or character as a dynamic system; and *reflect* when the choreographer and performer takes a high degree of artistic and creative liberty to abstract away from the representational. According to Foster, "Although all four might appear in any given dance, one usually predominates, and this mode, as it signals worldly experience, implies a stance toward the world that is crucial to the dance's meaning" (65). Foster's representation can be further interpolated by the Indian aesthetic theory of art reception where representation takes a particular valence moving from the personal to the impersonal. Abhinavagupta's concept of *Sadharanikarana* (universalization) refers to the process by which individual emotions depicted in a work of art (like a play or poem) are universalized, allowing the audience to experience them not as the private emotions of a specific character, but as generalized, shared feelings. It incorporates a second step in the cognitive, emotional, and physiological registers that detach from personal context (Higgins 2007). It transforms personal, mundane emotions into an aesthetic experience, transcending the ordinary and evoking a deeper and more universal response. In this manner, the aesthetic experience becomes a collective elevated emotional experience. While there is the artistic choice-making, creative intent, and technical capacity of the artwork to represent through degrees of abstraction, the hermeneutic capacity of the artwork that focuses in great detail on *representation for* the viewership further nuances Foster's modes of representation.

In *A Rasa Reader: Classical Indian Aesthetics* author Sheldon Pollock draws the intellectual development of the history of Indian aesthetics across two millennia. He notes how aesthetic appreciation can be a technical acuity, a creative capacity, a viewing response, and a transaction across the appreciator and the appreciated (Pollock 2016). The reception of the artwork, therefore, can be "analytically disaggregated" resembling the "taste" it metaphorically references" (26). The creative process in *Shilpanatanam* builds on such an aggregate of the formal capacity of the dance delving into a plethora of psychological, physical, and psychophysical states as well as the hermeneutical ability of performance for actualizing aesthetic elements during their visual-kinesthetic reception. The combination of *Sthayibhava* (basic emotions), *Vibhava* (foundational factors), *Uddipana* (stimulants), *Vyabicaribhava* (transitory emotions), *Anubhava* (physical reactions), and *Sattwikabhava* (psychophysical responses) points to the dramaturgical unfoldment as well as the performative and receptive emotional registers. The hermeneutical capacity is further explored through the notion of savoring, also broadly termed as *Rasa*, enabling the reception of the artwork as an agential exercise that encumbers the physical, the mental, and the affective.

Shilpanatanam relies on *Rasa* for meaning-making. The primacy of its performance lies in its ability to evoke *Rasa* through emotion and dynamism. In this manner, it adheres strongly to *Natyasastric* vocabulary and the long development of *Rasa* theory over the centuries.

Its approach to accomplishing the savoring of *Rasa* is uniquely creative and different from the mechanisms embedded in the classical Indian dance formats. In the latter, such as Odissi, meaning-making is largely adhered to gesture—one that is intricately and painstakingly elaborated in traditional texts through an array of symbolic uses of different parts of the body. This approach presupposes an elitist audience well-versed in the codes and conventions of the dance-texts. *Shilpanatanam*'s approach to movement is democratic since it does not adhere to the ancient textual injunction on gesture. According to the Nandikeshvara's *Abhinaya Darpana* as translated by Ananda Coomaraswamy in *The Mirror of Gesture*, meaning in dance "must be shown by the hands" (1917). Thus, per the *Abhinaya Darpana*, hand-gesture is the most important modality among a series of body-parts—head, eyes, neck, feet, arms, sides of the body, etc.—with detailed usage involving a textual interpretative valence to physical materiality and gestural meaning-making. *Shilpanatanam* branches out from this point of departure of a linear correlation across text and gesture, rupturing the textual continuity through meaning-making. Rather, it relies on dynamic elaboration of meaning through kinesthetic, energetic, and geometric modalities. In this way, it builds a basic emotion through its progression in movement in order to ensure its reception by an audience across varying degrees of experience. *Shilpanatanam*, in this way, poses a direct critique of conventional meaning-making in classical Indian forms.

I elaborate upon this theoretical critique below by demonstrating how there is an unfolding of a primary state of being, which is not static as such, but unfolds through progressive stages of development throughout the performative exercise. The *Sthayibhava* (basic emotion) is stable and dominant throughout the performance. For example, in the solo work *Rati Vilap* (2023) based upon mythology, storytelling, and emotion, the dominant mood is pathos. Here, the act of grieving is explored through multiple stages of delusion, denial, anger, and acceptance. The dance deploys multiple emotions in the portrayal of grief, however, the stable encounter with *Soka* (grief) goes through numerous changes and variations. Multiple other fleeting emotions enter the narrative—such as *Rati* (love), *Hasya* (mirth), *Krodha* (anger), *Utsaha* (enthusiasm), *Bhaya* (fear), and *Vismaya* (wonder)—to create the dramaturgical arc. The entire exercise of the unfolding of the basic emotion is through a myriad of physical expression in the form of contractions and releases, verbal information communicated through text on the projection screen or the use of text in the song-lyric, costuming conventions that find creative ways to depart from the worlds of symmetry and harmony of classical Indian aesthetics, and deeply felt, experienced, and exaggerated facial expressions.

Alambana (foundational factors) refers to the basis of perception, such as the primary characters portrayed. In *Rati Vilap*, the protagonist—a female mythical figure named Rati, a harbinger of sense-pleasure and enjoyment—is the basis of perceptual consciousness. All experiences in the dance filter through her characteristic portrayal. It creates the primary vehicular containment for the dancer for the narrative appeal. Although, *Rasa* is at the center of artistic performance and reception in Odissi, its foundational elements lie in the physical attributes of curvilinearity, spiraling, and groundedness. However, in *Shilpanatanam*, *Rasa* is at the center. So, *Alambana* and not the quintessential *Tribhangi* (S-curve) become the technical support, the silent repetition of which throughout the dance is like a meditative exercise for the dancer. Postural grounding is substituted with the dynamic mental states of literary characterization and imaginative personification. My prior investments of geometric framing transcend toward conceptual precepts to find subtle openings within curvilinear postural containment. The sinusoidal trajectory of the traditional postural parameters superimposes onto the world of the emotive and the imaginative. The dancer needs to return to the objective basis of the metaphorical allusion—a process that simultaneously fosters creativity and sustains focus—instead of a formal physical injunction as imposed by the vehicular containment within the four basic postures of Odissi.

Between the foundations and basic emotions, there is a plethora of stimulants, transitory emotions, physical reactions, and psychophysical responses that color perception and reception. The space-time continuum is addressed by the *Uddipana* (stimulating factors), which foster the arising sentiment. For grief, some of the stimulants might be darkness, smoke, rugged terrain, dry earth, dust, etc., progressively intensifying the sentiment of grief. Transitory emotions (*Vyabicaribhavas*) and involuntary expressions manifesting as a result of emotional intensity (*Sattvikabhavas*) further leads to the nuancing of the creation of *Rasa*. As delineated in the sixth chapter of the *Natyasastra*, there are thirty-three transitory emotions (dejection, depression, suspicion, jealousy, intoxication, weariness, laziness, helplessness, anxiety, passion, recollection, boldness, shame, fickleness, joy, agitation, stupor, arrogance, despair, inquisitiveness, sleep, epilepsy, dream, awakening, intolerance, concealment, ferocity, knowledge, sickness, insanity, death, fright, and doubt) and eight psychophysical responses (stunned, sweating, thrill, break in voice, trembling, pallor, tears, and swoon). The passing emotions that contribute to the creation of *Rasa* are classified as *Sancari-bhava*s. The physical involuntary expressions that manifest themselves as a result of the intensity of emotion in the mental plane are called *Sattvika-bhavas*. Bharata states that a configuration of these forty-nine emotions promotes the creation of *Rasa* in the minds of the sympathetic audience.

All these varying factors weigh in appropriately on the performance to ensure the register of the stable emotion of grief only to propel its aesthetic distillation by the viewership. *Rasa* is not a linear emotional landing of *Sthayibhava* from the dancer to the viewer. Rather, the savoring process of *Rasa* is a completely mental process where there is a significant gap between the creative demonstration of the emotional parlance and its aesthetic appreciation. *Representation of* remains in conversation with *representation for* in order for meaning-making to occur. The performative act is simultaneously colored by characteristic portrayal in the dance and the perceptual interpretation in its reception. The wide-ranging milieu offered by transitory emotions and involuntary responses nuance the stable emotion and its foundational cause for the viewership. The actual time-space-circumstance of character portrayal become mere secondary detail. Rather, the nuanced and well-rounded portrayal of the stable emotion lands as an argument across nonlinear progression of images and episodes of meaning-making. Thus, the aesthetic elements, often termed by ancient Indian thinkers as *Vibhavadi* (Pollock 2016, 67) make grounds for the simultaneous individuation and communizing the actualization of aesthetic savoring. While the entire process is deeply material through kinesthetic sweeps across the stage or percussive rendering of time through heel/toe articulations of the foot or through facial expressivity across the *Sthayibhavas*, *Vyabhicaribhavas*, *Sattvikabhavas*, the process of *Rasic* success lies in the joining of the representation with the means and the ends of the representative act. Pollock notes that this savoring or the state of identification occurs in the heart of the receiver and the producer blurring material distinctions between the two. Based on these theoretical grounding, *Shilpanatanam* relies on this performative abstraction from the material while exploring materiality in choreographic terms. Characters are taken time to fully flourish through movement expressive of basic emotion, foundational and stimulating factors, and ephemeral sensations, feelings, reactions, and responses. The experiential landing of its artistry can further operationalize the aesthetic appreciation through phenomenological registers and hermeneutical capacities.

The rationale for such meticulous detailing of representative abstraction comes from the inherent assumption of prioritizing the embodied experience of the viewer in the creative act. The viewer is held in high esteem and deep sympathy in the mechanics of the creative act where the evoking of *Rasa* is prioritized in the creative-making itself. The dramatic intensity created by the narrative and expressive folds of my Odissi body within *Shilpanatanam* realizes the opening of the choreographer and the dancer to its receptivity in the viewer, bringing the spectator at the heart of the aesthetic experience. This is the reason why affective intensities evoked in performance and reception alongside the preconscious emotional intensity and the embodied emotive capacity, remain at the center of *Shilpanatanam* as opposed to postural containment and the grounded languid of Odissi's quintessential flair. Emphasizing feeling as relational, dynamic, and often ineffable shows how emotions circulate through texts, bodies, and cultures much like how *Rasa* functions in dramaturgy to foster collective emotional resonance (Sedgwick 2020).

Steady Your Eyes!

In my experience of *Shilpanatanam*, the choreography is not of movements—shapes, geometric patterns, poses, and footwork—but of moods. I have noted that while there is exacting choreography of hands, feet, and eyes, there remains infinite scope of the performer to make the performance one's own and present with individuated artistic impressions. In this way, the dramatic arc characterizes the extent of kinesthetic expansion or contraction, a spatial pattern, or a percussive footwork choreographed to exacting beats of corresponding drums. This assumes that the dancer stays present in the moment, reflecting on energetic conjuring and psychological progression during the performance instead of dancing from muscle memory. This requires the dancer to never let go but be fully present in the performative act in order to ensure that analytical improvisations occur. It takes the shape of structured improvisation where music provides definite goalposts for the performance.

Shilpanatanam is an imagistic exploration of meaning-making through movement where movement is an external manifestation of the dramaturgical intent and intensity. The primacy of the spectator requires *Shilpanatanam* to remain mindful of differences across the subjective positioning of the performer and that of the spectator. Keeping at the center, the embodied experiential vector of the spectator or *Rasa*, this style prioritizes difference at the heart of meaning-making. While there is sympathetic unity in the act of creation and its meaning-making in reception, the primary set of differences in subjective positioning allow for empathic unity of the choreographic act with the viewership. The choreography keeps in mind the ideal situation in which the *representation for* the viewer will be successfully realized. In this case, the understanding of choreographic intent is secondary to the climactic generation of *Rasa* as the viewer is no longer invested in the emotional narrative of the dramatic act but stays immersed within the dramatic intensity—one that has been aesthetically distilled with the cognitive, emotive, and material elements as delineated in the above section. Every enactment is not identical. It is mere actualization of affective potential with its own relational dynamic within the embodiment of the dancer (Hermans 2023). Every instant is, thus, an exercise in differentiation and actualization far from the repetitive strictures usually deployed in the conventional repertoire.

Earlier in the book, I have theorized the *kinesthetic pause* as necessary to weave in the expressive storytelling with the assumption of a riveted viewer. The sculptural stasis quintessentially characteristic of Odissi braids with the affective quotient to generate varying degrees and qualities of silence in the dance. The stasis due to physical posture looks different from one that choreographically allows for performative registering of content and bringing aesthetic viewership into the dancing fold. So, how is narrative storytelling different in *Shilpanatanam*? First, Kulkarni's movement structure does not presuppose the ebb and flow of curvilinear Odissi movement that usually feels like a wave between one sculptural stasis to another. While the physicality is strikingly different, the emotional mapping is also one with a difference. Previously, I argued that Odissi remains ambiguous about the locus of *Rasa* regarding its generation in the performer or the viewer, but *Shilpanatanam* leaves no such ambiguity in place. Its basis lies on *Abhinavabharati*'s injunctions where the aesthetic experience of viewership remains the priority. However, in order to reach its goal, it does not rely on prior assumptions about audience perception and preparation, but relies simply on choreography and performative structures that make possible the evoking of *Rasa*. Not depending on the viewing audience's degree of aesthetic attunement and culturally specific knowledge, *Shilpanatanam* operates on the functional principle that the ultimate goal of performance lies in generating a state of awareness simulating perception (Lancaster 1957). Aesthetic evocation leads to vivid cognition that, while not based on direct sensory input, functions like a perceptual event. This simulated perception is a heightened form of consciousness arising from the intentionally crafted presentation of emotive and situational cues, which momentarily suspend mundane cognition and immerse the spectator in a shared suprapersonal experience.

There is a poetic mode of synthesizing kinesthetic and affective actions enmeshing both text and music. Whatever be the task at hand—either the psychological development of a character or visual exploration of natural imagery—the performance starts with the conceptual abstraction in material configurations. In this way, the choreographic intent aside, the performer's body-mind is implicated likewise. Semantic theories, knowledge of musical systems, and aesthetics of theatrical dance influence performative acting in *Shilpanatanam*, in which all three are woven through improvisation. Improvisatory exploration of ideation, rather than counting of steps or muscular expansion remain primary. Here, I use improvisation in a definite capacity where the thought experiment determines the intent, intensity, shape, size, and reach of a movement. "Practice it enough times so that you recognize the feeling," says Kulkarni. This mode of dancing is very different from practicing a phrase where the movement becomes muscle memory. But, if we are to listen to postmodern dancer and filmmaker Yvonne Rainer's famous comment about the mind being a muscle, Kulkarni's imperative about practice makes sense (McManus 2010). When a movement is practiced a number of times, it becomes second nature through muscle memory. Similarly, the practice of an affective section can continue to generate similar neural pathways and degrees of familiarity. At the center, remains a preoccupation with the nature of aesthetic reception of the creative product and not accurate delivery of a series of choreographed movements to music. Key structures are set in place synced with music, text, and movement cueing. However, the thrust of the continuity lies in seamless exploration of a series of experiential feelings, emotions, and sensations through the nuanced craft of *Abhinaya*. For example, a dominant emotion or the *Sthayibhava* is explored through a series of transitory emotions or *Vyabicaribhava*. The process is based on the complex field of Indian aesthetics concerning verbal meaning and experiential nature of human emotion channelized through expressive performance. Text, music, and movement weave intricately into one another to create a tapestry of visual imagery. Prose or poetry has literal meaning as well as a related meaning, both of which make obvious the authorial intent. There is a third possibility of suggested meaning where the literal borders on the poetic imagination of the receiving end. Music, in a similar fashion, evokes its own set of corresponding moods and imageries. Finally, the entire *Rasa-Bhava* theory undergirds the performative making taking the audience toward an aesthetic exposition of the affective potential.

Artistic dexterity lies in evoking *Rasa*, which has been defined by Abhinavagupta as the manifestation of state of awareness simulating perception. This is theoretically brought about by an efficient play of aesthetic elements that play on the dramatic appeal of the content. The dramaturgical performance experientially brings to light an elaborate process of the generation of *Sthayibhava*. Baring the psychological and affective landscape heightens the perceptual apparatus for the viewer who is then able to connect to higher degrees of conscious awareness. This awareness is content-independent. That is, improvisatory choreographic structures building on narrativity and ideation can possibly evoke a state of awareness simulating the nature of perception itself. There lies an aesthetic distance between the story—the narrative content—and the experience of perception that the evoking of *Rasa* permeates through the body-mind complex of the viewer. The viewer feels a sense of intense enjoyment or bliss in sync with the degrees of intensity made possible by the dramatic mapping where the details of the cause of dramaturgical narrative are mere incidentals. Now that we have meditated on theories of aesthetics undergirding reception, let us now reflect on the creative process within *Shilpanatanam*.

The creative process begins with a kernel of an idea that can emerge from within text or from music. This ideation could have folkloric, philosophical, fable-esque, sculptural, political, ideological, and/or musical inspiration. The translation of the idea into a dance script requires interplay of textual denotation, abstract rhythmic composition, and affective intensity. Sometimes, text becomes the starting point of a choreography. At other times, text is added as sonorous texture. However, the meaning of the text, ranging from the intention of the author to its deciphered meaning by the receiver, remains in a dynamic relationship with the choreographer's motive. Multiple meanings of the text are used to enact a particular scene. The literal verbal meaning merges with related aspects of the same expression. Finally, there is a suggested meaning that takes flight from the poetic imagination of the given text. The denoted meaning stands parallell to the literal and suggested connotations of the same text.

Poetic manifestation of suggestions as the primary meaning-making ethos plays with aspects of delivery, display, and organization. The organization of the movements play a significant role as movement clusters create affective resonances. Physical display of embodiment is only secondary to psychological responses and energetic reactions. Depending upon the structure of the piece, music, text, and movement create a sense of harmony despite ornate and complicated sonorous structures and kinesthetic embellishments demanding a high degree of versatility across technical proficiency and emotive appeal.

Literal laying out of the narrative eventually leads to processual abstraction and dissolution. The subjective and the objective aspects are followed by a processual composition of the characters themselves. The cognitive representation and reception of a narrative abstraction is then ornamented with the sensory, perceptual, and subsidiary strengthening. For example, in *Impossible Romance* (2022), the portrayal of a bedazzling lightning is presented through the sensation of fear in the cloud who has helplessly fallen in love with the electrifying beauty although cognizant of his fearful dissolution in the hands of desire. The cognitive, the sensory, and the contemplative together create the dissolution of the narrative to the simultaneously nonsubjective and nonobjective. Causally brought about or inferred from the presence of narrative appeal, this relished state is beyond subjectivity and objectivity. It is a cultivated sense of enjoyment and stasis—one that quietens the continuous flow of thoughts, emotions, and ideas into a universalized sense of restfulness. This comes from the journey away from the particular to the universal bringing forth an aesthetic enjoyment that borders upon the non-dual contemplation foregrounding the realization of the self. So, the journey in *Shilpanatanam* is one from the imagistic to the ineffable—from *Shilpa* (sculpture, painting, visual aesthetics) to *Rasa* (experiential fervor or bliss as the relishing of an after taste)—in dance.

Kulkarni's creative world-making across degrees of abstraction, from material to subtle visualization, depends on the gaze. The gaze connects the dance to the dancer as well as the dance to the audience. Dance, dancer, and gaze remain windows for moving toward and away from the self. However, the primary condition for this exercise is the ability to grasp the audience's attention through artistic honing of the gaze. The gaze becomes the primary tool of maneuvering between the various elements of a story—characters, personality traits, environmental conditions, and emotional conditions. This remains an exercise of constant and consistent unmooring of the subjective across the registers in order to effectively present the material dimensions of the story. The cultivation of a focused gaze requires introspection, internalization, and study of the subject matter as well as the translation of the perceptual, sensory, and the intellectual into the performative. This requires continued practice as suggested in Kulkarni's injunction *Steady your gaze, Kaustavi!*. Often, acting is seen as alien to physical abstraction of movement that forms the basis of choreography in Western concert dance practice (Chliara 2018). However, *Shilpanatanam* does not create false binary structures between movement, on one hand, and music and narrative expression, on the other. *Shilpanatanam* becomes an exercise of deep focus that allows for a constant shift in registers—intellectual, emotional, kinesthetic, and subjective—as the dancer, through both stasis and motion as well as via abstract movement and narrative expression, remains the witness to the story responsible for imprinting on the viewer the choreographic essence.

Initial sketches of movement generated either via Kulkarni's gestural mapping or my experiments with her verbal cues go through a process of aesthetic and emotional distillation.

FIG. 18: Distortion: Author Performing *Rati Vilaap* at Moving Images, Martha Graham School of Contemporary Dance, New York City, November 9, 2024. Reproduced with permission from Jeff Cravotta.

The contours of the body emerge according to visual symmetry—such as the back-bends or *Tribhangi* footwork. Emotional modulation of the body becomes equally important to deepen the movements according to the mood, feeling, and sensation of the piece. The aesthetic conduits amd the behavioral mannerisms determine the tenor of a piece. The creative process in *Shilpanatanam* canvasses intellectual, emotional, kinesthetic, and subjective dimensions of the performing artist. The intellect and the body implicate themselves in the constant back and forth between the dramaturgy and the dynamism, each informing and reinforcing the other. The emotional faculties modulate the narrative dimension imparting modulation to the storytelling exercise as the subjectivity of the performer provides the material basis of the performative storytelling.

Story Is King!

The above is yet another aphorism by Kulkarni that guides her desire to create across the literary and legacy perspectives. Dance creates the story, the text, the narrative that takes the audience along a journey of intense emotional churning. Every movement is uniquely generated that evokes a sensory response in the viewer. As a researcher, I disagree with Kulkarni about the basic definition of *Shilpanatanam*. She calls it a vocabulary, and I perceive it as a creative process.

FIG. 19: Extension: Author Performing *Rati Vilaap* at UNC Charlotte Dance Faculty Concert, Charlotte, January 26, 2024. Reproduced with permission from Jeff Cravotta.

It is possible that she projects onto it her desire of a lasting legacy that has been usually through the creation of a fully fleshed out form. Despite the quibble between our perspectival differences, in this chapter, I build upon my felt performative agency across intracultural difference. By focusing on my collaboration as a soloist trying to expand performative repertoire, I discuss how pluralistic foundational precepts between the choreographer and the dancer offset conventional modes of art-making. In the next few sections, I elaborate upon choreography as the kinesthetic intermediary breaking open the siloed binary of the visual image and the affective *Rasa* through the focused gaze. I develop the dramaturgical analysis across three solo works: *Rati Vilap* (2023), *Impossible Romance* (2022), and *Woman with a Parrot* (2021), as case studies.

Case Study I: *Rati Vilap* (2023)

Rati is the goddess of love who does Vilap, mourning the death of her beloved in the hands of Siva. Siva is meditating while a demon is on a rampage to conquer the three worlds. Siva can stop this demon. The gods hatch a plot to break Siva's meditation. They invite Madana, Rati's consort, to shoot an arrow at Siva. As the arrow awakens Siva, he becomes angry at Madana. An enraged Siva opens his third eye and fire rages forth destroying everything around including the god of desire. Seeing her husband die by Siva's fiery gaze, Rati faints away. On awakening, she looks around in utter despair. Everything has been reduced to ashes. She cannot recollect anything. The first act introduces a delusional Rati in a daze. Rati recollects fond memories of her beloved in springtime colors during the second act. Everything around reminds her of her beloved—bees perching on the nectar of flowers, elephants splashing in the water making triumphant love, and the Cakora (the bird who lives on the rays of the moon) gazing at the moon. Siva opens the third eye and there is total destruction. The Ganges plunges out of his matted locks; the snakes slither around his neck; the universe dissolves away. Everything is burnt to ashes. The third scene focuses on the role of anger in the midst of grief. The fourth scene takes us back to where we started. Rati is prone. Now, when she wakes up, she knows what has happened. She is in denial; lamenting and mourning the death of her beloved. She sees the burnt heap of ashes in front of her and asks Madana if he is alive. She embraces the figure only to find her hands and breasts covered in ashes.

Rati Vilap is the fourth canto of ancient Indian poet Kalidasa's epic literary creation called *Kumara Sambhavam* (Wilson and Dwivedi 1966). Kalidasa's immaculate poetic imagery in Sanskrit language is visualized in a four-act production called *Rati Vilap*. The piece explores grief in its multiple stages of psychological states where the object of grief is handled in different ways. The emotional progression charts out changing tones of grief. The dance goes through four acts exploring emotional registers of delusion, denial, anger, and acceptance sequentially.

Clinging to a hope that he might still live, Rati only sees the form of a man and nothing but ashes shaped by Siva's fiery wrath on the ground.

These emotions are enlivened through narrative elements translated from selected verses from the fourth canto, also known as *Rati Vilap*, of Kalidasa's *Kumarasambhavam*. While Rati is one of the many characters in Kalidasa's creative writing, she is central to Kulkarni's choreography. In its theatrical structures, visual arrangements, kinesthetic choices, textual interventions, and musicality, *Rati Vilap* is performative churning of emotions—the progression of which determine the choreographic arcs and their energetic valence.

Rati Vilap premiered in 2023 at the *University of North Carolina at Charlotte Faculty Dance Concert*. Reviewer John O. Perpener III comments on the use of nuanced facial expressions served as the vehicular conduit "to move through the emotional transitions of the narrative with a clarity and elegance that was remarkable" (2024, 6). Analyzing the four acts reclaims technical grounds, performative efficacy, and power of emotion in gesture. Kulkarni questions conventional reliance on gestural codification where meaning is condensed via the verbal interpretation of gesture. In contrary, *Rati Vilap* uses gesture sparsely and when it does, it pays attention to accessibility. Gestural usage does not presuppose prior knowledge and experience of the audience. The use of the gesture is not located in the hands and fingers. Rather, gestural interpolation is elaborated with physicality, energetic arcs, and kinetic dimensions to ensure readability without diluting creative freedom. The creative sensibility lies in gestural unpacking, which is quite similar to writing—how a topic sentence is followed by further explanation. In a similar manner, the gestural interface supplements or complements other kinesthetic structures that falls on the representational domain of the real. This critiques the secondary role of gesture as decorative in dance (Desmond 1997, 258). *Shilpanatanam* reclaims gesture as central to theatrical performance as both physical and verbal; both visual and emotional.

The presence of the lying dancing body evokes weighted vulnerability, a physicality that is deeply grounded and explores lower levels in motion. Heaviness of grief is drawn forth through weighted movements. Moving in a whirling delirium across denial and remembrance, joy and anger, eventually plunges into grief's abyss.

The curtain rises to reveal the silhouette of a bejeweled solo dancer supine on the stage surface. On the cyclorama, one can see words appearing about a story of love and loss.

> *Act I Sambhrama: Delusion: Rati wakes up in delusion unable to remember the death of their consort, Madana, who has been reduced to ashes by the fury of Siva.*

Sambhrama means delusion, a condition that best describes Rati as the once consummated love with Madana is now reduced to ashes. The write-up leaves the reader with an ambiguity of gender rendering a progressive gender politics onto Kalidasa's original story. The text pushes back against gender-assignment and heteronormativity to the audience's reading. Rather, the viewers can assign their own take on the exchange between Rati and Madana. As the words fade away, light shines on the soloist deepening into a backbend arching the neck before turning toward the audience. The dancer makes way to a standing posture, slipping and falling in the act of getting up. This adds to the dramatization of delusion not just in facial expression–crunched eye brows, clenched eyes, fearful eyes, and tense cheek muscles—but also in the physicality lacking purpose, intention, drive, focus in motion, raised shoulders, and tense rib cage. Rati notices the parrot who is Madana's friend, confidante, and transport. Reaching out to the parrot, Rati seeks answers about their beloved. Not receiving any news, Rati whirls into a dizzy and crashes on the floor as the stage goes dark, marking the end of Act I.

The stage goes dark before each of the subsequent acts as Rati goes through stages of denial, anger, and acceptance. Each act is preceded by a text presenting a summary of what to expect in the sections. In Act II, Rati begins their playful and light prancing movements ranging from slight pecks on lips to orgasmic union. The words appear on the projection screen:

> *Act II Smarana: Recollection: Rati is in denial of their grief. They remember and celebrate their love. Birds, elephants, deer, flowers, bees, the moon, and the moon-lily, all remind them of Madana.*

Smarana means recollection as Rati remembers Madana. At the beginning of Act II, lights turn on the soloist who is still seated. This time the face is no longer confused and deluded. Rather, the face is lit and joyful. The scene begins with *Ubhayakartari*, a gesture that signifies romantic union but also looks like a tender touch across two separate entities. The tips of the little finger, the ring finger, and the tall finger meet and then subsequently touch the similar configuration of the other hand. Like in Act I, there is an increasing intensification of emotion. While the dancer intensified the feeling of being distraught in Act I, Act II marks a rising temperature in passionate encounters. Love birds, the bees on a flower, elephants, deer, moon-lilies, the moon, and the famous *Cakora* birds of mythic origin accentuate the romantic mood in sequence. Projected images of natural imagery complement the gestural, postural, energetic, and kinesthetic physicalizing of the same. Humor is built in as elephants and deer court each other, seek consent, and then make love. The *Cakora* birds thrive on moonlight. Their absorption of moon-rays refers to the climactic union of Rati and Madana as the dancer descends once more to the floor and the weighted vulnerability of Act I paves way to ecstatic joy.

The sharp, high-pitched sound of the conch shell bookends Act III as the soloist maneuvers the stage with loud and fast footwork, large kinespheric extensions, big eyes, and sharp turns. The cyclorama projects:

> *Act III Tandava: Destruction: Shiva is infuriated with Madana's prank that woke them from deep meditation. Shiva's third eye opens with fire gushing out, engulfing the entire universe.*

This is then followed by an image with iconography from Hindu male deity Shiva who is known for his austerity, power, and anger. *Tandava*, meaning destruction, focuses on strength and force. The soloist draws movement inspiration both in replication and in imitation in Foster's terms from some of the iconography visible on screen. Serpentine qualities of snakes wrap around Śiva symbolizing desire and its subordination. Predatory instincts of the tiger-skin wrap around Shiva's waist. Gushing flood waters of the uncontrolled Ganges are quelled through Shiva's matted locks. Shiva's third eye opens to burn the universe, reminding of the cyclical nature of life where all things eventually come to an end. The driving force of this piece is the universality of emotion while the narrative and symbolic structures add variety and scaffolding to achieving that emotional breadth. The performative qualities—serpentine, gushing, and scorching—are cues for the elaboration of the emotional tenor. The first three acts are precursor build-ups to the main component of the piece, encapsulated by crying out aloud in grief in *Act IV: Vilap*, the namesake of the whole work.

Act IV begins with the projected text:

> *Act IV Vilap: Mourning: Rati is in the process of accepting their grief having gone through the various stages of denial, anger, and delusion. The earth and the skies bemoan the loss.*

This act begins the exact same way as Act I, reminding the viewers about the nonlinear temporal progression of the piece. It is as it one feels like living the same reality while engaging with multiple emotions—angst, denial, delusion, and grief. The dancer remains prone for the majority of this act, imagining a corpse lying in front parallel to the front edge of the stage. Through gestural elaboration, Rati says:

> *Are you alive? On the ground, I only see a shape reminiscent of you. But, it's just ashes left by the fire of Shiva's anger. My pain is fierce, my hair is wild, I am soaked with the earth's dust. The earth partakes in my suffering .....*

The piece, then, engages in intense *Angik Abhinaya* (physical expression) by generating a series of contortions and extensions. Waves of denial follow those of acceptance as horizontal splits contract into the fetal position with head buried into the knees and knees crunched into the chest. The light fades away from downstage left as we see on screen:

> *The earth and the skies bemoan ... grief awakens in us newer horizons.*

Rati Vilap feels heavy due to the subject matter as well as its treatment of movement. Grief feels like a downward vector. This directional quality frames Acts I, III, and IV although Act II feels light. The contrast aids in building variations in the script. The degrees of abstraction from grief (delusion in Act I, denial in Act II, and anger in Act III) explore the multifaceted psychological progression in the experience and expression of grieving. Waves of anger follow those of denial and delusion and vice versa. A nonlinear depiction of this psychological state through varying abstractions aid in the narrative efficacy. The earthy texture prioritizes a choreographic motif building throughout the work—one that focuses on consummate grieving, the experience of which enables newer possibilities. Absorption of grief through the process of grieving is elaborately explored in Act IV with the body rolling on, melting into, and embracing the floor—the grounds of existence. Through such absorptive maneuvers, grief makes transformation possible. *Rati Vilap* is an energetic and powerful churning–one that the dancer goes through in sync with the viewer. It does not evoke sadness or any particular emotion in the viewer but rather makes it possible to experience an experiential churning that reclaims power embedded within emotion.

Indian aesthetician Kapila Vatsyayan laments the loss of aesthetic stylization as the primary content of performance (1992). For Vatsyayan, the presentation of *Bhava*'s (emotional content) associated narrative, chronology, and meaning-making, rarefied into *Rasa* (aesthetic distillation) should create the epicenter of the performance. However, in actual execution, the emotional and aesthetic distillation often becomes secondary to the formal building blocks. I argue that in centering the affective, *Shilpanatanam* holds true Vatsyayan's claim of a *Rasic* centrality around which the sensory, the perceptual, the philosophical, the narrative, the spiritual, and the emotional revolve. In this way, the primary purpose of the piece lies in its unequivocal realization of a "special kind of reflexive consciousness that consists of the light of the bliss that is one's own pure consciousness...tasting, savoring, rapture, relishing, enjoyment, experience" (Pollock 2016, 221). Cognition, feeling, and sensitivity are all implicated in such a performative experience. Traditional Odissi, also imbued with *Rasa*, poses formal limitations onto itself. *Shilpanatanam*, in this case, does not pose itself any embodied restrictions. Rather, it delves into the *Rasic* premise in order to realize its promise in front of an audience.

Case Study II: *An Impossible Romance* (2022)

The Impossible Romance (2022) illustrates the dynamization of imagistic stasis through bodily materiality and dramatic intent. *The Impossible Romance* is a love story between the cloud and the lightning leading each other to their imminent demise at the point of their climactic union. The arbitrator in this story is a peacock who is bored out of its wits on a sultry afternoon and looking for something to get it going. It decides to lure the pompous cloud toward the dazzling lightning. Inviting the cloud to a tête-à-tête, the peacock starts conniving how to create mischief. Falling for the peacock's trap, the cloud descends on the earth for a conversation. The two-way dialogue starts with the cloud boasting about its apparent all-pervasive nature—comparing itself to the lotus blooms, the oceanic waves, the torrential rains, the mountains, the vegetation, and the divine creator of conventional religion. The cloud believes itself to be the source of life.

The peacock is visibly annoyed and plots to teach the cloud a lesson by creating suspense around the character of lightning. Slowly revealing about the lightning, the peacock is

FIG. 20: Plotting Peacock: Shalini Basu during a photoshoot sponsored by Greater Columbus Arts Council and Ohio Arts Council, April 25, 2022. Reproduced with permission from Jeff Cravotta.

FIG. 21: Dissolution: Author Performing *Impossible Romance* at UNC Charlotte Dance Faculty Concert, Charlotte, January 23, 2023. Reproduced with permission from Jeff Cravotta.

successful in rousing curiosity and desire in the cloud. The cloud then searches impetuously for the lightning, eventually discovering its electricality. The dazzling sight unnerves the cloud who is taken aback by the blinding magnanimity of the lightning. Unable to contain its desire, the cloud reaches out to the lightning. The lightning, on the other hand, warns the cloud to stay away. Thus, ensues a romantic chase between the cloud and the lightning, resulting in a climactic embrace—one that marks the kiss of death for both. *Shilpanatanam*'s imagistic exploration of the content is episodic in nature as images diffuse into one another. Static images such as a peacock lying lazily in siesta, the peacock excited upon seeing a pompous cloud, the cloud boasting about its life-giving capacity, the peacock luring the cloud to the lightning, the cloud chasing the lightning, and eventually, the cloud meeting its imminent dissolution, find kinesthetic resonance through gestural, postural, and emotional engagement.

The fable-esque approach of the choreography visualizes characters (peacock, cloud, and lightning), situations (sultry afternoon, ecological imagery), conversations (the manipulative peacock with the gullible, pompous cloud, the brilliantly honest lightning with the helpless cloud), and transformations (the ultimate diffusion of the cloud and the lightning as ether) metaphorically. Human experiences of manipulation find metaphorical lives through the characterizations of animal and natural entities. The choreographic approach brings on the same plane secular and religious narratives to the notional use of building a storyline. Unlike the centering of the spiritual motif in traditional Odissi, *Shilpanatanam* democratically treats the male deity of *Jagannath* as one among a series of ecological and imaginative motifs. Exaggeration of emotions and physical expressions drive home a notion of absolute absurdity of the narrative itself and its choreographic visualization through physical movement, costuming, and emotional charge. The piece itself becomes electrified with stasis and movement complementing one another across geometric (large extensions, *Chauka* and *Tribhangi* postures) and kinesthetic (percussive footwork, neck-eye-head maneuvering, hip motion) conjuring of space and time, visualizing an impossible romance between the cloud and the lightning. This aspect of Kulkarni's work where the experience is artistically honed through storytelling is captured by behavioral sociologist Robert Perinbanayagam (2023). In his book-length compilation of essays called *Dialogues, Dramas, and Emotions*, Perinbanayagam notes that in Kulkarni's choreographic visualization, "characters and situations are transformed into metaphors for one human experience or another" (41). As noted by Penrinbanayagam, the metaphorical syntactic approach becomes the binding force of the visualization of the experiential through choreography. The entire dramatic act happens without any verbal content. Percussive intonation and embodied expression carry forward this dramatic intent.

Dhei Karataka Dhei Ta Dhei
Taka Ta Thin Thinaka
Thina Kita Dhini Thina Kita Dhini Taka
Dhei Karataka Dhei Ta Dhei
Taka Ta Thin Thinaka
Thina Kita Dhini Thina Kita Dhini Taka

The above entry sequence is a percussive segment as the dance establishes a bored peacock looking out into the world to find comic relief. Odissi's languid upper body depicted by gestural cascading and echoing torso emerge as lagged responses to percussive sharpness of footwork. Departure from Guru Kelucharan Mohapatra style is also visible with the sidewise hip motion; a tease registering the mischief-maker in the characterization of the peacock.

Tat Dhei Karataka Gadi Ghene Dhei
Takita Takita Dhini
Karataka Gadi Ghene Dha
Karataka Gadi Ghene Dha
Karataka Gadi Ghene Dha
Tat Dhei Karataka Gadi Ghene Dhei
Takita Takita Dhini
Karataka Gadi Ghene Dha
Karataka Gadi Ghene Dha
Karataka Gadi Ghene Dha
Tat Dhei Karataka Gadi Ghene Dhei
Takita Takita Dhini
Karataka Gadi Ghene Dha
Karataka Gadi Ghene Dha
Karataka Gadi Ghene Dha

The *Tihai* (three times repetition of the exact rhythmic structure to mark a culmination of a section) ramps up the playfulness as the peacock continues to deploy eye glances and shoulder twists to continue prancing about its way, looking for a perfect prey. The *Tihai* ends with the peacock overjoyed at spotting the pompous cloud up and above, floating boastfully in the sky. Thus, the plotting begins.

One can say the intended meaning of the percussive act is to display speed, technical precision, and momentum in motion. However, the expressive dramaturgy clearly denotes personification and imagistic deepening of a particular character. Throughout the rhythmic act, the suggestion of bird-like gaits and mannerisms continue to ornament the poetic quality of the movement. Thus, one can see the multiple layers of meanings—literal or percussive, denoted or expressive, and suggested or inferred—compounded poetically in the construction of the choreographic narrative. Choreography becomes the intermediary between the imagistic and the ineffable *Rasa*. The energetic dissolution is palpable as the imagistic materiality dissolves into affective ineffability. Reviewer Lea Marshall writes that "like the story's lightning, she electrifies the air around her, connecting earth and sky through a deeply rooted plié extending up through a sinuous spine, energy radiating from and beyond her arms, hands, and face" (2023, 8). While Marshall's technical translation of Odissi's *Mandala Pada* (wide grounded stance with well-bent knees) into a "plié" is culturally informed, her writing underscores the choreographic visualization and its eventual dissolution that *Shilpanatanam* offers. Through choreographic dissolution, the visual and the verbal merge into kinesthetic materiality to further dissipate into

FIG. 22: Author Performing *Woman with a Parrot* at "Tridha: Three Parables," an online webinar sponsored by Aalokam, New York City, March 15, 2021. Reproduced with permission from Toby Shearer.

the aesthetic experience of *Rasa*during which the narrative, kinesthetic, choreographic, and dramatic do not exist as separate identities.

Case Study III: *Woman with a Parrot* (2021)

Woman with a Parrot is a solo work that premiered on March 15, 2021, as part of *Tridha: Three Parables*. Composer Sudha Raghuraman created a musical sketch comprising of vocal renditions articulating abstract syllabic constructs conveying percussive meaning. I began this chapter with a dramatic hook elucidating the narrative arc of this solo. This piece presents a relationship between a woman and a parrot, sculpturally represented in stone in the famous Hampi temples of southern India, and choreographically explored in movement narrative. It shows human experiences of love, playfulness, and agony through a relationship between a woman and a parrot. The narrative arc of this piece is consolidated within two acts. The first act establishes the parrot as an object of love and affection for the woman. The second act shows the agony of separation felt by the woman as the parrot wants to go away. The stark contrast between the two acts is differentiated predominantly through changing affective tenor.

> *The shocking expression on my face indicates the transition between the two acts. The berry I use to lure my beloved parrot slips away from my hand. I am shocked at what I hear. I remain in denial for a moment. My emotional pitch remains tense as I convey my disapproval. I REFUSE TO LET HIM GO. Why does he want to go out into the unknown? I try to coax and cajole, locking the door of the cage. I hear wailing. Tear droplets emerge from his eyes making his feathers wet. I cannot bear his anguish. But, I shudder at the thought of letting him go. He stays adamant.*
>
> *I hug his cage. With heavy breathing and loud heart palpitations, I open the cage doors. He perches on my index finger. I gather my tears in my hands and comb the back of his neck with my fingers. I softly hold his warm and fuzzy body with my hands one last time before letting him go. I follow him as he flies around me one last time. I see him perch on my ceiling bars before making his final leap toward the horizon. My eyes follow his tiny body until he is no longer visible. My heart is pounding hard at this point. My breathing is audible. My life has just flown away from me. I die of a broken heart.*

Music and dance cyclically informed one another as composer Sudha Raghuraman's score provided us an initial tool kit to choreograph movement. Here, Kulkarni would gesturally show her patterns in space. I would take her patterns of the upper body and design it in the vehicular containment of the Odissi *Bhangis* (postures) with complementing footwork. The sketch of the dance took about six sessions to develop. Once we knew the overall arc of the piece, we returned to the composer to infuse our necessary changes in terms of repetitions and musical changes. The final music was then created based on the choreographic requirements. When I received the final music, I spent many hours setting my dance exactly to it. This is an osmotic process since with deeper the understanding of the music, we have a better integration of physical geometry, mental communication, and soulful evocation of the performative. Repetition is key because it is important for the solo artist to make this second nature. However, in each repetition there lies a deeper understanding and a corresponding shift in emotional, dramatic, temporal, or even geometric facility of the dance. *Woman with a Parrot* created a montage of my emotional and visual geometry that was aided by the musical composition and delivery by Sudha Raghuraman and Kulkarni's choreographic acumen.

Gestural articulation and dialogical back-and-forth brought the parrot to life. Play remains at the center during the first half as the playful interaction between the main characters physically establish a duality—the chirpy parrot and the obsessive woman whose obsession lies with her bird. Gesturally through *Kapitha* (single-handed *Mudra* describing a small bird) and *Garuda* (double-handed *Mudra* describing a large bird), the bird is established in flight, playing pranks, sitting on and walking along the woman's shoulders and hands, and pulling her hair. The woman, on the other hand, is established via *Aaharya Abhinaya* (costuming). The costume has been designed after the sculpture of the woman holding a parrot from the Hampi temple. Recreation of sculpture dominates the costuming in this work. Inspired from the sculpture, Kulkarni wanted to create a new look creatively rehashing the sculptural fabric, hairstyle, jewelry, and persona. I used hair extensions and stone-studded jewelry to recreate the hair design of my sculptural counterpart. Instead of the conventional stitched costume, I wrapped a green *Bomkai Sari* (Odisha handloom fabric) as a *Dhoti* (loose pants). The draping of the *Sari*, golden ornamentation, elaborate hair braiding, and kohl-stained eyes establish a youthful woman, enlivening the same one from the sculpture.

The contours of the solo dancing body in motion as well as in stillness captures the two characters throughout. In the second act, the dancer's gaze toward the parrot in the cage signifies the dual characters. At the very end, the flight of the bird results in the woman's death with arched backs, heavy breathing, and the climactic collapse. Using call and response and catch and flight principles, the piece establishes the narrative arc. Yet, the dramatic intensity lies in poignant arcs of communicative exchange between the woman and the parrot. For example, when the woman shows the various bird-activities such as somersaulting and other chirpy antics, she stylizes pedestrian expressions and movements. These activities help establish the bond shared between the two. Thus, the dramaturgy focuses on character building as well as dialogical exchange through dance.

Conclusion

Storytelling remains at the center of processual choreographic building-up and tearing-down. The story can emerge from the choreographer's own thoughts or from a traditional poet such as Jayadeva or Kalidasa. Sculptural motifs inspire Kulkarni who then builds an entire narrative around them. The presentation is often projecting the inner landscape of human emotion in all its shades and variegated differences. The outer world is abstracted through a plethora of techniques involving sensory, conceptual, linguistic, and philosophical immediacy. Portraying warmth and affection via slight fluttering of hands, rising of shoulders, and a gentle smile, *The Woman with a Parrot* (2021) abstracts the relational intimacy between a human and a bird. Obsession, control, and excessiveness are larger concepts that are explored through dramaturgical insight and technical proficiency in *Abhinaya*—an alchemy of being and enactment.

Such ineffable nonconceptual pure sensation is sometimes partnered with humanistic insight about desire and its dissolution as demonstrated through the choreography that will be discussed in detail later in the chapter. The emotional resonances can come through poetic verses demonstrating authorial intent. In such case, the literary provides the primary inspiration for the sensory and emotive presentation. The linguistic and the sensory carry a dialogical conversation with one another as the performative captures the realistic portrayal sieved through the choreographer's volition. In a given moment, the performer channelizes sensory perception alongside cognitive and conceptual development sparked through emotional fabrication of the physical world.

What is the immediacy of the cognitive and the emotional in this choreographic fabrication? The cognitive and the emotional faculties are both simultaneously and sequentially at play during the performance. The cognitive maps the contextual elements as the dancer gestures at the bird jumping along the cornice and then perching on the shoulder. The gestures created by the neck, eye, head, and hand movements note the sensory reactions of the woman in dialogue with the parrot, introducing a degree of immediacy to the process of narrative build-up. So, the performative introduces the element of immediacy that is central to the storytelling process. This element is unique to the dancing body given the aesthetic capacity to process the sensory, the emotive, and the cognitive in real-time to portray a narrative moment imbued with humanistic intent and potential. Amplification of the emotive appeal through abstract physical imagery is the critical appeal of *Shilpanatanam* as the dancer is constantly implicating the cognitive, the sensory, and the perceptual faculties through careful choreographic crafting so that the metaphoric appeal of the performative shines through.

The construction of the dance centers on the literary through stylized performative enactments. The gaze is key in this fabrication because it takes the audience across the entire performance. The trajectory of the dance is controlled by the focusing of the gaze. The face does most of the work with a paucity of gesture. Body adds color to the face while gesture remains an aid to the storytelling in a minimal capacity entailing a Rasic expansion of the body. Hands are positioned such that they frame the body. Physical movements require directionality, intentionality, and development through the expressive valence. The geometric alignment matters while the bending of the body espouses measured clarity. Clarity of movements is sought after given the importance of clean lines in this presentation.

The energetic detailing of the dancing body is marked by its acculturation within Odissi's circularity, curvilinearity, spiraling pivots, and controlled-contained performativity. Display of technical rigor is secondary to the dramatic build-up of the narrative structure stretching the idiom to accommodate the choreographer's vision. Churning via dramaturgy then often might break free from perceived and practiced conventional limits. Abstraction of reality through emotional intensification guides generation, proliferation, and deepening of movement. Sketching dynamic contours requires constant and consistent play in the creative process and the final choreographic product. An element of playful exploration is founded on a philosophy that honors the infinite possibilities that a single thought, emotion, action, personality, or characteristic trait creates.

Note

1. However, Kulkarni worked with Guru Kelucharan Mohapatra over one summer in her six-decade career in Bharatnatyam in order to expand her performing repertoire.

References

Allen, M. 2012. "Body Mapping, Kinesthesia, and Inclusive Awareness." In *What Every Singer Needs to Know About the Body*, 2nd ed., edited by M. Malden, MJ. Allen, and K. A. Zeller. Plural Publishing.

Bose, M. 1991. "The Nāṭyaśāstra and the Concept of Dance." In *Movement and Mimesis: The Idea of Dance in the Sanskritic Tradition*. Springer.

Chliara, A. 2018. "Acting as Tool for Dance Performance." Master's thesis, The University of Lincoln, USA.

Cuneo, D. 2015. "Rasa: Abhinavagupta on the Purpose (s) of Art." In *The Natyasastra Anthology*. McFarland.

DeLahunta, S. 2000. "Dance Dramaturgy: Speculations and Reflections." *Dance Theatre Journal* 16 (1): 20–25.

Desmond, J. 1997. *Meaning in Motion: New Cultural Studies of Dance*. Duke University Press.

Foster, S. L. 1986. *Reading Dancing: Bodies and Subjects in Contemporary American Dance*. University of California Press.

Ghosh, M. 1951. *Natyasastram Ascribed to Bharata Muni: A Treatise on Ancient Indian Dramaturgy and Histrionics*. Chaukhamba Surbharati Prakashan.

Ghosh, M., ed. 2006. *Nāṭyaśāstra of Bharatamuni: Text, Commentary of Abhinava Bharati by Abhinavaguptacarya and English Translation*. New Bharatiya Book Corporation.

Hermans, C. 2023. "Let's Play: Reenactment of Affective Traces Through Dance Improvisation." *Journal for Emerging Affect Enquiry* 3 (1): 61–79.

Higgins, K. M. 2007. "An Alchemy of Emotion: Rasa and Aesthetic Breakthroughs." *The Journal of Aesthetics and Art Criticism* 65 (1): 43–54.

Kapur, A. 2024. "Abhinaya." In *The Routledge Companion to Performance-Related Concepts in Non-European Languages*, edited by E. Fischer-Lichte, T. Jost, and A. Schenka. Routledge.

Lancaster, C. 1957. *The Aesthetic Experience According to Abhinavagupta. Artibus Asiae* 20 (2/3): 220–22.

Marshall, L. 2023. *University of North Carolina at Charlotte Faculty Dance Concert*.

McManus, W. 2010. "Being Watched: Yvonne Rainer and the 1960s/Yvonne Rainer: The Mind is a Muscle/Feelings Are Facts: A Life." *Art Journal* 69 (3): 131.

Nandikeśvara, and A. K. Coomaraswamy. 1917. *The Mirror of Gesture: Being the Abhinaya Darpana of Nandikeśvara*. Harvard University Press.

Nannyonga-Tamusuza, S. 2015. "Music as Dance and Dance as Music: Interdependence and Dialogue in Baganda Baakisimba Performance." *Yearbook for Traditional Music* 47: 82–96.

Perinbanayagam, R. 2023. *Dialogues, Dramas, and Emotions: Essays in Interactionist Sociology*. Bloomsbury.

Perpener, J. O. 2024. "Discussion of Faculty Concert on January 26 and 27, 2024."

Pollock, S. 2016. *A Rasa Reader: Classical Indian Aesthetics*. Columbia University Press.

Roche, Jenny, and Stephanie Burridge. 2022. *Choreography: The Basics*. Routledge.
Sedgwick, E. K. 2020. *Touching Feeling: Affect, Pedagogy, Performativity*. Duke University Press.
Varma, K. 1960. "The Basis of Indian Classical Drama." *Zeitschrift der Deutschen Morgenländischen Gesellschaft* 110 (2): 317–29.
Vatsyayan, K. 1992. *Indian Classical Dance*. Publications Division Ministry of Information and Broadcasting.
Vatsyayan, K. 1963. "Notes on the Relationship of Music and Dance in India." *Ethnomusicology* 7 (1): 33–38.
Wilson, H. H., and R. P. Dwivedi. 1966. *Kumara Sambhavam or the Birth of War-God= Kumāra sambhavam*. Indological Book House.

Conclusion

A Pedagogy of the Self

SOLO DANCING HAS BEEN around for a long time but remains under-represented, misunderstood, and exoticized in scholarship as well as popular perception. What is the meaning-making mechanisms behind solo performance? Studying the solo Odissi dancing body across traditional repertoire and new choreographic experiments lead to an improved understanding of the self. Scholars have noted how breath, sensation, listening, and visualization are important tools for fostering self-awareness (Richards 2009). Movement brings all four elements into conversation with one another as in performing, one is deeply attuned to one's cognitive and physical processes in order to create worlds of visualization for the audience. The self is constituted in and through performance via a variety of creative, technical, and psychological mechanisms as investigated throughout the course of the text. *Shaping S-Curves: Choreographic Process in Odissi* delves into the implications of curvilinearity across technical precepts, philosophical reasoning, creative process, and musical and textual influences (Chatterjee 2024).

The *Gitagovinda* (twelfth-century masterpiece written by poet Jayadeva) has been a part of ritual service in Odishan contexts. The text holds a significant place in Odissi dance repertoire for its cultural and historical value (Citaristi 2022). Dancers expose themselves to the large pantheon of Odishan literature toward their scripting for new compositions (Panda 2020). Text and music remain equally important players with dance forming a triangular creative process. Each holds proportionate relevance, continuing to inform another during various stages of the creative process. While *Pallavi* (melodic exposition in the third element of the traditional Odissi repertoire) emphasizes melody in conjunction with rhythm, *Abhinaya* places greater weight on text during the compositional process. However, text and music are not exclusive to the *Abhinaya* (expressive section in the fourth element of the traditional Odissi repertoire) and *Pallavi*, respectively, as texts form an integral element of *Sabhinaya Pallavi* (*Pallavi* composition involving theatrical elements such as facial expression, gestural encoding, and text) while *Abhinaya* is often known for its musical development.

Technical and philosophical expositions of the curvilinear aesthetic across material, experiential, and psychological dimensions further explain the uniqueness of the choreographic process. Spiraling in the physical body, such as the turning of the torso as an echo of a footwork connected to a distinct percussive beat on the *Mardala* (two-headed drum accompanying Odissi dance), becomes analogous to the philosophical turning toward non-duality as the dance and the dancer juxtapose one another with cognitive, emotive, and narrative elements. The apparent independent subjectivity of the dancer merges with the supposed objectivity of the dance in a call and response process of what scholar Nandini Sikand deftly describes as *Languid Bodies Grounded Stances* in her book title (Sikand 2016). The languid makes its way in discussions involving deepening the traditional curvilinear aesthetic alongside a marked departure from it in contemporary experiments in choreography by Dr. Rohini Dandavate and Dr. Maya Kulkarni, respectively.

The methodology remains true to the title of this book as the author engages in multiple new solo works to investigate the creative process from conception to performance. This is the first book-length investigation of the solo dancing body where movement becomes an epistemological process of investigating the self, alongside a thorough reflection on the presence of the creative being. The act of spiraling, then, becomes a full circle of the self's navigation across plurality and multiplicity only to return to its subjecthood with reinvigorated perception, action, and thought (Sen-Podstawska 2019).[1]

The solo moving body becomes a microcosm of the cosmologies that it encompasses (Spencer 1996). This is not a directly imitative association that simplistically addresses the objective with the embodied. This connection is married across the philosophical, the technical, and the aesthetic. Creative choices weave the technical precepts of posture-gesture-gait with the musical and the textual. Furthermore, aesthetic choices of costuming manifest deeper significance, which is encoded to the trained eyes of the keen observer. The dancing body is an excellent example of cognitive, emotive, kinesthetic, and sensory processing in real-time with the observer. Communicating aesthetic ideals, narrative stories, or percussive complications, the dancer combines being, knowing, and enacting. The mind visualizes the objects represented gesturally. The assumption of the objective in embodiment follows the curvilinear aesthetic of the form in discussion. Parity across the sensory perception and objective materiality reduces the distance between the body as a separate entity in the world. This formal assumption of the objective by the subjective body-mind complex through aesthetic configurations of performance creates an immediacy between the knower, the object to be known, and the mechanism of knowing (Loy 2012).

Philosopher Dhirendra Mohan Datta notes that "the mind flows out to the object through the sense and assumes the form of the object and establishes thereby a sort of identity between the mind and the object" (1967, 78). Performance transforms space and time through a play on formal elements, such as (a)symmetry, levels, geometric patterns, etc. The artist's aesthetic sensibility filters the gathering, processing, and manifesting of kinesthetic perception as movement engages in a play across text, melody, and rhythm. Artist and scholar Aloka Kanungo innovates by adhering to *Desha* (space), *Kala* (time), and *Auchitya* (aesthetic sensibility) while addressing aesthetic needs of her production. Using red flowers as a hair ornament in lieu of the usual *Tahia* (circular head garment representing temple architecture) gives Kanungo the rationale to better depict the energetic configuration of *Dasamavidyas* (a group of ten female goddesses across a range of religious traditions). Reorienting from the architectural to the energetic furthers the embodied valence of movement. Meaning-making across the representative dimensions adheres to the controlled channeling of inner strength that is further accentuated with the aesthetic choices on colors and contours. Floral contours differ in edge and curvature from the spikes of the *Tahia*. If the *Tahia* depicts circular notions of time, the red flowers deepen the inner expansion in space. However, when performing solo in another context, Kanungo chooses to wear the *Tahia* instead of donning the red flowers. This conscious choice could be to communicate to the larger audience the defining elements of the Odissi costuming convention especially where different traditional dances were being showcased. Kanungo's aesthetic sensibility remains key to the translation of the content to the larger public where she keeps in mind the larger contexts of the purpose and communicative appeal of her performance (Kanungo 2020).

Much of the discussion in this text revolves around the dancer's perspective, especially in the non-dual processing by the sensory and the aesthetic. Performative processing of the kinesthetic reaches to an apotheosis where the dance and the perceiver literally become enmeshed into one continuous perception; the sense of a self as a separate entity that is engaged in dancing fades while the dance ceases to be something exterior. This discussion is quite similar to philosopher David Loy's description of nond-ual perception of music where he says: "No matter how well I may know the work, I cease to anticipate what is coming and become that single note or chord which seems to dance" (2012, 71). This is a cultivation of presence, a skill that is honed time and again by the dancing body. Dance assumes a pedagogical role of nurturing presence where the past and the futurity of linear temporal construction fade away. What remains is absolute immediacy where the moment becomes of paramount importance as the dance between the sensory and the aesthetic. The immediacy refers to the energetic contouring well besides the representative and the cognitive meaning-making. In the earlier paragraph, such an energetic characterization occurs in Aloka Kanungo's choices in *Aharya* (costuming convention that adheres to an impactful expressive ethos).

The self always dances in alchemical bouncing of energy with the audience (Higgins 2007). Such energetic configurations also cease to thrive in the non-dual stillness of emergent presence that is the ultimate goal in performance. Thus, the dancer and the dance remain in curvilinear vibration as presence, immediacy, and expansion of the perceived moment remain central in the non-dual experience of the subjective merging with the objective. Such heightened consciousness cannot be reinvigorated through mere formulaic repetition. The presence in question is perhaps the sheer ability of the solo artist to actually take the curvilinearity of the form into a spiraling toward the self. This realizes greater fruition through the dialogical cycle established with the audience as the viewer is brought inside the energetic circle of the artist not as a passive spectator but rather as an active arbitrator in the process of creating performative exuberance.

This moment of presence in the perceptive Odissi body is described best by *The New York Times*'s dance critic Jennifer Dunning as a moment of complete joyous abandon, apparently stripped of form and narrative yet retaining the S-shape (2008). Formal retention of geometric shape with the simultaneous abandonment retains the exemplary moment of the dancer becoming the dance and vice versa. Author Karen Greenspan further vouches for the absolute liberating intensity of such a performance as she articulates how the dancer "leads the audience to an inspired state of sublime, undiluted rapture-moksha" (2018, 55). As noted by Greenspan, *Moksha* (freedom) remains the ultimate purpose of Odissi dance where the freedom refers to the removal of ignorance about the true nature of the self. Acclaimed soloist of *Nrityagram* (the globally famous premier Indian dance company), Bijayini Satpathy, feels she could explore *speaking through Odissi* for the rest of her life as she finds infinite freedom within its S-curves (Harss 2019, 18). Satpathy's curricular updates with live dancing demonstration via video tutorials for *Dance Teacher* break down the S-pattern into bite-size lengths (Wingenroth 2023). This demonstrates how shape is a chiseling of artistic intention alongside the burden of tradition as formal clarity becomes ingrained into the persona and presence of the artist.

Dance becomes a manifestation of acculturation where each moment presents a certain assumption of form and/or content from an array of choices where decision-making happens in real-time, maximizing the ultimate goal of freedom. Technical encoding of a nonlinear core with an S-shape is rooted in the cultural identity of Odisha. Abundance of S-shapes are easily found in the temple sculpture of the *Alasakanyas* (stone sculptures of languid female personalities). But the languid does not stay restricted to the languid feminine (Sharman 2020). There are many male sculptural figures that also demonstrate the S-shape to its fullest extent. Such an ethnologic containment of dance and culture bleeds into the aesthetic and the philosophical (Kaeppler 1972). As noted earlier, Satpathy searches for infinite freedom within the curvilinear aesthetic noting how the spiraling motion itself is an intentional crafting of presence. It takes a long duration of at least three years to have the groundedness from which a nonlinear spine can emerge. Different teaching lineages pay varying levels of attention to the degree of rootedness. While bent knees are characteristic of every lineage, often the buoyancy of the grounded stance depends on the particular teacher's comfort zone.

As part of this research, I exposed myself to a range of teachers and pedagogical patterns available in this field. I found an entire spectrum of grounded bodies. Guru Debaprasad Das style has primary emphasis on the square stance. So, its groundedness quotient seems to be the highest to the eye. However, I found that Guru Kelucharan Mohapatra style pays primary attention to the oppositional quality of the lower upper. Stamping the right foot results in the echoing of the torso toward the left reducing side-to-side swaying motion to the least. This oppositional technique causes an illusion of fluidity given the lyrical nature of the upper body. Despite the illusion of the lyrical, the grounded, when partnered with a carefully metered echoing upper body with immobile hips as practiced in Guru Kelucharan Mohapatra Nrityabasa (the premier Odissi institution in Bhubaneswar, Odisha), requires significant practice. It is an act of centering from the sideways sway that in other styles might have greater degrees of oscillation.

The technical coordination of limbs and the spine remains central to navigating the core. This is the primary emphasis that mandates nonlinearity of the S-shape. The S-shape, either in visually explicit physical designs or in implicit technical parameters, requires practice and repetition for the body to automatically recognize it. The default posture of the S-shape functions as a strong motif in the Odishan landscape. The two postural parameters of the square and the S-shape dissolve within one another in choreographic compositions. Vehicular containment within these two alongside *Sama* (straight posture) and *Abhanga* (slightly bent posture) continue to differentiate the traditional form with contemporary experiments and expansions such as *Yorchha* (dance technique combining yoga, martial art form Chhau, and Odissi). The engaged core holds the curvilinear aesthetic and the periphery enhanced by gestural limits of

Padabheda (foot posture) and *Mudra* (hand gesture) signify verbal meaning-making. Choreographic and performative intent is restricted to the peripheral limits as the core holds the curvilinear aesthetic in its grounded languidity. So, the verbal meaning emerging from the periphery is distilled with the vehicular judgment of the curvilinear. Such a communicative appeal is a self-spiraling mechanism as the primary activity results from a turning inwards the core S. A break in the narrative communication occurs with the intentionless functioning of the spiral. There is a simultaneous turning inward and a turning toward where layers of meaning across technique, choreography, and melodic sketches fade away into insignificance. What remains is an inchoate vibration—a nonlinear impulse reaching out from the dancing body toward itself through an alchemical outreach to the audience member. The peripheral limits tend to develop a trajectory, a purpose, a narrative, or a communication of joy directed toward an intended receiver. Yet, the reception is only an alchemical first step in the spiraling art. The final step is the spiraling within and emerging into the S with its promise of intentionlessness and the freedom that comes with such a non-teleological activity. In this capacity, verbal meaning-making takes a seat secondary to the durational acculturation within the infinite degrees of freedom of the S.

The goal of such acculturation is simply to provide a tool kit of choices for the dancing body to make decisions in real-time. Such decisions can range across verbal, emotive, cognitive, psychological, and kinesthetic registers. The registers provide a plethora of combinations that can be drawn from or made up at an instant's notice by the dancer. Such choices at the spur of the moment make the dance look stripped of intention, narrative, emotion. However, these are effused within through the process of mindful repetition and incessant practice of deep engagement of the focused mind. In this manner, the dancing body with its spiraling gestures becomes a pedagogy of focus. At the moment of its final deliverance, it simply functions intuitively without deliberate intention, a moment also recognized by Jennifer Dunning as a combination of abundance and abandonment (2008).

Manifestation of thought in movement has been studied from the perspective of cognitive theories to conclude how creating and performing dance involve episodic memory in performance, occasional labelling of movement phrases in rehearsal; an augmentation of which occurs through expressive nuance and communicative intent that is not characteristic of other movement-based procedural tasks (Stevens and McKechnie 2005). Before delving deeper into the interpretation of thought in motion later in this concluding chapter, I make a case for the subjective interpretation of the solo artist in moment-to-moment decision-making. This occurs as a balancing act of coordinating multiple elements, such as the physical, the verbal, the ornamental, and the emotional, into a coherent whole. Such quick changes of emotion or affect is possible with efficacious and practiced repetitions where the dancer is able to recreate experientially felt sensations and emotions alongside spatially and temporally distinct movements. This is interspersed with the function of a constant communication with the audience. So, in a way, what rises subsides to ensure that the communication channel is kept friction-free. This communicative efficacy requires simultaneous disidentification with the content with experientially felt performative practice. The point is that I do not act joy, but rather feel joy in my enactment even though I might have to switch to a completely different emotion in the very next instant. So, the communicative property also serves as a sewing thread, changing the tone of the performance. The dance needs decision-making every instant as the body-mind complex works through the multiple layers of movement, text, and music in a curvilinear unfolding. The curvilinearity of the visual form is also true in terms of its treatment of choreographic content with an alternative rising and subsiding of affective intensity and melodic intonation. Different choreographers focus on various aspects of the curvilinear form in their choreography. Choreographer Meera Das focuses on *Lalitya* (softness) as she reimagines the iconic canonical piece *Batu* (foundational elements). Das reimagines Guruji's *Batu*, bringing alive the musical instruments *Veena* (string instrument), *Benu* (flute), *Mardala* (percussion), *Khola* (percussion instrument), *Manjira* (metal cymbals), *Ghanta* (bell), and *Khanjani* (metal plates strung on wood) in greater degrees of dynamism and curvilinearity.

Intentionality, agency, and meaning-making occur in thoughtful integration of movement with verbal codes. As an active participant in the choreographic process, the solo dancing body on whom pieces are commissioned, is privy to the entire gamut of thought arcs. Choreographic agency lies in the dancing body that translates the verbal instructions, thoughtful imaginations, and lucid visualizations of the choreographer. The choreographic process involves inspiration, observation, and visualization. The creative thought process is key to crafting movement that repurposes basic elements and source materials as geometric patterns or evocative emotionality. Life incidents and memories play a crucial role in the creative process. Inspiration comes to artists from observing performances. An autobiographical imprint remains in the choreographic creation, emerging out of distinct choices of following a thought process or discarding certain movements based on instinct. The artist's life experiences and perceptions develop the instinctual and intuitive capacity (Merritt 2015). The aesthetic disposition puts a personal stamp on the creation. Like transition in movement needs to remain smooth in the lyrical aesthetic, similarly loss of focus from one thought to another is unallowable in the advanced technique of expressive repertoire. Continuous looping in of thoughts is an important performative trait, especially for the *Abhinaya* repertoire that has an array of emotive range.

Thought patterns remain a significant performative tool for the dancing body in order to remain present in every passing moment of a durational solo recital that can range anywhere from forty minutes to over two hours. Intensity of the dancer's focus is key to maintaining the audience's attention.

In conclusion, it is safe to say that choreography is an immersive and multidimensional exercise in a complex art form such as Odissi where movement, music, text, and context are constantly shaping and reshaping embodiment and expression. Even during its incipient stages, choreography has been at least a constant back-and-forth between the melodic, the rhythmic, the textual, and the motility as crafted by the choreographer. Both rhythm and emotion color the gestural and the postural based on which movement—intentionally choreographed curvilinear arc—takes place. Layers of significance and meaning drawing from the cultural, the religious, the spiritual, and the philosophical, perhaps, leave little room for embodied creativity. In contrast, perhaps the infinite depths of the dancing body open up a plethora of possibilities where the same movement can be performed in innumerable affectations. Thus, choreography is not restricted to the externally visible motion but also extends to the internal crafting of emotion. Attitudinal differentiation becomes the key marker of virtuosic motion in the form,

FIG. 23: Self-Inquiry: 2025 Ohio Arts Council Traditional Arts Apprentice Ayshani Atarshi Performing at "Jugalbandi," Columbus, June 25, 2025. Reproduced with permission from Toby Shearer.

a concept that is totally unavailable to the conceptualization of choreography as solely physical movement. The embodiment within Odissi requires varying degrees of immersive attention given the interdisciplinary nature of the creative process. The choreographic process in Odissi is a multidimensional construct that is simultaneously immersive within the layers of construction—musical, percussive, gestural, postural, melodic, literary, and performative—as well as infinitely expansive. Odissi dancer and scholar Sabina Sen-Podstawska describes the immersive experience in the act of dancing where "a dancer undergoes a rainbow of embodied experience that carries meaningful threads in realizing herself/himself, the dance and the world the artist inhabits" (2018, 303).

Note

1. The Conclusion forms the philosophical basis of the *Dance and Community Research Institute* where multiplicity is fostered across a series of culturally situated initiatives. This institute brings South Asian artists, scholars, educators, and youth together to create systemic change within and beyond the arts and build infrastructure for South Asian arts. The Institute's handbook covers the operational basis of its multiple activities across scholarship, education, and outreach (Appendix A).

References

Chatterjee, S. 2024. "Performing Odisha, Performing Odissi: Tracing Interdependencies Among the Allied Performance Practices of Odisha." Master's thesis, University of California, Riverside.

Citaristi, I. 2022. *Odissi and the Geeta Govinda*. Routledge.

Datta, D. M. 1967. "Epistemological Methods in Indian Philosophy." In *The Indian Mind: Essentials of Indian Philosophy and Culture*, 118–35. University of Hawai'i Press.

Dunning, J. 2008. "Spirits That Fly High While Rooted in Tradition." *New York Times*, 157 (54227): E6 (L)-E6 (L).

Greenspan, K. 2018. "A Day in the Life of Nrityagram." *Dance Research Foundation, Inc.* 46: 51–55.

Harss, M. 2019. "Conjuring Gods and Demons.: *New York Times*, 15 (L)-15 (L).

Higgins, K. M. 2007. "An Alchemy of Emotion: Rasa and Aesthetic Breakthroughs." *The Journal of Aesthetics and Art Criticism* 65 (1): 43–54.

Kaeppler, A. L. 1972. "Acculturation in Hawaiian Dance." *Yearbook of the International Folk Music Council* 4: 38–46.

Kanungo, A. 2020. "007 Mahavidya - Aloka Kanungo." *Odissi Dancers Forum Kolkata*. YouTube, https://www.youtube.com/watch?v=TD-hYCrks2s.

Loy, D. 2012. *Nonduality: A Study in Comparative Philosophy*. Prometheus Books.

Merritt, M. 2015. "Thinking-Is-Moving: Dance, Agency, and a Radically Enactive Mind." *Phenomenology and the Cognitive Sciences* 14 (1): 95–110.

Panda, S. P. 2020. "A Text to Speech System in Odia Language."In *Language, Literature, Culture & Integrity*, Vol. II, edited by S. K. Prusty et al., 139–46. Institute of Odia Studies and Research.

Richards, C. E. 2009. "Toward a Pedagogy of Self." *Teachers College Record* 111 (12): 2732–2759.

Sen-Podstawska, S. S. 2018. "Why Dancing the Sensual Sculptures Matters?: Considering a Sensory Paradigm for Odissi Dance." In *Dance Matters Too: Markets, Memories, Identities*, edited by P. Chakravorty and N. Gupta. Routledge India.

Sen-Podstawska, S. S. 2019. "The Transient 'Ideals' of the 'Odissi Body' and the Changing Place and Role of Odissi Dancers in History." *Świat i słowo* 1 (32): 133–51.

Sharman, S. 2020. "Secular Female Imagery in Orissan Temple Architecture: The Case of Alasa Kanyas." *Chitrolekha Journal on Art & Design* 4 (2).

Sikand, N. 2016. *Languid Bodies, Grounded Stances: The Curving Pathway of Neoclassical Odissi Dance*. Berghahn Books.

Spencer, P. 1996. "Dance and the Cosmology of Confidence." In *The Politics of Cultural Performance*, edited by D. Parkin and H. Fisher. Berghahn Books.

Stevens, C., and S. McKechnie. 2005. "Thinking in Action: Thought Made Visible in Contemporary Dance." *Cognitive Processing* 6 (4): 243–52.

Wingenroth, L. 2023. "Bijayini Satpathy Teaches an Odissi Step." *Dance Teacher*. https://danceteacher.com/bijayini-satpathy-teaches-an-odissi-step/#gsc.tab=0.

RESOURCES FOR PRACTITIONERS

GLOSSARY

Aanvikshiki	Science of inquiry
Abarta Puspita	Cycle of a flower from bud to bloom
Abhanga	Slightly bent posture
Abhinaya	Expressive movement; Fourth element of the traditional Odissi repertoire
Abhyasa	Practice
Advaita Vedanta	Non-dual textual exegesis in Indic traditions
Agni	Fire
Aharya	Costuming convention that adheres to an impactful expressive ethos
Alambana	Foundational factors
Alap	Slow unmetered introduction to a melodic mode
Alapadma	Full-bloom
Alasakanyas	Stone sculptures of languid female personalities
Alolita	Head circle
Angik Abhinaya	Physical expression
Anondo	Joy
Antara	Musical variation building upon the *Sthayi*
Anubhava	Physical reactions
Arasa	Rhythmic interlude
Asamyukta	Single-handed gesture
Ashtapadis	Eight-versed songs
Atman	Self
Auchitya	Aesthetic sensibility
Bana	Bow
Bandhani	One-legged balance
Bansuri	Flute
Bastra	Clothes
Baul	Mystic minstrels dressed in saffron
Benu	Flute
Bhaga	Compartmentalization of the units in the *Tala*
Bhakta	Devotee
Bhakti	Devotional quotient
Bhangis	Postures
Bharatnatyam	Southern Indian classical dance form
Bhasa	Full-bodied gesture depicting the flow of water
Bhava	Emotion
Bhaya	Fear

Bhramari	Rotation
Bichhedo	Separation
Bichitro	Strange
Bomkai Sari	Odisha handloom fabric
Bol	Mnemonic syllables accompanying percussion
Brahman	Non-dual consciousness
Cakora	Bird who lives on the rays of the moon
Chakkar	Pirouettes
Chamara	Female holding a fly whisk
Champu	Combination of prose and poetry
Chatura Mudra	Single-handed gesture with thumb placed at the base of the ring finger
Chaturang	Compositional format having four distinct musical sections
Chauka	Square
Chhapaka	Sling-shot movement
Chhau	Eastern Indian martial art form
Cittavritti	Alterations of the mind
Dalamalika	Holding a branch like a garland
Darpana	Holding a mirror
Darshan	Relational viewing or visualization
Dasamavidyas	A group of ten female goddesses across a range of religious traditions
Desha	Space
Dhaivat	Sixth note in the octave
Dhoti	Loose pants
Drishti	Focused gaze primarily for maintaining focus and partners with balance
Ektali	A four beat rhythmic cycle with one clap
Ektara	One-stringed instrument
Ga	Short for *Gandhār*, *Ga* is the third note in the basic scale
Gabakshya	Window grills
Gamakas	Musical ornamentations
Garuda	Double-handed *Mudra* describing a large bird
Ghanta	Bell
Gitagovinda	Twelfth-century masterpiece written by poet Jayadeva
Gunthana	One who hides herself
Hasya	Mirth
Hameer	A nighttime melodic mode known for its dramatic and regal character
Jaya	To praise and elevate
Jhala	Fast-paced rhythmic section
Jhor	Developmental music between free-flowing *Alap* and rhythmic *Jhala*
Jhunk	Downward lilting accent specific to Odissi's curvilinearity
Jyoti	Light
Kala	Time
Kapitha	Single-handed *Mudra* describing a small bird
Karanas	Embodied postures with elaborate detailing
Karuna	Sadness

Katamukha	Single-hand gesture indicating a bud
Kavya	Words
Ketakibharana	Ketaki blossom
Khali	Indicator of a directional change in the *Tala*
Khanjani	Metal plates strung on wood
Khola	Percussion instrument
Komal	Flat musical mode
Krodha	Anger
Lalita Parsni Paada Sanchara	Serpentine heel-led forward gait
Lalitya	Softness
Laya	Movement of the units in the *Tala*
Manas	Fixed syllables that repeat three times in the same pace and end on *Sama*
Mandala Pada	Wide grounded stance with well-bent knees
Mangalacharan	Auspicious beginning; first invocation in Odissi repertoire
Manini	Offended
Manjira	Metal cymbals
Mardala	Two-headed drum; sculpture of a female-drummer
Margam	Traditional repertoire
Matrmurti	Sculpture of other
Mayur	Peacock
Milono	Union
Moksha	Freedom
Mudra	Hand gesture
Mugdha	Innocent
Nartaki	Dancer
Natanam	Dance
Natya	Acting
Natyasastra	Ancient Indian treatise on performing arts
Navakshari	Poem where nine letters are grouped together
Nayika	Female protagonist
Nritta	Pure dance
Nrityagram	Premier, globally renowned Indian dance company reputation
Nupurpadika	One wearing anklets
Padabheda	Foot posture
Pada	Sung lyric with narrative meaning
Padartha	Word-by-word
Padma	Full bloom
Padmagandha	Smelling the lotus
Pallava	Cascading of fingers
Pallavi	Melodic exposition in the third element of the traditional Odissi repertoire
Parampara	Lineage
Pataka	Fingers joined and held in extension of the forearm
Pradeepa	Oil-wick lamp
Prakampita	Forward and backward neck motion

Pramana Grantha	An intense deliberation on the methodology of argumentation
Puspa	Flower
Raga	Melodic mode
Shudhha Saarang	Afternoon melodic mode
Rasa	Mood; sentiment; emotional tone
Rati	Goddess of love
Sabhinaya Pallavi	Composition involving theatrical elements and melodic proliferation
Sakhya	Friendship
Sama	Straight posture
Sambalpuri	Odishan handloom
Sambhrama	Delusion
Samprada	Triad of song, music, and dance
Samprada Nijoga	Daily ritual offering
Samyukta	Double-handed gesture
Sanchari	Expressive elaboration of sung lyric through elaborate imagery
Sangeet	Triad of song, music, and dance
Saptak	Seven notes
Sargam	Melodious arcs
Sari	Long piece of fabric pleated near hips and shoulders
Sastric	Sanskrit literary, philosophical, and theoretical texts
Sattwikabhava	Psychophysical responses
Setu	Bridge
Shabda	Sounds that do not correspond to verbal meaning-making
Shikhara	Thumbs-up
Shilpa	Sculpture, painting, visual aesthetics
Shilpanatanam	Creative movement process dramatizing visual imagery
Shishya	Student
Shudh	Natural
Shukasarika	One playing with a parrot
Sithilapataka	Hand gesture with slight cascading of fingers
Smarana	Recollection
Sringara	The sentiment of love
Sthayi	Opening and principal section of a musical composition
Sthayibhava	Basic emotions
Suchi	Exaggerating the index finger
Sukhachanchu	Coy
Sutradhar	Storyteller to an audience
Swara	Melodic notations
Taba	Yours
Tahia	Circular head garment representing Odishan temple architecture
Tali	Claps
Tambula	Betel leaf
Tandava	Destruction
Tarana	Nonverbal sonic structures in a fast pace
Teora Taal	Seven-beat rhythmic cycle in Hindustani classical music

Tihai	Three times repetition of a rhythmic structure at the end of a section
Timiro	Darkness
Tirascinna	Diagonal chin-raise
Torana	One forming an arch
Tribhangi	S-curve
Tripata Taal	Seven beats rhythmic cycle in traditional Odissi music
Ubhayakartari	Gesture signifying romantic union
Uddipana	Stimulants
Umad-Ghumad	Rolling
UNESCO	United Nations Educational, Scientific and Cultural Organization
Utkal Sammelani	Organization founded fortify Odishan cultural heritage
Utsaha	Enthusiasm
Vadya	Percussive syllables
Vakyartha	Meaning of a sentence
Varnam	Traditional musical compositions in southern Indian dance
Veena	String instrument
Veera	Boldness
Vibhava	Foundational factors
Viniyogas	Intended usage
Vinyasa	Well-groomed
Virabhadrasana	Warrior pose
Vismaya	Wonder
Vilap	Mourns
Vyabicaribhava	Transitory emotions
Yorchha	Dance technique combining yoga, martial art form Chhau, and Odissi

Model Progressions

BELOW IS A SPIRAL ODISSI curriculum from Pre-K through Grade 12, aligned to the NCAS in Dance (Create–Perform–Respond–Connect) as a comprehensive K–12 Odissi Dance Teaching Toolkit. Each stage will expand on movement, technique, cultural literacy, creativity, and critical reflection. Safety Guidelines constitute notes on warming up, respecting limits, noncompetitive environment, and culturally sensitive teaching tips.

Spiral Growth Summary

- Pre-K–Grade 2: Exploration, joy, storytelling through body.
- Grades 3–5: Structure, vocabulary, rhythm, and pure dance.
- Grades 6–8: Repertoire beginnings, rhythm literacy, *Abhinaya*, and cultural context.
- Grades 9–10: Master repertoire, choreography, and history.
- Grades 11–12: Mastery, pedagogy, choreography, research, and performance.

Age Group: 3–5 years

Pre-K – Foundation in body, *Mudras*, rhythm, expression, and nature.
Theme: Exploration – "My Body, My Story"

- Units: Postures, Mudras, Rhythm, Expression, Nature, Celebration.
- Goals: Joyful play, body awareness, and creative exploration.

Framework: National Core Arts Standards (NCAS) in Dance – Create, Perform, Respond, Connect
Style: Odissi Classical Dance (introductory, embodied, and imaginative)

1. Learning Objectives
   - Develop body awareness, coordination, and spatial understanding through Odissi movement.
   - Cultivate expressive abilities through *Abhinaya* (gesture, facial expression, storytelling).
   - Experience cultural knowledge by listening to stories, music, and rhythms from Odisha.
   - Foster focus, imagination, and joy in group learning environments.
   - Connect dance with other arts (visual storytelling, music, language).

2. Standards Alignment (NCAS)
   - Creating: Explore movement ideas; use imagination to embody characters, animals, and nature from Odissi stories.
   - Performing: Practice basic stance (*chauka, tribhangi*), hand gestures (*Mudras*), and rhythm games.
   - Responding: Observe dance; share feelings and ideas about what they see.
   - Connecting: Link Odissi to cultural stories, songs, and visual art traditions of India.
3. Unit Outline

Unit	Theme	Skills/Focus	NCAS Link
1	My Dancing Body	Shapes, square posture (*chauka*), balance	Creating, Performing
2	Hands that Speak	Basic *Mudras* (flower, bird, water, sun)	Creating, Connecting
3	Rhythms in My Feet	Clapping, stamping, simple patterns	Performing
4	Faces Tell Stories	Emotions (happy, sad, surprised, angry) with *Abhinaya*	Creating, Responding
5	Dance with Nature	Embodying animals, trees, rivers (Odissi motifs)	Creating, Connecting
6	Celebration	Simple group sequence combining posture, *Mudras*, rhythm, and expression	Performing, Connecting

4. Sample Lesson Plans

Lesson 1: *My Dancing Body – Shapes & Posture*
- Warm-Up: Wiggle → stretch → freeze in shapes.
- Introduce: *Chauka* (square stance) → call it "strong like a temple pillar."
- Explore: Kids try making tall, wide, and tiny shapes.
- Creative Task: Make a "temple dance statue pose."
- Assessment: Share statue pose with a partner, talk about what shape they see.

Lesson 2: *Hands That Speak – Mudras*
- Warm-Up: Finger play (open–close, wave).
- Introduce: *Pataka* (palm flat, like a flag). Use to show sun, stopping, blessing.
- Explore: Other simple *Mudras*: *Tripataka* (tree), *Arala* (drinking water).
- Storytime: Tell a short story of a flower blooming using *Mudras*.
- Assignment: Draw your favorite hand shape at home.

Lesson 3: *Rhythms in My Feet*
- Warm-Up: Clap names in rhythm.
- Introduce: Stamp feet twice (dhaa-dhaa) in *chauka*.
- Explore: Teacher plays drum (*mardala*) → kids stamp to match beat.
- Creative Task: Make your own foot sound (soft–loud).
- Assessment: Perform a 4-beat stamp pattern for the group.

Lesson 4: *Faces Tell Stories*

- Warm-Up: Funny faces (mirror game).
- Introduce: Four emotions → Happy, sad, angry, surprised.
- Explore: Pair emotion with gesture: "Happy with flower," "Sad with rain."
- Creative Task: Act out "sun goes down and moon rises" with face + *mudra*.
- Assignment: Show a family member one "emotion dance face."

Lesson 5: *Dance with Nature*

- Warm-Up: Animal walks (elephant, peacock, deer).
- Introduce: Odissi motifs → Peacock (*Mayura mudra*), Deer (*Mriga mudra*).
- Explore: Dance like a peacock opening feathers; deer jumping.
- Creative Task: Kids create short nature dance (choose animal/plant).
- Assessment: Share nature dance with the class.

Lesson 6: *Celebration Dance*

- Warm-up: Quick review of all learned postures, *Mudras*, rhythms.
- Sequence: Put together 1 posture + 1 mudra + 1 rhythm + 1 emotion.
- Performance: Present as a group in circle.
- Reflection: "What was your favorite dance part?"
- Assignment: Tell someone at home the story of your celebration dance.

5. Assignments/Assessments (Play-based)
   - Portfolio: Drawings of *Mudras*, dance poses, and nature dances.
   - Show & Tell: Share one movement/gesture learned each week with family.
   - Mini Performance: End-of-unit sharing circle with parents.
   - Reflection: Teacher prompts with simple questions ("What made you happy in dance today?").

Grades 1–5 (Elementary)

Play-based learning becomes more structured; focus on rhythm, simple sequences, and cultural storytelling.

Grades 1–2 (ages 6–7)
Theme: Foundations – "Dance as Story"

- Objectives:
  - Refine posture (*chauka*, *tribhangi*).
  - Learn 8–10 single hand *Mudras*.
  - Explore 4-beat and 8-beat patterns.
  - Tell short stories with gesture and movement.

- Units:
  0. Shapes & Postures in Odissi.
  1. *Mudras* for Animals & Nature.
  2. Rhythmic Games (claps, stamps).

3. Story Dance (Ganesha, Peacock, River).
4. Performance Circle (group sequence).

- Sample Assignment: Draw a story in 3 pictures (beginning–middle–end) → perform it using dance.

Grades 3–5 (ages 8–10)

Theme: Structure – "Dance as Pattern"

- Objectives:
  - Execute *chauka* and *tribhangi* with control.
  - Memorize a basic *batu* (pure dance sequence).
  - Explore *Abhinaya* through simple songs (child-friendly *Jayadeva* or folk tales).
  - Learn *tala* cycles (e.g., 4, 6, 8 beats).
- Units:
  0. Dance Grammar (postures, torso bends).
  1. *Mudra* Vocabulary (hasta viniyoga).
  2. Rhythm Play (*khandi*, *tala* patterns).
  3. Pure Dance (basic *batu* sequence).
  4. *Abhinaya* (short story-song).
  5. Sharing/Showcase.
- Sample Assignment: Keep a weekly "movement diary" – write or draw one dance move they remember.

Grades 6–8 (Middle School)

Introduction to technique, choreography, notation, and analysis.
Grades 6–8 (ages 11–13)
Theme: Development – "Dance as Language"

- Objectives:
  - Learn full *batu nritya* and one simple *Abhinaya*.
  - Introduce Odissi repertoire structure (*mangalacharan*, *batu*, *pallavi*, *Abhinaya*, *moksha*).
  - Understand rhythm notation (symbols, *bols*).
  - Connect dance with music and visual art.
- Units:
  0. Dance Warm-Ups & Fitness (alignment, strength).
  1. Odissi Repertoire (*batu*, *pallavi* basics).
  2. Rhythm & *Mardala* (*khol*, clapping, reciting *bols*).
  3. *Abhinaya* Workshop (episodes from *Ramayana*).
  4. Research & Response (watch a performance, write feelings).

- Sample Assignment: Watch an Odissi video at home → identify 2 *Mudras* and 1 posture.

Grades 9–12 (High School)

Mastery, critical dance studies, performance, choreography, pedagogy, and research.
Grades 9–10 (ages 14–15)
Theme: Expansion – "Dance as Art Form"

- Objectives:
  - Perform multiple repertoire items (*pallavi*, *Abhinaya*).
  - Explore improvisation in *Abhinaya*.
  - Analyze Odissi's history and aesthetics.
  - Introduce choreography tasks (short solos/duets).

- Units:
  0. Technique Lab (pallavi training).
  1. *Abhinaya* & Expression (*Bhakti* poetry).
  2. Odissi History (Gotipua, Mahari, Jayantika revival).
  3. Choreography Task (short duet using *mudra* + *tala*).
  4. Reflective Practice (journals, peer feedback).

- Sample Assignment: Write a one-page reflection – "How does Odissi show devotion?"

Grades 11–12 (ages 16–18)

Theme: Mastery – "Dance as Research & Expression"

- Objectives:
  - Prepare for *Arangetram*/solo recital.
  - Master technique across repertoire.
  - Create original choreography (solo/ensemble).
  - Conduct research paper/project on Odissi's cultural, historical, or social context.
  - Mentor younger students/lead workshops.

- Units:
  0. Advanced Repertoire (*pallavi*, *Abhinaya*, *moksha*).
  1. Dance & Philosophy (*Rasa* theory, *Natya Shastra*).
  2. Choreography Lab (student-created solos/duets).
  3. Pedagogy Module (assist Pre-K–Grade 5 classes).
  4. Capstone (*Arangetram* or research + performance).

- Sample Assignment: Research essay: "Compare Odissi *Abhinaya* with another Indian dance form's storytelling."
- Capstone Project: Full solo/ensemble recital or research–performance presentation.

Building Infrastructure and Best Practices

As K–12 and higher education plan on including teaching and learning of Odissi, it needs sustained attention to generating foundational resources for the community including (but not only restricted to) the following:

- Teacher Guidebook: Philosophy of Odissi, historical overview, learning goals by grade band (elementary, middle, high).
- Student Workbook: Illustrated and age-appropriate explanations of key ideas, with reflection questions and activities.
- Glossary: Simple definitions of Odissi terms (e.g., *tribhangi*, *chauka*, *Abhinaya*, *pallavi*).
- Visual Reference Charts: Posters of basic stances, *Mudras*, costume elements, musical instruments.

2. Movement & Technique
   - Progression Framework: Sequenced syllabus of skills:
     - *Elementary*: posture, rhythm games, story-dance exercises.
     - *Middle School*: basic *chauka* & *tribhangi*, simple *adavus* (steps), hand gestures with meaning.
     - *High School*: *jatis*, *pallavis*, *Abhinaya* exploration, choreography projects.
   - Warm-Up & Conditioning Routines: Adapted for young bodies (safe alignment, joint mobility, stamina).
   - Step Notation Sheets: Simplified movement scores or diagrams.
   - Video Library: Demonstrations of movements from multiple angles.

3. Music & Rhythm
   - Audio Tracks: Recorded *mardala bols*, Odissi *ragas*, and practice loops at different tempos.
   - Rhythm Cards: Visuals of *tala* cycles (*eka tala*, *triputa*, *jhampa*) for clapping and recitation.
   - Call-and-Response Exercises: Teacher–student clapping or recitation of *bols*.

4. Storytelling & *Abhinaya*
   - Narrative Materials: Short, age-appropriate stories from Jagannath culture, *Gitagovinda*, *Panchatantra*, and *Odia* folk tales.
   - Gesture Cards: *Mudras* illustrated with meaning + activity suggestions.
   - Improvisation Prompts: "Show me how Radha feels when Krishna teases her" → encourages emotional literacy.
   - Drama Integration: Scripts for short dance-theater pieces.

5. Cultural & Interdisciplinary Context
   - History Timeline: Odissi from temple ritual → court → stage → contemporary global practice.
   - Temple Architecture Connections: Activities linking body postures to Konark Sun Temple sculptures.

- Music Integration: Basics of Odissi music, introduction to *ragas* and *talas*.
- Art Connections: Drawing costumes, designing a stage backdrop.
- Social Studies Links: Odisha's geography, Jagannath traditions, cultural festivals.

6. Assessment & Reflection Tools
   - Progress Checklists: Mastery-based "I can" statements (e.g., "I can perform tribhangi with balance").
   - Portfolio System: Students collect reflections, drawings, choreographic notes, video snippets.
   - Rubrics: Age-specific criteria (technique, rhythm, expression, creativity).
   - Peer & Self-Assessment Templates: Guided observation sheets.
7. Teaching Aids & Materials
   - Flashcards: *Mudras*, poses, instruments, Odissi vocabulary.
   - Costume Pieces: Simple scarves, jewelry replicas, or masks to simulate dressing up.
   - Props: Diyas (lamps), lotus cutouts, or symbolic items for storytelling.
   - Digital Companion Platform: Access to recordings, worksheets, and interactive rhythm tools.
8. Teacher Development Support
   - Pedagogy Notes: How to adapt for K–12, classroom management in dance, differentiation strategies.
   - Sample Lesson Plans: 30–45 minute templates for different age groups.
   - Cross-Curricular Project Guides: e.g., Dance + Poetry (*Gitagovinda* excerpts), Dance + History (temple heritage).
   - Safety Guidelines: Injury prevention, cultural sensitivity notes.

This toolkit can be modular: Teachers can use the core movement and storytelling modules and expand with cultural or interdisciplinary modules depending on grade level and available time.

Pre-K Odissi Dance – 36 Week Syllabus

Framework: NCAS in Dance – *Create, Perform, Respond, Connect*
Age Group: 3–5 years
Theme for the year: *"My Body, My Story"*
Unit Breakdown

- Unit 1 (Weeks 1–6): My Dancing Body – Shapes, posture, balance
- Unit 2 (Weeks 7–12): Hands that Speak – Basic *Mudras*
- Unit 3 (Weeks 13–18): Rhythms in My Feet – Stamping, clapping, *tala* play
- Unit 4 (Weeks 19–24): Faces Tell Stories – *Abhinaya* (emotions, expressions)
- Unit 5 (Weeks 25–30): Dance with Nature – Animals, trees, rivers in Odissi
- Unit 6 (Weeks 31–36): Celebration – Group sequence, reflection, sharing

Weekly Scope & Sequence

Unit 1: My Dancing Body (Weeks 1–6)

- Week 1: Wiggle–stretch–freeze → make "statue shapes." *Assignment:* Show a shape at home.
- Week 2: Learn *chauka* (temple pillar stance). *Assignment:* Draw a square for *chauka*.
- Week 3: Practice balance (stand on one foot). *Assignment:* Try balancing for 5 counts at home.
- Week 4: Introduce *tribhangi* (3-bend posture). *Assignment:* Show *tribhangi* to family.
- Week 5: Combine *chauka* + *tribhangi* in short play. *Assignment:* Choose favorite pose to share.
- Week 6: Mini showcase of postures. *Assessment:* Teacher notes focus, control.

Unit 2: Hands That Speak (Weeks 7–12)

- Week 7: Finger play → *Pataka mudra* (flag). *Assignment:* Show "stop" or "sun."
- Week 8: *Tripataka* (tree). *Assignment:* Draw a tree.
- Week 9: *Arala* (drinking water). *Assignment:* Show drinking gesture at home.
- Week 10: *Mayura* (peacock). *Assignment:* Dance like a peacock.
- Week 11: Storytime – "A flower blooms" (using *Mudras*).
- Week 12: Review of 4 *Mudras* + storytelling circle. *Assessment:* Identify 2 *Mudras*.

Unit 3: Rhythms in My Feet (Weeks 13–18)

- Week 13: Clap names in rhythm. *Assignment:* Clap your name at home.
- Week 14: Stamp feet twice (dhaa-dhaa). *Assignment:* Show 2 stamps to family.
- Week 15: Stamp + clap combo. *Assignment:* Try 4 stamps at home.
- Week 16: Stamp in *chauka*. *Assignment:* Show *chauka* + stamp.
- Week 17: Teacher plays drum → kids copy beat.
- Week 18: Mini rhythm performance. *Assessment:* Stamp in 4-count.

Unit 4: Faces Tell Stories (Weeks 19–24)

- Week 19: Mirror game – silly faces. *Assignment:* Make happy face at home.
- Week 20: Happy + *flower mudra*. *Assignment:* Draw a flower.
- Week 21: Sad + *rain mudra*. *Assignment:* Tell a "rain" story.
- Week 22: Angry + *stop mudra*. *Assignment:* Show an "angry face."
- Week 23: Surprised + *sun mudra*. *Assignment:* Act surprised at home.
- Week 24: Storytelling circle (sun goes down, moon rises). *Assessment:* Identify 1 face + 1 *mudra*.

Unit 5: Dance with Nature (Weeks 25–30)

- Week 25: Animal walks (elephant, deer). *Assignment:* Walk like an elephant.
- Week 26: *Mayura mudra* (peacock). *Assignment:* Show peacock to family.
- Week 27: *Mriga mudra* (deer). *Assignment:* Draw a deer.
- Week 28: Tree dance – grow roots, branches. *Assignment:* Be a tree at home.
- Week 29: River dance – flowing arms. *Assignment:* Show "river arms."
- Week 30: Nature dance circle (choose animal/plant). *Assessment:* Perform 1 nature dance.

Unit 6: Celebration (Weeks 31–36)

- Week 31: Review postures + *Mudras.*
- Week 32: Review rhythms + expressions.
- Week 33: Choose favorite movements for final dance.
- Week 34: Practice group sequence.
- Week 35: Rehearsal with music + storytelling.
- Week 36: Final Sharing Celebration (parents invited). *Assessment:* Participation, joy, and memory of sequence.

Assessment Tools

- Teacher observation checklists (focus, posture, participation).
- Portfolio of drawings (*Mudras*, dance shapes).
- Family engagement (show/share assignments).
- Final celebration performance.

Manchapravesh: Dance Studies Approach

As a dance studies scholar, my research in Odissi expands my network into the Indian diaspora in the United States. I work with varying populations ranging from community youth to professional artists. Since 2012, I have been teaching Odissi in the Indian community in Ohio and have graduated five students from the diaspora. Here, I discuss the graduation recital of two students, Shalini Basu and Tanisha Mukherjee. The dancers perform alternatively with verbal introductions to their respective pieces. This event, "Manchapravesh-Shifting Stages," took place on September 27, 2021, in Columbus, Ohio (https://www.youtube.com/watch?-v=AfYpgJ5-e-0). Manchapravesh literally implies entry to the stage. It supposedly marks the beginning of a career in dance for the artist. However, I qualify the traditional nomenclature with "Shifting Stages" to more accurately determine the trajectory of the diasporic youth who navigates their cultural domains in the familial space and a world of difference outside. This particular event took place in the middle of the pandemic. The performance took place in the proscenium theater without any audience. However, it was live-streamed on YouTube to audiences worldwide. While discussing the flow of the Odissi repertoire in this performance, I delineate how I deliberately depart from the traditional *Margam* for the soloist primarily for three reasons. First, I focus on the strengths of each dancer to curate the evening. Second, I ensure the pieces complement one another to create an overall flow for the entire performance instead of following a pedantic *Mangalacharan* to *Moksha* for each artist. Third, I curate the event through a dance studies approach by incorporating analysis and critique alongside the creative process by ending with a panel discussion called "Indian Dance in Diaspora" with historians, arts administrators, and feminist theorists.

While choosing pieces for the dancers, I pay attention to a nuanced representation of femininity inspired by choreographic imposition as well as the dancers' lived experiences. The performance flows from the conventional progression of invocation to emancipation while making it relevant to the dancers' realities in the diaspora. While all the pieces are performed solo, the culminating *Moksha* is performed as a duet where Shalini and Tanisha acknowledge their shared journey in dance over a period of eight years. Rather than theoretically connecting to a prescribed spiritual yearning, I choreograph their duet as an emancipatory celebration of community and friendship. The evening starts with *Navadurga*, an invocation to the goddess by Tanisha portraying various attributes of the powerful *Shakti*, or female force. Shalini dances *Varsha,* a rhythmically intricate piece celebrating the monsoons in India. "Shalini's dance on Varsha (rains), a rhythmical presentation on the rains created a beautiful ambience of sights and sounds in nature typical to the torrential Indian monsoons" (Dandavate 2021). This was noted in a review by dance-scholar Rohini Dandavate. It is necessary to pay attention to the fact that the performers jumped from the category of *Mangalacharan* to *Pallavi* by skipping *Batu*. However, I focus on displaying the acquisition of advanced skills. Since *Batu* focuses on fundamental technical precepts, I categorically do not choose a representation from this category. This shows that the curator often departs from the so-called *Margam* and organizes the flow according to creative impulse and audience assessment. Tanisha returns with *Sakhi Hain*, an advanced expressional dance from the revered *Gitagovinda*, the twelfth-century lyrical masterpiece written by poet Jayadeva. Tanisha's expressive strength comes through in this piece as noted in the review by Dandavate. Shalini returns with *Durga* to thematically explore the powerful image of the goddess through her strength and beauty. Shalini devotes the first half to exploring centering and grounding in grace while the second half is all about the practicality of fighting war via the deployment of weapons and strength.

An intermission of ten minutes is provided for costume change after which Tanisha displays her rhythmic acumen through *Hamsadhwani Pallavi*. Shalini presents her nuanced expressivity in the *Ardhanariswara*, quickly transitioning between the male and the female perspectives. Tanisha performs more items than Shalini while Shalini's pieces are all longer than Tanisha's at twenty minutes in duration . Tanisha's last solo is an emotionally rich piece called *No Ja Jomuna* that foregrounds female bonding and friendship. This piece is an easy transition to their last duet celebrating their friendship. Aligning myself with the philosophy of transcendence, I do not want to end on the note of *Sakhya* (mortal friendship). Hence, I perform *Amrita Mantra*, a piece celebrating emancipation of voice through freedom of expression. It is customary of the teacher to perform with the students in a *Manchapravesh*. Given social distancing and pandemic-related strictures, I have had to improvise by performing a solo while ensuring the continuity and arc of the *Margam* for the day.

I curated the evening in a dance studies approach bridging higher education and community contexts. In the panel discussion, attendees spoke from various perspectives including higher education in the US, South Asian diaspora, arts administration in India and the US, and feminist theory. Further, the dancers participated in the panel speaking from their own vantage points regarding their inspirations and aspirations. Shalini acknowledges dance as her connection to the Indian community while Tanisha expresses her relationship to dance with her best friend. In the chapter "Natyasastra: Emerging (Gender) Codes and the Woman Dancer" in the book *Engendering Performance: Indian Women Performers in Search of an Identity*, authors Urmimala Sarkar Munsi and Bisnupriya Dutt argue how prescribed notions of gendered identity imposition occur during the learning of dance. Munsi and Dutt notes that "learning and understanding one's cultural heritage (again a favorite endeavor of parents of the dancers of Indian diaspora), and also internalizing the traditional concepts of femininity, art of female representation and gendered behavior traditionally expected of Indian women follow hand in hand as well" (2010, 12). Given this danger of creating docile bodies, I ask the panelists to comment on the critique of the inculcated discipline within dance especially as it pertains to the diaspora. I qualify the question by bringing the perspectives of dance scholar Priya Srinivasan in the midst who has critiqued extensively the justification and rationale of such dance graduation recitals in the Indian diaspora.

In the ensuing discussion, multiple ways of looking at the female body, plural embodiment of femininity, and gender fluidity are acknowledged in technical rigor, conceptual clarity, and creative expression. Tanisha and Shalini note how Odissi adds strength and nuance to their sense of femininity. Shalini notes her strategies of connecting to divine masculinity and femininity engaged in the creative impulse through her piece *Ardhanariswara*. Shalini's point drives home the lacunae of contextual analysis and philosophical rigor in conservatory dance education as vocational training. Feminist historian Mytheli Sreenivas notes that higher education can push the envelope by bringing the university and community spaces through such events where the questioning spirit remains at the center and self-reflexivity and critique significantly contribute to the creative instinct. India-based artist and academic Parwati Dutta insists on creating cultural ecologies of sustainability by creating more dialogue with communities. The rigidity and conservatism that plague Odissi sometimes is antithetical to critical thinking. Sreenivas concludes the discussion by urging diasporic youth to invest in more thoughtful work in their dancing by contextualizing and connecting with their movement for performance through a rigorous regimen of practice and conceptual preparation.

APPENDIX II

Continuing Education: A Student's Praxis

By Dr. Monali NandyMazumdar

WORKING WITH AN *ABHINAYA*-CENTRIC repertoire is always challenging, often requiring students to traverse unfamiliar emotional terrains. Yet *Bichitro Anondo*, choreographed by Dr. Rohini Dandavate on my *Guru* Dr. Kaustavi Sarkar, felt immediately approachable. From my first class, the choreography struck a chord, largely because it drew so richly from the textures of daily life. The chosen text, a Bengali poem by Rabindranath Tagore, articulates the dualities of existence with startling simplicity, naming both *Mrityu* (death) and *Anondo* (joy). The dance mirrors this polarity through embodied contrasts: grief in the face of pandemic alongside the renewal of blooming nature; the fear of night tempered by the serenity of moonlight; the sweetness of union inseparable from the ache of separation. What remains most compelling is the soothing, lyrical quality of the movements—never over-embellished, always holding space for *Bhava* to emerge organically. True to its place within the *Pujo* (translated by me as ritual) section of Tagore's magnum opus text *Geetanjali*, the choreography sustains a sense of quiet consolation even as it acknowledges life's most painful truths.

My experience of learning this work was shaped by Dr. Kaustavi Sarkar's pedagogy. In the senior community class, she began by opening the text's larger meanings, then introduced the *Nritta* (pure dance) passages before moving to *Abhinaya* (expressional repertoire). The expressive sections resonated deeply with my own lived experiences—memories of images from India, birds I had filmed with my father, peacocks spotted in West Virginia at New Vrindavan, or childhood games of *Fugdi* (resembling Ring a Ring o' Roses) in Mumbai. These personal echoes helped me internalize the *Abhinaya* more fully, making the gestures and expressions feel less like study and more like remembrance. Kaustavi's patient word-by-word explanations, her demonstrations, and the recorded sessions provided further scaffolding for my learning.

In a younger batch, however, her approach shifted. Here, the focus was more on steps and rhythm, acknowledging that children could not fully grasp emotions of sorrow or mortality. Attending both classes offered me a rare comparative perspective: the same choreography adapted for different developmental stages. It impressed upon me how pedagogy itself can become a choreography of responsiveness, shaping learning according to students' capacities.

Another layer of reflection came through the work's musicality. Matching bodily lyricism to the cadence of Tagore's song demanded conscious effort. In every class, Kaustavi emphasized flow, gaze, and technique as inseparable from emotional gestures. Later, when I trained with her in person in Columbus, OH, I began to understand what she meant by "musicality." Her corrections—small but transformative—clarified my technique and opened new possibilities for expressivity. Here are my own notations of the musical sketches that imprint themselves choreographically onto my body-mind complex:

Aalap: 7*2 counts, before admiring the changing colors of the skies (surroundings) and spotting the peacock and admiring the beauty.

7-Beat Cycle

Dhei (1)	*Tajhe* (2)	*Naam* (3)	*Tajhe* (4)	*Naam* (5)	*Tajhe* (6)	*Naam* (7)	Repeats
			Sthai				
Jhimi	*Ta*	*Jhimi*	*Jhena*	*Kita*	*Jham*	*Tari*	2
Jhimi	*Ta*	*Jhimi*	*Jhena*	*Kita*	*Jham*	*Tari*	
Jhimi	*kita*	*jhimi*	*jham*	*kadataka*	*jhenu*	*jhena*	2
Jhimi	*kita*	*jhimi*	*jham*	*kadataka*	*jhenu*	*jhena*	
Jhimi	*kita*	*jhimi*	*jham*	*kadataka*	*jham*	*kadataka*	2
Jhimi	*kita*	*jhimi*	*jham*	*kadataka*	*jham*	*kadataka*	
Jhena	*jhenu*	*kina*	*kadataka*	*jham*	*kadataka*	*Jhena*	*Tihai*
jhenu	*kina*	*kadataka*	*jham*	*kadataka*	*jhena*	*jhenu*	
kina	*kadataka*	*jham*	*kadataka*	*jham*	*takadataka*	*jham*	
			***Sthai* Variation**				
Ta	*Jham*	*ta*	*ri*	*ta*	*jham*	-	4
jhe	*nu*	*ta*	*ri*	*ta*	*Jham* (*jhena*)	-	
Ta	*Jham*	*ta*	*ri*	*ta*	*jham*	-	
jhe	*nu*	*ta*	*ri*	*ta*	(*jhena*)	-	
Music	Music	Music	Music	Music	Music	Music	
Ta	*Jham*	*ta*	*ri*	*ta*	*jham*	-	2
jhe	*nu*	*ta*	*ri*	*ta*	*jham*	-	
Ta jham	*ta*	*rita*	*jham*	-	*Ta jham*	*ta*	
rita	*jham*	-	*tari*	*kita*	*kukun*	*dari*	

Ta	*Jham*	*ta*	*ri*	*ta*	*jham*	-	2
jhe	*nu*	*ta*	*ri*	*ta*	*(jhena)*	-	
			Swara Jati				
Ni sa	*re ma*	-	*re ma pa*	-	*ni dha pa*	*ma pa*	
Re ma	*pa dha*	-	*ma pa ni*	-	*pa ni re*	*sa*	
Dhei kadataka	*dhei ta*	-	*dhei dhei ta*	-	*Dhei kadataka dhei*	*tat dhei*	
Dhei kadataka	*dhei ta*	-	*dhei dhei ta*	-	*Dhei kadataka dhei*	*ta*	
Ma re	*sa ni*	-	*ni dha pa*	-	*ma re*	*sa ni sa*	2
Ma re	*Sa ni*	-	*Dha pa ma*	-	*Ga re ma*	*Pa ni*	
Ta	*Jham*	*ta*	*ri*	*ta*	*jham*	-	
jhe	*nu*	*ta*	*ri*	*ta*	*(jhena)*	-	
Music	Music	Music	Music	Music			
			***Sahitya*-1 (*Mukhda*)**				
					Jo	*yo*	2
to	*bo*	*bi*	*chi*	*tro*	-	*aa*	
non	*do*	-	*he*	-	*ko*	*bi*	
jo	*yo*	*toma*	*ro*	*ko*	*ru*	*na*	
-	-	-	-	-	*jo*	*yo*	
to	*bo*	*bi*	*chi*	*tro*	-	*aa*	
non	*do*	-	*sargam*	*s*	*s*	*s*	
s	s	s	*s*	*s*	*jo*	*yo*	
to	*bo*	*bi*	*chi*	*tro*	-	*aa*	
non	*do*	-	*sargam*	*s*	*s*	*s*	
s	*s*	*s*	*s*	*s*	*jo*	*yo*	
to	*bo*	*bi*	*chi*	*tro*	-	*aa*	
non	*do*	-	*sargam*	*s*	*s*	*s*	
s	*s*	*s*	*he*	-	*ko*	*bi*	
jo	*yo*	*toma*	*ro*	*ko*	*ru*	*na*	
-	-	-	-	-			

(*Continued*)

Dhei (1)	*Tajhe* (2)	*Naam* (3)	*Tajhe* (4)	*Naam* (5)	*Tajhe* (6)	*Naam* (7)	Repeats
			Sahitya-2 (Anondo/Koruna)				
Sargam	*s*	*s*	*s*	*s*	*s*	*s*	
s	*s*	*s*	*s*	*s*	*he*	-	
ko	*bi*	*jo*	*yo*	*toma*	*ro*	*ko*	
ru	*na*	-	-	-	-	-	
Sargam	*s*	*s*	*s*	*s*	*s*	*s*	
s	*s*	*s*	*s*	*s*	*he*	-	
ko	*bi*	*jo*	*yo*	*toma*	*ro*	*ko*	
ru	*na*	-	-	-	-	-	
Sargam	*s*	*s*	*s*	*s*	*s*	*s*	
s	*s*	*s*	*s*	*s*	*s*	*s*	
s	*s*	*s*	*s*	*s*	*he*	-	
ko	*bi*	*jo*	*yo*	*toma*	*ro*	*ko*	
ru	*na*	-	-	-	-	-	
Sargam	*s*	*s*	*s*	*s*	*s*	*s*	17
s	*s*	*s*	*s*	*s*	*jo*	*yo*	
to	*bo*	*bhi*	-	*sho*	*no*	-	
sho	*bo*	*ko*	*lu*	*sho*	-	*na*	
-	*sho*	*no*	*ru*	-	*dro*	*ta*	
-	-	*Sargam*	*s*	*s*	*s*	*s*	
s	*s*	*s*	*s*	*s*	*s*	*s*	
s	*s*	*s*	*s*	*s*	*s*	*s*	
s	*s*	*s*	*s*	*s*	*jo*	*yo*	
to	*bo*	*bhi*	-	*sho*	*no*	-	
sho	*bo*	*ko*	*lu*	*sho*	-	*na*	
-	*sho*	*no*	*ru*	-	*dro*	*ta*	
Sargam	*s*	*s*	*s*	*s*	*s*	*s*	3
Jo	*yo*	*o*	*mrito*	*to*	*bo*	-	
Sargam	*s*	*s*	*s*	*s*	*s*	*s*	
jo	*yo*	*mri*	*tyu*	*to*	*bo*	-	
Sargam	*s*	*s*	*s*	*s*	*s*	*s*	

jo	*yo*	*sho*	*k*	*to*	*bo*	-	
Sargam	*s*	*s*	*s*	*s*	*s*	*s*	
jo	*yo*	*shan*	*To*	*na*	-	-	3
Jo	*yo*	*to*	*bo*	*bi*	*chi*	*tro*	
-	*aa*	*non*	*do*	-	*he*	-	
ko	*bi*	*jo*	*yo*	*to*	*ma*	*ro*	
ko	*ru*	*na*					
			***Arasa-*1**				
		(*Dhei*	*tathin*	*da*	-	-	4
tathin	*daka*)	(*Dhei*	*tathin*	*da*	-	*dhei*	2
Tathin	*da*)	(*Dhei*	*tathin*	*da*	*tathin*	*da*	2
tathin	*da*)	(*Dhei*	*tathin*	*da*	*tathei*	*Ta ka*	2
dhei	*dhinta*)	(*Dhei*	*tathin*	*da*	*Tinthina*	*kititaka*	4
Thina kita	*thini taka*)	(*Mare*	*nisa*	*rema*	*pani*	*mapa*	3
nisa	*pani*	*sare*	*sa*	-)			
sargam	*s*						1
			Antara				
		(*Ta*	*jhe*	*nu*	*jhe*	*na*	2
jhe	*nu*	*Jhe*	*na*	*ta*	*ri*	*ta*	
jhe	*na*)	(*Ta*	*jhe*	*nu*	*jhe*	*na*	2
jhe	*nu*	*jhe*	*na*	*ta*	*ri*	*ta*	
jhe	*na*)	(*Tajhe*	*nu*	*tamta*	*jham*	-	3
tajhe	*nu*	*tamta*	*jham*	-	tarikita	kititaka	
tarikita	*kititaka*)	*Ta*	*Jham*	*ta*	*ri*	*ta*	
jham	-	*jhe*	*nu*	*ta*	*ri*	*ta*	
(*jhena*)	-	*Sargam*	*s*	*s*	*s*	*s*	
s	*s*						
			Bol				
		Na kita	*Kiti taka*	*tarikita*	*Kiti taka*	*dhik*	
dhalangataka	*dhalanga*	*Gadhi ghene*	*dhei*	-	*Na kita*	*Kiti taka*	

(*Continued*)

Dhei (1)	*Tajhe* (2)	*Naam* (3)	*Tajhe* (4)	*Naam* (5)	*Tajhe* (6)	*Naam* (7)	Repeats
			Bol				
tarikita	*Kiti taka*	*dhik*	*dhalangataka*	*dhalanga*	*Gadhi ghene*	*dhei*	
-	*Na kita*	*Kiti taka*	*tarikita*	*Kiti taka*	*dhik*	*dhalangataka*	
dhalanga	*Gadhi ghene*	*dhei*	-	-	-	-	
			***Sahitya*-3 (*Timiro/Jyoti*)**				
Jo	*yo*	*pur*	*no*	-	*ja*	*gro*	2
to	-	*jyo*	*ti*	-	*to*	*bo*	
jo	*yo*	*ti*	*mi*	*ro*	*ni*	*bi*	
ro	*ni*	*shi*	*thi*	*ni*	-	-	
bho	*yo*	*da*	*yi*	*ni*	-	-	
Jo	*yo*	*pur*	*no*	-	*ja*	*gro*	
to	-	jyo	*ti*	-	*to*	*bo*	
-	-	*Sargam*	*s*	*s*	*s*	*s*	
s	s	*s*	*s*	*s*	*s*	*s*	
Jo	*yo*	*pur*	*no*	-	*ja*	*gro*	
to	-	*jyo*	*ti*	-	*to*	*bo*	
Sargam	*s*	*s*	*s*	*s*	*s*	*s*	
s	*s*	*s*	*s*	*s*	*s*	*s*	
Jo	*yo*	*pur*	*no*	-	*ja*	*gro*	
to	-	*jyo*	*ti*	-	*to*	*bo*	
Sargam	*s*	*s*	*s*	*s*	*s*	*s*	
s	*s*	*s*	*s*	*s*	*s*	*s*	
Jo	*yo*	*pur*	*no*	-	*ja*	*gro*	
to	-	*jyo*	*ti*	-	*to*	*bo*	
jo	*yo*	*ti*	*mi*	*ro*	*ni*	*bi*	
ro	*ni*	*shi*	*thi*	*ni*	-	-	
bho	*yo*	*da*	*yi*	*ni*	-	-	
-	-	*sargam*	*s*	*s*	*s*	*s*	
s	*s*	*s*	*s*	*s*	*s*	*s*	
s	*s*	*bho*	*yo*	*da*	*yi*	*ni*	
-	-	*Sargam*	*s*	*s*	*s*	*s*	
s	*s*	*s*	*s*	*s*	*s*	*s*	
s	*s*	*s*	*s*	*s*	*s*	*s*	

Jo	*yo*	*ti*	*mi*	*ro*	*ni*	*bi*	
ro	*ni*	*shi*	*thi*	*ni*	-	-	
bho	*yo*	*da*	*yi*	*ni*	-	-	
Sargam	*s*	*s*	*s*	*s*	*s*	*s*	3
Jo	*yo*	*ti*	*mi*	*ro*	*ni*	*bi*	
ro	*ni*	*shi*	*thi*	*ni*	-	-	
bho	*yo*	*da*	*yi*	*ni*	-	-	
-	-	*Sargam*	*s*	*s*	*s*	*s*	
s	*s*	*s*	*s*	*s*	*s*	*s*	
s	*s*	*s*	*s*	*s*	*s*	*s*	
Jo	*yo*	*ti*	*mi*	*ro*	*ni*	*bi*	
ro	*ni*	*shi*	*thi*	*ni*	-	-	
bho	*yo*	*da*	*yi*	*ni*	-	-	
Jo	*yo*	*pur*	*no*	-	*ja*	*gro*	
to	-	*jyo*	*ti*	-	*to*	*bo*	
jo	*yo*	*ti*	*mi*	*ro*	*ni*	*bi*	
ro	*ni*	*shi*	*thi*	*ni*	-	-	
bho	*yo*	*da*	*yi*	*ni*	-	-	

Antara Returns

Ta	*jhe*	*nu*	*jhe*	*na*	*jhe*	*nu*	4
Jhe	*na*	*ta*	*ri*	*ta*	*jhe*	*na*	
Ta	*jhamta*	*rita*	*jham*	-	*ta*	*jhamta*	3
rita	*jham*	-	*tarikita*	*kititaka*	*tarikita*	*kititaka*	
Ta	*jham*	*ta*	*rita*	*jham*	-	*jhe*	1
nu	*ta*	*ri*	*ta*	*jhe*	*na*	-	
Sargam	*s*	*s*	*s*	*s*	*s*	*s*	

***Arasa*-2**

Dhei	*tathin*	*tathin*	*takta*	*tathin*	*tathin*	*ta*	2
Ta	*tathin*	*tathin*	*takta*	*tathin*	*tathin*	*ta*	
Tathin	*tathin*	*tathin*	*tathin*	*thina*	*thinta*	*thini*	1
Tathin	*tathin*	*tathin*	*tathin*	*thina*	*thinta*	*thini*	

(*Continued*)

Dhei (1)	*Tajhe* (2)	*Naam* (3)	*Tajhe* (4)	*Naam* (5)	*Tajhe* (6)	*Naam* (7)	Repeats
			Arasa-2				
Ta	*tathin*	*tathin*	*takta*	*tathina*	*tathin*	*thina*	2
Dhini	*tathina*	*takta*	*tathin*	*tathin*	*tak*	*thinitaka*	2
(*Dhini*	*tathina*	*takta*	*tathin*	*thina*)	(*Dhini*	*tathina*	
takta	*tathina*	*thina*)	*Dhini*	*tathina*	*takta*	*tathin*	
ta	-	-	-	-			
			Sahitya-4 **(*Milono/Bicchedo*)**				
					Jo	*yo*	2
pre	*mo*	-	*mo*	*dhu*	*mo*	*yo*	
mi	*lo*	*no*	*to*	*bo*			
					jo	*yo*	2
o	*sho*	*ho*	*bi*	-	*chhe*	*do*	
be	*do*	*na*	-	-			
					Jo	*yo*	
pre	*mo*	-	*mo*	*dhu*	*mo*	*yo*	
mi	*lo*	*no*	*to*	*bo*	-	-	
Sargam	*s*	*s*	*s*	*s*	*s*	*jo*	
yo	*pre*	*mo*	-	*mo*	*dhu*	*moyo*	
mi	*lo*	*no*	*to*	*bo*	*Sargam*	*s*	
s	*s*	*s*	*s*	*s*	*Jo*	*yo*	
pre	*mo*	-	*mo*	*dhu*	*mo*	*yo*	
mi	*lo*	*no*	*to*	*bo*	*Sargam*	*s*	
s	*s*	*s*	*s*	*s*	*Jo*	*yo*	
pre	*mo*	-	*mo*	*dhu*	*mo*	*yo*	
mi	*lo*	*no*	*to*	*bo*	*jo*	*yo*	
o	*sho*	*ho*	*bi*	-	*chhe*	*do*	
be	*do*	*na*	-	-	*Aalap*	*a*	
a	*a*	*a*	*a*	*a*	*jo*	*yo*	
o	*sho*	*ho*	*bi*	-	*chhe*	*do*	
be	*do*	*na*	-	-	*Aalap*	*a*	

a	*a*	*a*	*a*	*a*	*jo*	*yo*	
o	*sho*	*ho*	*bi*	-	*chhe*	*do*	
be	*do*	*na*	-	-	*Aalap*	*a*	
a	*a*	*a*	*a*	*a*	*Jo*	*yo*	
pre	*mo*	-	*mo*	*dhu*	*mo*	*yo*	
mi	*lo*	*no*	*to*	*bo*	*jo*	*yo*	
o	*sho*	*ho*	*bi*	-	*chhe*	*do*	
be	*do*	*na*	-	-			
			Sahitya-End				
					jo	*yo*	
o	*mri*	*to*	*to*	*bo*	*jo*	*yo*	
mri	*tyu*	-	*to*	*bo*	*jo*	*yo*	
shok	-	*to*	*bo*	-	*jo*	*yo*	
shan	*to*	*na*	-	-	*jo*	*yo*	3
to	*bo*	*bi*	*chi*	*tro*	-	*aa*	
non	-	*do*	-	-			
					Jo	*yo*	
to	*bo*	*bi*	*chi*	*tro*	-	*aa*	
non(sargam)	*do (s)*	*s*	*s*	*s*	*s*	*s*	
Final *S*	-	-					

Upon the internalization of the broader meaning and the steps from Kaustavi, I had the opportunity to interact with the choreographer of the piece, Dr. Rohini Dandavate, and deepen my understanding of the process and the embodiments to further improve my rendition. Rohini's guidance on *Abhinaya* and gestural advocacy deepened my ability to inhabit the poem's emotional registers. From the choreographer's own perspective, I have reflected upon my interaction with her during which I came to understand the significant features of her creative process. Identifying and engaging with three critical elements—technical accuracy, the evocation of emotion, and musicality—have been instrumental in refining my performative abilities. This interaction and my narrative response have been published by Dr. Rohini Dandavate (2023).

Learning *Bichitro Anondo* continues to be a process rather than a product. Each session with Kaustavi offers something new—sometimes a technical refinement, sometimes a shift in emotional understanding. Virtual learning has made this continuity both fragile and precious: I try to treat every class performance as though it were live, attentive to detail, body alert, mind engaged. The work insists on carrying its questions and resonances beyond class, so that practice itself becomes a kind of reflective thinking. Over time, I feel the choreography slowly inscribed itself into my body—not only as a sequence of movements, but as lived knowledge shaped by memory, emotion, and conscious practice.

Reference

Dandavate, R. 2023. "A Dancer's Reflections on the Choreographer's Creative Process." *Medium*. https://medium.com/.

APPENDIX III

Shilpanatanam

A Pedagogy of Focus

Rationale

IMAGINE A DANCE EDUCATION setting in an Indian context: the teacher (*guru*), the student (*Shishya*), and the practice space—whether in a formal studio, a temple courtyard, or the intimate room of a guru's home. The guru's first task is to decide on the content to begin with. She chooses the action concept *Bhramari* (rotation): a circular movement of the body as a whole, or of specific limbs, central to both classical and folk vocabularies. But she pauses: What is the difference between a *Bhramari* that is executed merely as a step and one that is *performed* with intention, rhythm, and emotion? The difference lies in how repetition is embodied, observed, and transmitted. This distinction reflects the limits of human cognition, the aesthetic values of Indian culture, and the pedagogical traditions of dance training.

Another decision arises: should she teach through imitation (*do as I do*) or through verbal instruction, using mnemonic syllables and *Sanchari* imagery (*do as I say*)? A pivot initiated on the left leg recalls the codified *Karanas* (embodied postures with elaborate detailing) of the *Natyashastra*. A spiraling wrist that opens the palm suggests the eloquence of *Hasta Mudras*, carrying symbolic meaning that transcends pure physicality. Perhaps one should consult an anatomical chart, realizing that while the wrist joint itself does not rotate fully, the subtle coordination of forearm and palm allows the gesture to appear as if it does.

Dance educators in the Indian context face a myriad of questions about what and how, why and who, where and when to teach dance. These questions underscore that instruction itself is socially constructed, shaped by cultural histories and lineages of practice. The *guru–shishya Parampara* (lineage) exemplifies humanity's unique relational capacity to learn transmitting complex artistic and cultural knowledge from generation to generation. For educators, this suggests that teaching dance is not merely about passing on movement, but about enabling learners to thrive within the evolving ecosystems of tradition and innovation.

Dance, in India, is a quintessential form of social learning. To learn dance is to enter a world where rhythm, gesture, myth, and devotion are interwoven with social formations and cultural memory. From a child imitating *Abhinaya* in play, to audiences witnessing a staged *Margam* (traditional repertoire), human beings experience dance as part of everyday life and across the lifespan. To teach dance, however, is to enculturate learners into systems of *Mudra*,

Nritta, *Abhinaya*, and *Rasa*—a pedagogy of meaning in movement. Indian dance educators focus on how transmission occurs—through demonstration, repetition, metaphor, and embodied experience—*Abhyasa* (practice) transforms the dancer, and the dancer transforms the practice.

Pedagogy is shaped by institutional syllabi (as in universities, University of Hyderabad, Sri Sri University, etc., and boards like Kalakshetra, Gandharva Mahavidyalaya, etc.), by the demands of performance, by assessment structures in competitions, and by cultural values attached to mentor-mentee transmission. Still, its focus is on the art and science of teaching dance. Lee Shulman's concept of pedagogical content knowledge—the interplay of what is taught and how it is taught—resonates strongly here (Vollmer and Klette 2023). A teacher must know not only how to physically instruct a movement sequence but also how to convey its rhythmic, symbolic, and aesthetic dimensions so that the learner experiences both technique and meaning.

To become a successful dance teacher, then, one must confront content and pedagogy simultaneously. The object of teaching is not only to train the body but also to generate situations where the learner apprehends meaning—whether through cultural expressivity, narrative storytelling, or contemporary reinterpretations of classical forms. This requires weaving together physical and conceptual, rhythmic and relational, emotional and experiential, historical and cultural facets. Indian dance is both a medium of creative expression and a method of cultural transmission, connecting individuals to others, to environments, to society, and to worlds imperceptible to our immediate sensory apparatus.

The motivation for teaching lies in advancing such embodied understandings and cultural competencies for both learner and teacher. This has always been central to Indian dance pedagogy, from the Sanskritized codifications of the *Natyashastra* to the innovations of Rukmini Devi Arundale, Uday Shankar, Chandralekha, and other modern practitioners. As in global contexts, Indian dance education today grapples with questions of how to advance the field, how to define, evaluate, standardize, and improve teaching, and how to situate tradition in dialogue with contemporary practice. In this sense, pedagogy reflects a layered inheritance: oral traditions, embodied demonstrations, codified texts, institutional frameworks, and contemporary re-imaginings. What emerges is a complex, evolving field where teaching is both the preservation of lineage and the creation of new knowledge through embodied practice.

Pedagogical Content Knowledge in *Shilpanatanam*

In the framework of *Shilpanatanam* (a creative movement process centering visual imagery in dynamic expression), *pedagogical content knowledge* becomes more than the intersection of subject matter and teaching method—it is the meeting point of tradition, imagination, and re-interpretation. Classical technique is not only taught as a formal vocabulary but contextualized within literary, visual, and philosophical sources. For instance, a simple *hasta* may be taught alongside its depiction in sculpture, its invocation in Sanskrit poetics, and its expressive potential in performance. The teacher, therefore, must not only demonstrate the physical mechanics but also convey how cultural memory, textual resonances, and aesthetic intention infuse movement. In *Shilpanatanam*, pedagogical content knowledge is thus expanded to include the artist-scholar's ability to activate multiple cultural layers, guiding the learner to experience technique as a living archive. Particular importance lies in postural stance where the sides of the body (not as used in conventional *Margam*) gets the centerstage. Alignment is key as the head, neck, shoulders, and arms remain in a productive visually palpable tension. Drawing of the space is larger than the actual body as the visualizing potential scales up the proprioceptive and the kinespheric capacities. Teaching content simultaneously resorts to metaphorical language and embodied imagery.

Shilpanatanam aligns naturally with the ethos of critical dance studies, which interrogates the political, historical, and cultural dimensions of movement. Here, analysis is embedded within practice: the dancer learns not just to reproduce but to question, contextualize, and reinterpret. For example, exploring a *Nayika*'s (female protagonist) longing in *Abhinaya* is not limited to codified gestures but may involve examining representations of desire in Sanskrit poetry, temple sculpture, or oral folk traditions, as well as reflecting on contemporary gender dynamics. *Shilpanatanam* insists that criticality is not an external commentary but an embodied inquiry. The dancer-scholar becomes both performer and critic, able to trace how forms have been shaped by social power, devotional practice, and artistic innovation. In this way, *Shilpanatanam* makes critical dance studies an internalized, creative practice that bridges textual exegesis, performance reconstruction, and imaginative reinterpretation.

The "inside–outside" dynamic takes on a particular resonance in *Shilpanatanam*. The *inside* refers to the dancer's embodied immersion—technique, breath, rhythm, and emotional identification—while the *outside* points to the expansive worlds of history, literature, sculpture, and philosophy from which material is drawn. *Shilpanatanam* thrives on the constant interplay between these poles: a movement sequence drawn from a temple frieze must be internalized (*inside*) through bodily practice, but also analyzed and reframed (*outside*) in light of contemporary relevance and aesthetic choices. This oscillation between inward embodiment and outward contextualization allows dancers to create performances that are both deeply rooted in tradition and strikingly original. In Kulkarni's vision, the creative process depends on this circulation—where the dancer's inner experience of movement continuously dialogues with outer worlds of cultural meaning.

Dance pedagogy, across cultures, is often contested—between preservation and innovation, between practice and theory. In *Shilpanatanam*, Maya Kulkarni proposes an alternative framework: dance pedagogy as a layered creative process where rehearsal itself becomes the site of cultural memory, aesthetic inquiry, and personal formation. Unlike pedagogies that separate "studio practice" from "research," *Shilpanatanam* insists that learning, making, and reflecting are inseparable. A sculptural fragment, a Sanskrit verse, or a ritual gesture may enter the rehearsal room as readily as rhythm, space, and anatomy. Here, the signature pedagogy of *Shilpanatanam* emerges not from universal rehearsal norms but from the distinctive way dancers are led to think and move through three modalities: *engagement, uncertainty, and formation*. These pedagogies are not abstract categories but embodied practices that shape the dancer's way of knowing, being, and creating.

Imagine a rehearsal where a group of dancers sit in a circle around a Chola bronze. The teacher invites them: *"Notice the turn of the torso, the spiral of the hip, the lifted hand. Now let your body converse with the sculpture — not by imitation, but by listening."* The space becomes a shared laboratory, where each dancer's exploration feeds into the collective imagination. Engagement in *Shilpanatanam* is dialogic: the teacher does not dictate form but facilitates a conversation between dancer, text, and iconography. A gesture is first encountered in the body, then reflected against poetry or visual art, and finally re-embodied with new resonance. Improvisation is not random but tethered to cultural referents; repetition is not mechanical but exploratory. The pedagogy of engagement honors multiplicity, asking dancers to move as individuals and as participants in a shared cultural continuum.

In *Shilpanatanam*, uncertainty is cultivated deliberately. A dancer might be asked to embody the word *Sanchari* (wandering), guided only by the sound of a verse and the image of a figure carved half-eroded in stone. The instruction is at once precise and vague: embody the "wandering" without knowing its destination. Frustration and dissonance inevitably arise, as dancers grapple with ambiguity. Yet it is in this discomfort that new meaning emerges. The pedagogy of uncertainty in *Shilpanatanam* resists the closure of fixed technique. Instead, it asks dancers to linger in the unknown, to "wait with the gesture" until something unexpected surfaces — perhaps a shift in rhythm, perhaps a new *Rasa*. The teacher's role is not to supply answers but to hold the rehearsal in a state of tension where curiosity becomes the engine of learning.

Formation in *Shilpanatanam* is not only about perfecting technique but about shaping aesthetic disposition and cultural identity. Repetition is central here—not for mechanical mastery, but for cementing meaning into muscle and memory. A wrist circle repeated a hundred times does not merely train coordination; it inscribes into the body the lineage of sculpture, ritual, and narrative that gesture carries. Through such labor, dancers cultivate patience, discipline, and a malleable relationship between multiple facets of the self—the body, the mind, the intellect, and the ego. Fatigue is not seen as failure but as a threshold: when the body is exhausted, the movement may become more resonant with the cultural weight it bears. Formation thus builds character as much as skill, instilling values of respect for tradition, attentiveness to detail, and openness to reinterpretation.

Together, these three modalities shape the distinctive pedagogy of *Shilpanatanam*. Engagement connects dancers to cultural memory and to one another through dialogue; uncertainty keeps the process open, generative, and resistant to easy answers; formation imprints values and dispositions through embodied repetition. *Shilpanatanam* preserves tradition while preparing dancers to reimagine it, enabling them to live within the paradox of continuity and change. Its "signature" lies not in prescribing a style but in cultivating dancers who can move between text and body, history and imagination, tradition and innovation.

In this sense, *Shilpanatanam* expands dance pedagogy into a form of cultural scholarship: every rehearsal is simultaneously an act of training, interpretation, and creation. To learn within *Shilpanatanam* is to apprentice oneself not just to a teacher, but to a constellation of texts, sculptures, memories, and philosophies. It is to become, in Maya Kulkarni's vision, an artist-scholar whose body is both archive and laboratory. Based on my research with Kulkarni and my lectures and workshops across universities, museums, and community studios, I have created a sketch for a fifteen-week course structure in a graduate curriculum that can be used by *Shilpanatanam* educators in their teaching preparation.

MFA Seminar: *Shilpanatanam — Embodiment, Text, and Creativity*

Learning Outcomes:
By the end of the course, students will:

- Demonstrate embodied understanding of sculpture, text, philosophy, and rhythm as sources for choreography.
- Critically apply the pedagogies of engagement, uncertainty, and formation.
- Develop individual choreographic works grounded in *Shilpanatanam*.
- Articulate theoretical and reflective writing connecting practice to research.

Course Length: Twelve weeks
Format: One seminar (Two hours) + One studio/lab (Two hours) per week
Final Output: A performance-research project (solo or group) with a written reflective essay.
A fifteen-week MFA-level course on *Shilpanatanam* should weave together theory, practice, and research, just as Maya Kulkarni intended: sculpture, text, philosophy, and performance interlaced through embodied exploration. At the graduate level, students should not only *learn* the framework but also *apply and extend* it in their own research/creative practice. One needs to train deeply in technique, aesthetics, and interdisciplinary creativity in order to then research and create in the vein of *Shilpanatanam*. Here is a semester-long syllabus structure with weekly exercises and lesson plans:

Week 1	**Introduction: What is *Shilpanatanam*?** • Topics: Origins of Shilpanatanam; Maya Kulkarni's method in dialogue with Indian aesthetics, sculpture, and performance traditions; Guided improvisation using one image of sculpture (Chola bronze of Nataraja); Kinesthetic adaptation of sculpture.
Objective	• Introduce Maya Kulkarni's framework of *Shilpanatanam*. • Situate it within Indian dance history and philosophy. • Begin first embodied explorations from sculpture.
Seminar	• Lecture on Maya Kulkarni's vision: sculpture, poetry, philosophy as movement sources. • Contrast *Shilpanatanam* with Bharatanatyam pedagogy, Laban literacy, and somatic models. • Collective circle improvisation: one dancer begins from sculpture, others join sequentially.
Studio	• Begin with body awareness warm-up (breath, grounding). • Teacher shows an image of Nataraja bronze. • Students: "Stillness to Life"—embody the sculpture, then let the pose dissolve into improvisation.
Readings	• Selections from *Natyashastra* (*Karanas*) + Kulkarni's writings/interviews.
Assignment	• Reflective journal: "What does sculpture reveal that notation or instruction does not?" • Short reflective writing: How does sculpture "speak" to your body?

(*Continued*)

Week 2	**Sculpture as Archive** • Topics: Iconography of dance in temple art (*Natyashastra Karanas*, temple reliefs); Students select one sculptural fragment (hands, torsos, torsions) and attempt to re-embody it in multiple tempos; Learning about Padma Subramanynam's *Bharatha Nrityam.*
Objective	• Deepen relationship with sculpture as cultural memory. • Explore stillness and motion.
Seminar	• Lecture on temple architecture as a dance archive (Chidambaram, Konark, Hoysala temples). • Discuss how sculpture preserves movement but also transforms it.
Studio	• "Fragment Work": each student selects one body fragment from a relief (arm, torso, leg). • Explore how the fragment initiates whole-body motion. • "Stillness to Motion" exercise: hold pose for 1 minute, release into phrase.
Readings	• Read Sumana Sen Mandala's Master's thesis "Paradoxes to Intersections—Discovering the Invitations as a Bharata-Nrityam Teacher in the United States."
Assignment	• Create a visual diary of 3 sculptures, annotate possible choreographic impulses. • Create a tabular representation of meaning in sculpture and movement through a study of the *Karanas.*
Week 3	**Text as Movement Source** • Topics: Poetics and dramaturgy (*Abhinaya Darpana, Rasasutra, Kalidasa*).
Objective	• Explore Sanskrit poetry as choreographic impulse. • Translate word to gesture.
Seminar	• Read verses from Kalidasa and Jayadeva. • Discuss how metaphor creates movement. • Introduce concept of *Sanchari Bhava.*
Studio	• "Word-to-Body": Each dancer assigns body articulations to each word of a verse. • Pair work: One dancer literalizes text, another abstracts it. • Select one verse and prepare a short danced interpretation for peer sharing.
Readings	• Read Peter Smagorinsky and John Coppock's "The Reader, the Text, the Context: An Exploration of a Choreographed Response to Literature"; • *Natyashastra*, Chapters 6 and 7; • Kalidasa's *Kumarasambhavam*; • Jayadeva's *Gitagovinda.*
Assignment	• Embody one Sanskrit *shloka* or Tamil *padam* through gesture and rhythm; compare literal vs. interpretive embodiment. • Prepare a 1–2-minute solo from one verse for in-class sharing in Week 4.
Week 4	**Philosophy and Gesture** • Topics: Philosophical resonances—Vedanta, Shaiva, and Shakta cosmologies in dance; Explore oppositions (stillness/motion, contraction/expansion) as philosophical principles.
Objective	• Link philosophy (Vedanta, Shaiva, Shakta) to embodied practice. • Explore oppositional energies.
Seminar	• Lecture: *Advaita* and duality, Shaiva cosmology, the five acts of Shiva. • Discuss gesture as philosophy-in-motion.

Studio
- "Opposites": contraction vs. expansion, stillness vs. motion, center vs. periphery.
- "*Advaita* Through Motion": begin with dual gesture, resolve into unified phrase.

Readings
- Read Śarma Candradhara;s The Advaita Tradition in Indian Philosophy: A Study of Advaita in Buddhism, Vedānta and Kāshmīra Shaivism;
- Read John George Woodroffe's *Shakti and Shakta*.

Assignment
- "*Advaita* Through Movement" – Begin with duality (two contrasting gestures), resolve into oneness.
- 2-page essay: How does philosophy shape your movement research? How does philosophy shape choreographic choices?

Weeks 5–9 **Rhythm, Time, and Circularity**
- Exercise: Rhythmic Echo"– Move a sculptural phrase in 3 different *talas*
- Assignment: Document how rhythm transforms meaning of the same phrase.

Objective
- Embrace ambiguity as generative.
- Work with incomplete sources.

Seminar
- Lecture: absence, fragmentation, uncertainty as choreographic provocations.

Studio
- Dancers given fragmentary sculpture/text.
- "Negative Space" – Embody what is missing.
- Explore frustration/discomfort and transformation through improvisation.

Assignment
- Reflective essay: Describe one moment of uncertainty that opened new meaning.

Week 10 **Critical Dance Pedagogy in *Shilpanatanam***

Seminar
- Gender, caste, coloniality in Indian dance histories.

Studio
- Reinterpret a *nayika* archetype through a contemporary lens.

Exercise
- "Critical Re-Embodiment" — Embody a historical trope, then disrupt/reclaim it.

Assignment
- 2–3-page critical reflection: How does *Shilpanatanam* allow critique inside choreography?

Week 11 **Sharpen Creativity and Focus**

Seminar
- Read Mihaly Csikszentmihalyi's *Creativity*

Studio
- Work on honing one's creative practice across theory and embodiment

Exercise
- Create a script to be enacted by a peer in class

Assignment
- Change the script based on in-class workshopping

Week 12 **Research-to-Performance**

Seminar
- How scholarship and choreography merge; performance as research.

Studio
- Each student develops a short choreographic study (3–5 mins) from their chosen source material.

Exercise
- Peer feedback circle: focus on integration of *Shilpanatanam* elements.

Assignment
- Submit project proposal (performance + reflective essay plan). Write your own story about flowers; shy, flirtatious, bold (sunflower). Attribute these things and create an appropriate storyline and movements for your own *Shilpanatanam story*. Write three statues. The story must have a dramaturgy, draw on the *Rasa Bhava* theory for it to be engaging to the audience.

Shilpanatanam for K–12

K–12 Foundation (Grades K–12, ages ~5–18)

Goals: Spark curiosity, build body literacy, introduce cultural context, and nurture creativity/play.

Elementary (K–5)

- Focus: Playful embodiment + storytelling.
- Activities:
  - Basic postures and gestures from Indian dance (e.g., simple *Mudras*).
  - "Dance the Sculpture": Children strike temple-figure poses and animate them into short dances.
  - Storytelling through movement: retelling Panchatantra tales with gesture and rhythm.
- Learning Outcome: Children understand that movement carries story, symbol, and cultural meaning.

Middle School (6–8)

- Focus: Form, rhythm, and cross-cultural imagination.
- Activities:
  - Introduction to *adavus* (basic steps), simple rhythmic patterns (*tala* claps).
  - "Movement Diary": Each student sketches sculptures/temple motifs and turns them into phrases.
  - Improvisation games ("If this sculpture could speak, how would it move?").
- Learning Outcome: Students begin connecting body, history, and imagination.

High School (9–12)

- Focus: Critical awareness and creative experimentation.
- Activities:
  - Compare Bharatanatyam *adavus* with Western dance vocabularies (ballet plié vs. *araimandi*).
  - Mini-research: Pick a verse from Indian poetry and choreograph a short solo.
  - Introduce reflective writing (journals on cultural meanings, gender roles in dance, etc.).
- Learning Outcome: Students recognize Indian dance as both cultural tradition and creative medium.
- Capstone Project (Grade 12): A short choreographic work inspired by sculpture/poetry + artist statement.

Undergraduate (BA/BFA, ages ~18–22)

Goals: Deepen technical mastery, critical inquiry, and interdisciplinary experimentation. Serve as bridge between cultural literacy and graduate-level research.

Year 1–2 (Foundation)

- Technique Training: Core *adavus*, rhythmic cycles, expressive basics (*Abhinaya*).
- Coursework:
  - Intro to Indian aesthetics (Natya Shastra, *Rasa* theory).
  - Dance history (Devadasi tradition, colonial reforms, global modernities).
- Creative Practice:
  - Sculpture Studies I: Analyze and embody *karanas*.
  - Text & Gesture Lab: Translating Sanskrit/Tamil poetry into choreography.

Year 3–4 (Advanced Practice)

- Coursework:
  - Dance theory: Critical race, gender, and postcolonial studies in Indian dance.
  - Comparative performance studies: Indian vs. global choreographic frameworks.
- Studio Practice:
  - Improvisation and composition labs drawing on *Shilpanatanam* (text + sculpture + philosophy).
  - Collaborative projects (pairing dancers with art historians, musicians, and philosophers).
- Capstone (Final Year):
  - Research + Performance Project: 10–15-minute solo/group work based on archival research (temple, text, or philosophy).
  - Written reflection (10 pages): Link creative choices to cultural sources.

Undergraduate Learning Outcomes:

- Solid technique in Indian classical movement vocabularies.
- Critical ability to contextualize Indian dance historically and socially.
- Ability to create short works inspired by *Shilpanatanam* principles (sculpture, text, philosophy).

MFA Level (Graduate)

Goals: Advanced research-creation, pedagogy, and contribution to dance scholarship.

- Pipeline Connection:
  - MFA assumes K–12 grounding in cultural appreciation, undergrad mastery in movement/text, and critical inquiry.
  - MFA extends this into original choreographic research (practice-as-research), pedagogy, and contribution to the field (e.g., publishing, conference presentations).

Core MFA Features (from the 15-week seminar we built):

- Signature Pedagogies (engagement, uncertainty, formation).
- Inside–Outside Dialogue (somatic vs. archive).
- Research-to-Performance (critical reflection + choreography).
- Capstone Project (performance + scholarly essay).

Bibliography

Allen, M. 2012. "Body Mapping, Kinesthesia, and Inclusive Awareness." In *What Every Singer Needs to Know About the Body*, 2nd ed., edited by M. Malden, MJ. Allen, and K. A. Zeller, p. 1. Plural Publishing.

Bose, M. 1991. "The Nāṭyaśāstra and the Concept of Dance." In *Movement and Mimesis: The Idea of Dance in the Sanskritic Tradition*, pp. 108–30. Springer.

Chliara, A. 2018. "Acting as Tool for Dance Performance." Master's thesis, The University of Lincoln, USA. https://www.academia.edu/37961991/ACTING_AS_TOOL_FOR_DANCE_PERFORMANCE.

Cuneo, D. 2015. "Rasa: Abhinavagupta on the Purpose (s) of Art." In *The Natyasastra Anthology*. McFarland.

DeLahunta, S. 2000. "Dance Dramaturgy: Speculations and Reflections." *Dance Theatre Journal* 16 (1): 20–25.

Desmond, J. 1997. *Meaning in Motion: New Cultural Studies of Dance*. Duke University Press.

Foster, S. L. 1986. *Reading Dancing: Bodies and Subjects in Contemporary American Dance*. University of California Press.

Ghosh, M. 1951. *Natyasastram Ascribed to Bharata Muni: A Treatise on Ancient Indian Dramaturgy and Histrionics*. Chaukhamba Surbharati Prakashan.

Ghosh, M. 2006. *Nāṭyaśāstra of Bharatamuni: Text, Commentary of Abhinava Bharati by Abhinavaguptacarya and English Translation*. New Bharatiya Book Corporation.

Hermans, C. "Let's Play: Reenactment of Affective Traces Through Dance Improvisation."

Higgins, K. M. 2007. "An Alchemy of Emotion: Rasa and Aesthetic Breakthroughs." *The Journal of Aesthetics and Art Criticism* 65 (1): 43–54.

Kapur, A. 2024. "Abhinaya." In *The Routledge Companion to Performance-Related Concepts in Non-European Languages*, edited by E. Fischer-Lichte, T. Jost, and A. Schenka, pp. 516–22. Routledge.

Lancaster, C. 1957. *The Aesthetic Experience According to Abhinavagupta*. *Artibus Asiae* 20 (2/3): 220–22. https://doi.org/10.2307/3249400.

Mandala, S. S. 2020. "Paradoxes to Intersections—Discovering the Invitations as a Bharata-Nrityam Teacher in the United States." Master's thesis, Arizona State University.

Marshall, L. 2023. *University of North Carolina at Charlotte Faculty Dance Concert*. Anne R. Belk Theater, Charlotte, NC.

McManus, W. 2010. "Being Watched: Yvonne Rainer and the 1960s/Yvonne Rainer: The Mind Is a Muscle/Feelings Are Facts: A Life." *Art Journal* 69 (3): 131.

Nandikeśvara, and A. K. Coomaraswamy. 1917. *The Mirror of Gesture*. Harvard University Press.

Nannyonga-Tamusuza, S. 2015. "Music as Dance and Dance as Music: Interdependence and Dialogue in Baganda Baakisimba Performance." *Yearbook for Traditional Music* 47: 82–96.

Nityaswarpananda, S. 1953. *Ashtavakra Samhita: Text With Word-for-Word Translation, English Rendering, and Comments*. Advaita Ashrama.

Perinbanayagam, R. 2023. *Dialogues, Dramas, and Emotions: Essays in Interactionist Sociology*. Bloomsbury Publishing PLC.

Perpener, J. O. 2024. "Discussion Of Faculty Concert on January 26 and 27, 2024."

Pollock, S. 2016. *A Rasa Reader: Classical Indian Aesthetics*. Columbia University Press.

Śarmā, C. 1996. *The Advaita Tradition in Indian Philosophy: A Study of Advaita in Buddhism, Vedānta and Kāshmīra Shaivism*. Motilal Banarsidass Publishers.

Sedgwick, E. K. 2020. *Touching Feeling: Affect, Pedagogy, Performativity*. Duke University Press.

Smagorinsky, P., and J. Coppock. 1995. "The Reader, the Text, the Context: An Exploration of a Choreographed Response to Literature." *Journal of Reading Behavior* 27 (3): 271–98.

Varma, K. 1960. "The Basis of Indian Classical Drama." *Zeitschrift der Deutschen Morgenländischen Gesellschaft* 110 (2): 317–29.

Vatsyayan, K. 1963. "Notes on the Relationship of Music and Dance in India." *Ethnomusicology* 7 (1): 33–38.

Vatsyayan, K. 1992. *Indian Classical Dance*. Publications Division, Ministry of Information & Broadcasting.

Vollmer, H. J., and K. Klette. 2023. "Pedagogical Content Knowledge and Subject Didactics–An Intercontinental Dialogue?" In *Didactics in a Changing World: European Perspectives on Teaching, Learning and the Curriculum*, edited by F. Ligozac, K. Klette, and J. Almqvist, pp. 17–33. Springer.

Wilson, H. H., and R. P. Dwivedi. 2023. *Kumara Sambhavam or the Birth of War-God= Kumāra sambhavam*. Prachya Vidya Bhawan.

APPENDIX IV

Dance and Community Research Institute

A Resource Guide for Diasporic Dance Teachers
Society for Diasporic Indian Arts for K–12 and Adults

Table of Contents:

Welcome Message

UNC Charlotte Dance has created an outreach program for diasporic arts education called Dance and Community Research Institute (dNc). We work with dance educators across various genres to help them shape next generation arts leaders. The university does programming tailored toward strategic development of students' academic merit, dance expertise, and leadership/ civic engagement. Here, we work with students (scouts) as well as teachers (guides) toward creating more responsible leaders. Our goal is to leverage students' dance training in their college applications by induction into the National Honor Society for Dance Arts (NHSDA) and preparing students for numerous fellowship programs (Young Arts, Lotus Fellowship, NHSDA Award , etc.). We believe in the six-pronged structure of:

1. *Darshan* (philosophy);
2. *Drishti (vision)*;
3. *Avahan* (curious and open-minded);
4. *Titiksha* (self-efficacy);

5. *Parichay* (networking);
6. *Nishtha* (social justice).

Welcome to the Dance and Community Research Institute (dNc), a dynamic and inclusive space dedicated to fostering a deeper understanding of the intersections between dance, community, and culture. Whether you are here as a student, researcher, performer, or community member, we hope you find the resources, support, and inspiration you need to contribute to the world of dance and community-driven initiatives. It is a research project embedded within the Department of Dance at the University of North Carolina at Charlotte. Founded in 2020, the Dance and Community Research Institute is a hub for artistic development, cultural exchange, and academic inquiry. dNc works at the intersection of dance and social science, bringing together practitioners, scholars, and community members to explore how dance can be used to address social issues, promote healing, and build community bonds.

Vision: To create a global network where dance becomes a catalyst for positive social change, cultural understanding, and community building.

Mission: dNc is dedicated to promoting the study, practice, and appreciation of dance as an art form while fostering research and community engagement. We strive to provide a collaborative environment for scholars, artists, and communities to explore, create, and connect.

Core Values:

- Inclusivity: We welcome individuals from all backgrounds, abilities, and identities to participate in dance and research.
- Collaboration: We believe that community-driven initiatives amplify the impact of our work.
- Integrity: We uphold the highest ethical standards in both artistic and academic practices.
- Innovation: We are committed to pushing the boundaries of what dance can achieve in research and social practice.

Four Pies

Dance and Community Research Institute, UNC Charlotte Dance (dNc) has been working in the Indian diaspora in the United States in the fields of South Asian aesthetics, dance education, performance research, theorizing praxis, scholarly mentoring, and peer-reviewed publications. It has had Fulbright scholars, renowned choreographers, and important artists working through federal, state, and regional grant funded opportunities. Kaustavi Sarkar, as dNc convenor, has been coordinating the multiple pipelines of activities at this institute, which include the peer-reviewed journal *South Asian Dance Intersections*, the online professional certification through UNC Charlotte called *Indian Classical Dance Pedagogy Certificate*, and the performance wing, *Dance and Community Ensemble*. This institute is born out of research in technique, education, aesthetics, choreography, and cultural studies perspectives within South Asian dance practice especially with a focus on Odissi from the eastern Indian state of Odisha.

Education, Research, Artistry, and Infrastructure are the four pies of the Dance and Community Research Institute.

1. Pedagogical excellence through examinations and professional development
2. Fostering research in theory, history, and practice
3. Promoting artistic excellence in new works and preserving canonical works
4. Create infrastructural support for artists, educators, and scholars

Objectives:

The institute's objectives are as follows:

- To promote the recognition, development and understanding of South Asian dance.
- To facilitate communication and exchange among dance individuals, institutions and organizations interested in South Asian dance.
- To provide a forum for discussion of matters relating to South Asian dance.
- To encourage and support the research, education, criticism, creation and performance of South Asian dance.
- To liaise, coordinate, and participate in activities with other dance organizations in the world.
- To create more awareness, appreciation, and pedagogical systemization of South Asian dance in the United States.

dNc Scouts and Guides Program

(dNc Scouts and Guides is for students from Pre-K to Grade 12)

The Honors Program for Dance Education within the US diaspora is a distinguished academic and artistic pathway designed for highly motivated students seeking to deepen their understanding of dance within diverse cultural contexts. This program integrates rigorous coursework in dance theory, history, pedagogy, and performance with a strong emphasis on the unique experiences of diaspora communities in the United States. Students will engage with a broad spectrum of dance forms from traditional and contemporary genres to regional dance practices that reflect the varied cultural heritages of the South Asian diaspora.

In addition to cultivating technical proficiency and artistry, this program nurtures critical thinking about the role of dance in society and the importance of cultural representation. Graduates of the program will be equipped to contribute to the thriving field of dance education in schools, arts organizations, and communities, fostering a deeper appreciation for the intersection of dance, culture, and identity. Through a blend of academic research, performance opportunities, and community engagement, the Honors Program for Dance Education will develop future leaders who can inspire with an inclusive, culturally aware perspective, ensuring the preservation and evolution of dance traditions within the American context. Attending the Honors Program for Dance Education offers several K–12 benefits that can significantly enrich students' educational journeys and personal development:

1. Cultural Awareness and Diversity: Students in the program gain a deep understanding of various cultural traditions and dance forms, fostering respect and appreciation for the diverse communities within the US diaspora. This experience helps them navigate and appreciate cultural diversity, an essential skill in today's global society.
2. Enhanced Critical Thinking and Creativity: The interdisciplinary approach encourages students to think critically about dance, its history, and its role in society. This fosters creativity, problem-solving, and innovation—skills that extend beyond dance and benefit academic performance in other subjects.
3. Academic Excellence and Leadership: By engaging in challenging coursework and performance projects, students develop strong academic habits, discipline, and leadership skills. The program nurtures personal responsibility and leadership abilities, preparing students to take on leadership roles in their future careers and communities.
4. Physical and Emotional Well-Being: Dance provides numerous physical benefits, including improved strength, flexibility, coordination, and overall fitness. Additionally, the emotional expression inherent in dance can support mental health, help reduce stress, and improve emotional resilience, contributing to students' overall well-being.
5. Collaborative and Communication Skills: Through group projects, performances, and community engagement, students develop excellent teamwork and communication skills. These abilities are crucial for building relationships, navigating group dynamics, and excelling in future academic and professional endeavors.
6. Preparation for Teaching and Mentorship: The program equips students with teaching and mentoring skills that can be applied to future careers in education. They gain hands-on experience in leading dance classes and working with younger students, creating a strong foundation for those interested in pursuing teaching careers or community engagement through the arts.
7. Global Perspective and Innovation: Exposure to the global dance community and innovative dance education methods prepares students to think broadly and creatively. They develop a global perspective on dance and the arts, enhancing their adaptability and capacity to contribute to evolving artistic practices.
8. Scholarship and College Readiness: By participating in this honors program, students gain a competitive edge for college applications and scholarship opportunities, particularly those seeking to pursue further studies in dance, arts education, or related fields. They also build a strong portfolio of work and performance experience that highlights their academic and artistic accomplishments.
9. Building a Lifelong Passion for Dance: Students who engage in the Honors Program for Dance Education are given the tools to cultivate a lifelong passion for dance, whether as a profession, a form of personal expression, or a community activity. They leave the program with a deep, lasting connection to the art form.

10. Training as an Arts Professional: Students receive training in historically marginalized art forms that have limited to no representation in higher education and professional arts contexts so that they have a voice and a pathway to follow their passion.

In sum, this program not only nurtures academic and artistic growth but also prepares students to thrive in diverse, inclusive environments, making them well-rounded individuals ready for success in the twenty-first-century world.

dNc Scouts and Guides:

I. Institutional Membership: Recruitment of Guides.

dNc honors critical difference in movement and youth voice. Toward that mission, it wants to provide a social and cultural infrastructure for dance teachers. Institutions with an identified Academic Lead, also known as dNc Guide, affiliate with the dNc Colloquium by working with the dNc Convenor and completing the preliminary paperwork. Together, they create academic protocols that are specific to the chapter's needs and strengths. This is not just an issue of compliance but rather an opportunity to simultaneously grow the individual chapter as well as dNc Colloquium as it adjusts and remains flexible for diasporic needs and differences.

II. dNc Induction

Eligible Scouts are inducted into the dNc Colloquium. Students can then work up the ranks of proficiency standards.

A. dNc Assessment:

Project-Based Assessment

dNc Convenor works with Academic Lead to determine the project-based 10-week assessment initiative. Students enter into the following gold standards.

Grade	Gold Standard
Pre-K	Tots
K	Tots Plus
1	Wakers
2	Dreamers
3	Deep Sea Movers
4	Turiya Stars
5	Juniors
6	Intermediate [NHSDA Eligible]
7	Proficient [NHSDA Eligible]
8	Exemplary [NHSDA Eligible]
9	Accomplished [NHSDA Eligible]
10	Apprentice [NHSDA Eligible]
11	Scholar [NHSDA Eligible]
12	Professional [NHSDA Eligible]

Opportunities:

1. Scouts and Guides are able to participate in UNC Charlotte Department of Dance events that are subsidized for diasporic outreach and research initiates. There are three events every academic year (Fall, Spring, Summer).
2. Scouts and Guides can take advantage of a larger network of students and teachers working in the field of Indian arts.
3. Scouts can find a pathway to academic and professional success in the mainstream arts contexts.

B. dNc Annual Evaluation:

Once a student is eligible to be inducted in dNc, they go through annual evaluations to gain proficiency standards.

Opportunities:

1. Scouts are able to participate in leadership roles for new inductees.
2. Scouts can gain credit for volunteering activity.
3. Scouts can participate in ongoing dNc research in Indian arts and gain research experience in working with leading experts in the field of South Asian Studies.

dNc Student Examinations

The dNc Student Examinations are a graded evaluation system that enables dNc Certified Teachers to receive personalized, constructive feedback on their methods. Not only are the Student Examinations a useful tool for dance educators, but they also provide feedback for participating students regarding their technique and artistry.

1. Prior Prathamik I (PPI) Under 10
2. Prior Prathamik II (PPII) Under 13
3. Invocations (13–14)
4. Foundations (14–15)
5. Ornamentations (15–16)
6. Elaborations (16–17)
7. Emancipation: Mancha-Pravesh (17–18)

The exact curriculum design for each level is decided by the dNc Coordinator in consultation with affiliated schools, educators, and lab school. The exams need to be conducted by external examiners. A Google Form is shared by the dNc Coordinator where students fill out their details and pay the examination fee ($100).

A model for community dance studio *Sai Nritya Sangam* in Ohio, led by Narayani Mukherjee and focusing on the Guru Kelucharan Mohapatra style of Odissi, uses the following template.

1. Prior Prathamik I (PPI):
Technical Fundamentals:
Chauka, Tribhangi

Foundations: Head, Neck, Eyes, Hands, Feet
Slokam

2. Prior Prathamik II (PPII):
Technical Fundamentals:
Chauka, Tribhangi
Foundations: Head, Neck, Eyes, Hands, Feet
Slokam, Siva Mangalacharan

3. Invocations:
Technical Fundamentals:
Chauka
Tribhangi
Foundations: Head, Neck, Eyes, Hands, Feet
Basic Items:
Namami, Shiva Mangalacharan, Sai Mangalacharan, Sthyayee, Basant Pallavi

4. Foundations:
Technical Fundamentals:
Chauka, Tribhangi
Foundations: Head, Neck, Eyes, Hands, Feet
Basic Items:
Namami, Shiva Mangalacharan, Sai Mangalacharan, Sthyayee, Basant Pallavi
Intermediate Items:
Shantakaram, Batu, Jaya Mahesh, Kasturi Tilakam

5. Ornamentations:
Technical Fundamentals: *Chauka, Tribhangi*
Foundations: Head, Neck, Eyes, Hands, Feet
Basic Items:
Namami, Shiva Mangalacharan, Sai Mangalacharan, Sthyayee, Basant Pallavi
Intermediate Items:
Shantakaram, Batu, Basant Pallavi, Kasturi Tilakam, Jaya Mahesh, Bichitro Anondo, Mohona Pallavi, Dash Avatar, Moksha

6. Elaborations:
Deepening of *Abhinaya*
Ability to demonstrate strong skills in Odissi Music
Thorough knowledge of Odissi Rhythms
Thorough knowledge of Oriya Literature

7. Emancipation:
Mancha-Pravesh: Debut graduation recital
In 2024–2025, two students have been recognized for this process. This is the first time students will graduate from this program.

In addition to the above curriculum, students are required to also cover the following:

1. Watch at least 3 concerts per year
2. Participate in community dance events for performance experience
3. Complete research-projects in dance-affiliated topics

III. dNc National Honor Society: Induction and Graduation

Exceptional Scouts in middle and high school programs are eligible to apply for National Honor Society for Dance Arts (NHSDA) Induction affiliated to the National Dance Education Organization (NDEO). Academic Lead will be educated about the point tracking system. Scouts can take advantage of scholarships open for NHSDA inductees.

dNc Chapter NHSDA Induction: A student is inducted into the Junior Program (middle school) and the Secondary Program (high school). Students will receive certificates from NDEO.

dNc Chapter NHSDA Graduation: Graduation with Honors comes with a sponsor printed certificate and a medallion. Graduating students also receive the blue/white NHSDA cord.

IV. dNc Fellows: Adult Programming

dNc Fellows is for adults. dNc provides programming exclusively for adults. Whether you are an adult beginner or a seasoned dancer hoping to professionalize your training, dNc has created performance, teaching, and research pathways. You can sign up as a dNc Fellow through a two-step procedure: A 10-week project with formative and summative assessment.

A. dNc Induction and Annual Evaluation:

Project-Based Assessment

dNc Convenor works with Academic Lead to determine the project-based 10-week assessment initiative. Adult Fellows follow the apprentice-learning methodologies while interning with the research institute for holistic education around dance writing, dance history, and dance criticism. They work with both the institute and the academic lead to ensure a global and plural perspective in the arts. Leadership, performance, and research opportunities are available in UNC Charlotte programs, namely

1. The international academic journal: *South Asian Dance Intersections*
2. The annual Indian dance conference, *Odissi Odyssey*
3. The annual Summer Leadership Institute

B. dNc Annual Evaluation:

If interested, the adult learner can also participate in annual evaluation procedures. The gold standards for the adult beginner are as follows:

1. F&C: Foundations and Conditioning
2. VE: Vocabulary Expansion
3. ER1: Expressive Repertoire
4. RB: *Rasa* (sentiment) and *Bhava* (Feeling) Deepening
5. ER2: Expanding Repertoire and Expressive Range

6. FR: Full-Length Repertoire
7. PV: Personal Voice
8. AA: Advanced Artistry

Important Dates *
dNc/ NHSDA Fall 2025 Registration: August 15–30
dNc/ NHSDA Spring 2026 Registration: January 15–30
dNc/ NHSDA Summer 2026 Registration: June 15–30
*Rolling Registrations are available as per consultation with dNc Convenor and Academic Leads.

Resources for Educators: Daily Dance Technique Practice Protocol

1. Preparation (5–10 min)
   - Centering: Quiet standing or floor work to bring awareness to breath and alignment.
   - Mental check-in: Set an intention for the practice (e.g., focus on clarity of arms, musicality, or stamina).
2. Warm-Up (15–20 min)
   - Joint mobilization: Ankles, knees, hips, shoulders, spine.
   - Dynamic stretches: Swings, lunges, cat-cow, torso spirals.
   - Core activation: Planks, balance holds, pelvic tilts.
   - Rhythmic coordination: Light footwork, or *tatkar* (in Indian classical), tendus (in ballet), or simple isolations (in jazz/hip-hop).
3. Foundational Technique Drills (20–30 min)
   - Postural alignment: Rehearse basic stance (*araimandi*, first position, parallel).
   - Basic vocabulary: Foot articulations, arm pathways, torso bends, isolations.
   - Rhythm/musicality drills: Clapping patterns, reciting *bols/sollukattu*, or marking phrases with counts.
   - Repetition sets: Choose 3–5 key movements and repeat in slow, medium, and fast tempos.
4. Combination Practice (20–25 min)
   - Short phrases: Put foundational movements into 4–8-count sequences.
   - Spatial focus: Practice facing different directions, traveling across the floor.
   - Dynamic variation: Perform the same sequence with changes in tempo, energy, and size.
   - Expressive focus: Layer intention or emotion (*nritta* vs. *Abhinaya* in Indian forms, or dramatic vs. abstract in modern).
5. Repertoire/Choreography Work (20–30 min)
   - Rehearse sections of a dance piece with focus on technique + artistry.
   - Break down difficult transitions or jumps/turns.
   - Work in segments (don't always run full pieces).
   - Alternate between full-out execution and marking with detail to conserve energy while refining clarity.

6. Conditioning/Cross-Training (10–15 min)
   - Strength: Core, glutes, legs (squats, bridges, TheraBand work).
   - Balance & proprioception: One-legged holds, relevés, yoga poses.
   - Cardio bursts: Short intervals (skips, fast footwork) to build stamina.
7. Cool-Down & Reflection (10–15 min)
   - Gentle stretching: Hamstrings, quads, calves, back, shoulders.
   - Breath work: Return heart rate to normal.
   - Journaling/verbal reflection: Note what felt strong, what needs improvement, and set goals for next session.

Weekly Structuring

- 5–6 days practice (alternating intensity).
- Light day: Focus on fundamentals, flexibility, notation/journaling.
- Medium day: Technique drills + short combinations.
- Heavy day: Full-out run of choreography + stamina training.
- Rest/recovery day: Gentle stretching, yoga, or mindful walking.

Tips for Sustainability

- Always begin with alignment and breath awareness.
- Keep hydration and breaks built into long practice sessions.
- Alternate between technical precision and artistic expression so practice doesn't become mechanical.
- Track progress weekly (video, notes, self-assessment).

Resources for Educators: Practice Protocol for Dance Expression

1. Grounding & Awareness (5–10 min)
   - Sit or stand in stillness. Focus on breath, posture, and softening facial muscles.
   - Gentle massage of face, jaw, and hands to release tension.
   - Mirror check: neutral face → identify baseline presence.
2. Facial Technique Warm-Up (10–15 min)
   - Isolations: Eyebrows up/down, eyes wide/narrow, cheek lifts, lip shapes (smile, pout, neutral).
   - Transitions: Move smoothly from one expression to another (anger → surprise → joy).
   - Mirror & no-mirror practice: First with mirror for accuracy, then without for internalization.
3. Gesture & *Mudra*/Hand Expression (10–15 min)
   - Practice codified gestures (*Mudras* in Indian classical/expressive hands in modern/jazz).
   - Pair each gesture with intention (showing water, offering, calling).
   - Repeat gesture with and without facial expression to notice the difference.

4. Voice & Rhythm Integration (10–15 min)
   - Speak or recite while moving (poetry, text, *sollukattu*, or simple counting).
   - Practice lip-synching or reciting lyrics while gesturing.
   - Explore pacing: slow delivery vs. fast, soft vs. loud tone (even if silent).
5. Improvisation for Emotional Range (15–20 min)
   - Pick an emotion (joy, grief, anger, longing, devotion).
   - Express it using:
     1. Only face.
     2. Face + gesture.
     3. Face + gesture + whole body.
   - Use music prompts: Dance the same movement phrase to three different soundtracks (e.g., sad *raga*, upbeat drum, silence).
6. Narrative/Storytelling Practice (20–25 min)
   - Choose a short narrative (myth, personal memory, or character scene).
   - Break into beats: beginning → middle → climax → resolution.
   - Perform it once with clear narrative gestures, then again with subtle internal focus (imagining the feeling rather than "showing").
   - Alternate between over-exaggeration and minimalism to expand expressive range.
7. Partner/Audience Exercises (15–20 min)
   - Practice maintaining eye contact with a partner or "invisible audience."
   - Perform an expressive phrase facing:
     1. Mirror.
     2. A friend/peer.
     3. Empty space (imaginary audience).
   - Get feedback: Did the emotion read clearly?
8. Cool-Down & Reflection (5–10 min)
   - Gentle stretches for face and body.
   - Breathing exercise: inhale emotion, exhale release.
   - Journal: What emotion felt most natural today? Which was challenging?

Weekly Structuring

- 3 days focused on *technique of expression* (facial isolations, gestures, voice).
- 2 days on *narrative work* (storytelling, character, acting through dance).
- 1 day on *improvisation* (free exploration of emotion with music).
- 1 day on *performance run-throughs* (simulate stage presence, stamina in expression).

Tips for Developing Expressivity

- Film your practice and review: Does the emotion "read" across the screen?
- Study reference material: classical *Abhinaya* (Natya Shastra, Odissi, Bharatanatyam), modern masters (Martha Graham's dramatic tension, Pina Bausch's psychological depth).
- Always connect expression to breath and inner intention—avoid surface-level exaggeration.
- Train empathy: read poetry, watch theater, observe human emotions in daily life.

Resources for Educators: Protocol for Professionally Logging Dance Hours

1. Categories of Dance Activity to Track

Break down hours into clear categories so records are meaningful:

- Technique Class: Structured practice of foundational vocabulary.
- Rehearsal: Choreography, staging, polishing repertoire.
- Improvisation/Composition: Creative exploration or choreographic research.
- Conditioning/Cross-Training: yoga, Pilates, cardio, strength.
- Performance: Live or recorded shows.
- Pedagogy/Teaching: Leading or assisting classes.
- Research/Study: Reading, watching archival footage, note-taking.

2. Information to Record Daily

Each log entry should include:

- Date
- Start + End Time (24-hour or AM/PM)
- Duration (hrs/mins)
- Category (from above)
- Activity Description (specifics: "Bharatanatyam *adavus* drills," "Odissi *Pallavi* rehearsal," "Martha Graham floorwork warm-up")
- Location (studio, home, theater, gym, etc.)
- Instructor/Collaborators (if applicable)
- Reflections/Notes (progress, challenges, injuries, artistic insights)

3. Weekly/Monthly Summaries

At the end of each week/month:

- Total hours spent per category.
- Observations (e.g., "Technique improving, but stamina lacking; need more conditioning.")
- Adjustments (e.g., "Add 2 more hours of cardio next week.").

4. Tools for Logging

- Digital Spreadsheet (Google Sheets/Excel) → flexible, allows for totals and charts.
- Specialized Apps → Toggl, Clockify, or even fitness trackers.
- Dance Journal (Paper) → if reflection and embodiment notes matter more than data crunching.
- Hybrid System → spreadsheet for official records + journal for qualitative notes.

5. Professional Formatting Standards

- Use consistent time units (hours in decimals: 1.5 = 1 hour, 30 minutes).
- Keep logs legible and auditable (grant bodies and institutions prefer clean spreadsheets).
- Store in monthly folders or one master sheet.
- Include signatures/verification if logging for certification under a teacher.

6. Example of a Daily Log Entry

Date	Start	End	Duration	Category	Activity Description	Location	Instructor	Notes
2025-09-16	10:00	11:30	1.5 hrs	Technique	Odissi *chauka* + *tribhangi* drills	Studio A	Guru XYZ	Improved stamina, knees sore.
2025-09-16	14:00	15:30	1.5 hrs	Rehearsal	*Pallavi* run-through, spacing	Studio A	Self	Need to refine arm pathways.

Daily total: 3 hours
Weekly running total (so far): 9.5 hours

7. Verification for Professional Settings

If required by a program, institution, or guild:

- Get logs signed weekly by instructor/rehearsal director.
- Attach performance programs, rehearsal schedules, or attendance sheets.
- Keep digital backups.

8. Reflection Component

Add a short weekly reflection (150–200 words):

- What improved?
- What was difficult?
- What to focus on next week?

This transforms the log from a time sheet into a professional development tool.

Resources for Educators: Writing Assignments

Ten full assignment handouts on dance criticism with word counts, evaluation criteria, and suggested readings. They are scaffolded so that students develop both critical writing skills and theoretical engagement. Together, these assignments build from description → analysis → comparison → context → ethics → positionality, giving students both practice in writing and engagement with dance criticism as a scholarly and creative practice.

Assignment 1: Descriptive Criticism – Writing the Dance

Prompt:

Watch a live or recorded performance of your choice. Write a descriptive account of the piece, focusing only on what you see and hear—movement vocabulary, costuming, staging, sound, atmosphere. Avoid interpretation or judgment. Your goal is to translate dance into words with clarity and precision.

- Length: 800–1,000 words
- Evaluation Criteria: Accuracy of description, clarity of language, sensory detail, avoidance of interpretation.

- Suggested Readings:
  - Sally Banes, *Writing Dancing in the Age of Postmodernism* (Introduction)
  - Deborah Jowitt, *Time and the Dancing Image*

Assignment 2: Formal Analysis

Prompt:

Choose a short excerpt (2–5 minutes) from any dance work. Break down its choreographic elements: space, time, dynamics, phrasing, motif, repetition, and structure. Discuss how formal choices create rhythm, coherence, or emotional intensity.

- Length: 1,000 words
- Evaluation Criteria: Attention to choreographic detail, analytical clarity, use of dance vocabulary.
- Suggested Readings:
  - Susan Leigh Foster, *Reading Dancing*
  - Ann Cooper Albright, *Choreographing Difference* (selected chapter)

Assignment 3: Comparative Review

Prompt:

Compare two dance performances from different genres (e.g., Bharatanatyam and contemporary modern dance). Critique the works in terms of embodiment, cultural reference, technique, and audience reception. Discuss both similarities and differences.

- Length: 1,200 words
- Evaluation Criteria: Depth of comparison, cultural sensitivity, critical insight, structure of argument.
- Suggested Readings:
  - Brenda Dixon Gottschild, *Digging the Africanist Presence in American Performance*
  - Avanthi Meduri, *Bharatanatyam as a Global Dance*

Assignment 4: Criticism and Context

Prompt:

Find a historical review of a dance work (print, online, or archive). Write a response analyzing the critic's language, assumptions, and biases. How do history, politics, and ideology shape critical reception?

- Length: 1,000–1,200 words
- Evaluation Criteria: Engagement with historical context, depth of textual analysis, awareness of critical positioning.
- Suggested Readings:
  - Arlene Croce, *Writing in the Dark, Dancing in* The New Yorker
  - Sunil Kothari, *New Directions in Indian Dance*

Assignment 5: The Audience's Eye

Prompt:
Attend a live performance. Write two short reviews:

1. From the perspective of a professional dance critic.
2. From the perspective of a first-time dance audience member.

Compare how framing, vocabulary, and expectations affect each review.

- Length: Two 600-word reviews (total ~1,200 words)
- Evaluation Criteria: Ability to shift perspective, voice, and tone; clarity of contrast; critical reflection.
- Suggested Readings:
  - Deborah Jowitt, *Dance Beat: Writings on Dance*
  - Sanjoy Roy, reviews for *The Guardian* (online archive)

Assignment 6: Choreographer–Critic Dialogue

Prompt:
Research one choreographer (e.g., Martha Graham, Chandralekha, Akram Khan). Analyze how their works were reviewed by critics over time. Compare choreographic intent with critical interpretation.

- Length: 1,500 words
- Evaluation Criteria: Research depth, synthesis of sources, critical insight into dialogue/tensions between artist and critic.
- Suggested Readings:
  - Ramsay Burt, *The Male Dancer* (contextual chapters)
  - Uttara Asha Coorlawala, "Classical and Contemporary Indian Dance: Performing Gender, Culture, and the New Nation"

Assignment 7: Ethics of Dance Criticism

Prompt:
Write a critical essay on the ethics of reviewing dance. Should critics evaluate technique, cultural authenticity, innovation, or emotional impact? Who defines the standards? Use case studies of reviews that sparked debate or controversy.

- Length: 1,200–1,400 words
- Evaluation Criteria: Critical argumentation, ethical reasoning, use of evidence, clarity of stance.
- Suggested Readings:
  - André Lepecki, *Exhausting Dance*
  - Gay Morris, *Moving Words: Re-Writing Dance*

Assignment 8: Language and Dance

Prompt:

Write two versions of a dance review:

a) Academic/theoretical style (dense with references and frameworks).

b) Poetic/evocative style (imaginative, sensory-driven).

End with a short reflection on how language transforms the reader's reception of dance.

- Length: Two 800-word reviews + 500-word reflection
- Evaluation Criteria: Mastery of multiple registers, creativity, meta-reflection on writing.
- Suggested Readings:
  - Yvonne Rainer, *Work 1961–73* (selected texts)
  - Adrienne Rich, "When We Dead Awaken: Writing as Re-Vision"

Assignment 9: Dance, Media, and Criticism

Prompt:

Select a filmed dance (YouTube, TikTok, or a professional dance film). Write a review that considers how camera work, editing, and digital platforms shape choreography and audience perception.

- Length: 1,200–1,500 words
- Evaluation Criteria: Critical media literacy, attention to digital aesthetics, integration of dance and media analysis.
- Suggested Readings:
  - Sherril Dodds, *Dance on Screen*
  - Harmony Bench, *Perpetual Motion: Dance, Digital Cultures, and the Common*

Assignment 10: Personal Position Paper

Prompt:

Write a self-reflective essay on your positionality as a dance critic. Consider your training, cultural background, aesthetic values, and personal biases. How do these shape your approach to watching, interpreting, and writing about dance?

- Length: 1,200–1,500 words
- Evaluation Criteria: Depth of reflection, self-awareness, articulation of critical voice, honesty.
- Suggested Readings:
  - bell hooks, *Art on My Mind: Visual Politics*
  - Brenda Dixon Gottschild, *The Black Dancing Body*

Resources for Educators: Research Assignments

Ten full research assignment handouts for a dance studies course. Like the criticism ones, they include prompts, word counts, evaluation criteria, and suggested readings. These move from exploratory research → contextual studies → critical frameworks → independent research.

Assignment 1: Dance Research Foundations – Mapping the Field

Prompt:

Write a short research paper introducing the field of dance studies. Identify at least three approaches (e.g., ethnographic, historical, choreographic analysis, cultural studies) and explain how they shape research questions.

- Length: 1,000 words
- Evaluation Criteria: Understanding of field, clarity, organization, correct use of sources.
- Suggested Readings:
  - Alexandra Carter & Janet O'Shea, *The Routledge Dance Studies Reader* (Introduction)
  - Andre Lepecki, *Dance* (Very Short Introductions)

Assignment 2: Archival Research

Prompt:

Locate and study archival material related to a dance form, choreographer, or performance tradition. This may include photographs, programs, reviews, or oral histories. Write a paper analyzing what these sources reveal about the performance and its cultural context.

- Length: 1,200 words
- Evaluation Criteria: Source analysis, contextualization, originality of insights.
- Suggested Readings:
  - Ann Cooper Albright, *Traces of Light: Absence and Presence in the Work of Loie Fuller*
  - Gay Morris, *A Game for Dancers*

Assignment 3: Ethnographic Fieldwork Exercise

Prompt:

Attend a rehearsal, workshop, or community dance class. Take detailed field notes and write a reflective report describing what you observed. Consider questions of participant observation, embodiment, and ethics.

- Length: 1,200–1,400 words
- Evaluation Criteria: Depth of observation, reflexivity, ethical awareness, clarity of writing.
- Suggested Readings:
  - Deidre Sklar, "Five Premises for a Culturally Sensitive Approach to Dance"
  - Ananya Chatterjea, *Butting Out: Reading Resistive Choreographies Through Works by Jawole Willa Jo Zollar and Chandralekha*

Assignment 4: Historiography in Dance

Prompt:

Choose a dance form (e.g., Odissi, ballet, hip-hop) and trace how its history has been written. Compare at least two sources (scholarly vs. popular, insider vs. outsider). Analyze the narratives, silences, and tensions.

- Length: 1,500 words
- Evaluation Criteria: Engagement with historiography, source comparison, critical analysis.
- Suggested Readings:
  - Susan Manning, *Ecstasy and the Demon: Feminism and Nationalism in the Dances of Mary Wigman*
  - Janet O'Shea, *At Home in the World: Bharata Natyam on the Global Stage*

Assignment 5: Dance and Identity

Prompt:
Research how dance functions as an expression of identity (race, gender, sexuality, class, or nation). Choose one case study and analyze the interplay of movement, embodiment, and politics.

- Length: 1,200–1,500 words
- Evaluation Criteria: Depth of case study, theoretical application, clarity of argument.
- Suggested Readings:
  - Brenda Dixon Gottschild, *The Black Dancing Body*
  - Thomas DeFrantz & Anita Gonzalez, *Black Performance Theory*

Assignment 6: Dance and Globalization

Prompt:
Study the globalization of a dance practice (e.g., salsa, K-pop choreography, Bharatanatyam in diaspora). How does transnational circulation transform style, pedagogy, or meaning?

- Length: 1,500 words
- Evaluation Criteria: Research depth, cross-cultural analysis, use of theory.
- Suggested Readings:
  - Yutian Wong, *Choreographing Asian America*
  - Priya Srinivasan, *Sweating Saris*

Assignment 7: Dance and Media

Prompt:
Research how media (film, television, TikTok, YouTube) shapes the production, dissemination, and reception of dance. Choose one platform or dance phenomenon as a case study.

- Length: 1,200–1,500 words
- Evaluation Criteria: Integration of media theory, depth of analysis, originality of case.
- Suggested Readings:
  - Sherril Dodds, *Dance on Screen*
  - Harmony Bench, *Perpetual Motion: Dance, Digital Cultures, and the Common*

Assignment 8: Dance and Interdisciplinary Research

Prompt:
Write a research paper that connects dance with another discipline (e.g., neuroscience, anthropology, visual art, musicology, philosophy). How does this interdisciplinary lens deepen our understanding of dance?

- Length: 1,500–1,800 words
- Evaluation Criteria: Creativity, strength of interdisciplinary connection, quality of sources.
- Suggested Readings:
    - Maxine Sheets-Johnstone, *The Primacy of Movement*
    - Mark Franko, *Dancing Modernism/Performing Politics*

Assignment 9: Critical Literature Review

Prompt:

Select a topic (e.g., postcolonial dance studies, dance and disability, improvisation). Write a literature review summarizing and analyzing at least 6 scholarly sources. Identify gaps in the research and suggest future directions.

- Length: 2,000 words
- Evaluation Criteria: Organization, depth of synthesis, clarity of critical perspective.
- Suggested Readings:
    - Rebekah Kowal, Gerald Siegmund, & Randy Martin (eds.), *The Oxford Handbook of Dance and Politics*
    - Carrie Noland, *Agency and Embodiment*

Assignment 10: Independent Research Paper (Final Project)

Prompt:

Design and carry out an independent research project on a dance topic of your choice. Incorporate at least one primary source (archival, ethnographic, performance analysis) and situate your study within existing scholarship.

- Length: 3,000–3,500 words
- Evaluation Criteria: Originality, research depth, engagement with theory, quality of writing, scholarly rigor.
- Suggested Readings:
    - Encourage students to return to the full course bibliography and readings that align with their topic.

Resources for Educators: Point System for Awards and Fellowships

dNc works with educators to nurture next-generation artists and arts entrepreneurs. Following is the point structure that could be used as a model template for students.

Award Point Schemata (Starting Grade 9)

1. Technique & Training
    - Weekly Dance Classes (studio, school, community, or conservatory):
        - 1 point per 45 hours of instruction of in-chapter instruction.
        - Example: Ballet, modern, jazz, hip hop, Odissi, Bharatanatyam, etc.
    - Summer Intensives/Workshops:
        - 2 points per full day of participation.

- Private Lessons:
  - 1.5 points per hour.

2. Performance & Production
   - School Performances/Recitals/Studio Concerts:
     - 3 points per performance.
   - Community or Professional Performances:
     - 5 points per performance.
   - Choreographing a Piece (for class, concert, festival):
     - 3–5 points depending on length and scope.
   - Stage Crew/Production Help:
     - 1 point per rehearsal, 2 points per performance.

3. Scholarship & Research
   - Dance-Related Research Paper or Project:
     - 3–5 points (graded or presented).
   - Program Notes/Essays for Performances:
     - 2 points per piece.
   - Conference Presentations/Workshops Led:
     - 5 points each.
   - Book/Article Reviews in Dance Studies:
     - 2 points each.

4. Leadership & Service
   - Dance Club/NHSDA Chapter Leadership (officer, organizer):
     - 3 points per semester of service.
   - Mentoring Younger Dancers:
     - 1 point per hour of teaching/assisting.
   - Community Engagement/Outreach (teaching in schools, libraries, senior centers):
     - 2 points per session.
   - Volunteer Work at Dance Events:
     - 1–2 points depending on task.

5. Creativity & Original Work
   - Original Choreography Presented:
     - 5 points (solo or group).
   - Dance Film/Multimedia Project:
     - 5 points per completed work.
   - Improvisation Showcase/Composition Lab:
     - 2 points per event.

6. Professional Engagement
   - Attending Performances (with reflection/essay):
     - 1 point per live performance (with written reflection).
   - Attending Masterclasses:
     - 1 point per hour.

- Dance Competitions/Festivals:
  - 3 points per event (extra if winning/placing).
- Dance-Related Certifications (e.g., yoga, Pilates, injury prevention):
  - 5 points per certification.

Tracking System

- Students should maintain a Dance Points Log beginning in Grade 9.
- Each entry should include: Date, Activity, Hours/Details, Supervisor Signature (if possible), and Points Earned.
- A suggested target is 30–40 points per year starting in Grade 9, so that by Grade 12 students are well-prepared for induction and recognition.

NHSDA Award Point Schemata (Starting Grade 10)

NHSDA induction usually requires 30 points minimum, but students aiming for the NHSDA Award (especially seniors) should target 60+ points across multiple categories. This schemata guides preparation from Grades 10–12.

1. Technique & Training
   - Weekly Classes (school, studio, conservatory, community):
     - 1 point per 45 in-chapter instructional hours.
     - Example: Ballet, modern, jazz, hip hop, Odissi, Bharatanatyam, etc.
   - Summer Intensives/Workshops:
     - 2 points per full day of training.
   - Private Coaching:
     - 1.5 points per hour.

Suggested Goal by end of Grade 10: 15–20 points

2. Performance & Production
   - School/Studio Performances: 3 points each.
   - Community/Professional Performances: 5 points each.
   - Choreography for Class/Showcase/Festival: 3–5 points (depending on scope).
   - Stage Crew/Production Work: 1 point per rehearsal, 2 points per performance.

Suggested Goal by end of Grade 10: 10–12 points

3. Scholarship & Research
   - Dance Research Papers or Presentations: 3–5 points each.
   - Program Notes/Written Analyses: 2 points each.
   - Book or Article Reviews in Dance Studies: 2 points each.
   - Dance Conference Presentations/Talks: 5 points each.

Suggested Goal by end of Grade 10: 5–8 points

4. Leadership & Service
   - NHSDA Chapter Officer/Dance Club Leadership: 3 points per semester.
   - Peer Mentoring/Teaching Assistance: 1 point per hour.
   - Community Outreach (school, library, senior center, nonprofit): 2 points per session.

- Volunteering at Dance Events: 1–2 points per event.

Suggested Goal by end of Grade 10: 5–8 points

5. Creativity & Original Work
   - Original Choreography Presented: 5 points each.
   - Dance Film or Multimedia Project: 5 points each.
   - Improvisation/Composition Showcase: 2 points per event.

Suggested Goal by end of Grade 10: 3–5 points

6. Professional Engagement
   - Attending Performances (with reflection/essay): 1 point per performance.
   - Masterclasses/Guest Workshops: 1 point per instructional hour.
   - Dance Competitions/Festivals: 3 points per event (+bonus if awarded).
   - Certifications (yoga, Pilates, first aid, safe body practices): 5 points each.

Suggested Goal by end of Grade 10: 3–5 points

Yearly Point Targets

- Grade 10: 40–50 points
- Grade 11: 50–60 points
- Grade 12: 60+ points (NHSDA Award eligible)

Tracking Method

Students should keep a Dance Points Log with:

- Date
- Activity
- Hours/Description
- Category (Training, Performance, Service, etc.)
- Points Earned
- Teacher/Advisor Signature (if applicable)

This gives students a clear 3-year progression plan to build their portfolio, not just for NHSDA but also for college dance applications, scholarships, and resumes.

NHSDA Award Point Schemata (Starting Grade 11)

Students need 30 points minimum for induction into NHSDA, but for the National Award, they should target 60+ points by graduation. If starting in Grade 11, the goal is to earn ~30–35 points per year in two years.

1. Technique & Training
   - Weekly Classes (school, studio, conservatory, community):
     - 1 point per 45 hours of in-chapter instruction.
   - Summer Intensives/Workshops:
     - 2 points per full day of training.
   - Private Coaching:
     - 1.5 points per hour.

Target for Grade 11: 12–15 points

2. Performance & Production
   - School/Studio Concerts: 3 points each.
   - Community/Professional Performances: 5 points each.
   - Choreography for Showcases/Festivals: 3–5 points.
   - Stage Crew/Tech/Costuming Help: 1–2 points per event.

Target for Grade 11: 10–12 points

3. Scholarship & Research
   - Research Paper/Dance Essay/Critical Reflection: 3–5 points each.
   - Conference Presentation/Symposium Participation: 5 points.
   - Book or Article Reviews: 2 points each.
   - Program Notes/Written Analysis for Performance: 2 points.

Target for Grade 11: 5–7 points

4. Leadership & Service
   - NHSDA Chapter or Dance Club Leadership Role: 3 points per semester.
   - Peer Mentoring/Teaching Assistance: 1 point per hour.
   - Community Dance Outreach (schools, libraries, senior centers): 2 points per session.
   - Volunteering at Dance Events (ushering, backstage, organizing): 1–2 points.

Target for Grade 11: 5–7 points

5. Creativity & Original Work
   - Original Choreography Performed: 5 points.
   - Dance Film/Multimedia Project: 5 points.
   - Improvisation/Composition Showcase: 2 points per event.

Target for Grade 11: 3–5 points

6. Professional Engagement
   - Attending Performances (with reflection): 1 point each.
   - Masterclasses/Guest Workshops: 1 point per instructional hour.
   - Competitions/Festivals: 3 points per event (+bonus for awards).
   - Certifications (yoga, Pilates, safe practices, injury prevention): 5 points each.

Target for Grade 11: 3–5 points

Grade 11–12 Roadmap

- Grade 11 Goal: 35–40 points
- Grade 12 Goal: 30–35 points
- By Graduation: 65–70 points (Award Eligible)

Tracking Method

Students should maintain a Points Log with:

- Date
- Activity

- Category (Training, Performance, Research, Service, etc.)
- Hours/Description
- Points Earned
- Advisor Signature

This plan ensures even a late start in Grade 11 can still lead to both induction and the NHSDA National Award.

Here's a Grade 12–focused point schemata:

NHSDA Award Point Schemata (Starting Grade 12)

- Minimum for induction: 30 points
- National Award eligibility: ~60 points (possible in one year if students commit strategically)

1. Technique & Training
   - Weekly Dance Classes (school, studio, conservatory, community):
     - 1 point per 45 in-chapter instructional hours.
   - Summer Intensives (if before Grade 12):
     - 2 points per full day.
   - Private Coaching:
     - 1.5 points per hour.

Goal: 15–20 points (through weekly technique + workshops/masterclasses)

2. Performance & Production
   - School/Studio Concerts: 3 points each.
   - Community/Professional Performances: 5 points each.
   - Original Choreography (solo/group/festival): 5 points.
   - Stage Crew/Lighting/Costume Help: 1–2 points per event.

Goal: 12–15 points (maximize by choreographing AND performing in multiple events)

3. Scholarship & Research
   - Dance Research Paper/Critical Essay: 3–5 points each.
   - Program Notes/Analysis for Performance: 2 points.
   - Conference Presentation/Symposium Participation: 5 points.
   - Book or Article Reviews: 2 points each.

Goal: 5–7 points (write one strong research essay + 1–2 shorter reflections)

4. Leadership & Service
   - NHSDA Chapter Leadership/Dance Club Officer: 3 points per semester.
   - Peer Mentoring/Teaching Assistance: 1 point per instructional hour.
   - Community Engagement (school visits, library, senior center, nonprofit): 2 points per session.
   - Event Volunteering (ushering, organizing, backstage): 1–2 points per event.

Goal: 5–8 points (serve as a mentor/assistant + volunteer at events)

5. Creativity & Original Work
   - Original Choreography Presented: 5 points.
   - Dance Film/Multimedia Project: 5 points.
   - Improvisation/Composition Showcase: 2 points per event.

Goal: 5–7 points (one major project + smaller creative works)

6. Professional Engagement
   - Attending Performances (with reflection): 1 point per performance.
   - Masterclasses/Guest Workshops: 1 point per instructional hour.
   - Dance Competitions/Festivals: 3 points per event (+bonus if awarded).
   - Certifications (yoga, Pilates, first aid, injury prevention, safe practices): 5 points each.

Goal: 5–7 points (attend performances + masterclasses + at least one certification)

One-Year Roadmap (Grade 12)

- Fall Semester:
  - Focus on technique, choreographing, leadership/service, and writing a short research paper.
  - Aim: ~25 points.

- Spring Semester:
  - Focus on performances, creative work, and professional engagement (competitions, certifications).
  - Aim: ~30–35 points.

By Graduation: 60+ points → NHSDA Award Eligible

Tracking System

Each student should maintain a Points Log, with:
- Date
- Category (Technique, Performance, Service, etc.)
- Hours/Details
- Points Earned
- Teacher/Advisor Signature

Even if starting in Grade 12, this focused plan ensures students can still reach induction + National Award recognition with intentional, high-yield choices.

Resources for Educators: NHSDA Point Schemata for Solo graduation recital in Indian Dance

1. Technique & Training

(Years of preparation leading up to solo graduation recital)
   - Weekly Classes (regular training with guru): 1 point per one-on-one instructional hour.
   - Private Coaching for Solo Graduation Recital items: 1.5 points per hour.

- Rehearsals (solo or with musicians): 1 point per hour.
- Summer Intensives/Masterclasses (Indian dance or related forms): 2 points per full day.

Estimated Points: 20–25 (over 1–2 years of prep)

2. Performance & Production
   - Full Solo Graduation Recital (90–120 min): 15 points (major performance milestone).
   - Invited Previews/Informal Run-throughs: 3–5 points per showing.
   - Participation of Musicians/Technical Team (coordinated rehearsals): 2 points per rehearsal.
   - Stage/Costume/Lighting Management: 2 points per event.

Estimated Points: 20+ (recital + supporting rehearsals + previews)

3. Scholarship & Research
   - Program Notes/Research Essay on items performed (history, music, meaning, choreography): 5–8 points.
   - Documentation of Solo Graduation Recital (portfolio, video archiving, reflective essay): 5 points.
   - Talk/Presentation (sharing the significance of Solo Graduation Recital at school/with community): 3–5 points.

Estimated Points: 10–15

4. Leadership & Service
   - Mentoring Younger Dancers (helping with rehearsals, group classes, teaching basics): 1 point per instructional hour.
   - Community Engagement (lecture-demonstrations in schools, libraries, temples, cultural centers): 2 points per session.
   - Volunteer Contributions at Dance Events (ushering, backstage support for others' solo graduation recitals): 1–2 points per event.

Estimated Points: 5–10

5. Creativity & Original Work
   - Choreographing a Short Item (*varnam*, *tillana*, or modern thematic piece): 5 points.
   - Dance Film/Multimedia Documentation of Solo Graduation Recital: 5 points.
   - Improvisation/*Manodharma* Segments (*alapadma*, *sanchari*, *Abhinaya* exploration): 2 points per event.

Estimated Points: 7–10

6. Professional Engagement
   - Attending Live Indian Dance or Music Performances (with reflection): 1 point per event.
   - Workshops with Visiting Gurus: 1 point per instructional hour.
   - Participation in Festivals/Competitions Before or After Solo Graduation Recital: 3 points per event.

Estimated Points: 5–7

Point Summary for a Solo Graduation Recital

- Technique & Training: 20–25
- Performance & Production: 20+
- Scholarship & Research: 10–15
- Leadership & Service: 5–10
- Creativity & Original Work: 7–10
- Professional Engagement: 5–7

Total Potential Points: 70–85+

Completing a Solo Graduation Recital not only qualifies a student for NHSDA induction (30 pts) but can single-handedly prepare them for the NHSDA National Award (60+ pts), since it demonstrates artistic mastery, academic research, leadership, and community engagement in one integrated event.

www.ingramcontent.com/pod-product-compliance
Lightning Source LLC
LaVergne TN
LVHW060629110826
845147LV00014B/881

* 9 7 8 1 4 6 9 6 9 8 7 7 9 *